THE CONTEMPORARY DISCUSSION SERIES

World Religions
and
Global Ethics

WORLD RELIGIONS AND GLOBAL ETHICS

EDITED BY
S. CROMWELL CRAWFORD

A NEW ERA BOOK

PARAGON HOUSE
NEW YORK

First edition, 1989

Published in the United States by

Paragon House Publishers
90 Fifth Avenue
New York, NY 10011

A New Ecumenical Research Book

Manufactured in the United States of America

Library of Congress Cataloging-in-Publication Data

World religions and global ethics/edited by S. Cromwell Crawford.
p.   cm.
"A New Ecumenical Research Association book"—
Includes bibliographies and index.
ISBN 0-913757-57-8
0-913757-58-6 (PBK)

1. Religious ethics.   I. Crawford, S. Cromwell.
BJ1188.W67 1988
291.5—dc19   87-21883
                                                          CIP

TO A. DURWOOD FOSTER
A teacher, first and foremost,
whose classroom is the world.

Contents

Acknowledgements

The idea for this book developed in the lush beauty of Puerto Rico, during a conference of the New Ecumenical Research Association. I am grateful for the support and encouragement given me by the conference organizers, John Maniatis, Executive Director of New ERA, and Senior Consultants, M. Darrol Bryant, Richard Quebedeaux, and Frank K. Flinn.

The prime movers of this volume are the contributors who, coming from different parts of the globe and representing diverse religious and cultural traditions, have provided spice and substance to the ecumenical array of offerings in ethics. I am most grateful for their enthusiastic co-operation.

I am also much indebted to colleagues at the University of Hawaii who shared their expertise: Robert Bobilin, Chungying Cheng, Lenn Goodman, David Kalupahana, Michael Saso, Lee Siegel and K. N. Upadhyaya. The book title was suggested by K.L. Seshagiri Rao of the University of Virginia. Marjorie A. Sadgunn, from her conning tower in London, supplied helpful insights which sharpened the East/West focus of the book.

In the preparation of the manuscript I am appreciative of the limitless labours of Roberta Mau whose secretarial skills proved invaluable.

Finally, I must thank the publishers for their expert assistance and remarkable patience.

INTRODUCTION
Ethics in an Interdependent World

Once you see that the knee bone is connected to the thigh bone and the thigh bone is connected to the hip bone, you can no longer pretend that they are separate. And if you are going to make them work, you're going to have to deal with them in combination.

Elliott Richardson

Global interdependence has emerged as the distinguishing mark of the contemporary international system. Physically and politically, this has become a hard—and often painful—reality. Political leaders and social scientists share a consensus that "interdependence constitutes the common challenge facing mankind in the latter part of the twentieth century."[1]

"Global ethics" is a response to this challenge. By developing principles that reflect the reality of global interdependence, global ethics promote a world order based on reciprocal understanding and cooperation.

Moral philosophers have long struggled with the task of bringing about a world community by fashioning a global ethic from the multiple strands of discrete cultures, each with its own system of ideas, values, and loyalties. Today that enterprise takes on special urgency because, in the contemporary world, community is no longer the goal; it is the starting point. It is not the case that "first we have to do this . . ." but "first we have to do everything . . ." Yesterday's virtue is today's necessity.

Both the peril and the promise of world community have been brought about in our generation by the convergence of two forces of universality, one very old and one very new. Reinhold Niebuhr anticipated this phenomenon soon after World War II. As he saw it:

For the first time in human history the communal order, which rests upon, and is limited by, forces of national particularity, stands under a double challenge. The old force of universality which challenges nationalistic particularism is the sense of universal moral obligation, transcending the geographic and other limits of historic communities. The new force of universality is the global interdependence of nations, achieved by a technical civilization.[2]

Niebuhr traces the ancient force of moral universalism to the "high religions and philosophies" that displaced the earlier tribal and imperial religions two to three thousand years ago.

> Primitive society felt no strong sense of obligation to life outside of the tribal community, which was held together and limited by the principle of consanguinity. The early empires were achievements of human freedom over the limits of nature in the sense that they extended the boundaries of effective community beyond the limited force of consanguinity. They were artifacts of the human imagination in which the soldier's skill and the priest's manipulation of religious loyalties achieved a wider community than merely natural impulses could have held together. But these imperial communities were informed by a culture which culminated in an imperial religion, unable to envisage a universal history or to comprehend the totality of human existence in its universe of meaning.[3]

Next, we turn to the second force toward universalism—the reality of global interdependence. The catalysts of modernization that have brought it about are revolutions in the fields of economics, communication, transportation, science, and technology. These developments have unified our world so that it has become a single unit for mankind. In Marshall McLuhan's flamboyant phrase, "Ours is a brand-new world of allatonceness. 'Time' has ceased, 'space' has vanished. We now live in a global village . . . a simultaneous happening."[4] Business consultant Peter Drucker, with an eye to the genuine world economy ushered in by the global corporation, calls our new world a "global shopping center."[5] Whatever the phrase, the fact remains that human inventiveness has created a unitary world.

This phenomenon of interdependence confronts our era with a new situation. For thousands of years our national and cultural groupings, each with its private interests and loyalties, were challenged merely from *above* by the forces of universal moral obligation in the world's religions. The impact was minimal. Calls to a world community appeared naively utopian—mere "pie in the sky bye and bye." Even as recently as the forties when Wendell Willkie published his *One World,* the notion seemed like a dream. But yesterday's dream threatens to become today's nightmare. Today's shrunken world cannot permit the luxury of particularism. The entrenched status quo that has lasted interminably is now being pressured from *below* by the forces of modernity. Their message is clear: interdepend or perish! Our technological civilization leaves us in no doubt: interdependence is not a theory, but a fact; not an ideology, but a condition. Technologically, economically, politically, and morally, interdependence in international relations is inescapable. No more can any single nation be the master of its own fate and the captain of its own soul.

A dramatic example of interdependence is the current AIDS epidemic. The global spread of this disease confounds national boundaries. It demands global remedies. No single nation or group of nations, no matter how technologically advanced, possesses the capabilities or resources to arrest the deadly virus independently. What was first dubbed as an "African problem" or a "Haitian problem" has now surfaced, like some hydra-headed monster, as a global problem.

AIDS is the latest in a long list of earlier problems—poverty and hunger, environmental decay, resource depletion, population pressure, international terrorism, and nuclear proliferation—that once were neatly and logically discussed within the closed categories of the "life-boat" ethic. But in an interdependent world, there are no life-boats! Like the king who discovered that his royal command could not stop the tide, no country can place "No Entry" signs upon its national borders against any of these problems.

Thus, the coming together in our time of the two forces of universality, one moral, the other technical, are creating, as Niebuhr prophesied, "a powerful impetus toward the establishment of a world community."[6]

Each author in this volume brings out the element of moral universalism in his own tradition and attempts to demonstrate its relevance to the solution of our global problems.

For our part, we draw on these traditional insights and proceed to construct the outlines of a global ethics. Our purpose is to give systematic definition to the range of ideas and attitudes presented by the individual authors.

Global ethics starts with the assumption that as human beings we are *already involved* in global society, whether we know it or not; whether we like it or not. Biologically, we all belong to "a single, common species of life," and therefore we all partake in several common features. Ecologically, we are part of the planet's biosphere and are rooted in the earth's material and energy system. Historically, in matters of language, religion, arts, and technologies, the separate wells from which we drink are all fed by subterranean streams. Culturally, we are multinational and the whole world is becoming a melting pot. Spiritually, increasing numbers are embarked on a journey of self-discovery through interreligious dialogue. Ewert Cousins states:

> In an unprecedented way, the religions of the world are meeting one another in an atmosphere of trust and understanding. The members of the different traditions not only wish to understand the others, but to be enriched by them. As the traditions meet, each individual can become heir to the spiritual heritage of the human community as a whole. With this enrichment, consciousness can expand its horizons to encompass the entire human community, with its accumulated heritage of spirituality in a new interrelated, global consciousness.[7]

If our involvement in global society is something *given,* it follows that the ethics based on this assumption must be pluralistic. Ethical pluralism is open and inclusive. It is liberated from the interests, biases, and habitual attitudes of any particular political, economic, and cultural scheme, or from any pretensions of religion and morality to know "the only way."

Pluralism accepts cultural differences among people as the product of social conditioning. Every person is born into a particular culture that becomes his or her window upon the world. Actually, there is no such thing as "the world," but only historic views of the world. The "world" is a mediated phenomenon that often reveals more about the perceiver than about the perceived. Thus, social heterogeneity can be accounted for in terms of "a common human nature influenced by different social institutions and different ideologies."[8]

By "common human nature" we are not suggesting something fixed and unchanging—the sort of stuff traditional ethical systems used as blueprints for their brands of "natural law," *"dharma",* *"tao",* etc. Global ethics rejects all such substantialist views of human nature. Instead, by "common human nature" it refers to certain properties, qualities, and energies that are universal, indestructible, and creatively expressed through personal styles. Erich Fromm has this dynamic view of human nature in mind when he says:

> Man is not a blank sheet of paper on which culture can write its text; he is an entity charged with energy and structured in specific ways, which, while adapting itself, reacts in specific and ascertainable ways to external conditions. . . . Human evolution is rooted in man's adaptability and in certain indestructible qualities of his nature which compel him never to cease his search for conditions better adjusted to his intrinsic needs.[9]

Stated in terms of the one and the many: cultural life styles on this planet are indeed many, but the many are manifestations of the one. To apprehend the one in the many is to discover the *raison d'etre* for the pluralistic stance of global ethics.

A well-known argument for pluralism among several of the world's religions is the theory classically expressed in the fable of the blind men and the elephant. The spirit of tolerance in religions such as Buddhism, Jainism, and Hinduism flows from this sort of epistemology that affirms that historic human consciousness impedes our perceptions of reality, and hence respect is the appropriate attitude toward the belief and conduct of people who differ from us.

Today we can take a step beyond this traditional argument. Science has come to the aid of epistemology and supplies us with more positive reasons for cultural pluralism based on findings from biological systems. The fact is that nature in her biological wisdom never puts all her eggs in one basket. "Species develop and differentiate as a response to environmental changes, and animals and plants have emerged that can survive and flourish under almost any conceivable condition of temperature, altitude, atmosphere, and the like. If some major disaster were to befall the world, there is a good chance that somewhere in all that diversity there would be some organism that could survive the holocaust and begin anew."[10]

Thus, "pluralism" is nature's own strategy for survival. It is the very stuff of reality. "Without multiplicity, without the many others, our world—from atoms to molecules to plants to bugs to humans—would not be able to function and exist. Reality is essentially pluriform: complex, rich, intricate, mysterious."[11]

This book documents a variety of life styles that flourish around the globe, each suited to different societies and circumstances. Brought together, they help us correct our limited, monocultural views and develop alternative and more flexible solutions to our global problems. Futuristically, they point to a new breed of people who can act as links between the cultures of the world—people who are aware of the world as a whole; who believe in the unity and inviolability of our variegated existence; who are cognitively flexible and ethically relativistic. In classical Greece such individuals were known as "seers" or *thereroi*. Their task was to penetrate foreign cultures in order to discover how others lived so that life back home could be improved by contact. Our modern *seers* have this same natural curiosity to find out how other cultures think, feel, and behave, and they help us regulate our untutored imagination by reality, so that instead of thinking how things may be, we *see* them as they are.

S. CROMWELL CRAWFORD
Honolulu, Hawaii

Notes

1. Gerhard Mally, *Interdependence* (Lexington, MA: Lexington Books, 1976), 3.
2. Reinhold Niebuhr, *Children of Light and Children of Darkness* (New York: Charles Scribner's Sons, 1944), 154.
3. *Ibid.*, 154, 155.
4. Marshall McLuhan, *The Medium Is the Massage* (New York: Bantam Books, 1967), 68.
5. Richard J. Barnet and Ronald E. Muller, *Global Reach* (Taipei: Imperial Books, 1974), 14.
6. Niebuhr, 159.
7. Ewert H. Cousins, "Interreligious Dialogue: The Spiritual Journey of our Time," *IRF* (A Newsletter of the International Religious Foundation, Inc.), 11, no. 1, (Jan–Feb), 1987, 2.
8. Lindsay Birker, "Foreword," in Thomas Welty, *The Asians* (New York: J.B. Lippincott, 1963), iv.
9. Erich Fromm, *Man for Himself* (New York: Holt, Rinehart and Winston, 1964), 23.
10. Stephen Bochner, "The Mediating Man and Cultural Diversity," in *Culture Learning*, ed. Richard W. Brislin (Honolulu: University Press of Hawaii, 1977), 10, 11.
11. Paul F. Knitter, *No Other Name* (New York: Orbis Books, 1985), 6.

Part I
SOUTH ASIA

1

Hindu Ethics for Modern Life

S. CROMWELL CRAWFORD

Satyam eva jayate nanritam.
Truth alone is victorious and not falsehood.

India's contribution to the field of ethics is both very old and very young; old as the ancient civilization itself and young as Mahatama Gandhi's formulation of *Satyagraha* or "Truth-Force" as the means for winning Indian independence in 1947.

The Sanskrit word for ethics is *dharma* (*dhar,* "to hold"). It signifies that which upholds or embodies law, custom, and religion, and is very much analogous to the concept of "Natural Law" in Christian ethics, though the idea of "law" should not detract from its dynamic character. *Dharma* is activity, mobility, and is possessed of catalytic qualities. By contrast, *a-dharma* is stasis, stoppage, and to that extent, unnatural. Philosopher K. N. Upadhyaya points out that *dharma* is one of the most common, yet most abstruse terms of Indian religio-philosophical thought. "From the very dawn of Indian civilization, the Indian mind is found to be chiefly concerned with it. The persistence and intensity with which the inquiry into *dharma* has been pursued is mainly on account of the firm conviction of the Indian people that *dharma* constitutes the differentia of man, whereby he is distinguished from brutes; just as in the West, following Aristotle, rationality is regarded as the distinguishing mark of man."[1]

In the earliest days of the Rig Veda, *dharma* is predominantly understood in sacerdotal and cosmological terms. However, its ethical foundations are firmly laid in the cognate concept of *Rita,* which, in addition to its ritual aspects, carries the ontological meaning of immanent order and the theological meaning of "divine law." Gods Varuna and Mitra, who preside over *Rita,* have fully developed moral personalities, and their hymns are reminiscent of the high moral tone found in the Hebrew Psalms. The epistemological meaning of *Rita* as "truth" reinforces its ethical character. The roots of *Rita* are to be found in the Avestan *(asha)* and Achaemenid *(arta)* literature which, as Filliozat declares, "indicates a common origin in prehistoric time."[2]

5

In my study, *The Evolution of Hindu Ethical Ideals,* I have documented the changing meanings of *dharma* within the colorful development of Hinduism itself, up to the dominance of *ahisma,* which, with the impact of Jainism and Buddhism, became the cardinal virtue of Hindu ethics. Here is presented an overview of the religio-philosophic structure of Hinduism from which the ethics is derived. What then is the nature of Hinduism?

Philosophic Assumptions

Our investigation begins with the Upanishads in which the unique quality of Indian speculative wisdom is seen as essentially cosmic. Unlike the Semitic religions, which view creation in anthropocentric terms, the Upanishadic seers behold the Supreme Being as manifest in all creation, "Verily, this Soul is the overlord of all things, the king of all things. As all the spokes are held together in the hub and felly of a wheel, just so in this Soul of all things, all gods, all worlds, all breathing things, all these selves are held together."[3]

This cosmic manifestation of the Supreme Being is delineated in evolutionary terms. Evolution is progressive and spiritual. It starts with matter in which the Spirit lies dormant. From a lifeless stone, Spirit rises to the level of life and manifests itself in the vegetable kingdom. It then ascends to the level of consciousness, manifesting itself in the animal kingdom. From consciousness it progresses to the level of intelligence, and takes form in the kingdom of man. The most perfect state is that of pure Spirit in which matter lies dormant and Spirit manifests itself as bliss in the Supreme Spirit. Thus, all the world is a stage and all forms of life merely players. They have their exits and their entrances as One Spirit plays many parts. Matter struggles with Spirit, but Spirit, step by step, comes into its own. The Bhagavad Gita summarizes this cosmic scenario thus: "Unmanifest is the origin of beings, manifest their mid-most stage, and unmanifest again their end."[4]

That which precedes and succeeds the evolutionary process is shrouded in mystery because it is outside the pale of time. As mortals in this planetary theater, we cannot apprehend how the Divine Actor divided itself into subject and object and commenced this evolutionary show; nor can we tell how Spirit shall prevail over matter so that the original perfection is finally restored. All that we know at this stage of history is that there is movement; that this movement is spiritual and progressive, and that the divine plan for human life is that we join the creative ascent of the Spirit. To have this knowledge is to be able to distinguish the relative merits of material, biological, intellectual, and spiritual values.

Such is the cosmic vision of Hinduism. It is rationally held, but it derives its strength from subliminal springs. The conviction is religious, but it permeates the whole culture including all the arts and sciences. Even when the Hindu speaks in the language of the particular, the words and sentences assume a global grammar. With the tongue he may invoke his chosen deity, but in the Spirit he transcends all names and forms.

Having defined the essence of Hinduism in terms of cosmic awareness, let us examine how this attitude serves as a creative catalyst in formulating the Hindu's relationship to himself, to the deity, and to the world.

Man's Relation with Himself

First is man's relation to himself. The Hindu philosophy of human nature is basically dualistic. It precisely demarcates the essential self from the empirical self. Our immediate, daily experience is of the latter. It constitutes our world of sense experience, but is unreal to the extent that it is the product of original ignorance *(avidya)*. Exactly how the operation of *avidya* brings about the loss of identity between the essential self and the Supreme Being is beyond philosophic inquiry and must remain eternally wrapped in mystery. However, Hindu psychology probes into the nature of the empirical self that the real self takes on during its bondage in the phenomenal world. It makes a rigorous analysis of the body-mind complex and describes man's role in the world in terms of three bodies.

There is the physical body fabricated of five elements that return to their physical source upon death. There is the subtle body with its vital, mental, and intellectual functions that are closely associated with the essential self. It is the locus of individuality, the bearer of moral consequences, and is subject to the law of *karma* as it undergoes numerous transmigrations. It ceases when the Supreme Self is recognized. Finally, there is the causal body out of which the physical and subtle bodies arise and dissolve. It is known through the state of deep sleep in which the subtle and physical bodies are completely quiescent.

Each individual is possessed of a certain character conditioned by different aggregations of three *gunas* (subtle elements that make up matter). When the *sattvic* qualities prevail, the person's bodily, vocal, and mental actions are characterized by knowledge; when the *rajas* and *tamas* qualities prevail, the actions are of passion and ignorance, respectively.

The point to note is that Hindu psychology is aware of the law of spiritual progression even in its characterization of the empirical self. Spirit is active in and through matter. Whereas in less imaginative systems spirit and matter are treated antithetically, here, matter is not alien to Spirit but serves as the vehicle for the realization of Spirit. This is possible because material phenomena are hierarchically understood, as in the case of the three bodies and the three gunas. Therefore, not only are spiritual values affirmed, but intellectual, biological, and material values as well. Each level is respected, cared for, and nurtured as a *necessary* step in the total process of spiritual progression. This psychology of personal development proceeds from the Hindu's cosmic vision and evolutionary view of life in the world.

Of course, the vision shines brightest as we turn from the empirical self to the essential self. Descriptions of the essential self vary, but the most common view is that the essential self is of the nature of pure self-consciousness, and is to be radically distinguished from the physical and mental states that it assumes with individuality. The classical formula is that of *sat* (pure existence), *chit* (pure consciousness), *ananda* (bliss).

The cosmic purpose is realized when the essential self discovers its identity with the Supreme Reality through a mystical experience that goes beyond our normal states of consciousness. The experience of liberation is difficult to achieve, entailing many stages of transmigration, but the underlying view of spiritual evolution is a sustaining source of confidence that the goal shall be reached, that *moksha* is a birthright.

The chief feature of *moksha* is the shift of an individual's attitude from that of individuality to universality: *Aham Brahmasmi* (I am Brahman). The techniques for achieving this goal are imaginatively devised with sensitivity to individual differences. Innovation, not imitation, is the salient feature of yogic discipline.

Man's Relationship with God

Secondly, we examine the innovative impact of Hinduism's cosmic outlook upon the Hindu's relationship with God. The principle of spiritual progression provides Hinduism with the flexibility to entertain a theistic posture side-by-side with the philosophic stance discussed above. In many religious systems the contending claims of monism and theism are considered contradictory but in Hinduism these two interpretations exist in creative tension. This is possible because its evolutionary scheme allows a legitimate place for the relative beside the absolute. In absolute terms, Reality is *Nirguna* (without attributes), but in relative terms, Reality conceived as God is *Saguna* (full of attributes).

For most persons in the course of their long ascent toward philosophic knowledge, it is sufficient that they proceed on the level of religious knowledge. Higher knowledge is available at all times but the seeker's state of inner evolution dictates a regimen in accordance with capacity. This is the meaning of the doctrine of *adhikara*, the notion that religious instruction should be graded according to the competence of the student.

The knowledge best suited to those who have graduated from the level of idols and rituals is dualistic. God is perceived as the "Other." He is worshipped as befits his name and form and is praised for His infinite grace, holiness, and power. Imaginative images of the deity with many arms, feet, and eyes give strength and comfort to the devotee who believes his chosen deity is indeed omniscient, omnipotent, and omnipresent. In truth, deity is devoid of description. The finite cannot comprehend the Infinite. But since no description can lay claims to finality, all descriptions are allowed. God may be worshipped in any form as long as worship produces likeness, and moral and spiritual character is advanced. Thus, epistemology and psychology conspire to legitimate the relative status of theistic knowledge and allocate to it an instrumental role within the cosmic purpose. Such sensitivity to religious need is yet another mark of Hindu tolerance.

Man's Relationship with the World

Thirdly, we review the effect of Hinduism's cosmic outlook upon man's relation to the world. Here, too, the law of spiritual progression is innovatively at work. The operative word is *dharma*. *Dharma* is the solvent that bonds Spirit with matter, time with eternity, the ideal with the actual, and the individual good with the social good. To understand how this takes place is to appreciate the religious imagination of the Hindu mind.

The divided nature of the self envisioned by Hindu philosophy creates obvious problems when one ponders man's relation to the world. "Man" in this context is certainly not the *atman*, for the essential self has nothing to do with the phenomenal world.

The status, therefore, of the world and of life in the world is, philosophically considered, inferior. However, though the world is deemed inferior in the light of the philosophic end, it has the significance of being the necessary means toward that end. If life is the cosmic evolution of the Supreme Spirit from pure matter in which Spirit lies dormant to pure Spirit in which matter lies dormant, betwixt the two extremes is a mingling of matter and Spirit whereby matter becomes a stepping stone for Spirit. In practical terms this means that while the individual good of a person may be the renunciation of the world in order to realize his essential self or the attainment of *moksha,* his social good is to be involved in the world and so fulfill his *dharma.* As the domain of ethics, *dharma* is inferior to *moksha;* at the same time, *dharma* is the *sine qua non* of *moksha. Prajnana* or saving knowledge only arises in the tranquil mind.

The instrumental relation between *dharma* and *moksha* reflects the position of the empirical self to the essential self. Both are rooted in a complex antrhopology. The human being is perceived as an intricate organism in whom there is an ascending scale of values represented by the four *purusharthas* or values of life: *kama, artha, dharma,* and *moksha.* From one perspective, the first three values, representing the needs of the empirical self, are distinct from the fourth value, which represents the need of the essential self. Viewed under the law of spiritual progression, together they belong to a creative continuum. Thus, within the holistic anthropology of Hinduism, seemingly divisive claims of this world and the next are innovatively aligned.

The practical task of bringing out all human values is expedited within a social scheme known as *Ashramadharma* or the Four Stages of Life. This institution attests to the psychological astuteness with which Hindusim perceives differences within people.

Contrary to the Freudian view that personality is fixed in early childhood and that what appears to be later developments are actually adjustments to new cultural expectations, Hinduism advances an evolutionary view of life based on alternating stages of stability and transition. Contemporary support for the psychology of the *ashrama* scheme comes from the research of scholars such as Jean Piaget, Erik Erikson, Lawrence Kohlberg, Daniel Levinson, and Roger Gould. They are attuned to the stages of human development and have charted life's steps from childhood to adulthood. Central to progression is the faith that persons are endowed with higher values that unfold with experience and maturity. Each stage has its unique richness and the last stage, like good wine, is the richest of all!

Not only are these differences *within* people, Hinduism perceives differences *among* people. Awareness of this is institutionalized in the scheme of *Varnadharma,* which is the ethical organization of the social life of the Hindu. Here, too, the law of spiritual progression is evident.

The structure of the ideal society envisioned in *Varnadharma* is built around the belief that each individual functions most efficiently in the social slot for which nature has endowed him. Not birth or status, but qualification and merit are the regulating principles of the earliest social order. The injunction is that you do not place a square peg in a round hole. Allowance is also made for change and growth. Culture and cooperation are ends to be sought, but character and responsibility are deemed the highest good.

The possibility of progress entails the risk of regress and, in time, *varna* (color) turned to *jati* (caste). Stability is preferred to search, order to progress, and conformity to experiment. One way of assessing this phenomenon is to say that the evolutionary view of Hinduism is not one of psychological determination, but that participation in the forward movement of the Spirit is one of human autonomy.

Our brief inquiry into the fundamental relations of human existence has shown that the essence of Hinduism lies in its cosmic outlook, which functions as a *code* for the understanding of its civilization, and as the *canon* by which progress is measured. This view is dynamically held, innovatively expressed, and progressively realized.

Principles for Ethical Decision-Making

Hindu assumptions concerning man's relation to God, to himself, and to the world provide the philosophic framework from which certain ideals are derived that serve as principles of ethical action. These ideals are catalogued under the rubric of *Samanya* or generic duties and are to be distinguished from the *Vishesha* or specific duties we discussed in the scheme of *varnashramadharma.* The generic duties or *sadharanadharma* are common in the sense of being independent of caste and station in life, and are categorical imperatives binding upon man as man—not as an individual with certain membership.

Since human rights precede communal rights, *sadharanadharma* provides the basis for *varnashramadharma* and also defines its boundaries. For instance, a Brahmin wanting to make a sacrificial offering is not at liberty to acquire the object of sacrifice by stealing it, for *asteya* or non-stealing is a universal duty. One could go further and claim that the offering itself is illegitimate because it contravenes the principal of *ahimsa* or nonviolence. A modern example of the ethical priority of *sadharanadharma* would be Gandhi's opposition to the traditionally hallowed practice of untouchability. He argued: "Untouchability is repugnant to reason and to the instinct of mercy, pity, and love. A religion that establishes the worship of the cow cannot possibly countenance or warrant a cruel and inhuman boycott of human beings."[5]

The motivation behind *sadharanadharma* is two-fold: the sacredness of life and gratitude for life. The unity of man is deemed deeper than his diversity. Out of this unity the sense of sacredness is born. We are not *brahmacharis* or *brahmins*, not *sannyasins* or *shudras* who happen to be people, but people who happen to occupy this particular station or that particular caste, both of which are relative and changing.

Secondly, there is the same sense of gratitude operant in *sadharanadharma* as in *ashramadharma*. Man is indebted to his community and therefore sacrifices; but even more so he is culturally and experientially indebted to humanity and must therefore serve the universal good.

Cardinal Principles

The cardinal principles found in most Hindu sects are: purity, self-control, detachment, truth, and nonviolence. Each of these ideals has its own inner evolution and is therefore a mixture of ingredients not easily understandable to the outsider. Thus, purity has a history of ritualism and ceremonialism, but progressively all of the rules pertaining to ablutions, food habits, and the like, are internalized as signifying the purification of heart and mind. So also, self-control, on one level, refers to the physical and mental senses. In the history of Hinduism such preoccupation has glorified asceticism and has made heroes of fanatics who have destroyed their sight glaring at the sun or atrophied their limbs through yogic acrobatics. On a higher level, self-control has gradually been perceived as a means for harmonizing all of one's calls and claims toward the development of a happy and healthy personality.

The ideal of detachment also has a long history representing the perennial tension between the ideals of *dharma* and *moksha*—of world-affirmation and world-negation. The early Mimamsa espoused the ideal of *dharma* so that the purpose of ethical action was that of enjoyment, both in this life and the next. The Mimamsa consequently ridiculed ascetics who practiced renunciation. In time, under the influence of Jainism and Buddhism, Vedic orthodoxy adopted the *moksha* ideal and thereby ethics became the instrument for the attainment of liberation. However, even when it incorporated this new ideal into its philosophy, the Mimamsa continued its former emphasis upon activity in the world. Against the objection that such activity, even when it is good, keeps one bound to the wheel of *samsara,* because a man must reap what he sows, the Mimamsa responded that action performed in the spirit of detachment is emotionally empty and therefore not subject to the operation of karma.

The Bhagavad Gita built on the ethical stance of the Mimamsa. Its formulation of ethical activism is a refined synthesis of two orthodox though conflicting modes of discipline: *pravritti* (active life) and *nivritti* (quietism).

Devotees who embraced the first ideal engaged in Vedic rituals and duties prescribed by the *Kalpa-sutras* with a view to reward in heaven. Devotees who embraced the second ideal abandoned all such works and relied solely on *jnana* or knowledge as the pathway to liberation. They reasoned that since all actions—good and bad—must have their consequences in reincarnations, the most direct way to escape the evil of rebirth was to minimize all activity.

The Gita counters the above argument that karma is evil and should be abandoned because it leads to rebirth, by making a shrewd analysis of human behavior. It does not stop with karma, but goes beyond karma to *kama.* Behind the deed lies the desire. Aversions and attachments determine a person's behavior, therefore a person's real enemies are not actions but passions.[6] Actions are only the motor manifestations of the impulse to love or to hate.

The implication of this analysis is that the power to bind one to continued existence resides in *kama,* not karma. Accordingly, karma without *kama* has no consequence for rebirth. Once desire is removed from the deed, the deed loses its fateful sting. He who knows this is wise. He can work and yet does nothing. In the Gita's words, "Having no desire, with his mind and self controlled, abandoning all possessions, performing actions with the body alone, he commits no sin."[7]

The Gita's analysis of action as the extension of desire, along with the inference that detached action *per se* has no binding power, brings one to the conclusion that what is ethically required is not "renunciation *of* action" but renunciation *in* action."[8]

The Gita's nomenclature for detached activism is karma-yoga. Karma-yoga treats the act as an end in itself and not as a means to another end. The classic formulation of karma-yoga is contained in the admonition, "In action only hast thou a right and never in its fruits. Let not thy motive be the fruits of action; nor let thy attachment be to inaction."[9]

Thus, in the principle of karma-yoga the Gita synthesizes the positive elements of *pravritti* and *nivritti*. "While it does not abandon activity, it preserves the spirit of renunciation. It commends the strenuous life, yet gives no room for the play of selfish impulses. Thus it discards neither ideal, but by combining them refines and ennobles both."[10]

The next two ideals, truth and nonviolence, are combined, and are regarded as Hinduism's highest ideals.

The ethical imperative of truthfulness flows from the metaphysical concept of Truth as Reality. Gandhi utters Upanishadic insight when he says, "Truth is by nature self-evident. As soon as you remove the cobwebs of ignorance that surround it, it shines clear."[11] Earlier, Gandhi believed that God is Truth, but subsequently he revised it to: Truth is God. By taking this step he felt he could include in the fold of believers all persons who were lovers of Truth and yet could not subscribe to any theistic ideology. His seeming innovation was not far removed from the Sanskrit word for Truth *(Sat)* which literally means "Being." The ontological meaning of *Sat* as "being" or "existing" is translated into the ethical meaning of *Sat* as "good."

The cardinal virtues reach their apex with the concept of *ahimsa*. It is *Paramo Dharma* (highest virtue). The word is a compound of *a* = "not" and *himsa* = "harmful." It literally means, "Not to injure or harm." *Ahimsa* is a correlate of Hinduism's cosmic outlook and therefore its moral mandate comprehends the whole created order.

As with the other cardinal virtues that have been tried and tested through the centuries, *ahimsa* has ancient origins. There is some speculation that it began as a "protest against blood sacrifice." The ambitious Aryan settlers were hardly disposed to the values of *ahimsa*, judging by their records of wars and their aftermath.[12] By

the time of the Upanishads, when the meaning of sacrifice was eth-
icized, truthfulness and nonviolence were given prominence. The
Chandogya Upanishad says, "Austerity, almsgiving, uprightness,
harmlessness, truthfulness—these are one's gifts to the priests."[13]

Strict adherence to *ahimsa* was observed by Buddhism, and more
so by Jainism. Classical Hinduism, while maintaining the primacy
of *ahimsa*, adjusted the ideal to political realities and developed a
"just war" theory not unlike its Christian counterpart.

The strict interpretation of *ahimsa* without qualifications or cave-
ats continued to appear in Hindu scriptural texts. For instance, in
the Yoga Sutras of Patanjali, *ahimsa* provides the ethical framework
for all the other virtues classified under *Yama* (restraint). *Ahimsa* is
more than nonviolence, it is non-hatred *(vairatyagah)*. Its scope is
universal. It is "not limited by life-state, space, time, and circumstance."[14] That is to say, *ahimsa* cannot be relativized by a series of
"ifs," "ands," and "buts."

The individual who served as a bridge to bring the pristine character of *ahimsa* into the twentieth century was Mahatma Gandhi
(1869–1948). This man, who Churchill once referred to as that
"naked fakir," is hailed today as "The Man of the Century." What
separated him, then and now, from other practitioners of nonviolence was his application of this principle to national and global
affairs. *Satyagraha* (nonviolent protest) was the technique by which
he put *ahimsa* into action.

Gandhi acknowledged that "nonviolence is common to all religions," but found its "highest expression and application in Hinduism (I do not regard Jainism or Buddhism as separate from Hinduism). Hinduism believes in the oneness not merely of all human
life, but in the oneness of all that lives. Its worship of cow, is in my
opinion, its unique contribution to the evolution of humanitarian-
ism. It is a practical application of the belief in the oneness and,
therefore, sacredness of all life."[15]

On the point of cow protection, Gandhi thought is was "the gift
of Hinduism to the world." It symbolized the protection of the
weak by the strong. It subsumed everything that feels. Causing pain
to the weakest creature on earth incurred a breach of the principle
of cow protection.[16]

Gandhi discovered nonviolence in his pursuit of Truth. He found
that *ahimsa* and Truth were so intertwined that it was impossible to
disentangle them. Even so, *ahimsa* was the means and Truth the
end. "Means to be means must always be within our reach, and so

ahimsa is our supreme duty. If we take care of the means, we are bound to reach the end sooner or later."[17]

To achieve *ahimsa,* strenuous discipline was necessary. "The perfect state is reached only when mind and body and speech are in proper coordination."[18] One must be fearless. "The votary of nonviolence has to cultivate the capacity for sacrifice of the highest type in order to be free from fear."[19] Nonpossession is essential. "If we are to be nonviolent, we must then not wish for anything on this earth which the meanest or lowest of human beings cannot have." One must be prepared to suffer for the sake of love. "The *satyagrahi* seeks to convert his opponent by sheer force of character and suffering. The purer he is and the more he suffers, the quicker the progress."[20]

This concludes our discussion of the cardinal virtues of Hindu ethics which serve as principles for decision making. All of these ideals ensue from Hinduism's cosmic outlook. Fundamentally, they teach respect for all forms of life and the duty to do good to all creatures.

We shall apply the ethical principles of Hinduism to three bioethical issues: population, abortion, and the environment.

Application of Ethical Principles

Population

India's population problem has to be viewed in its global setting. The world's population continues on a spiral course upward despite some success in slowing down its rate of growth. In 1985 another 85 million persons were added to world population—the equivalent of adding seventeen El Salvadors or one Mexico in one year. By the middle of 1987 the population will hit 5 billion and is expected to climb to 6.3 billion by the year 2000. More than ninety percent of that growth will take place in the less developed countries.[21] The figures are multiplying fastest in urban areas. Warns Lee-Jay Cho, Director of the Population Institute, East-West Center, Honolulu:

> The increasing urban concentration is an important aspect of demographic change affecting both rural and urban development efforts. Urbanization in the next two decades will bring about drastic changes in social, economic, and political life. The increasing number of people in cities thwarts governmental efforts to improve the quality of life for current and future generations. When such growth

becomes unmanageable—that is, when jobs and public facilities lag behind the demand for them—then urbanization becomes a serious concern of public policy.[22]

With 785 million people, India is at the epicenter of the population problem. Geographically, Indians inhabit an area that is 2.4 percent of the world's land mass, yet they number one-fifth of humanity. With a crude birth rate (annual number of births per 1000 population) of 35, and a crude death rate (annual number of deaths per 1000 population) of 13, India's annual rate of population growth is now 2.3. That means, at a minimum, the population escalates by an astounding 15 million annually, or makes the addition of one Australia per year. The population doubling time now stands at 31 years. By the year 2000, India's population will explode to 1,017.000. These statistics are grim by any measurement. In economic terms, India's per capita GNP (1983, US $) was 260, which places it among the poorest countries in the world. The comparable US figure is 14,080.[23]

Statistics are impersonal. To witness their human side, we must pay a visit to its great urban centers where twenty-three percent of the people live.

The city of Calcutta is described by its deputy mayor (1986), Mani Sanyal, as a "necropolis, a city of the dead and the dying." He calls it "a gas chamber with sixty percent of its inhabitants suffering from respiratory ailments due to intolerable levels of effluents saturating the atmosphere." The river is so choked with untreated waste that the annual fish yield is decimated. The noise pollution is twenty-five decibels higher than the World Health Organization's safe standard, which suggests that "however the city suffers, it does not do so in silence." The current population of 11 million is projected to 16.6 million by the year 2000.[24] It will then be the fourth largest city in the world.

Bombay, a metropolis of 10.1 million, is described by its mayor (1986), Datta Nalawade, as a city that developed "by chance." As the nation's financial and commercial center, Bombay attracts some 350 new residents per day. As a result, some sections of the city have a net density of 10,000 people per hectare. By the year 2000, Bombay's population is expected to soar to 16 million. It will then follow Calcutta as the fifth largest city in the world.[25]

Aside from urban areas, the population problem is most acute in Uttar Pradesh, Bihar, Madhya Pradesh, Andhra Pradesh, and Rajasthan. Actually, some eighty districts are responsible for over sixty percent of the population growth over the past decade. By contrast, the family planning program has prospered in Kerala, Tamil Nadu, Maharashtra, and Orissa.[26]

Factors responsible for India's population problem are many and complex:

- the decline of infant mortality from 220 per thousand in 1920 to 110 per thousand in 1986
- the decline of death rate from 48 per thousand in 1921 to 13 per thousand in 1986, without matching reduction in rate of birth
- low age of marriage
- extreme poverty
- low status of women
- lack of education in matters of sex and family planning methods
- logistical problems in delivering family planning services to a nation that is seventy-six percent rural
- social and attitudinal factors
- cultural, religious, and ethnic diversity
- setbacks in the seventies due to overzealous attempts to impose population control measures

The Indian government, which was the first to adopt a national policy aimed at reduced fertility, has made population strategy a major part of its current Five-Year Plan (April 1985), especially after the shocking revelation that in its 1981 census it had underestimated the population by some 12 million.

In a recent interview, Rami Chabra, adviser to India's Ministry of Health and Family Welfare, declared that the present population strategy is to achieve a crude birth rate of 27; a crude death rate of 10; an infant mortality rate of 87; and a contraceptive prevalence rate of 42 percent of the nation's reproductive couples. The goal of this strategy is to reach "a net reproductive rate of unity" by the year 2000 when married women of reproductive age will replace themselves with one daughter.[27]

"There are 130 million couples now in the productive age group," says Chabra. "Of these, 40 million are protected against pregnancy and we expect this to rise to 170 million by the end of the century."

She also points out that, while ninety percent of India's couples eligible for family planning have an awareness of some birth control device, only one-third make use of it. "To bridge the gap between awareness and adoption of a method at a faster pace," she notes, "we must understand that permanent methods of contraceptives cannot work for younger couples who will not accept them."[28]

Among other factors of the population strategy, Chabra stressed the need for community participation, increasing the legal age of marriage (which if raised to twenty could reduce the birth rate by thirty percent), and child survival programs. There is evidence that women in the Third World have fewer children when they can be certain that the ones they have will survive.

In his President's Message on the eve of Republic Day, 1987, Rajiv Gandhi said:

> The real benefits of development can be had in the long run only if we tackle our population growth effectively. In this task the active participation and cooperation of the people have to be enlisted. Family welfare should be developed into a mass movement. Social and attitudinal changes have to be brought about through sustained endeavours. Voluntary organizations have to supplement the efforts of the Government in this regard.[29]

In response to the President's challenge, the question arises: What part can Hindu ethics play toward supplementing the effort of the government, especially in terms of bringing about necessary social and attitudinal changes?

First, as we have pointed out, *dharma* is a dynamic concept, open to change. The *dharma* of the Vedas was to beget "ten sons."[30] That made sense in times when warfare, an agricultural economy, and high rate of infant mortality were the order of the day. For most of India's history, these exigencies have prevailed, and hence it has become hallowed tradition to have large families. But today the same principle of welfare dictates a radical shift in attitude both toward fertility and toward fertility as a requirement of *dharma*. Bluntly stated, yesterday's *dharma* is today's *a-dharma*. "The rules of *dharma* are the mortal flesh of immortal ideas and so are mutable."[31]

Today it is ethically irresponsible to say, "God sends children into the world" and that "man should not interfere with the will of God." In Hindu ethics, that which distinguishes civilization from the jungle is man's capacity to control nature, including his own. Sexual restraint is the infrastructure of the *ashrama* scheme in which procreation is limited to the householder stage. It is also a rationale for sanctions against sexual intercourse on a number of auspicious days and seasons.

But, having emphasized restraint in the face of the popular belief that God sends children, it is not our purpose to recommend that this age-old Hindu virtue be used as a method of birth control. That was Gandhi's solution to the problem, "I want limitation of pop-

ulation, but the method which we adopt is the method of abstinence, austerity, and self-control."

Radhakrishnan opposed Gandhi on this point:

> There is no doubt that it [abstinence] is the best method, but, I should
> like to ask, whether it be by self-control or abstinence, or austerity
> of living that limitation of population is brought about, is not that
> interference with nature? If we do not control ourselves, we will pro-
> duce more, and if we do control ourselves, we will produce less.
> There is an interference with nature even there, and so far as we are
> concerned most of us are human beings striving to be saintly, but
> have not yet become saints.[32]

The last point reflects the thinking of another Hindu sage,
Rabindra Nath Tagore. Contrary to Gandhi's plea for abstinence,
he said:

> I believe that to wait till the moral sense of man becomes a great deal
> more powerful than it is now and till then to allow countless gen-
> erations of children to suffer privations and untimely death for no
> fault of their own is a great social injustice which should not be
> tolerated.[33]

Indians need control, but they need contraceptives first. Seshagiri
Rao correctly states:

> Generally, Hindus show little resistance to the idea of birth control.
> There is no objection to contraception on religious or moral grounds.
> Brihadaranyaka Upanishad spells out a method of birth control for a
> man "who desires his wife, but does not want her to conceive"
> (VI.4.10). A temperate exercise of sex instinct by the householder is
> recommended in the shastras . . . ; and contraception helps in avoid-
> ing unwanted and undesirable pregnancies. Hence contraception is
> generally acceptable to the Hindus and is to be encouraged in the
> interests of domestic felicity and welfare of society.[34]

Family planning should be more than the distribution of contraceptives. One mistake of the past has been to treat contraceptives in
isolation. What needs to be emphasized is the integration of family
planning with family welfare, environmental sanitation, child
nutrition, literacy, and freedom and economic independence for
women. This "package" approach versus the piecemeal approach is
ethically more sound because it does justice to Hinduism's concern
for the whole person.

Two remaining factors that are essential to a population ethic
involve marriage and offspring.

Traditional Hindu marriage has a five-fold purpose: pleasure *(rati)*, parenthood *(prajati)*, companionship *(sakhya)*, sacrificial service *(yajna)*, and spiritual bliss *(ananda)*.[35] Due to the historic need for large families, it is understandable how the primary meaning of marriage developed around the notion of *prajati* (parenthood). This identification of marriage with procreation has tended to define the wife's role as biological. The young bride only becomes a fully fledged member of the husband's family when she produces a child, preferably a son. Without this, her traditional status has been in jeopardy. Today, with the need to limit the size of families, the social and spiritual purposes of marriage ought to be cultivated around the goal of *sakhya* or companionship. A wife is a friend, not a factory. This sentiment is expressed in the words of the groom to the bride in the marriage hymn of the Rig Veda, "I take thy hand in mine for happy fortune that thou mayst reach old age with me thy husband."

Finally, in developing a population ethic, Hindus are obligated to face honestly the issue of equality of offspring. Prejudice and injustice run deep. They are hallowed by religion and flourish in an ethos that is patriarchal to the core. Success in this area could not only mean a moral victory but reduction of the birth rate by a substantial percentage. Signs of hope can be seen on family planning billboards that dot the landscape. They promote the "value of female babies in an effort to open a new perspective for many Indian couples who feel their family is incomplete unless they have at least one male child."[36]

The need for "a new perspective" grows out of Hinduism's traditional preference for male offspring. The religious basis for this preference is the belief that the son rescues the souls of departed ancestors from hell. Manu says:

> By a son one conquers the worlds, by a son's son one attains the infinite, by the son of a son's son one attains the region of the sun.
> Since a son succours his father from the hell called *Put;* hence, the self-begotten one (Brahma) has called a son, *Putra* (lit, deliverer from the hell of *Put*).[37]

The status of the eldest son in the Hindu family is unique. He has the right to offer the funeral cake *(pinda)* at the time of the *shraddha* ceremony marking the anniversary of the death of the father and ancestors.

Responsibility for performance of rites for the forefathers stems from the notion that the sins of commission and omission done by parents are visited upon their children. Retribution can be averted by means of the *shraddha* rites. These household ceremonies are conducted every month for one year after the death. During this time it is believed that the deceased father moves in the air, not having been admitted to the company of the forefathers. At the conclusion of the year, a ceremony is performed by which the deceased is admitted to the assembly of the forefathers and thereby becomes a *pitri.*

Manu states that the first-born son on whom the father passes his debt *(rinam)* and by whom he gains immortality *(anantyam)* is the only child begotten for the sake of *dharma (sa eva dharmajah putrah);* all others are the fruit of passion *(kamajah).*[38]

The importance of the *shraddha* rites elevates the role and status of the son and devalues the daughter. When the dowry, which the father must give upon the marriage of the daughter, is also calculated, her liability increases as compared with a son who is an asset to his father in every way. No wonder there are always accounts of infanticide. *Hinduism Today* reports:

> In India, female infanticide is an ugly reality not easily faced or solved by state governments. It is common among low-caste families. Female infanticide is an offshoot of both the generally negative status for women and the dowry. In Hindu social dynamics, sons are prized and girls mean bankrupting dowries. The parents reluctantly poison the newborn girl, justifying it as a shortening of her suffering from one life to one hour.[39]

It is time that Hindus reevaluated the unethical accretions which have grown around their eschatology. Hindu beliefs are held on progressive levels of sophistication, but *shraddha,* though philosophically low, is not recognized as such because it caters to a host of nonreligious factors that assume male superiority and are difficult to eject in a patriarchal society. Philosophically viewed, the declared function of a son "as an instrument for cleansing his ancestors in the funeral rites" is purely magical. The private performance of *shraddha,* out of the sight of eunuchs, outcastes, heretics, or pregnant women, for fear that it might be rendered "unclean"[40] is both magical and superstitious. It demeans Hindu ethics to be associated with beliefs about collective guilt, about doing good deeds to acquire merit, and about the notion that offerings (excluding "unconsecrated grain or lentils, gourds, garlic, onions, or red vegetable extracts," and salt) somehow nourish the ethereal bodies of the departed ancestors, enabling them to perform works of merit that will advance them toward their goal of union with *brahman*.[41]

Hindu eschatology is more rationally served by the philosophic belief in *karma,* which asserts that each person makes his or her own heaven and hell. Moreover, our deeds are private and therefore cannot accrue for good or for ill to other persons aside from the natural impact of socially conditioned forces. Most importantly, a religion that views life unitively is ethically inconsistent when it elevates the salvific value of one sex over the other. It is strange that a religion that establishes the worship of animals should discriminate against its daughters. In today's world of exploding populations there is a more ethical way to affirm the continuity between the generations and to honor and immortalize the names of beloved ancestors. This is done by performing good deeds, the most dharmic of which may be limiting the size of one's family.

Abortion

The US Agency for International Development (AID) issued a call in January 1986 for global family planning as a means of reducing widespread abortions. The AID administrator, M. Peter McPherson, asserted:

> When couples want fewer children and family planning services are not accessible, abortion is often resorted to. This is true, whether or not it is legal.

McPherson observed that an estimated 25 million abortions are performed in Third World countries every year, compared with 113 million births.[42]

In India it is estimated that "annually there may be 6 million abortions . . . of which 3.9 million cases may be induced, and the rest spontaneous."[43]

Abortion is causing complex problems in India where the Hindu scriptures condemn it as *garbha batta* (womb killing) and *bhruna hatya* (killing undeveloped soul stuff). A Hindu newspaper reports a scenario which it claims "takes place in reality on the average of three thousand times a day in India."

> With rhythmic, anesthetized breathing, a 25-year old woman lies limp on an operating table, surrounded by sophisticated diagnostic gear and green-gowned surgeons. She is a Saivite Hindu, a lingam locket dangling from her neck, the holy ash she wore on her forehead when she entered the hospital that morning now scrubbed off.

She had spent the early dawn hours in prayer and puja at a temple.
But it hadn't erased her guilt. She was two months pregnant. Her
surgery was an elective abortion—her choice to abort because the
pregnancy was out of wedlock and a stumbling block to her legal
career.

The surgical team was also Hindu by faith. The chief surgeon's
youngest son just had his first-feeding ceremony. His mind was split
3 ways between a religious ache that he was killing a human life
form, a biological concept that the fetus at that stage was in insen-
tient sculpture of cells and his professional duty as a surgeon. In cases
where the abortion is therapeutic—necessary to save the life of the
mother—his mind was more easy. Today it wasn't. Within minutes
the fetus was pumped into a bag labeled "products of conception"
with "suction abortion" equipment. The patient was back in her
Madras, India, apartment that day.[44]

Abortion is referred to by *Hinduism Today* as "India's hushed epidemic."[45] Hindu society does not want to talk about it and government agencies are unwilling to distribute abortion information.
"But most significantly, Hindu spiritual leaders are not addressing
this huge societal problem."[46] Government statistics are available
from the state of Tamil Nadu. They recorded (1984) some 69,000
medical terminations of pregnancies (MTP's), 62,317 of which
were done on Hindu women, and the rest on Muslim and Christian
women.

The age group of women having abortions is mostly between
18–30. Of these, government figures indicate that only thirty percent have abortions for health reasons or because of fetal deformity.
A few are rape cases. The remaining cases are classified as due to
"unrevealed causes." There are good reasons to believe that these
statistics are faulty on the downside, but if they are representative,
abortion is being resorted to as a birth control method. *Hinduism
Today* surveyed an abortion clinic in New Delhi, which reported
that "25% of 15,000 abortions performed yearly are for unwed
mothers."[47]

Before the religious and ethical issues these statistics present are
discussed, we must point out that, when the Government of India
passed the Medical Termination of Pregnancy bill of 1971, abortion
was not intended to become a mechanism for birth control. The
bill clearly states two indications for terminating pregnancy:

(1) The continuance of the pregnancy would involve a risk to the
life of the pregnant woman or of grave injury to her physical or mental health; or (2) there is substantial risk that, if the child were born,

it would suffer from such physical or mental abnormalities as to be seriously handicapped.

Two appendices follow:

Explanation 1—Where any pregnancy is alleged by the pregnant women to have been caused by rape, the anguish by such pregnancy shall be presumed to constitute a grave injury to the mental health of the pregnant woman.

Explanation 2—Where any pregnancy occurs as a result of failure of any device used by any married woman or her husband for the purpose of limiting the number of children, the anguish caused by such unwanted pregnancy may be presumed to constitute a grave injury to the mental health of the pregnant woman.[48]

The quality of *daya* (compassion) clearly lies at the heart of this legislation and is manifest in its effects. The legalization of abortion has removed it from unsanitized backrooms and the butchery of unscrupulous opportunists, and has placed it in government hospitals and clinics run by qualified medical staffs. However, the ethical questions do not go away, for abortion contradicts the fundamental Hindu principal of *ahimsa*.

The basic ethical question is: When does life begin? The whole ethics of abortion depends on how this question is answered.

For an answer we go to the *Caraka Samhita,* a classical work on Hindu medicine. In its chapter on the "Formation of the Embryo" it states:

When a man with unimpaired sperm and a woman with unafflicted genital tract, ovum and uterine bed, cohabit during the period of fertilization, the *jiva* (Soul) along with the mind descends into the zygote (combined form of the sperm and ovum) lodged inside the uterus. It grows, unafflicted, being nourished by the wholesome *rasa* (final product of digestions of mother's food) and being managed with proper regimen. Thereafter the fetus is formed with all the sensory and motor organs, possessed of all the limbs of the body and endowed with the excellence of strength, complexion, mental faculties and compactness for delivery in time (ninth or tenth month of gestation). This occurs due to the combination of the factors derived from the following sources: (1) Mother, (2) Father, (3) Soul, (4) Wholesomeness and (5) Rasa (digestive product of the mother's food).[49]

Thus, according to Caraka's account, conception takes place in the womb by the union of semen and ovum and when the soul, along with the mind, enters the zygote. The soul, representing the element of consciousness, is omnipresent. It does not migrate from one place to another. When the mind finds a particular locus in conformity to its past actions, consciousness is manifested there. This is why it is said that the soul transmigrates along with the mind. Once the embryo is thus constituted, its further development depends on the quality of the food and regimen to which the mother resorts.

The entire process whereby consciousness unites with the psycho-physical apparatus to form the embryo "takes place in a very short time."[50] The embryo is of unique constitution because it is a composite of the vital information it receives from both parents. It is this information that determines all of its idiosyncratic features with respect to sex, physical development, and mental qualities. In brief, the humanization of the individual takes place in the moment of conception and all future growth is only the actualization of conceptual potency.[51]

If Caraka's archaic formulation of scientific intuitionism is translated into current medical idiom, he seems to be saying that the new being receives its genetic code at conception, and hence it is in the act of conception that hominization occurs. A being with a human genetic code is indeed a human being. It therefore makes no sense to discriminate between different degrees of human potentiality in terms of "ensoulment," "viability," and "brain waves," because that which is conceived by two humans is possessed of full human potential. It is nothing short of a self-evolving being.

The modern Hindu believes that human life begins with conception, basing his position on the *shastras* and on the principle that genetic components are complete at conception and that, therefore, the individual is subject only to the environment for future development. This reasoning makes him affirm the inviolability of the fetus and reject abortion.

At the same time, Hindu ethics recognizes that its position on nonkilling cannot be absolutist when the equal rights of human beings come into conflict. Ethical dilemmas arise in cases of rape and incest and when the mother runs the risk of grave injury or death. In such situations, abortion may be considered justifiable because Hindu ethics places greater weight on maternal rights. The adult human being, having arrived at a karmic state where there is much more at stake for her spiritual destiny, and where there are existing obligations to be performed for family and society, is in a position to be favored over an equal human being whose evolution, in this life, is by comparison rudimentary, and who has not yet established a social network of relationships and responsibilities.

The line for justifiable abortion is drawn in the case of probable child deformity. New technology, which makes it possible to detect prenatal problems soon after conception, gives parents the option of terminating the pregnancy at an early stage, if desired. Hindu religious leaders oppose such abortion on the grounds that it is interference with the karmic development of the child. However, the issue is by no means settled.

What is not ambiguous in this discussion is the use of pregnancy tests to determine the sex of the child, which often leads to the abortion of a female fetus. This is patently immoral. It is but one aspect of female infanticide to which we have already referred. Indians shudder at the government-sponsored programs of abortion practiced in China, but India's frequent resort to female infanticide is no less of a global scandal.

Environment

Bhopal and Chernobyl are grim reminders that the greatest problems we face today are those of our own creation. Through our technological powers we have made our planet more *accessible,* but not *manageable,* and the new price of our survival is the management of our planet. Norman Cousins observes:

> With all his gifts, man has been able to effect vast change, making his life different from that of those who have lived before. His capacity for invention and his sense of creative splendor have constructed great civilizations. But he has never been in command of his own works. He has never been in balance. The result today is that, for all his brilliance, he has thrown himself all the way back to his primitive condition, in which his dominant problem on Earth was coping with his environment. . . . He has been hammering at the chain of life at its weakest link, impairing the ability of the forests and the seas to make oxygen, putting poisons in the air beyond the ability of his lungs to eliminate them, fouling his own soil and water so that they cannot provide him with food.[52]

The latest news from the environmental front comes to us through the World Watch Institute, a prestigious research organization in Washington, DC. In its fourth global report on, "State of the World 1987," it warns that worldwide events are inexorably leading us toward disasters which "could bring a wave of extinctions comparable to that which wiped out the dinosaurs and half of all other species 65 million years ago." We are left with one choice, says project director, Lester R. Brown, "Initiate the needed reforms in population, energy, agricultural and economic policies, or risk deterioration and decline."[53]

The most critical area of imminent decline is the ozone layer—the band around our planet which filters out harmful solar ultraviolet rays. The deterioration is caused by the effects of chlorofluorocarbons (CFCs) which are used for refrigerators, air conditioners, aerosol products, and for cleaning computer chips.

Once they enter the stratosphere, CFCs have the reactive effect of decomposing ozone molecules, thus thinning the ozone layer and allowing solar radiation. The consequences of radiation are alarming:

- Skin cancer
- Drastic climate changes
- Disruption of the marine ecosystem due to loss of plankton
- Widespread soil erosion
- Declining food production
- Changing levels of the ocean, causing coastal flooding.

One part of this problem is the loss of forests. India, for instance, has lost twenty-two percent of its tree cover in the past eight years. European and Central American countries have recorded similar losses. Deforestation is caused by a global warming trend—the "greenhouse effect"—brought about by air pollution from burning oil and coal. When the forests are denuded, especially the tropical rain forests, the earth's ability to absorb the carbon released by the burning of coal and oil is correspondingly diminished. The result is the depletion of the ozone layer. A *Nova* television documentary, "A Hole in the Sky," pinpoints this phenomenon over Antarctica. Scientists report that a piece of the sky, fifteen miles high and the size of the United States, has vanished over this area. They are uncertain whether the disapperance is due to the dynamics of nature or is chemically induced. Could this be the first signal that all is not well in the ozone layer?

The gravest threat to nature's umbrella against planetary radiation comes from the perils of nuclear war. Carl Sagan states in "Nuclear War and Climatic Catastrophe: Some Policy Implications," that nuclear explosions could hurl vast amounts of smoke and dust into the stratosphere where it would absorb solar heat and light, thus precipitating temperatures to fall, and killing all forms of life on a global scale.[54] In the Kafkaesque words of Jonathan

Schell, a nuclear war could reduce the United States to a "republic of insects and grass."[55]

It should be evident that the management of our planet requires global governance. This will involve not just a test of technology but philosophy, for "everything begins—or ends—with a view of life."[56]

The fact is that ethics precedes ecology. But the question is: What type of ethics? In his landmark article, "The Historical Roots of our Ecologic Crisis," historian Lynn White, Jr., argues that our Western religious beliefs have legitimized the exploitation of our environment. The case can be argued pro and con, but there is little doubt that the historical achievements of Christian ethics have lain more in the social arena than in care for the environment. Conservationist Aldo Leopold explains modern man's ethical dilemma:

> The first ethics dealt with the relationship between individuals. The Mosaic Decalogue is an example. Later accretions dealt with the relationship between the individual and society. Christianity tries to integrate the individual to society, Democracy to integrate social organization to the individual.
>
> There is yet no ethic dealing with man's relationship to land and to non-human animals and plants which grow upon it. Land, like Odysseus' slave-girls, is still property. The land relation is still strictly economic, entailing privileges but not obligations.[57]

This means that modern man has a third step to take as an ecological necessity. It is the judgment of this writer that this third step has indeed been taken by Hinduism.

There are three basic values in Hindu ethics that can supply guidelines for a proper relationship between ourselves and the environment.

The first value is that of interconnection as a fundamental principle of life. The monumental contribution of Charles Darwin to the ecology movement, as expressed in *The Origin of Species* (1859) and *The Descent of Man* (1871), was to establish scientifically the intricate and dynamic connections within the world of biological existence. He presented life as a web in which diverse parts are precariously held together in a complex balance.

Darwin's research prepared the way for the science of ecology with its central concept of an ecosystem. Within this system nothing is closed, isolated, separate, or unique. Rather, all things are in a state of organic process, marked by reciprocal interdependence. Here, individualism is an illusion, for while some species may be unique, they are individual manifestations of the whole. Unity precedes diversity.

Harmonizing with science, Hinduism posits the interconnection of all forms of life through its evolutionary view of creation. As previously stated, Spirit transforms itself progressively from matter to life, to consciousness, to intelligence, and finally, to the perfect stage of pure Spirit. Thus, each stage is cyclically interlocked with the other stages. The dead stone is linked to life in the vegetable kingdom, plants are linked to consciousness in the animal kingdom, animals are linked to the intelligence of *homo sapiens,* and man is connected to the Life Force within the cosmos. Everything and all processes are pervaded by this single Energy, and therefore all elements of the universe are worthy of care and dignity. The awareness that we are denizens of a *universe* and not a pluriverse, imparts to the Hindu an ecological conscience. The ecological conscience, as distinguished from a merely social conscience, views the world as a series of interrelated systems that are in a state of dynamic equilibrium within which man must play his part as a responsible spectator and participant. In the balance of ecology, the responsibility or irresponsibility of an act is defined by its ability either to preserve or to destroy the integrity of the biotic community.

A second value of Hindu ethics that helps us relate ecologically to physical nature is the value of restraint.

In view of Western man's *pleonexia*—his insatiable desire for more—the realization of the finite character of our natural resources is forcing us to redefine economic growth. Time-honored principles of industry such as economic growth based on increasing expansion and consumption, must now be questioned and corrected. Speaking before a congressional hearing on ecology, Dr. J. George Harrar has stated:

> We, in the more advanced nations at least, should put considerably less emphasis on that form of economic growth that simply multiplies production and consumption of material goods. Our resources are not limitless, and when those that are non-renewable are consumed or transformed, they can never be replenished.[58]

Harrar sees the problem not only as economic, but as moral. "Morally, no society has the right to overutilize the world's resources for its own contemporary and selfish interests."[59] The point is well made. Even though the United States consitutes six percent of the world's population, it utilizes fifty-three percent of the earth's non-recoverable resources.

Some will say the position is not hopeless, "Technology will find a way to solve the problems." But this hope is a fiction. Technology may indeed solve a given problem, but it inevitably creates new problems. Technology is intermixed with toxic and tonic capabilities, and we must be able to see the distinction. Technology can no longer be taken for granted. It must be thought about, not merely produced, celebrated, and accepted in all its manifestations as an irrepressible but essentially benign human phenomenon.

By challenging the myths of economic growth and technology, we are not implying that technology has no place in solving the problems of our environment. It is impossible to turn back the hands of the technological clock. Besides, technology will inevitably be needed in such processes as recycling resources. What we need in addition to technology is an ecological attitude. This attitude will be more concerned with the quality of life than with such artificialities as the "standard of living." The quality of life can be enhanced by changing from a growth system to an equilibrium system in which economic growth and technological development will be adapted to the limits of our planet.

One essential ingredient within this ecological attitude will be the ideal of restraint. This does not advocate a withdrawal from the world but a way of acting *in* the world, *with* the world, and *for* the world. Something may be technologically possible, but the possible is not always the desirable. Because we can deploy weapons in space is not an adequate reason for "Star Wars" to be built. In an era of restraint, we shall not only have to ask, is this technologically possible, but is it ecologically justifiable. There is a growing list of things we *can* do that we *must not* do.

The ideal of restraint lies at the heart of Hindu ethics, which is essentially one of progressive renunciation. An important mode in which this ideal of conservation is categorized is within the scheme of the *purusharthas* or values of life. One bonafide value is *artha* or wealth. However, as with all values in Hindu ethics, *artha* is relational. It is instrumental to *dharma*. This subordination of wealth to wisdom, of economics to ethics, has imparted a characteristic attitude of parsimony to Hinduism which, today, is a quality essential for a "spaceship society." This observation has prompted Kenneth Boulding to assert that an ethic of conservation is "more likely to be found in Eastern religions than in the Judeo-Christian tradition," and he therefore sees the need for the West to enter into a genuine dialogue with Asian religions. In his words:

It may be that India, for instance, had to adjust to a highly conservationist economy before the West had to do it, simply because the West has always been more expansionist geographically and hence could preserve the illusion of the illimitable plane for a longer period. There is a paradox here, in that the scientific revolution could probably have taken place only in the West, precisely because of the Western expansionism and aggressiveness and the concept of man as the conqueror of nature. The East has never had any illusions about being able to conquer nature, and has always regarded man as living in a somewhat precarious position, as a guest of doubtful welcome, shall we say, in the great household of the natural world.[60]

To conclude, Hindu ethics does not reject technology, for that would consign the Third World to continued poverty and disease, but it does seek the intervention of international agencies to control the depletion of our global environment and to initiate an equitable distribution of the economic and health assets of technology. Similarly, on the question of growth, Hindu ethics steers a path between "pro-growth" and "no growth" and advocates a position of "selective growth" based on equity and quality. In the words of Ian Barbour, "Global justice requires that in developed nations economic growth be channeled toward services that are not resource-intensive. Ecological wisdom requires research on technologies for recycling and waste reduction. . . . Both justice and ecology require that affluent nations practice restraint in consumption, for which changes in personal values and life-styles, and in national priorities and policies, will be necessary."[61]

The third value of Hindu ethics in respect to the environment is the notion of man's continuity with the rest of physical nature.

Until Darwin, we could speak of man as the only species "made in the image of God," distinct from the whole of the natural order, and thereby endowed with divine rights to "have dominion over the fish of the sea and over the birds of the air and over every living thing" (Genesis 1.26,28). Moreover, when God reveals himself, the medium fitting for his communication is *history*, not *nature*. Thus, nature is desacralized and, once emptied of gods and demons, it qualifies as the orderly domain for man's technological exploits. White maintains that it was this anthropocentricism which imbued Western man with "arrogance toward nature." Theoretically, Darwin demolished our anthropocentric view of the world by tracing man's continuity with other forms of life. As it transpires, this is a scientific version of what Hinduism has believed and practiced from its inception. Its cosmic view of the self is expressed in such passages as:

> The essential self or the vital essence in man is the same as that in a gnat, the same as that in an elephant, the same as that in these three worlds, indeed the same as that in the whole universe.[62]

The general idea behind this text is that the individual *atman* is one with the universal *Brahman*. *Brahman* literally means "the growing or increasing force" *(brih)*. This *Brahman* force is manifest in the divinities of heaven, and in human, animal, and plant life on earth. All of these entities live an apparently independent existence, but they all emanate from *Brahman* and are finally reabsorbed into it. *Brahman* itself is infinite, and is therefore greater than the sum of all its manifestations: past, present, and future.

This belief in *Brahman* provides the philosophic basis for the Hindu's veneration of the natural world and man's participation within it. He sees nature, not as a commodity to possess, but a community to which he belongs. This universe appears to be material, but it is indeed the universal consciousness or *Brahman*. Since all is one, the conquest of nature cannot be true to reality, and our anthropocentric sense of separateness, isolation, and egotism are plainly the products of ignorance.

When ignorance is replaced by wisdom, the enlightened person can only truthfully embrace the virtue of *ahimsa*. *Ahimsa* does not reduce man to nature, but equates transcendence with responsibility.

Notes

1. K.N. Upadhyaya, *"Dharma* as a Regulative Principle," unpublished paper.

2. J. Filliozat, *Ancient and Medieval Science* (134) in Margaret and James Stutley, *Harper's Dictionary of Hinduism* (Harper and Row: New York, 1977) 252.

3. Brihadaranyaka Upanishad, 2.5.15, in *Thirteen Upanishads,* R.E. Hume trans., 2d. rev. ed. (London: Oxford University Press, 1971), 104.

4. Bhagavad Gita, 2.28.

5. *Harijan,* January 30, 1937.

6. Bhagavad Gita, 111.34.

7. Bhagavad Gita, 4.21.

8. M. Hiriyana, *Outlines of Indian Philosophy* (London: Allen and Unwin, 1970), 121.

9. Bhagavad Gita, 11.48.

10. Hiriyana, Outlines, 121.

11. *Young India*, 27.5.26, 189.

12. Atharva Veda 8.8.10; Rig Veda 10.89,9. Stutley, *Dictionary*, 7,8.

13. Chandogya Upanishad, 3.17,4.

14. Yoga Sutras, 11.31.

15. *Harijan*, January 30, 1937.

16. *Young India*, June 8, 1921.

17. M.K. Gandhi, *From Yeravda Mandir*, 2d. ed. (Amhedabad: Nava Jivan Press, 1935), 13.

18. *Young India*, 1.10.31, 287.

19. *Harijan*, 1.9.40, 268.

20. Mahadev Desai, *With Gandhiji in Ceylon* (Madras: S. Ganesan, 1928), 132.

21. *Popline*, 8, no. 3 (March 1986), 4.

22. Lee-Jay Cho, "The Population Institute," *East-West Center Program Prospectuses* (1982–1983): 1.

23. *1986 World Population Data Sheet*, Population Reference Bureau, Inc., Washington, DC.

24. "A City of Dead and Dying," *Popline*, 8, no. 6 (June 1986): 6.

25. "Bombay," *Popline*, 8, no. 6 (June 1986): 6.

26. "Population," *Darshan* 1 (January 1982): 16.

27. Hal Burdett, "Ambitious Targets Highlight India's Population Strategy," *Popline*, December, 1986, 4.

28. Ibid.

29. "President's Message," *Indiagram*, January 26, 1987, 2.

30. Rig Veda, 10.85.44–45.

31. S. Radhakrishnan, quoted in S. Chandrasekhar, "How India is Tackling Her Population Problem," *Foreign Affairs*, 47., no. 1 (October 1968): 145.

32. S. Radhakrishnan, *Planned Parenthood* (New Delhi: Central Family Planning Institute, 1969), 11.

33. H.C. Ganguli, "Religion and the Population Explosion," *Religious Pluralism and the World Community*, E.J. Jurji, ed. (Leiden: E.J. Brill, 1969), 208.

34. Seshagiri Rao, "Population Ethics: A Hindu Perspective," *Encyclopedia of Bioethics*, Warren T. Reich, ed., vol. 3 (New York: The Free Press (Macmillan), 1978), 1271.

35. Ibid.

36. Burdett, Hal, "Ambitious Targets Highlight India's Population Strategy," *Popline*, December 1986, 4.

37. Manu Samhita 1aX.137,138 in *Dharam Shastra*, M.N. Dutta, ed., 5 (New Delhi: Cosmo Publications, 1979), 334.

38. Ibid., 9.107.

39. "China's Forced Abortions, India's Female Infanticide," *Hinduism Today,* (July-August, 1986): 23.

40. Stutley, *Dictionary,* 284.

41. Ibid.

42. "Global Family Planning Aid Needed to Reduce Abortions," *Popline,* January, 1986, 3.

43. Bishen Lal Raina, "Family Size Norms," *Population Problems of India: A Symposium,* A.R. Kamat, ed., CFPI Monograph Series, no. 11 (New Delhi: Central Planning Institute, 1969), 45–61. Cited in Rao, "Population Ethics," 1272.

44. "Abortion Raises Complex Problems Among Hindus," *Hinduism Today* (March 1, 1986) 8, no. 2: 1.

45. Ibid.

46. Ibid., 21.

47. Ibid.

48. O.P. Jaggi, "History of Medical Ethics," *Encyclopedia of Bioethics,* vol. 3, 910.

49. *Caraka Samhita,* R. Sharma, Bhagwan Dash, eds., vol. 2 (Varanasi: Chowkambha Sanskrit Series Office, 1977), 366, 367 (3.1,2).

50. Ibid., 390 (4.8).

51. Ibid., 2.23–27.

52. Norman Cousins, "A Philosophy for the Environment," *Saturday Review,* March 7, 1970, 47.

53. John Christensen, "Making the Earth Uninhabitable," *Honolulu Star Bulletin,* March 9, 1987: A-13.

54. William French, "Technology and Ethics: Reflections after Chernobyl," *The Christian Century,* July 30-August 6, 1986: 676.

55. Ibid., 676.

56. Cousins, "Environment," 47.

57. Aldo Leopold, *Readings in Conservation Ecology,* George Cox, ed. (New York: Appleton-Century-Crofts, 1969), 585.

58. Paul Montgomery, "Ecologic Ethic," *The New York Times,* April 12, 1970, 16.

59. Ibid.

60. Kenneth Boulding, *Contemporary Religious Issues,* D.E. Hartsock, ed. (Los Angeles: Wadsworth, 1968), 123, 124.

61. Ian G. Barbour, "Environment and Man: Western Thought," *Encyclopedia of Bioethics,* vol. 1: 373.

62. Brihadaranyaka Upanishad, 1.3.22.

2

Ethics of the Theravada Buddhist Tradition

P. D. PREMASIRI

This essay is an attempt to accomplish a twofold task: to present the fundamental tenets of the Buddhist ethical system according to the Theravada canonical tradition; and to clarify the implications of these fundamental ethical principles for some moral issues that raise fresh challenges to the moral agent in the contemporary global context.

Basic Tenets of Buddhist Ethics

The claim of the Theravada school, which in the history of the expansion of Buddhism took root in South East Asian countries such as Sri Lanka, Burma, and Thailand, is that it is *the* school that has preserved the teaching of the Buddha in its pristine purity. It recognizes the canonical literature preserved in the Pali language, broadly classified into three sections, viz., *Vinayapitaka, Suttapitaka,* and *Abhidhammapitaka,* as the most authoritative representation of the Buddha's doctrine. Most modern scholars who adopt a critical historical approach to the study of Buddhism believe that it is the doctrinal content in the *Suttapitaka* that is of paramount importance for the understanding of the original message of the Buddha. All later schools of Buddhism, seeking to establish the validity of their respective doctrinal positions, invariably appeal to the authority of the *sutta* literature that seems to consist of a commonly accepted core of doctrine. Therefore, in reconstructing the fundamental tenets of the Buddhist ethical doctrine, the *Suttapitaka* will be used as the primary source from which material will be drawn.

The Theravada canon does not consist of scriptures in the form of treatises devoted to a systematic discussion of moral doctrines or philosophical ethics. Yet, these scriptures serve as an invaluable source for the reconstruction of a coherent ethical system. There is conspicuous evidence of the use of a tremendously rich ethical terminology in terms of which all aspects of human life and behavior have been evaluated. The early Buddhist scriptures may be said to consist, on the one hand, of certain theoretical statements describing the nature of things and, on the other hand, of certain evaluative, prescriptive, and practical utterances involving the appraisal of human actions, behavior, practices, and modes of life. Moreover, they offer guidelines for people to adopt certain modes of behavior, cultivate certain mental dispositions, and aim at certain specific ends in life.

The primary postulate on which the entire ethical system of Buddhism rests is the fundamental premise that there is a supreme end in human life that all rational and intelligent persons ought to aim at achieving. This goal, the *summum bonum* of Buddhism, is referred to in the Pali *suttas* as *Nibbana*. It is the goal which is aimed at, either remotely or immediately, by both layman and recluse *(bhikku)*. The religious or holy life *(brahmacariya)* is said to be lived to attain this goal.[1] The Buddha himself valued *Nibbana* as the highest attainment.[2] The goal of *Nibbana* is the guiding principle for moral action in Buddhism. *Nibbana* itself is conceived as a state of moral perfection and purification. It is defined in the *suttas* as the elimination of lust and greed *(ragakkhaya/lobhakkhaya)*, the elimination of hatred *(dosakkhaya)*, and the elimination of delusion *(mohakkhaya)*.[3] It is characterized as the highest *kusala*.[4] *Kusala* is one of the principal terms of evaluation in the moral discourse of early Buddhism, and has, in many contexts, the same meaning as the English term "good." The Buddha is said to have undertaken a noble search *(ariyapariyesana)* consisting of the quest for what is *kusala (kimkusalagavesi)*, and this search is supposed to have ended in his realization of *Nibbana*.[5] Since *Nibbana* is valued in Buddhism as the highest good, while other activities that serve as a means to the attainment of this goal are also judged to be good, the Buddhist ethical system may be described as teleological.

However, the significance of the concept of *Nibbana* to Buddhist ethics has been undermined by later attempts to interpret this concept in metaphysical terms. *Nibbana* has been interpreted as a transcendental reality, beyond any forms of conceptualization or logical thinking. This has been largely the result of the influence of the absolutistic and transcendentalist views stemming from the Vedic tradition, which the Buddha in his own teachings characterized as falling within the class of eternalist *(sassatavada)* doctrine. Radhakrishnan, for example, attributed to the Buddha the conception of an absolute metaphysical Being: He says:

Nirvana is an eternal condition of Being, for it is not a *samskara,* or what is made or put together, which is impermanent. It continues, while its expressions change. This is what lies behind the *skandhas,* which are subject to birth and decay. The illusion of becoming is founded on the reality of *nirvana.* Buddha does not attempt to define it, since it is the root principle of all and so is indefinable.[6]

The weight of evidence in the Pali *suttas* is clearly against such an interpretation. The Buddha never spoke of *Nibbana* as the metaphysical ground that explains the empirical universe. Metaphysical concepts such as God, *Brahman, Atman, Purusa,* presenting ultimate metaphysical grounds as explanations, are discouraged in Buddhism. However, Radhakrishnan, in his enthusiasm to interpret the conceptions of Buddhist *Nibbana* in absolutistic terms, even tried to attribute the theory of timeless self to the Buddha. He states:

> ... *Nirvana* is timeless existence, and so Buddha must admit the reality of a timeless self. There is a being at the back of all life which is unconditioned, above all empirical categories, something which does not give rise to any effect and is not the effect of anything else.[7]

Such attempts at describing the nature of Buddhist *Nibbana* have transformed its character from being a concept having ethical and psychological significance to being a concept having metaphysical and ontological significance, and this seems to be contrary to what was intended by the Buddha. The consequence of this view on the nature of *Nibbana* has been that the relation between the *Nibbana* ideal and the ethical life of man has been distorted, resulting in the interpretation of Buddhist *Nibbana* as an escapist and life-denying ideal which involves the most radical form of salvation doctrine. Some have even gone to the extent of saying that the highest spiritual attainment in Buddhism transcends morality altogether. S. Tachibana, for instance, says:

> The *Bhikku,* the *Brahmana,* the Buddha *(sattha muni)* are said to be free from such distinctions as good and evil, pleasantness and unpleasantness, purity and impurity and so on. . . . When one reaches this state of culture, distinctive ideas will be absolutely abolished. . . . He has reached the mental condition where there is not consciousness of moral, aesthetical or logical distinction; the relative ideas therefore of good and evil, pleasure and pain, agreeableness and disagreeableness, right and wrong are all annihilated for him.[8]

The doctrines represented in the Pali canonical scriptures do not reflect such an attitude to morality. According to the scriptures, it is a person who attains spiritual perfection who is capable of making moral distinctions with confidence and conviction. A person who is enlightened is said to be perfect in knowledge and virtue *(vijja-caranasampanno)*. The view that Buddhism advocates a spiritual goal that transcends moral distinctions has been based on the misinterpretation of some ethical terms used in the moral discourse of Buddhism. It is true that the Buddha instructed his disciples to get rid of both *punna* and *papa*.[9] These two terms have often been translated into the English language, without any qualification, as "good" and "bad," respectively. It is important to note that these terms have specific meanings in the context of the Buddhist analysis of the nature of man's destiny in the universe. *Punna* and *papa* are terms used exclusively in connection with the Buddhist doctrine of rebirth and *kamma*. *Punna* refers to the volitional impulses that produce a happy consequence to the individual agent of action in the *samsaric* process, while *papa* refers to exactly the opposite. Within the Buddhist world view, *samsaric* existence in any form is thought to be associated with *dukkha* (dis-ease or unsatisfactoriness). The supreme goal is the cessation of becoming *(bhavanirodha)* that occurs with the perfection of knowledge and character or the elimination of all roots of evil *(akusalamula)*. Therefore, all impulses leading to the prolongation of the process of becoming are to be abandoned without residue. Both *punna* and *papa* (good and bad impulses that produce pleasant or unpleasant fruit in *samsaric* life) must necessarily be abandoned. This does not mean that the perfected saint transcends the sphere of morality in the sense that he is free to act in any way he likes. The perfection of the Buddhist saint consists primarily in his perfection of moral character and his elimination of the roots of evil *(akusalamula)*. The Buddha, for example, is described as a person who has abandoned all evil traits of mind *(sabbakusalammapahino)* and is endowed with wholesome mental traits *(kusaladhammasamannagato)*.[10] While the highest attainment itself is characterized as *kusala*, the person who attains it is described as one who is endowed with *kusala* and possessed of the highest *kusala (sampannakusalam paramakusalam)*.[11] The Buddha and his disciples were admired by their contemporaries for being endowed with noble *kusala* conduct.[12] Perfected persons are represented in Buddhism as ethical models to be emulated by others. They are considered persons most eminently qualified to dispense moral guidance to others and to provide moral direction for the whole of humanity. By virtue of the moral perfection they have attained, they are spontaneously capable of conducting themselves in a right and blameless manner. They do not confront the moral struggles that one short of spiritual perfection is bound to confront for they feel no conflict between duty and inclination. It is said that a person who reaches this state is psychologically incapable of falling into heedlessness and morally blameworthy practices *(abhabba te pamajjitum)*.

The scheme of moral evaluation in Buddhism can be clearly seen to be relative to the goal of *Nibbana*. In the moral evaluation of persons, one who has attained *Nibbana* is judged to be the most praiseworthy person. A disciple who has confidence in the Buddha and who has as his ultimate aim the attainment of *Nibbana*, is described as a noble disciple *(ariyasavaka)*.[13] The *Dhammapada* describes the *arahanta* as the highest being *(uttamaporiso)*.[14] It is said that as far as the abodes of living beings extend, as far as the end of the realm of becoming, the *arahanta* are the highest, the supreme beings in the universe.[15]

The Noble Eightfold Path of Buddhism

The life that conduces to the attainment of *Nibbana* is called *brahmacariya* (the higher life). This attainment is possible by the understanding of the *ariyasaccani* (noble truths). The path to its attainment is called *ariyamagga* (noble path). This path is usually enumerated as consisting of eight factors, namely, right view *(samma ditthi)*, right thought *(samma sankappa)*, right speech *(samma vaca)*, right action *(samma kammanta)*, right livelihood *(samma ajiva)*, right effort *(samma vayama)*, right mindfulness *(samma sati)*, and right concentration *(samma samadhi)*.

The Noble Eightfold Path of Buddhism, which the Buddha himself described as the Middle Way, can be called the quintessence of the Buddhist ethical system. It was called the Middle Way *(majjhima patipada)* because of the context in which the Buddha preached. During that time, there were those who believed that man's spiritual elevation depended on self-mortification, and there were those who completely disregarded spiritual values and preoccupied themselves with sensuous indulgence. The Middle Way of the Buddha is sometimes described as a scheme of the threefold moral training *(tayo sikkha)*, consisting of virtuous practice *(sila)*, mental composure *(samadhi)*, and wisdom *(panna)*. A detailed analysis of the factors of the Noble Eightfold Path or the Middle Way gives a clear picture of the nature of the ethical norms accepted in Buddhism.

The first step of this Path, Right View *(samma ditthi)*, draws attention to the ideological basis necessary for a satisfactory moral outlook on life. Although Buddhism does not encourage a dogmatic ideological stance *(ditthi)*, a right view is considered pragmatically necessary as a starting point. Therefore, any ideological approach to life that involves a total denial of moral responsibility and free will and denial of the power of human effort and initiative to transform oneself morally is condemned in Buddhism. Forms of strict determinism and fatalism *(niyativada)*, on the one hand, and forms of strict indeterminism *(ahetu appaccayavada)*, on the other, were seen by the Buddha as damaging to the ethical life of man. He rejected the view that all human experience is determined by the will of a supreme God *(issaranimmanahetu)*, and also the view that it is determined by past action *(pubbekatahetu)*.[16] He considered the strict determinism of Makkhaligosala, a well-known contemporary, to be very damaging to mankind on the grounds that it persuaded people to adopt an attitude of absolute inaction *(akiriya)*. The Buddha equally considered as false the materialistic or nihilistic world view that rejected the efficacy of the moral and spiritual life toward improving the lot of mankind and that denied the good or evil consequences of volitionally performed action and the reality of survival after death.

Right Thought *(samma sankappa)*, the second step in the Eightfold Path, consists of thoughts free from lustful attachment or greed *(nekkhammasankappa)*, free from malevolence or hatred *(avyapadasankappa)*, and free from violent intention *(avihimsasankappa)*. Such thoughts form the psychological basis of benevolent moral action. The emphasis on the connection between thought and action, and inquiry into the psychological roots of human behavior, are striking characteristics of Buddhism.

Right Speech *(samma vaca)*, the third step, consists first of the avoidance of false speech *(musa vaca)* and the cultivation of truthfulness and trustworthiness. Second, it involves the avoidance of slanderous speech *(pisuna vaca)* intent on causing dissension among people and the cultivation of speech that promotes unity among those who are divided *(samaggakaranim vaca)*, and it strengthens the bonds of those who are already united. Third, it involves the avoidance of harsh speech *(pharusa vaca)* and the cultivation of speech that is pleasant and delightful to hear *(nela kannasukha pemaniya hadayangama)*. Fourth, it consists of abstention from frivolous or vain talk *(samphappalapa)* and the cultivation of meaningful, purposeful, useful, and timely speech *(kalena sapadesam . . . atthasamhitam)*.[17]

Right Action *(samma kammanta)* is the fourth step. It is connected with abstention from wrongful bodily action and the cultivation of right bodily behavior. It first recommends abstention from injury to life and from all violent acts of terrorism, the laying aside of all weapons used to cause injury to living beings, and the positive cultivation of a mind full of love and compassion, expressing itself in corresponding action. Second, it recommends abstention from theft and fraudulent behavior and the cultivation of honesty. Third, it recommends abstention from wrongful gratification of the senses, especially in terms of sexual misconduct.

Right Livelihood *(samma ajiva)* is the fifth step. It emphasizes the necessity of adopting a morally acceptable means of livelihood, avoiding those occupations that might be materially rewarding but morally reprehensible. In Buddhism, engaging in any occupation that might result in harmful social consequences is considered as a wrong means of livelihood *(miccha ajiva)*. Trading in weapons, animals, flesh, intoxicants, and poisons are classified under such illicit occupations that ought to be avoided by the Buddhist layman. In the case of the Buddhist monk, conditions of right livelihood are even more stringent, being determined by the consideration that his life should be in conformity with a life of detachment and renunciation.[18]

Right Effort *(samma vayama)*, the sixth step, recommends constant vigilance over one's character, determination to prevent the growth of evil dispositions, and the cultivation of wholesome dispositions of character already acquired. The moral agent constantly confronts inner conflict in choosing between what he considers to be the right thing to do and what passions, emotions, and inclinations prompt him to do. Right effort is considered in Buddhism to be a vital factor necessary for the triumph of the moral will over the baser emotions.

Right Mindfulness *(samma sati)*, the seventh step, means watchfulness over the mind to prevent the entrance of evil thoughts. It guides all aspects of mental, verbal, and bodily behavior, giving them the right moral direction. It may be described as the alertness necessary to observe and check *akusala* (immorality).

The last step in the Eightfold Path is Right Concentration *(samma samadhi)*. It stands for the clear, composed, and uncon-

founded mental condition that is conducive to the dawning of the
wisdom that results in the final elimination of all evil dispositions,
culminating in the perfection of moral character. The various
methods of mental training recommended in Buddhism *(bhavana)*
that lead to progressively higher states of mental composure are
considered to be the means for cultivating Right Concentration.
Methods of mental training that are usually referred to under Buddhist meditation are closely connected with the ethical life of the
Buddhist, as they are considered instrumental in freeing the mind
of unwholesome emotions.

The Noble Eightfold Path is morally significant for the Buddhist
because it leads to the attainment of the highest moral end of Buddhism. The highest end is the total elimination of *lobha* (lust,
greed), *dosa* (hatred), and *moha* (delusion). When the Buddha is
requested to state briefly what in his opinion is moral evil, he mentions these three psychological dispositions.[19] They are also
described as the roots of immorality *(akusalamula)*.[20] The numerous
patterns of bodily, verbal, and mental behavior that are characterized in Buddhism as *akusala* are said to be rooted in these psychological dispositions. According to the *Sammaditthisutta*, there is a
tenfold manifestation in human behavior of the three roots of evil.
They are (1) killing *(panatipato)*, (2) stealing *(adinnadanam)*, (3)
wrongful indulgence in sense pleasures *(kamesu micchacaro)*, (4)
false speech *(musavado)*, (5) slanderous speech *(pisuna vaca)*,
(6) harsh speech *(pharusa vaca)*, (7) frivolous talk *(samphappalapo)*,
(8) intense greed *(abhijjha)*, (9) malevolence *(vyapado)*, and (10)
wrong view *(miccha ditthi)*.[21] This is the standard list of moral evils
recognized in the Theravada canonical literature. Buddhism
attaches ethical value not only to overt action, but also to numerous
mental states that often are expressed in the form of overt behavior.
The *Dhammadayadasutta*, for instance, enumerates a lengthy list of
evil mental traits that can be conceived of as by-products of the
three basic evil dispositions.[22]

Any mental trait that hinders clarity of mind and mental composure, and which becomes an impediment to *Nibbana*, is considered evil. Buddhism mentions five such mental hindrances, namely,
urge for sensuous gratification *(kamacchanda)*, malice *(byapada)*,
sloth and torpor *(thinamiddha)*, flurry and worry *(uddhaccakuk-
kucca)*, and doubt *(vicikiccha)*. They are, from the Buddhist point of
view, fit to be called a heap of immorality *(akusala)* because they
hinder a person's progress towards *Nibbana*.[23] The four bases of
mindfulness *(cattaro satipatthana)*, consisting of the analysis of all

physical and mental constituents with perfect self-possession and mindfulness, are said to be a heap of *kusala* in that they consist of the certain path to moral perfection and the attainment of *Nibbana.*[24]

All modes of conduct having a tendency to reduce the strength of the three fundamental evil dispositions—greed, hatred, and delusion—are considered morally good in Buddhism. While recommending the highest degree of vigilance and restraint in respect to those modes of behavior that tend to feed, nourish, and enhance those unwholesome dispositions, Buddhist ethics also recommend certain positive actions conducive to their elimination and the cultivation of the opposite wholesome dispositions.

It is in this light that the significance of the four *brahmaviharas* (divine abidings) mentioned in the Buddha's teaching have to be considered. *Metta,* the first *brahmavihara,* stands for an attitude of friendliness, a loving kindness which one can consciously cultivate through contemplative and meditative practice. According to the Buddha, this attitude of friendliness has to be boundless and all encompassing and should not be limited by the common bounds of attachment familiar in narrowly-defined human relationships, such as those of family, race, and religion. *Metta,* in its ideal form, amounts to a universalization of the mother's love to her one and only child. The *Mettasutta,* describing how such loving kindness should be cultivated, says:

> Let one cultivate boundless thoughts of compassion towards all beings thus: "May all beings be happy. Whatever living beings there are, weak or strong, long or great, middle-sized, short, small or large, seen or unseen, living far or near, born or seeking birth, may all beings be happy." Let no one deceive another or despise another in any place. Let one not, out of anger or resentment, wish harm to another. As a mother protects her one and only child, even at the risk of her life, so also let one cultivate boundless compassion towards all beings.[25]

In the same manner should sympathy *(karuna),* sympathetic joy *(mudita),* and equanimity, which involves impartiality and fairness *(upekha),* be cultivated towards all beings. The cultivation of *brahmaviharas* through contemplative exercise, conditions the mind for appropriate moral action. The four *sangahavatthu* (bases of benevolence) operate at the level of overt action. They may, on the one hand, be looked upon as the behavioral expression of the mental condition cultivated by the *brahmavihara* and, on the other hand, as the modes of behavior that feed and nourish the wholesome traits of mind associated with the *brahmavihara. Dana* (liberality), the first base of benevolence, is one of the cardinal moral virtues recognized in Buddhism. The sacrifice of personal possession for the benefit of others, whatever the possession may be—material wealth, knowledge, expertise, or labor— is considered a great moral virtue. *Piyavacana* (pleasant speech), *atthacariya* (service of others), and *samanattata* (equal respect for all) form the other three bases of benevolence.

The path to spiritual perfection in Buddhism may be based on a systematic doctrine of moral psychology. According to one of the principal formulations of the spiritual path, it consists of three stages of development: *sila* (moral practice), *samadhi* (mental composure), and *panna* (wisdom). *Sila* is interpreted as the method by which the activity of evil dispositions is curtailed at the grossest level. Evil dispositions find their expression in verbal and physical behavior in the form of killing, violence, stealing, wrong speech, etc.. The function of *sila* is to deal with evil dispositions at the most tangible level, that is, at the level of observable behavior. The behavioral expressions of evil dispositions have the effect of feeding those dispositions themselves, further nourishing and strengthening them. The starting point in the moral catharsis, therefore, has to take the form of a deliberate and conscious effort to refrain from such behavior that may further enhance the evil traits of mind. Hence, *sila* is presented primarily in the form of voluntary abstention from bodily and verbal behavior that is morally evil. *Sila* has, in addition to this negative aspect of refraining from evil action, a positive aspect of cultivating wholesome action. In both cases the goal is the same, that is, hindering the growth or reducing the strength of evil dispositions.

Secondly, evil dispositions express themselves at the level of inner mental experience *(pariyutthana)*. Lust, anger, envious thoughts, jealousy, etc., may set in motion a process of inner turbulence disturbing a person's inner tranquility. *Samadhi* (mental composure) helps in preventing the expression of evil traits at the level of inner experience and promotes the further weakening of those impulses. The various techniques of calming the mind *(samatha-bhavana)* recognized in Buddhism are supposed to help a person overcome the expression of evil dispositions at the level of inner mental experience.

The third and most subtle level at which these dispositions operate is the subconscious *(anusaya)*. Greed, hatred, and delusion may not always be expressed in physical and verbal action or in the form of an inwardly felt mental disturbance. Those tendencies may be inherently there to be expressed when a person is confronted with a certain type of situation. One may not always be exhibiting angry and aggressive behavior or feeling the pangs of anger, but one may be disposed to becoming angry when confronted with a certain situation. It is understanding or wisdom *(panna)* that eradicates evil at this subtle level. Insight into the three characteristics of all existence *(tilakkhana)*, namely, their transient nature *(anicca)*, their dissatisfying nature *(dukkha)*, and their unsubstantial nature *(anatta)* is considered the highest self-transforming knowledge that is hailed by Buddhism as the achievement of an enlightened, *nibbanic* individual.

Although the aims and goals of Buddhism, as well as the methods for achieving them, are thought of as universally applicable to all human beings, on certain practical considerations, the Buddha clearly seems to have indicated a difference in degree with regard to the moral precepts *(sila)* to be observed by Buddhist monks and those to be observed by Buddhist laymen. The life of the *bhikku* (monk) has to conform strictly to a life of full renunciation of worldly possessions. It is to be devoted fully to the contemplative exercise of purging one's mind of all defiling tendencies *(asava)* with alertness, self-possession, and intense self-analysis. The *bhikku* is not expected to pursue certain worldly occupations for his livelihood but is to depend on the faithful and generous laity for his material needs. The frugality and simplicity required in the life of the *bhikku* is amply illustrated in the enumeration of the moral precepts that the *bhikku* is expected to observe.[26] Thus, in addition to the main abstentions such as abstention from killing, stealing, and wrong speech, the *bhikku* is expected to be celibate, moderate in food, and not given to luxurious living. He should be content with the barest minimum of material requisites. Although the Buddha shuns self-mortification as a useless exercise leading to no elevation of the character, the life of the *bhikku* is expected to be free from the lower pursuit of material luxuries that could divert his attention from the higher spiritual ideals. The virtuous *bhikku* is referred to by the Buddha as one who does not inherit material luxuries *(amisadayada)* but one who inherits righteousness *(dhammadayada)*.[27]

The good society envisaged by the Buddha is one in which the *bhikku*, the *samana,* or the *brahmana* (all three terms stand for the person truly committed to the spiritual pursuit) has an important role to play in the general moral well-being of society. The monk's role in society was conceived by the Buddha as an exclusively moral and spiritual one. He may not rule, but he may give moral guidance to rulers. He may not engage in trade and business, but he may point out to laymen how to engage in such activities without violating the principles of good conduct. The moral direction given to society from such a detached and disinterested position is considered by the Buddha as very significant. The degree of detachment cannot be expected of an ordinary lay person who is bound by various ties and bonds of personal relationships and attachments. But a *bhikku* is one who has renounced everything—wealth, property, family ties. The *Singalovadasutta,* in which the Buddha outlines certain principles of conduct for the laymen, considers the spiritual community as the upper direction *(uttara disa)* that a virtuous layman ought to worship in place of the traditional, superstitious ritual of worshipping directions *(disa vandana).* The goal of the *bhikku* is moral perfection involving the eradication of all ties and attachments, including attachment to his own self. What is aimed at by such an ideal is not the production of a band of selfish seekers after individual salvation but spiritual leaders capable of setting the right moral pace for the whole society. Critics of the Buddhist ideal of *Nibbana* miss this aspect of the Buddha's moral teaching by concluding that Buddhism merely offers an individualistic, otherworldly, life-denying ideal of salvation.

To say this is not to deny that Buddhism aims at salvation in an individual sense as well. For Buddhism sees *samsara,* the cycle of becoming, as unsatisfactory *(dukkha)* and seeks to put an end to it. Escaping this cycle is considered the real well-being of each individual. However, it sees no opposition between this goal and benevolent, altruistic action. The path that leads to salvation is precisely one involving the eradication of evil tendencies of the human mind. Moreover, man is capable of becoming happy here and now by getting rid of evil dispositions that hinder his happiness. This ideal is one of immediate concern for the Buddhist monk, though it may not be for the layman. Once it is achieved, the Buddhist saint does not lapse into a state of inertia and inaction. Rather, by virtue of the new benevolence of heart that replaces the former selfishness, he is spontaneously moved to disinterested action for the well-being of humanity.

Buddhism admits that there are certain limitations to the degree of moral perfection that a layman may attain. It is said that a householder *(gihi)* cannot live the higher life *(brahmacariya)* in its most perfect form.[28] The life of renunciation *(pabbajja)* is said to be free from the encumbrances of lay life. Yet, this does not preclude the layman from reaching the same spiritual heights that a monk is capable of reaching, provided he trains himself in the same discipline. On practical considerations, however, the Buddha recommends to lay people, as a minimum moral requirement, that they observe the five moral precepts *(pancasila):* abstention from killing, abstention from stealing, wrongful enjoyment of sensual pleasures, false speech, and abstention from intoxicants. More detailed instruction regarding how the layman should strike a good balance between his economic and moral life has been given by the Buddha in several *suttas.*[29] Righteous acquisition of material wealth is praised as a virtue in the case of laymen. Energetic and industrious persons who make a success of their material condition in life, adhering to righteous principles, are praised while inert individuals who live purposeless lives are condemned. The conscientious performance of one's role in society as father, son, ruler, or teacher is praised. Sharing of one's material possessions with one's own family, friends, and relatives is highly commended. Caring for aged parents, fulfilling one's responsibilities towards members of the family, and safeguarding marital fidelity are considered important virtues of the lay life. Above all, the layman is expected to cultivate his spiritual welfare. Hence, he is periodically expected to visit spiritual teachers and recluses who can give him proper guidance on spiritual matters.

In the foregoing account, a general description of the content of Buddhist ethics has been presented. It is important, especially from the point of view of moral philosophy, to determine the formal characteristics of Buddhist ethics. Buddhism, like any system of religious morality, subscribes to a cognitivist position with regard to moral issues. In other words, Buddhism admits to the possibility of achieving ethical knowledge. It affirms that there are moral truths to be known. "Nothing is right or wrong, but thinking makes it so," is not a position favored by Buddhism. What, then, are the formal characteristics of the Buddhist ethical system? What light does Buddhism throw on the problem of the rationality of moral discourse?

The *Kalamasutta* can be considered the *locus classicus* for the interpretation of the Buddhist method of moral reasoning. The *sutta* can be said to have been preached by the Buddha in a typically ethical context. It raises a fundamental question that concerns the moral philosopher, namely, how do we know what is right or wrong? To what criterion can we make a rational appeal? The Kalamas were a people who were confronted with doctrines evidently involving mutually contradictory moral teachings propounded by numerous teachers who visited them. When the Buddha visited them they expressed their puzzlement and asked him to offer a sound criterion for making moral choices. On this occasion, the Buddha advised them to disregard tradition, revelation, authority, *a priori,* or speculative reason, and to use their own judgment based on what they themselves could observe objectively. The Buddha's attempt to resolve the moral problem which the Kalamas faced can be seen in the following dialogue:

> Now what do you think, Kalamas, when greed arises within a man, does it arise to his benefit or harm?
> To harm, Sir.
> Now Kalamas, this man, thus become greedy, overcome by greed, with his mind completely filled with greed, does he not kill a living creature, take what is not given, commit adultery, tell lies and induce others too to commit such deeds as those which conduce to disadvantage and unhappiness for a long time?
> He does, Sir.[30]

The same is said about malice and delusion. The Kalamas admit that greed, malice, and delusion *(lobha, dosa, moha)* are *akusala* (morally bad), *savajja* (blameworthy), *vinnugarahita* (censured by the wise ones), and when one is under their influence, the results are illness and suffering. The Buddha's attempt here is to show that the Kalamas can know for themselves the distinction between good and bad, without depending on external authority.

A similar exposition of the Buddhist criterion for distinguishing good and bad behavior is presented in the *Bahitikasutta* of the *Majjhimanikaya.* Here, bad conduct, censured by wise recluses and brahmins, is defined as conduct that involves injury or harm *(savyapajjha).* Injurious conduct, in turn, is described as conduct that has an unhappy consequence *(dukkhavipaka).* It is conduct that results in tormenting the agent, tormenting others, and tormenting both the agent and those affected by the action.[31] The *Ambalatthikarahulovadasutta* states the same criterion, emphasizing the need for a moral agent to reflect carefully on the general tendencies that particular actions can be known to possess.[32] Rahula is advised to reflect on the observable consequences of action of body, word, and mind before performing it, while performing it, and even subsequent to its performance.

It should now be clear that the Buddhist enumeration of moral virtues and moral precepts, and its recommendation of a supreme goal for rational beings, has conformed to a teleological or consequentialist criterion. The concepts of happiness and well-being play a central role in Buddhist ethics. The goal of *Nibbana* is a worthwhile ideal to pursue because it constitutes the real happiness that man can attain. *Nibbana* puts an end to *dukkha*. The highest happiness from the point of view of the individual is attained when there occurs a total emotional transformation. It is on hedonic considerations that *Nibbana* is conceived as the highest happiness. Individuated existence in the cyclic process of *samsara,* subjected to the hazards of birth, old age, disease, and death, and numerous other depressions, anxieties, and frustrations due to the transient nature of phenomenal existence, is *dukkha.* This process does not cease until the psychological defilements *(asava)* are laid to rest. The evil tendencies that function as the driving forces of *samsaric* life are precisely those mental traits that produce immoral behavior. At the root of all conflicts, dissensions, rivalry, and warfare are the basic evil dispositions *(lobha, dosa, moha).* From the Buddhist point of view, man is incapable of becoming happy as long as these evil bases are dominant in his behavior. Disharmony at a social level, and the resultant suffering produced by man himself in the form of violence towards fellow members of the society, discriminative treatment, and violation of the rights of others are all explained in Buddhism as being rooted in these evil dispositions.

Buddhism believes that observation and analysis of the facts of human experience should form the rational basis of a sound ethical system. Human behavior can be evaluated only on the basis of our knowledge of the nature of the human predicament. It is the facts about the nature of the human situation that reveal to us what, in the ultimate analysis, constitutes happiness and well-being. Buddhism accepts as facts about the human predicament the reality of *kamma,* rebirth, and *samsara.* Morally praiseworthy action is, from the Buddhist perspective, action that conforms to a hedonistic, consequentialistic, or teleological criterion. However, this hedonsim is universalistic in the sense that Buddhism admits that, in the ultimate analysis, there is a universal harmony of interests. One can be happy only by the development of a character that is conducive to the happiness of others as well. There is no opposition, in the final count, between one's own welfare and the welfare of others. The Buddha says:

> Monks, in looking after one's self, one looks after another. How, monks, does one in looking after one's self, look after another? By the practice, development, and cultivation (of wholesome qualities). . . . How, monks, does one in looking after another look after oneself? By endurance, non-injury, loving-kindness, and sympathy.[33]

The significance of this statement is that altruistic action, involving love and compassion, promotes the cultivation of the nobility of one's character, and that in turn promotes altruistic action. Buddhism insists that one cannot pull another person out of the mud unless one comes first out of the mud oneself.[34] One becomes suitable for acting as a liberator of mankind only when one is free from the moral depravities that prompt one to act in evil ways. Those who have no moral basis for their so-called social commitment usually end up doing more harm than good to society because of their depraved condition. The morally perfect man in Buddhism is one who is intent on the welfare of himself as well as of others.[35] The enlightened person intends the well-being of all, not only of himself.[36] The Buddhist emphasis on the moral significance of liberating the mind from evil dispositions as a causally necessary condition for one's own well-being cannot be interpreted as an egoistic doctrine. For, in the long run, there is no opposition between what conduces to one's own well-being and the well-being of others. According to Buddhism, such an opposition occurs only when our perception of a moral situation is confined to a narrow perspective.

The Buddhist claim is that it is possible to give good reasons in favor of an ethical judgment. Unlike contemporary non-cognitivist ethical theories, such as emotivism and prescriptivism[37] that claim there is, in the final analysis, no valid reason that can be given for having a particular moral attitude, nor for accepting a fundamental moral premise, the Buddhist position is that there is a certain limit to the kind of reasons that can be adduced in favor of a moral judgment. When Buddhism judges killing to be a bad action, it bases this judgment on one or more factual premises:

1. that such action springs from and enhances *lobha, dosa,* and *moha,* or any of those mental conditions or character traits that impede the individual's progress towards the highest happiness,
2. that killing has harmful *kammic* consequences to the individual in this life itself or in a future life,

3. that killing has harmful consequences resulting from the individual's guilty conscience, social and legal sanctions, etc.,
4. that killing results in unhappiness and harm to persons other than the individual agent of such action.

In favor of a judgment of the sort, *"X is kusala,"* one cannot adduce any arbitrary fact. "Giving food to A who is now suffering from hunger is a *kusala* deed" is not justified, for instance, by supplying some idiosyncratic reason as, "Today is Sunday." It is justified by the reason that it leads to the alleviation of another person's suffering, and to the cultivation of the benevolent character of the person who performs that action.

In terms of the above Buddhist position, one can be said to be mistaken about one's moral opinions under two conditions:

1. If one is mistaken about the relevant facts and lacks factual knowledge about what constitutes real happiness and well-being and the causal laws operating in the sphere of human action.
2. If one oversteps the legitimate sphere of morally relevant facts, that is, if one pays no attention to the consequences of an action but appeals to external authority, traditions, etc.

The above criteria for the evaluation of human behavior seem to conform to a utilitarian doctrine. However, it is often contended by those who are opposed to utilitarian or consequentialist moralities that the criterion of utility does not accord with some of our basic moral intuitions. It is argued that moral notions such as justice, fairness, and equal treatment of all persons cannot rest on a purely utilitarian criterion. Buddhism could answer this objection by pointing out that utility need not be the sole criterion of morality. For Buddhism explicitly uses another criterion within which moral notions other than those that fall under a utilitarian criterion can be included. According to an explicitly stated alternative pattern of moral and practical decision making advocated in the Pali Nikayas, one way in which a moral agent can reason in situations is as follows:

I do not want X to be done unto me.
Other beings who are like myself in this respect, too, do not want X done unto them.
I ought not to do unto others what I do not like to be done unto myself.
Therefore I ought not to do X.

This was a familiar ground on which the Buddha based his moral injunctions. In the *Dhammapada,* for instance, this pattern of moral reasoning is clearly exemplified.[38] It is this criterion that is called the Golden Rule of morality. Kant formulated a similar criterion and referred to it as the "moral law." R. M. Hare refers to it as the "Universalizability" of the moral imperatives.[39]

Buddhism accepts as fact that all sentient beings have in their psychological constitution certain common feelings, desires, and attitudes. No sentient being desires to be deprived of life, or to be subjected to torture, or to be deprived of possessions by force or theft. To have a moral attitude towards life is to have the ability to put oneself in the position of the other person who might be affected by one's action. Buddhism also seeks to establish seven moral values upon this criterion. These are frequently mentioned under the concepts of *sila* and *kusala*. The *Samyuttanikaya* contains an explicit instance of an application of this criterion:

> Here a noble disciple reflects thus: "I like to live; I do not like to die. I desire happiness and dislike unhappiness. Suppose someone should kill me, since I like to live and do not like to die, it would not be pleasing and delightful to me. Suppose I, too, should kill another who likes to live and does not like to die, who desires happiness and does not desire unhappiness, it would not be pleasing and delightful to that other person as well. What is not pleasing and delightful to me is not pleasant and delightful to the other person either. How could I inflict upon another that which is not pleasant and not delightful to me? Having reflected in this manner, he (the noble disciple) himself refrains from killing, and encourages others, too, to refrain from killing, and speaks in praise of refraining from killing. . . .[40]

Similar reflections are said to occur concerning theft, adultery, false speech, slanderous speech, harsh speech, and vain and frivolous talk.

In recommending the abstention from certain types of evil action and the positive performance of certain types of wholesome action, Buddhism seems to depend on this criterion as well. It should be pointed out however, that people may sometimes commonly desire what is not in their interest, and it would, under such circumstances, not be morally right to do an action that is not in the real interest of oneself or others. It is therefore necessary constantly to check this criterion against the former criterion of utility in order that it may genuinely become a moral criterion. It is often the case that, if people really understand what is in their real interest, they do not hesitate to pursue it. But this may not always happen, as one can ignore one's greater interest due to some weakness of will or addiction to base pleasure. Therefore, the mere fact that someone, in common with fellow members of a society, has certain desires does not imply that it is always right to work for the fulfilment of such desires without ascertaining the worthwhileness of those desires. Thus the criterion of utility along with the Golden Rule can be said to be the dual criteria for moral decision-making in Buddhism. They are to be applied as mutually supportive criteria in order to avoid certain conflicts that might otherwise occur with our common moral intuitions.

The foregoing account affirms that Buddhist ethics is not founded on the authority of a supernatural being. Certain modes of behavior are good or bad, not because God or any other authority has commanded them or prohibited them, but because people themselves can discover these distinctions on an autonomous basis. In any case, with reference to a moral precept that is accepted on the ground that God has commanded it, the question arises as to whether God has commanded it because it is good, or whether it is good because God has commanded it. To say that God commands only what is morally good reduces itself to a circular definition of goodness unless one accepts a criterion other than that a particular morality is commanded by God. Buddhism insists that the pursuit of morality is an autonomous exercise and that, as rational beings, men can determine what is right and wrong only after a comprehensive understanding of human nature and the human predicament. If this is the Buddhist attitude to moral questions, one might wish to know what is the difference between Buddhist morality and the morality of a scientific humanist. Although Buddhism is a nontheistic religion, it is not materialism. The Buddhist world view rests on an epistemological basis that is different from that accepted in the empirical sciences. Like the scientific humanist, Buddhism rejects revelation and external authority. But it admits certain special methods of knowing that, in the Buddhist scriptures, are referred to as *abhinna* (super-cognitive knowing). These cognitive abilities are said to be a consequence of mental composure *(samadhi)* attained in meditative training. These special cognitive abilities are supposed to enable the person to verify in his own experience the truth of survival after death and the operation of the laws of *kamma*. The consequentialist position of Buddhism sees the effects of action as extending beyond the span of a single lifetime. This is significant ground for a wide divergence of opinion between Buddhism and scientific humanism on specific moral issues.

Implications of Ethical Principles for Moral Issues

No system of morality is capable of supplying one with a ready-made set of moral rules that are applicable to all times and climes, although a moral system may be said to contain certain general principles in terms of which we may derive new moral rules to meet altogether new situations. Conditions of living have undergone vast changes and life has become much more complex today compared with the social milieu of the Buddha's day. Modern empirical science is increasingly wielding its influence on people's thinking and is generally recognized as the paradigm of cognitive activity. It has not only brought about changes in the way people perceive but has given them enormous skills with the aid of its technology. These developments in the realm of science and technology are raising new moral issues, especially for those whose outlook has been traditional. Therefore, the question, Can contemporary man adequately respond to these fresh challenges with the aid of the fundamental tenets of traditional moralities? is most significant. Our inquiry will focus on the extent to which Buddhist moral principles can still provide guidelines for moral choices, personally, socially, and on a global scale. The specific issues we shall address include the areas of population, abortion, sexual relationships, the family, and violence.

Population

The problem of the population explosion is a contemporary issue that modern communities expect to solve with the help of scientific technology. It is unlikely that anyone can deny the danger of a steadily increasing population on a global scale, especially under circumstances of limited resources, and in those areas where the boom is greatest. Several national organizations have already responded to this population crisis by adopting methods of birth control and family planning, despite opposition from traditional religious bodies. The question in our context is: What are the implications of Buddhist moral principles on the issue of population control?

It has already been stated that Buddhism does not derive its morality from a divine source. Human morality is based, first, on a concern for well-being that is to be determined on the basis of experientially observed facts, and second, on the Golden Rule that treats other sentient beings in the way one would want to be treated by others. There is no room for sacred commands that need to be observed as man's moral duty, irrespective of the consequences that would follow to oneself and others from such performance of duty. Buddhist ethical doctrine has a teleological rather than a deontological structure. It is in terms of this formal structure of Buddhist ethics in general that one has to determine the Buddhist moral response on an issue such as birth control.

A genuinely Buddhist response therefore has to be preceded by a careful investigation of facts related to birth control. An investigation of currently practiced birth control devices shows that they are mostly methods for the prevention of undesired conceptions. Contraceptive methods involve some form of interference with the natural order but do not involve causing any pain or affliction to a living being or the destruction of existent life. Buddhism definitely would raise moral objections to the destruction of existing life however minute that form of life may be, provided it is done with malicious or selfish intentions. But the mechanical or artificial prevention of unwanted conceptions, especially when the rise in population may have harmful consequences on society as a whole, would not be looked upon as a moral evil. Since man has a duty to promote the welfare of the community as a whole, Buddhism would rather consider it a duty to regulate deliberately one's social environment in order to make it conducive to harmonious and satisfactory living.

Abortion

While contraceptive birth control would not be objectionable from the point of view of Buddhist morality, abortion is definitely condemned on moral grounds. In the disciplinary rules for Buddhist monks, abortion falls under one of the four offenses of the highest gravity, as it is considered equivalent to the murder of a human being (manussa viggaha),[41] involving the destruction of a life that has already come into existence. One could, however, question whether abortion is unconditionally a moral evil from the Buddhist point of view. Situations with all sorts of dilemmas can arise that favor the moral rightness of abortion in those special instances. One instance may be the case in which it is medically determined that the child that the young mother is carrying is stricken with some complication that could result in its being born with serious abnormalities, and that the birth would be at the cost of the mother's life. Is abortion morally justified in this situation? The present case is certainly to be distinguished from one in which a young woman wishes to resort to the abortion of a fetus that has been conceived as a result of premarital or extramarital sex, and the woman is now concerned for the protection of her social prestige. There are no definite moral rules in Buddhism to deal with the former type of dilemma. The moral precept that has direct relevance to practical moral decision making with regard to abortion is the one concerning the destruction of life *(panatipata)*. The reasons given in Buddhism for abstaining from the destruction of life are, the evil nature of the psychological source of such action, the resulting damage to one's character, and a need for sensitivity to the interests of other sentient beings who have similar psychological, physical, and emotional constitutions. Therefore, in making moral choices in such dilemmatic situations, one cannot abide by any hard and fast moral rules. One needs to take into account the total situation, motives, and other moral factors, and then make one's choice with a full sense of responsibility. The physician, for instance, might hold the opinion that it is morally more worthwhile to save the mother, and that abortion is the best recourse in this difficult situation. The mother may, perhaps, reckon this situation as an opportunity to cultivate her moral character by determining to sacrifice her life for the sake of her child, even though she is aware that the child will most probably be abnormal. Such a decision may appear awkward in terms of scientific humanism or materialistic secularism that deny certain cardinal Buddhist doctrines, such as *kamma* and rebirth. But it would not be so from the Buddhist standpoint, for Buddhism views an individual as a pilgrim in a long *samsaric* journey, heading towards the ultimate goal of *nibbanic* perfection. Alternatively, however, the mother may weigh the various consequences of her decision, such as its effect upon the well-being of her other children, and, purely as a matter of choosing the lesser evil, she may opt for abortion. From the Buddhist point of view, what is of primary moral importance in situations of this sort is the goodness of the intention. Benevolent motivation partly depends on the type of consequences one intends to bring about by one's practical choice. Since Buddhism does not subscribe to a deontological system of ethics, moral action is not looked upon as mere obedience to sacred commands. There is enough room for independent deliberation on moral matters and flexibility in moral choices, depending on the peculiarities of a specific situation.

Sexual Relationships

Closely related to the specific issues of contraception and abortion is the more general subject concerning the contemporary attitude towards sexual relationships. Moral opinions in the sphere of human sexual relationships can be considered as a major area in which contemporary attitudes and traditional religious morality come into conflict. In most Western societies, the puritanical approach to sex has been discarded. The result has been an increasingly liberal attitude towards sexual relationships. People concerned about the moral outcome of this contemporary trend complain that it has led to increasingly promiscuous behavior among young adults, a growing disregard for the sanctity of the bonds of marriage, and the breakdown of the institution of the family. What should the Buddhist moral response be in this regard?

According to Buddhism, the sexual impulse in man is one of the strongest expressions of what it conceives as *kamatanha* (craving for sensuous pleasures). *Raga* (lust) is at the root of the sexual impulse, and it is one of the bases of unwholesome action that has to be completely eliminated in order to achieve full liberation from *dukkha*. The sexual relationship is itself referred to as the vulgar practice *(methuna-gama-dhamma)* from which the *bhikku* should completely abstain. Strict celibacy is enjoined for the Buddhist monk, and violation of this precept is one of the four gravest offenses for which the penalty is excommunication from the order of monks. Whatever form sexual offenses have taken, the Buddha condemned monks who committed them on grounds that they have acted completely contrary to the higher way of life they have avowedly chosen, that is, a life free from lust *(viraga)*. Although indulgence in sexual pleasure is conceived as an impediment to the highest form of spiritual perfection *(brahmacariya)* and is totally prohibited for the Buddhist monk, the Buddhist layman may enjoy sexual pleasures in moderation. It is taken for granted that the life of the layman is one in which there is sensuous enjoyment. Laymen are therefore referred to as those who enjoy sensuous pleasures *(kamabhogi)*. The third moral precept for the Buddhist lay devotee is abstention from wrongful gratification of sensuous desires. An explanation of the Buddhist ethical response with regard to human sexual behavior depends largely on the interpretation of this moral precept.

The Family

Buddhism seems to favor the institutional regularization of sexual behavior, and views unregulated sexual behavior, as among lower animal species such as dogs and cattle, as highly undesirable for the human community. According to the *Cakkavattisihanadasutta,* the disregard for family relationships and considerations of propriety in respect to one's sexual conduct is a mark of moral degeneration. In such a corrupt society, "There will not be mutual respect of the consideration that this is mother, mother's sister, mother's sister-in-law, or teacher's wife, or father's sister-in-law. The world will fall into promiscuity, like goats and sheep, fowls and swine, dogs and jackals."[42]

The ideal recommended for laymen in Buddhism with respect to sexual behavior is the satisfaction of this urge in a wholesome and lasting relationship between persons who are brought together by bonds of mutual love. It is on this basis that the institution of the family arises in human society. The family is considered a unit within which the layman can have his basic spiritual training by converting his self-centered urge for personal pleasure-seeking into a responsible and dutiful relationship of mutual love and respect. Parents, in their self-sacrificing care for their children, sublimate the sexual desires in the more wholesome relationships of parental love. Buddhism does not seem to conceive of a better alternative to the family unit as a foundation for a healthy lay society. The parental care and love that children receive within the family in the formative years of their growth is considered extremely conducive to the development of a healthy society. Buddhism considers parents to be worthy of veneration and respect. They are equal to the highest God, Brahma. The ideal form of love and fellow-feeling expressed through the concept of *metta* is derived from the mother's self-sacrificing love for her own child.[43] Looking after one's parents when they grow old is one of the cardinal virtues of a layman. In the *Anguttaranikaya*, the Buddha says:

> Monks, those families where the mother and father are worshipped in the home, possess *Brahma*. Those families where the mother and father are worshipped in the home possess the foremost teachers . . . the foremost deities. . . . *Brahma*, monks, is a name for mother and father, foremost teachers. . . . Foremost deities, monks, is a name for mother and father. Those worthy of gifts, monks, is a name for mother and father. What is the reason for this? Mother and father, monks, are of great assistance to their children; they bring the children up; nourish them and introduce them to the world.[44]

The relationship between parents and children operating within the institution of the family is believed to be essential to a harmonious social order. This relationship gives a mutual sense of security to both parents and children, the maintenance and continuance of which requires the fulfilment of mutual duties. It is under a stable marital relationship that such family bonds become possible. Therefore, Buddhism recognizes the great value of a wholesome marital relationship. Adultery is considered one of the cardinal sins in lay life. Although Buddhism does not condemn polygamous or other nonmonogamous forms of marriage, it evidently recognizes monogamy as the ideal form of bonding. Marital fidelity of both husband and wife are considered great virtues. The *Anguttaranikaya* mentions as the exemplary and ideal marriage relationship the one between the householder, Nakulapita (Nakula's father) and Nakulamata (Nakula's mother). The following passage illustrates the ideal form of marital relationship which won the approbation of the Buddha:

> Nakula's father said to the Exalted One: "Sir, ever since the housewife Nakula's mother was brought in marriage to me when I was a mere lad, and she yet a girl, I am not conscious of having been unfaithful to Nakula's mother even in thought, much less in physical action. Sir, we desire to be in the company of each other not only in this very life but also in the life to come."
>
> Then also the housewife, Nakula's mother, said this to the Exalted One: "Sir, ever since I was taken in marriage by Nakula's father, the householder, when he was yet a lad, and I yet a girl, I am not conscious of having been unfaithful to Nakula's father even in thought, much less in physical action. Sir, we desire the company of each other not only in this very life but also in the life to come."
>
> (The Exalted One said):
> "Herein householders, if both husband and wife desire the company of each other both is this life and in the life to come, and both are equal in faith, virtue, generosity, and wisdom, then they have each other's company not only in this very life but also in the life to come."[45]

Buddhism values stable marital relationships primarily because of the emotional stability that such relationships provide to the society as a whole. Marital relationships would not become stable if marriage was conceived merely as a means for gratifying one's sexual desires.

Although Buddhism may not look upon divorce as a sin against the commands of a supreme moral lawgiver, it would definitely agree that it is generally undesirable for the emotional stability of all members of society to have an increasing number of broken families. If individuals cease to enter a marital relationship without a sense of responsibility and, if they take it as a loose bond that may be dissolved once the initial infatuation wears off, then the institution of the family will not survive. It would seem to follow that the Buddhist moral attitude toward divorce does not support an extremely liberal position. There is, however, no explicit condemnation of divorce or remarriage. Therefore, in the absence of any hard and fast rules, the Buddhist standpoint advocates the examination of the merits and demerits of each case in making moral choices in this regard, while recognizing in general the desirability of preserving stable family bonds.

The Buddhist attitude toward sexual morality tends to differ from that of a theistic ethical system because Buddhism does not regard sexual conduct as consisting of a divinely ordained form of human behavior for the continuance of God's creation. Therefore the Buddhist attitude toward certain "deviant" forms of sexual behavior, such as homosexuality, does not bear the same degree of disapprobation as theistic moralities do. Buddhism disapproves of homosexuality, not because it is "deviant," but because it is the expression of lust. As such, there can be no room for permissiveness toward homosexuality because it widens the area for people to indulge their carnal appetites.

Violence

Another serious moral dilemma that most contemporary societies are confronting concerns the justification of violence as a means for achieving some morally desirable end. The global situation testifies to the increasing number of advocates of the theory that it is morally right to use violence to overthrow an unjust regime or to win the inalienable rights of a socially oppressed group. Associated with that is a similar ideology—the concept of "holy war." The problem of terrorism has also caused grave concern during the recent past and continues to hold the major cities of the world in the grip of fear. A major test not facing Buddhist morality is whether it can condone violence in situations where non-violent means for overcoming injustice have slim prospects for succeeding.

Buddhism accepted that violent revolutions, social upheavals, and conditions of disharmony and insecurity result as a sociological fact from unjust, tyrannical, and oppresive regimes. In the *Cakka-vattisihanadasutta* and the *Kutadantasutta* of the *Dighanikaya,* the Buddha's teaching cautions rulers against the creation of conditions that lead to economic disparities and unfair distribution of wealth. However, given its opposition to killing, bloodshed, and violence

as the foremost evils, is it possible for Buddhism to approve of violence as a method for securing the greater good? The categorical
answer is that, under no set of circumstances does Buddhist morality justify the use of violence as the means for achieving some
benevolent end. Instead, it calls for a sound causal analysis of situations and circumstances in which violence and social conflicts arise
and attempts to enlighten men on ways to prevent violence from
ever taking place.

Buddhism's opposition to violence stems from the analysis that
violence is psychologically rooted in *dosa* (hatred). This is a dispositional trait that is conditioned by malicious conduct and, in turn,
determines the way human beings behave. It is the fundamental
cause of a whole cycle of violence from which individuals and societies find it impossible to escape. Therefore, no matter what the
intended merits of a projected social order may be; if it is established
by violence, it will have to be perpetuated through violence, for
dosa can only beget *dosa*. Social change through nonviolent means
is the only *realistic* path to a stable social order. Buddhism does talk
about conquest but it is the conquest of righteousness *(dhammavijaya)* which, in root and in fruit, has nothing in common with the
notion of "holy war." In *dhammavijaya* conquest is effected without
the use of weapons *(adandena asatthena dhammena abhivijiya)*.[46]

Thus, Buddhism upholds the reality of an eternal law that hatred,
vengeance, and animosity can never cease as long as they are met
with hatred, vengeance, and animosity. These age-old forces of evil
can only be permanently disarmed by virtue of their opposites *(na
hi verena verani sammantidha kudacanam—averena ca sammanti esa
dhammo sanantano)*.[47] Hatred should be conquered by nonhatred,
unrighteousness by righteousness, miserliness by generosity, and
falsity by truth.[48] Fundamentally, the Buddha only permits a single
weapon to vanquish one's foes—compassion! He insists that the
training of his disciples in the practice of compassion should be such
that it would be a moral violation if they were to express the slightest irritation or anger, even if wily robbers were to lay hold of them
and cut them apart limb by limb with a double handled saw.[49] A
canonical *sutta* mentions an instance in which one of the Buddha's
immediate disciples, named Punna, was tested by the Buddha himself for his strength to withstand any form of harassment to which
he might be subjected by the atrocious people of Sunaparanta, and
that he did, in fact, succeed in winning them over through
compassion.[50]

We have also seen that the propensity to violence is addictive and causally forges a chain of reciprocal links. An example from the contemporary global situation is the build-up of nuclear weapons by the superpowers that threatens the survival of life on this planet. It is increasingly and ominously evident that mankind is now faced with two alternatives: either to let the reciprocal hatred and suspicion of arch rivals continue until its momentum achieves its end, or to abandon war as an outdated and inefficient means of resolving conflicts and explore, instead, avenues of mutual understanding, cooperation, and friendship. The consequentialist ethic of Buddhism is squarely on the side of the latter alternative. Buddhism does not have some private agenda whereby it seeks to impose a particular brand of morality from above. Rather, it attempts to give directions to people in all parts of the globe who are disillusioned with the false promises of greed *(lobha)*, hatred *(dosa)*, and ignorance *(moha)*, and to enable them, by the use of untapped resources, to make discoveries of lasting happiness in their own moral experience.

Notes

1. *Anupada parinibbanatthamkhoi avuso bhagavati brahmacariyam vussati. Majjhimanikaya*, Pali Text Society Edition (PTS) M. 1.148.

2. *Nibbanam paramam vadanti buddha. Dighanikaya* (PTS) D. 2.49.

3. *Yo kho avuso ragakkhayo dosakkhayo mohakkhayo idam vuccati nibbhananti. Samyuttanikaya* (PTS) S. 4.251.

4. D. 3.102.

5. M. 160.

6. S. Radhakrishnan, *Indian Philosophy* (London: George Allen and Unwin Ltd., 1929), vol. 1: 449.

7. Ibid., 452.

8. Shundo Tachibana, *Ethics of Buddhism* (Colombo: The Bauddha Sahitya Sab, 1943), 37–38.

9. *Suttanipata* (PTS) Sn. 522; 547; 790; *Dhammapada* (PTS) Dh. 267, 412.

10. M. 2.115.

11. M. 2.28.

12. *Anguttaranikaya* (PTS) A. 5.66.

13. M. 1.477.

14. Dh. 97.

15. S. 3.83.

16. A. 1.173–174.

17. A full description of good conduct in speech is found in D. 1.4–5.

18. S. 1.9–12.

19. M. 1.489.

20. M. 1.47.

21. Ibid.

22. M. 1.15; also see *Sallekhasutta* for a list of evil and wholesome traits of mind. M. 1.40.

23. S. 5.145.

24. Ibid.

25. *Suttanipata* (PTS) Sn. vv. 146–149.

26. D. 1.64–71.

27. M. 1.12.

28. *Nayidam sukaram agaram ajjhavasata ekantaparipunnam ekantaparisuddham sankhalikhitam brahmacariyam caritum.* M. 2.55.

29. Sn. 18–20; D. 3.180–193; A. 4.281.

30. A. 1.189.

31. M. 2.114.

32. M. 1.415.

33. S. 5.169.

34. M. 1.45.

35. A. 2.95.

36. A. 2.179.

37. For a fully developed emotivist meta-ethical theory, see *Ethics and Language,* C.L. Stevenson, Yale University Press, 1944; for a fully developed prescriptivist theory, see *The Language of Morals,* R.M. Hare, Oxford University Press, 1964.

38. Dh. 1129–131.

39. See *Freedom and Reason,* Richard M. Hare, Oxford University Press, 1965.

40. S. 5.354.

41. *Vinayapitaka* (PTS) 3.83.

42. D. 3.72.

43. Sn. v. 149.

44. A. 2.70.

45. A. 2.61.

46. D. 3.59.

47. Dh. 5.

48. Dh. 223.

49. M. 1.129.

50. M. 3.267.

3

The Ethics of Jainism

PREM SUMAN JAIN

Introduction

The Jain religion is primarily intended for monks. It prescribes a rigorous discipline involving penance and self-control by which the soul sheds its weight of evil actions and ascends to its pristine state of liberation. Jain saints analyzed the total form and function of the universe and cultivated diverse means of meditative techniques to enable the individual who had renounced the world to achieve final release.

When lay persons entered the movement, Jain saints evolved a system of ethical principles to guide their conduct in the world.

The purpose of this essay is to provide a survey of Jain ethics, lay and monastic. Prior to that we must take stock of its antiquity, its heroes, its literature and order, and its fundamental beliefs.

The Antiquity of Jainism

The Jain religion is the oldest religion of India. It began as a spiritual discipline for *Samanas, Arhats, Tirthankaras, Nigganthas,* and *Jinas.* They were called *Samanas* (Monks) because they believed in the equality of all beings and practiced nonviolence. They were called *Arhats* (worthy of worship) because they lived virtuous lives. As the originators of the spiritual path, they were known as *Tirthankaras* (Fordmakers). Being free from passions, they were called *Nigganthas* (detached). And because they had conquered all of their desires, they were identified as *Jinas* (Victors). Hence, the religion propounded by such conquerors is fittingly called the Jaina religion.

There are references to the Jaina *Tirthankaras, Samanas,* and *Arhats,* and to the ethical principles they espoused in the Rigveda, Yajurveda, and in the Puranas. Scholars have examined these sources and have concluded that these personalities must be pre-Vedic and that the religion they preached must have preceded the Vedic religion. According to Sarvepalli Radhakrishnan: "Jaina tradition ascribes the origin of the system to Rsabhadeva, who lived many centuries back. There is evidence to show that so far back as the first century B.C. there were people who were worshipping Rsabhadeva, the first *Tirthankara*. There is no doubt that Jainism prevailed even before Vardhamana or Parsvanatha. The Yajurveda mentions the names of three *Tirthankaras*—Risabha, Ajita, and Aristanemi. The Bhagvata-Purana endorses the view that Rsabhadeva was the founder of Jainism."[1] Likewise, J. P. Jain declares: "It is now no more necessary to prove that Jainism is an absolutely independent, highly developed, very comprehensive and ancient system, not unreasonably described as 'the oldest living religion', or the earliest 'home religion of India.' It is, indeed, found to have been in existence, in one form or the other, or under one name or the other, since the very dawn of human civilization, continuing without break throughout the pre-historical, proto-historical and historical times."[2] The images, seals, and other findings amongst the discoveries at Harappa and Mohenjodaro, and some earlier inscriptions of ancient India also lend support to the view that Risabhadeva was the founder of Jainism, which was non-Vedic in origin and probably pre-Aryan.

Jain Heroes

The tradition states that time is infinite and follows repetitive cycles of ascents and descents. During the phase of ascent there is a gradual increase of truth and goodness, and during the period of descent there is a decrease of happiness and righteousness. It is held that at the end of the third division of the period of descent, fourteen propounders of the faith appeared, and that during the fourth division of decline, sixty-three spokesmen arrived, of whom there were twenty-four *Tirthankaras*.

The fourteen propounders are credited for their progressive work. The Manu Nabhi, the last member of this group, had a wife named Marudevi, who gave birth to a son named Risabha who is generally credited with being the first Tirthankara. Tradition calls him the "harbinger of civilization." Having performed his role of educating the people in all aspects of culture, Risabha renounced the world he had civilized and retired to the forest where he attained supreme knowledge *(kaivalya-jnana)* and became a *Jina*. He then spent his time preaching his creed of love. "He was the first preacher of '*ahimsa dharma*,' the first prophet of salvation. In the end he attained nirvana at Mt. Kailasa (in Tibet)."[3]

Risabha was succeeded by twenty-three other *Tirthankaras*. The historical character of these heroes is not clear; even so, historian J. P. Jain has been able to link these personalities to pivotal milestones of ancient Indian history.[4] All of them preached the Jaina values of nonviolence, truth, nonstealing, nonpossessiveness, and dedicated their lives to the service of suffering humanity. Parsva, the twenty-third *Tirthankara,* was exceptional, his influence extended to Central Asia and Greece. Under the impact of his teachings, Vedic sacrifice diminished and the spiritualistic philosophy of the Upanishads began to rise. So remarkable was "his contribution to the creed of the *Tirthankaras* and his influence on contemporary religious thought and practice . . . that he is often described as the real founder of Jainism."[5]

The last of the twenty-four *Tirthankaras* was Vardhamana Mahavira ("the Great Hero"), a contemporary of Lord Buddha, born of royal parents in the year 599 B.C. His boyhood became the stuff of legends because of his expansive compassion toward all creatures.[6] At age thirty, he renounced the world and became a monk. After twelve years in deep meditation and severe austerities, Mahavira attained the state of perfect knowledge. At the age of forty-two he became an *Arhat,* a *Jina,* a *Tirthankara.* From then on he preached the tenets of the *sramana* cult in the popular language of the masses (Prakrit). He also introduced several innovations such as the vow of *brahmacharya* (celibacy) and the constitution of the community into a four-fold order consisting of monks, nuns, male householders, and female householders. His religion is aptly described as *Sarvodayatirtha* (an order for the upliftment of all). The doctrine of *sarvodaya* characterizes Mahavira's order as one in which "everyone has an equal opportunity to rise; everyone may attain the highest position; everyone has the full right to knowledge and happiness."[7] Having spent his entire ministry spreading the principle of *ahimsa* and self-realization, Mahavira attained *nirvana* (salvation) at the age of seventy-two, in the year 527 B.C. The event was celebrated with lights, signifying his friendship for all living beings. The celebration is continued today through the famous festival of Dipavali.

The Jaina Order and Literature

The history of Jainism after Lord Mahavira is recorded in the Jaina literature preserved in various Indian languages.[8] The most momentous event, which occurred about 80 A.D., was the division of the Jain community into two sects: *Svetambaras* (white-robed) and *Digambaras* (sky-robed). The split did not incur doctrinal or moral differences but only dissent on the basis of religious practices.

In the year 453 A.D. a major council was held at Vallabhi in order to establish Mahavira's teaching which had been preserved through oral traditions. The outcome of this council was the writing of the Jaina canon.[9] The *Svetambara* sect granted it full validity but the *Digambaras* questioned its authenticity. Instead, the latter canonized the literature of Acarya Kundakunda and his followers. The modern scholar must draw on both traditions to glean the truth of the original teachings of Lord Mahavira.

The Jaina literature is a rich compendium of diverse interests and is written in several Indian languages so as to reach all people. J. P. Jain describes the writings of these *acaryas* as having "manifold attractions" not only for those in Jaina studies but for lovers of literature, history, culture, philosophy, and comparative religion.[10] It is to this vast source that we now turn for an understanding of Jaina beliefs of the universe, religion, and morality.

Fundamental Beliefs

The Universe

Jainism has a unique view of the universe. It believes the universe is uncreated, self-existent, beginningless, eternal, and infinite. It is an aggregation of six substances *(dravyas):* Soul *(Jiva)*, Non-Soul *(Pudgala)*, Principle of Motion *(Dharma)*, Principle of Rest *(Adharma)*, Space *(Akasa)*, Time *(Kala)*. Substance consists of attributes and modes. Attributes are the essential features of the substance and always occupy the substance, whereas modes are the changing features of the substance. If substance is characterized in terms of its attributes, it is nonchanging and eternal. But if viewed from the perspective of its modes, it is regarded as changing and transitory.[11]

Jain cosmology refers to our limited world as *Loka*. Beyond this there is the unlimited world of *Aloka*.[12] The principles of *dharma* and *adharma* only operate in *Loka* where the Soul and non-Soul are located. *Loka* is divided into three parts: the upper universe where celestial beings dwell, the middle universe occupied by humans and animals, and the lower universe in which the wicked reside.[13]

The fundamental substances of Soul and non-Soul are thought of as interdependent.[14] This connection eventuates in the creation of pleasure and pain for the soul as a result of its involvement in karmic matter. This can be clarified by describing the human predicament and the role of karma.

The Human Predicament

Man's life in this world comprises many stages that he must pass through because of his bondage to karma. Salvation is achieved when he becomes enlightened sufficiently and is able to shed the weight of karma. The elements involved in this process are: Soul (Jiva), non-Soul (Ajiva), the inflow of fresh karmic matter (Asrava), karmic bondage (Bandha), the checking of karmic matter (Samvara), the shedding of karmic matter (Nirjara), and Liberation (Moksha).[15] In addition to the seven elements listed, there are two more elements that are fundamental to the Jain view of worldly exitence: sin and virtue or papa and punya. The proper content of Jaina ethics centers upon the two elements of checking and shedding karmic matter. It covers the conduct both of the monk and the layman. The whole purpose of ethics and religious exercises is the attainment of salvation.[16] This summum bonum is captured in the following adage: "Asrava (inflow of karmic matter causing misery) is the cause of mundane existence and Samvara (stoppage of that inflow) is the cause of liberation. This is the Jain view; everything else is only its amplification."[17]

The Doctrine of Karma

The role of cause and effect in the physical world corresponds to the role of karma in Jaina ethics. Every person is deemed responsible for bearing the fruit of his own deeds. It is also the rule of nature in practical life that the quality of the seed determines that of the fruit. Jaina philosophy theorizes that one achieves happiness by doing good deeds, and sorrow by doing evil deeds, hence the need to perform noble works that are at all times well intentioned. The self is free and fully competent to act as such. The self is the real cause of sorrow and joy. It is clearly pointed out in the Uttar-adhyana-Sutra, "My own self is the doer and undoer of misery and happiness; my own self is friend and foe, as I act well or badly."[18]

Jain philosophy has described the details of the process of the bondage of karma and its view must be distinguished from other formulations of the same.[19] The principle, "As a man gives, so he receives," is present in many philosophies. Often such types of karma theories are fatalistic because the past is seen as determining the present. In this way the karmic explanation of one's deeds delivers the doer from the bondage of some superintending divinity, but it only exchanges bondage to the supernatural for bondage to the unrelenting grasp of karma. This tells us why there have been so many popular views on the cause of happiness and sorrow in Indian philosophies. Time, Fate, Nature, Chance, Matter, Purusa, and combinations of all these, have been taken as the causes of joy and sorrow.[20] In all these the individual is stripped of his capacities to free himself from the force that holds him captive.

Jaina philosophy differs from such fatalistic renderings of karma. According to Jain ethics, man can increase or reduce the period of his karmas by his own effort and can reduce or increase their power of bearing fruit. It has been called *udirana:* the energy that makes possible the premature fruition of karmas. Similarly, a person can convert his *punyas* (virtues) into sins because of his evil deeds *(asat karmas)* and he can convert his sins into *punyas* (virtues) because of his virtuous activities *(sat karmas).* Udirana is called the energy that contributes to differentiation of karmas *(samkramana).*

The conversion is possible, in a positive sense, through right knowledge and self-control. The process is called *Upasamana.*[21] It is described in the *Karma-Sidhant* of Jainism. It saves a person from becoming a fatalist and imparts confidence to change the direction of one's life through virtuous actions *(sadacarana).* Thus the role of self-awakening and human effort within the framework of the doctrine of karma invest Jaina ethics with originality.[22] Its optimistic attitude toward the success of human efforts to cancel the effects of previous actions and to block the inflow of fresh karmic matter makes ethics a force for good.[23]

The Doctrine of Man .

The discussion of karma theory has made it plain that the human self is the center of ethical existence and that, by virtue of its knowledge and consciousness, it has infinite powers. However, these superior qualities are concealed for the developing individual due to the overlay of karma. It therefore becomes the ultimate goal of the individual to achieve the pure form of the self and to attain absolute being. Though difficult, this goal is possible because human nature is rational and voluntaristic. Only human beings can achieve this goal, hence the importance of human birth.[24] The Jaina *Agamas* state that even deities bow down to the person whose mind has reached the highest bliss characterized by noninjury and self-restraint.[25] The individual is capable of reaching such divine heights because the pure form of the self is itself divine and therefore relies on its own efforts.[26]

The Denial of God

The Jaina views of the nature of man and the universe render the notion of God unnecessary. All of nature is autonomous and is governed by its own laws. Man makes his own world for better or for worse. Jaina ethics is thus nontheocentric, unlike Judaism, Christianity, Islam and some forms of Hinduism.[27] In all of these religions, God functions as Maker, Ruler, Rewarder, and Judge. But for the Jainas "it is not necessary to surrender to any higher being, nor to ask for any divine favor for the individual to reach the highest goal of perfection. There is no place for divine grace, nor is one to depend on the capricious whims of a superior deity for the sake of attaining the highest ideal. According to Jainism each individual soul is to be considered as God, as he is essentially divine in nature."[28]

Though Jainism rejects the notion of a creator God, it does have a sort of "ethical heaven" inhabited by enlightened souls called *Arhats* and *Siddhas*. These pure beings are ones who have realized the true form of the self by conquering their senses. In the words of D. N. Bhargava: "These *siddhas* are far more above gods or deities. They neither create nor destroy anything. They have conquered, once and for all, their nescience and passion, and cannot be molested by them again."[29]

Jainism permits the worship of the *Arhats* and *Siddhas* but not in the conventional sense of seeking rewards. Instead, worship is ethically oriented for the sake of attaining their high qualities. It begins with penance.[30] It continues with progressive purification of one's actions. Jaina ethics specifies three grades of Self.[31] First, there is the Outer-Self, involved in worldly affairs, taking the body to be the soul. Second, there is the Inner-Self that understands the difference between body and soul and aims at the perfection of the latter. Third, there is the Enlightened Soul *(Parmatman)* that has realized its true form. It possesses infinite knowledge and joy unspeakable. In the practice of Jaina worship, one must renounce the Outer-Self and, through the conversion of the Inner-Self, move toward the *Parmatman,* which is the true goal of the mystic quest. This journey is "traversed through the medium of moral and intellectual preparations, which purge everything obstructing the emergence of potential divinity."[32] The spirit in which the Jaina devotee worships the *Paramatmans* is reflected in this verse, "Him who is the leader of the path to Liberation, who is the crusher of mountains of Karmas, and who is the knower of all reality, Him I worship in order that I may realize those very qualities of his."[33]

Thus the purpose of Jaina worship is not the deification of some savior figure, but the veneration and adoration of the ideals that figure represents.

Jaina Ethics and Morality

Jaina ethics is directed toward the liberation of the individual. Its orientation is therefore religious. Its end is the spiritualization of all areas of life in order to fit the individual for his final goal. Its primary precept applicable to king and commoner alike is, "Do your duty and do it as humanly as you can."[34]

Jainism permits no separation between religion *(dharma)* and morality because both are concerned with the well-being of the individual in the world, in keeping with his own nature. The word *dharma* signifies the nature of things *(vathu sahavo dhammo)*. It is the law which "leads, binds, or takes back a being to its essential nature; enables it to realize the divinity inherent in itself; helps it to extricate itself from the misery of mundane existences and reach the state of perfect beatitude."[35] All beings seek happiness and try to avoid pain and loss. The practice of *dharma* enables them to achieve this end. In the words of the well-known *Acarya* Samanta bhadra, "Religion is something which takes the living beings out of the worldly misery and establishes them in the highest bliss."[36]

This interconnection between religion and morality imparts to Jainism its distinctive feature. H. S. Bhattacharya finds the insistence of Jainism on spiritual movitation "the foundation" of all true religion and ethics and thinks it may well serve as "the basis of a universal code of moral and religious acts." The uniqueness of Jainism "lies not only in emphasizing this all-important condition of all religious and moral activities but in justifying their position by looking upon morality, not as an adjunct to human nature, but as part and parcel of it."[37]

The connection between religion and morality is often missed because Jainism delineates the pathway to spiritual perfection through the practice of yoga and demarcates stages of self-realization, but the roots of that perfection are in the soil of everyday life. "We have first to learn to live a good life in this world and then we can go higher to spiritual perfection."[38] In order to exclude none from the need for moral discipline, Jainism has formulated two levels of religious existence: one which sets moral standards for laymen, and one for monks.

For one who sets out on the path toward perfection, Jainism presents the practice of ten great virtues. They are: Supreme Forbearance, Humility, Straightforwardness, Perfect Truthfulness, Purity, Perfect Self-restraint, Austerity, Complete Renunciation, Nonattachment, and Celibacy. These virtues are to regulate thought, speech, and action. They are an essential part of Jaina ethics, and are like "ten inextinguishable lamps" which illuminate the path for the beginner.[39]

Three Spiritual Paths

Jaina religion encompasses a threefold path of spiritual practice. It includes right faith, right knowledge, and right conduct.[40] The three components are interrelated and interdependent and are known as "The Three Jewels," because of their value for salvation.[41]

Right faith is primary. It signifies belief in the omniscience of the spiritual teachers. It assumes a life of principled morality on the part of the householder. The scriptures describe the eight organs of right faith.[42] Yasastilakacampu states that right faith is the "prime cause of salvation."[43]

Right knowledge follows from faith. It is obtained by studying the teachings of the *Tirthankaras*. Because it is the basis of right conduct, Jaina philosophy explains it minutely.[44] It ranges all the way from sense knowledge to reasoning, clairvoyance, direct awareness of the thought forms of others, and infinite knowledge *(kevalajnana)*.[45] These represent progressive stages.

Right knowledge includes the nature of things in this world. In discussing the qualities of material particles, Jainism finds they are of infinite number and that some of these are apparently contradictory. Simply stated, the qualities of a thing are not exhausted by our comprehension of it, and there is more than meets the eye. Philosophically, this is known as the theory of nonabsolutism *(anekantavada)* and calls for an attitude of openness.[46] Our limitations of knowledge dictate a style of relativity. The linguistic manner of expressing various qualities of matter is called *Syadavada* (the doctrine of qualified assertion). The style of *Syadavada* allows no room for assertions. This Jaina theory of knowledge, incorporating the two principles of nonabsolutism and relativity, has made an esteemed contribution toward liberalizing the mind of man. It elevates the mystery of life and denigrates dogmatism.

The third jewel is right conduct. Jaina scriptures approach this developmentally—conduct for householders and for monks. For the former, the goal sought is the development of the individual and society; for the latter, it is self-realization.[47] All aspirants dedicate themselves to proper conduct through vows *(vratas)* and subvows. Vows are at the heart of Jaina morality and are undertaken with a full knowledge of their nature and a determination to carry them through.[48]

Principally, Jaina ethics specifies Five Minor Vows *(anuvratas)*, Three Social Vows *(gunavratas)*, and Four Spiritual Vows *(siksavratas)* to be carried out by the householder.[49] Being twelve in number, the texts speak of them as *Duvalasaviha Agaradhamma.*[50]

The Minor Vows are: nonviolence, truth, nonstealing, celibacy, and nonpossession. They are called "Minor" *(anuvrata)* because the householder observes them in a modified way. In their full observance by monks, they are called *Mahavratas.*

Nonviolence is the foundation of Jaina ethics. Mahavira called it pure, universal, everlasting religion. It says: "one should not injure, subjugate, enslave, torture or kill any animal, living being, organism or sentient being."[51] This is the essence of religion.[52] It embraces the welfare of all animals, visible and invisible.[53] It is the basis of all stages of knowledge[54] and the source of all rules of conduct.[55] The scriptures analyze the spiritual and practical aspects of nonviolence and discuss the subject negatively and positively.

Four stages of violence are described: Premeditated Violence—to attack someone knowingly, Defensive Violence—to commit intentional violence in defense of one's own life, Vocational Violence—to incur violence in the execution of one's means of livelihood, Common Violence—committed in the performance of daily activities.

Premeditated violence is prohibited for all. A householder is permitted to incur violence defensively and vocationally provided he maintains complete detachment. Common violence is accepted for all in the business of remaining alive, but even here, one should be careful in preparing food, cleaning house, etc. This explains the Jain's practices of filtering drinking water, vegetarianism, not eating meals at night, and abstinence from alchohol.[56]

The primacy given to *ahimsa* by the Indian people has nobly contributed to their character, most dramatically by Mahatma Gandhi.

"In the hands of Mahatma Gandhi, *Ahimsa*—the sword of self-suffering—became a mighty instrument" that wielded enormous social and political power with utmost significance for the future of mankind.[57] Jaina literature is a treasury of many such characters who exemplify the human potential for living nonviolently in this world.[58]

The second of the five minor vows is Truth. It is more than abstaining from falsehood; it is seeing the world in its real form and adapting to that reality. The vow of truth puts a person in touch with his inner strength and inner capacities. He becomes secure and fearless. There is then no need to steal—the third vow.

Celibacy is the fourth vow, applicable to monks and householders in differing degrees. Its basic intent is to conquer passion and to prevent the waste of energy. Positively stated, the vow is meant to impart the sense of serenity to the soul. The householder fulfills this vow when he is content with his own wife and is completely faithful to her.

Nonpossession is the fifth minor vow. As long as a person does not know the richness of joy and peace that comes from a consciousness of the soul, he tries to fill his empty and insecure existence with the clutter of material acquisitions. But, as Lord Mahavira said, security born of things is a delusion and must come to nought. To remove this delusion, one takes the vow of nonpossession and realizes the perfection of the soul. Nonpossession, like nonviolence, affirms the oneness of all life and is beneficial both in the spiritual and social spheres.

In addition to the Five Minor Vows, the householders observes three Social Vows that govern his external conduct in the world. Then there are the four Spiritual vows that reflect the purity of his heart.[59] They govern his internal life and are expressed in a life that is marked by charity *(dana)*.

The Jaina householder who observes these twelve vows progresses upon the spiritual path until he comes to the place where he must decide whether to observe the discipline of the monk's life. To enter this higher domain, he must pass through eleven successive stages called *Pritimas*. When the eleventh stage is reached, he can begin the conduct of a monk.

In order to preserve the integrity of the principal vows listed above, Jain thinkers have prescribed sub-vows as precautionary means. First, there is reference to the *Salyas* or disturbing factors such as ignorance, deceit, and self-interest, from which a person should free himself. The *salyas* represent the negative requirements for the perfect practice of the *vratas*. In addition, there are the four *bhavanas* (virtues) that represent the positive means of supporting the *vratas*.[60] These qualities, which a votary of nonviolence must possess, are *maitri* (love, friendship), *pramoda* (joy and respect), *karunya* (compassion), and *madhyastha* (tolerance toward living beings). Third, there are the twelve sub-vows known as *anupreksas* (reflections). Broadly stated, they are twelve topics of meditation that cover a wide field of teaching. They are designed to serve as aids to spiritual progress, produce detachment, and lead the devotee from the realm of desire to the path of renunciation. They are reflections upon the fundamental facts of life, intended to develop purity of thought and sincerity in the practice of religion.[61]

In this way Jaina ethics prescribes thirty-five rules of conduct for the householder. They are meant for the good of his entire personality. By observing these rules, he comes to possess all of the twenty-one qualities that a fully developed individual must manifest.[62]

Having observed all the rules of conduct and having passed through the eleven religious stages *(pratimas)*, the householder is now qualified to become an ascetic. The life of a monk is marked by the spirit of detachment. Through the practice of yoga and meditation, he finally attains the highest knowledge and becomes an enlightened soul. This is the ultimate end of Jaina ethics.

Viewed from the level of the life of a monk, Jaina ethics appears to be a rigorous discipline for the individual, aimed at cultivating his detachment from the world. From a broader view, including the life of the householder, Jaina ethics is not just individual and spiritual, but inclusive of all forms of life for the total upliftment of existence. The person who subjects himself to this form of ethics will be serious, good tempered, merciful, straightforward, wise, and modest. He will be sociable, careful in speech, reverent to age and custom. Renouncing ego and possessions, he will endure all manner of hardships until he attains the highest ideal of perfection.

Response to Contemporary Issues

Science and technology have created a new world of prosperity, but material gain has been purchased with a spiritual loss that has global consequences not only for human life upon this planet but for the planet itself. As a result, there seems to be a trend, often politicized, for people to return to their spiritual roots.[63] Jaina ethics are relevant to the quest of modern man for they satisfy not only the value-orientation of the individual, but of society. They find the basis of these values in a spirituality that is as deep as it is open and tolerant.[64]

The Jaina scriptures indeed show us the way to escape material bondage within this world, but the ethical path they prescribe takes us through all the highways and byways of this mortal life. Society is never overlooked.[65] Human welfare is at all times taken seriously.[66] The *Tirthankaras* whom Jains worship are known to have led full social lives before attaining salvation. Contemporary Jains are a prosperous community. There is therefore no modern custom or usage from which the Jain must abstain, as long as it does not conflict with the ethical principles of the Jaina faith.[67]

We turn now to the ethical issues of our own day. Eminent scholars of different religious traditions have addressed these problems with deep insights.[68] But the problems persist. We shall therefore make a modest attempt to find some solutions to these problems in the light of the principles of Jainism.

Social Issues

The Jain *Acaryas* have discussed some of the social issues that confront us today such as sexual relationships, marriage and family, and the role and status of women. Modern scholars also provide us with updated interpretations of ancient principles.[69]

On the matter of sexual relationships, Jainism sets celibacy *(brahmacarya)* as the norm. For the monk, the vow is defined as total abstinence but for the layman it means inner purity. The householder must be content with his own wife and must consider all other women as his sisters, mothers and daughters. The *Acaryas* had a realistic understanding of the power of sex and counselled against its indulgence through suggestive literature, sexual fantasies, and intimacy. Sexual deviations were to be avoided, including contact with lower animals and inanimate objects.[70] The scriptures provide many examples of positive sexual relationships that are applicable to the present situation.[71]

Unlike the Hindus who look upon marriage as a sacrament, Jains treat the institution as a contract. Its purpose is to make sex licit within a family. The role of sex between husband and wife is strictly procreational, so that its engagement is limited to the ovulation period.[72] Notwithstanding many of its own unique features, the Jain concept of the family is strongly influenced by the prevailing Hindu culture.[73]

Women have been accorded equal status to men within the Jain religion. As a matter of fact, there were more women in the order of Lord Mahavira than men. The scriptures record many tributes to exceptional women.[74] The care of women, especially in critical situations, is given a higher priority than that of men.[75] Mothers of the *Tirthankaras* are given special honor through communal worship. Legends abound in which heroines such as Brahmi, Sundari, Mallikumari, and Rajmati have come to the aid of men.[76] Women have also been celebrated for their learning and have been recognized for their exceptional contributions in the fields of education, culture, and religion.[77] So far as their legal and social status within the community is concerned, Jaina women are on a par with their Hindu sisters.

Jain egalitarianism rejects the Hindu division of society into higher and lower castes. It finds no basis for the idea that makes one caste superior to the other. On the contrary, it finds casteism an evil based on hatred, pride, and deluded vision. Lord Mahavira gave no ground for the supremacy of any caste by reason of birth. This explains why many slaves, untouchables, and low-caste people entered the Jaina fold, and some were able to prove their personal merit by rising to the level of saints.[78] Mahavira showed his feelings for the dignity of his fellows by eliminating the convention of caste distinctions in mutual address. He says, "Worthy beings! Take it as my command that henceforth no monk address another by the latter's caste."[79] He was very conscious that pride of caste is destructive of communal solidarity.

The eighth and ninth sermons contained in the Uttaradhayana-sutra ethicize the notion of caste so that virtue, not birth, is the hallmark of a person's standing. It is said, "One becomes a *Sramana* by equanimity, a *Brahmana* by chastity, a *Muni* by knowledge, and a *Tapasa* by penance. By one's action one becomes a *Brahmana,* or a *Ksatriya,* or a *Vaisya,* or a *Sudra.*"[80]

In a similar vein, Acarya Amatigati said that, "Good people should not have pride in any class as it leads to degradation, but they should observe good conduct which might give them high position."[81]

It is clear that there is no religious support for casteism in the Jaina tradition. However, in the course of history, because of certain social factors, the Jainas did form a large number of castes and sub-castes.[82] Even so, the Jaina community has been foremost in social services that cross all caste barriers and it has served as a cohesive force for national unity.

Social service is a prominent outcome of Jaina ethics. It prescribes six daily duties for every householder. These duties are: adoration of deity *(Jina),* veneration of the Gurus, study of literature and scriptures, practice of self-discipline, observance of fasts and curbing appetites, and charity.[83] All of these daily duties are related to the performance of social service for mankind.

The duty of charity *(dana)* sets the mood and manner of the layman's daily life. One performs charity, not on a cloud of sentiment, but following the details of scripture so that it is all done wisely, equitably, politely, and in a spirit of gratitude and humility.

One vow of spiritual discipline *(siksavrata)* that the householder takes is that of hospitality to monks *(Atithi-Samvibhaga-Vrata).* This involves the supply of food, books, medicine, etc. Acarya Samantabhadra calls the vow of hospitality physical service *(Vaiyavrattya).* It makes the householder into the parent of the monk. Sick, aged, and helpless monks are thus taken care of in their time of need. The practice of such physical service developed particularly in the area of medical charities *(Ausadhi-Dana).* Its effect was the creation of a communal sense of fearlessness *(Abhaya-Dana).*

Jaina ethics also makes the study of scriptures *(Svadhyaya)* an important service for monk and layman. This endeavor is known as *Sastra-Dana.* Its purpose is to advance knowledge, eliminate error, and to bring many others into its orbit of enlightenment. By following the duty of scriptural charity, Jain laymen have erected prestigious libraries containing numerous literary treasures. These *Grantha-Bhandaras* are not confined to Jaina works but contain collections which are of value for Indian culture at large.

This brief listing of social services should make it plain that there is no conflict in Jaina ethics between individual piety and social outreach. The six daily duties of the householder are personal, but not private; they extend into the community of which the individual is a part. Spirituality and practicality go hand-in-hand.

In addition to medical care for humans, Jainism is a leader among religions in providing hospitals for animals and birds.[84] Its epitome of true spirituality is when a monk, wrapped in contemplation, takes time to mend the broken wing of a little sparrow. His holy mission is to all creatures great and small.[85]

The Economic Order

A global problem that threatens the welfare of all people is the conflict between Communism and Capitalism. Though totally different, they have these things in common—an insatiable appetite for material consumption and a corresponding disregard for moral principles. The result is mass exploitation on both sides. The only way this materialistic tide can turn is by the introduction of moral considerations into global economics.[86] Jainism believes the only type of economics that can bring both peace and prosperity to all must have a moral base.

Jaina ethics enjoins upon the householder certain vows which are economically oriented: Truth, Nonstealing, Nonpossession, to mention only some. The vow of truthfulness requires a man to abstain from duplicity in his business and to conduct its affairs on the lines of honesty. Nonstealing permits no occasions for falsehood. All deceptions *(maya)* are prohibited, including dishonest gain through smuggling, bribery, and any sort of disreputable financial practice *(adatt-dana)*.[87] In this way truthfulness and honesty are the prerequisites for the practice of the vow of *Aparigraha* (nonattachment).

The essence of the economic virtue of *Aparigraha* is that one should set a limit to one's own needs and whatever surplus one may accumulate beyond these needs should be disposed of through charities. "By limiting one's property, the vow keeps in check the concentration of wealth and paves the way for its wider and more even distribution."[88] *Aparigraha* is the only means whereby the growing gulf between the rich and the poor can be peacefully bridged. Its message is that we live in a society from which we profit and that, for the economic health of that society, the fair distribution of wealth is essential. Therefore, business dealings must be conducted in the nonacquisitive spirit of *aparigraha*.[89]

The Idea of Ahimsa

One of the distinctive marks of Jainism has been its long tradition of nonviolence. Living as we do in an era of unparalleled violence, this feature of the Jaina ethic should stimulate contemporary interest for finding solutions to our global problems.

Ahimsa is a way of living that proceeds from the recognition of the spiritual value of man as man. It is supported by the values of *aparigraha* and *anekantavada* that develop an outlook of nonpossessiveness and nondogmatism. Greed, hatred, attachment, and intolerance give way to a mind and spirit that is sensitive to life, compassionate, benevolent, and open. It is never supposed that the practice of *ahimsa* is easy, for a person must go through many stages of purification. But once the discipline is mastered, *ahimsa* is the only way of ending all conflicts.[90]

The Jaina literature is full of stories, historical and legendary, that demonstrate that *ahimsa* can serve as a power for peace. For instance, there is the account of two kings, Bahubali and Bharata, who were about to engage in a bloody war with large armies. At the critical moment Bahubali suggested that instead of allowing this conflict to entail the lives of many soldiers, he and Bharata themselves engage in a show of strength to settle accounts. Thus a battle was fought without the shedding of blood. Such stories have kept alive the option of nonviolence as a way of resolving conflicts.[91]

The Jaina *Tirthankaras* and monks have been in the forefront of creating a world devoid of violence. Numerous episodes in the life of Parsvanatha record his strong opposition to violence. He was in the habit of countering hostile attempts upon his life with the response of *ahimsa*. It is said that he once saved a snake from being burnt by a mendicant in a sacrificial fire. The incident shows that he would not even permit violence for a religious purpose against any living creature. Similarly, several events in the life of Lord Mahavira also serve to establish *ahimsa* as the highest perfection of human life. Through his many acts of forgiveness and his firm faith in spiritual values, Mahavira demonstrated that violence cannot permanently resist nonviolence. If truly observed, *ahimsa* ultimately triumphs.

A few years ago, the prominence given to *ahimsa* by Jainism would have sounded idealistic; today it is not just nice but necessary. The old, practical ethics of justified killing belies the true conditions of human fulfillment and overestimates the power of violence against nonviolence. Thus, the principle of pacifism, which has surfaces on and off in the ethical consciousness of the human race, is found to be deeply rooted in the Jaina religion both in principle and in practice.[92]

In its fullest ramifications, *ahimsa* is more than pacifism as it is known in the Western world. Nonviolence is a principle of life that goes beyond human life to include birds, animals and all living beings. Jaina laymen are obligated to the daily practice of *Jivadaya*— showing mercy to all creatures. It was this vow that brought the Jaina saints into conflict with the Vedic practice of animal sacrifice. Acarya Somadeva says to the royalty who often paid for these elaborate sacrifices, "A king who constantly desires longevity, strength, and health must not cause injury to living creatures himself, nor allow it to take place when planned by others. One may give away the Meru mountain of gold as well as the entire earth. The result will not be equal to that of saving the life of a single sentient being."[93] It does not take much sensitivity to see that all living beings wish to live and are in fear of death. Therefore it is immoral to take away life for selfish ends.

Jaina literature has many examples of animal rescue. It is said that Neminatha, the twenty-second *Tirthankara,* staged a nonviolent demonstration by sacrificing his nuptial pleasures in order to save the helpless animals that were kept in cages for the occasion of his marriage.

Other stories make the point that, ironically, dumb animals better understand the meaning of *ahimsa* than intelligent man. There is the narrative of Meruprabha the elephant who was caught in a raging forest fire. All the animals and birds assembled in a field to escape the flames. The area was so packed that a small rabbit was unable to find a vacant space to lodge itself. Suddenly, Meruprabha lifted its leg to scratch its body. Immediately, the rabbit occupied the spot vacated by the elephant's foot. Knowing the move, the elephant kept its leg elevated so as not to allow it to come down on the rabbit. At the end of three days, the fire subsided and all the animals departed. But the elephant died in that place because of injury sustained in standing on three legs for three days.

The story of Meruprabha the elephant is a literary gem because it illustrates the beneficent law of the jungle.[94] To be sure, animals feed on one another but the carnage is not indiscriminate; fights are not to the death, and they do protect their young with their own lives. Man, to whom intelligence is given, is thereby placed in a position of greater ethical responsibility. He is Nature's eldest son who must use his superior powers to care for and protect beings who are less endowed. He must not act as though the world was made only for him and that animals were placed here as objects for human food or sport. The saints have understood better. *Ahimsa* is not just a social value but a natural value. "Nonviolence is for the welfare of all kinds of animals, visible and nonvisible."[95]

Vegetarianism is another important correlate of *ahimsa.* It is "an attitude of life which refuses to enjoy any pleasure at the cost of another's pain. It is the policy of living at peace with all beings as far as possible. It is a more radical innovation than any of the modern sciences to raise the cultural level of man. The rational conclusion of vegetarianism is that one should refuse anything for any purpose in which animals are slaughtered, even medicine and leather goods."[96]

Since the Jaina ethical code is based on nonviolence, the people are very particular about matters of food and drink. Every layman is required to possess *Asta-Mulagunas* that comprise the five *Anuvratas* plus abstinence from the consumption of flesh, wine, and honey. Numerous stories describe some of the *mulagunas,* and it is claimed that "flesh-eaters have no kindness, drunkards never speak the truth, and people who take honey and the Udumbara fruit feel no pity."[97]

Jainism's ancient advocacy of vegetarianism is receiving global attention due to severe food shortages and to the researches of the scientific community.[98] Vegetarianism is the only viable answer to world hunger, given the scarcity of resources. This is not tantamount to the taking of a backward step out of necessity, for it is now a fairly well established fact that "there is nothing necessary or desirable for human nutrition to be found in meats or flesh foods which is not found in and derived from vegetable products."[99]

There is one final aspect of *ahimsa* that needs some comment, namely, its bearing on euthanasia. The intent of euthanasia is to bring about a good death through the elimination of needless suffering on the part of a terminal patient.

Ahimsa does not warrant euthanasia because it does not find the source of pain in disease, nor does it find release from pain through death. The true locus of pain or joy lies in actions (karmas) of the individual in this life or in previous ones. Everyone is bound to bear the results of every action committed by him. Therefore it is futile to attempt to release the pain of any individual in this life through mercy killing. Nonviolence allows for no exceptions, including euthanasia. It also considers the violence committed in the mind as a source of pain. Whatever feelings of joy one may have in terminating another's life is going to be a source of severe pain for the individual for many lives. For these reasons Jainism is categorically opposed to the practice of euthanasia. Its intention might be benevolent but that does not change the fact that it is a violation of *ahimsa.*

A possible contradiction of the sentiments just expressed may be found in the Jain vow of *Sallekhana* (ritual death by fasting). In fact, it has nothing to do with suicide or euthanasia. This becomes clear when we consider the form and object of *sallekhana* as described in the scriptures.[100]

The vow of *sallekhana* is the highest amition of every pious person. Its object is *samadhi-marana* (peaceful pass away), *sannyasa-marana* (decease in asceticism), and *pandita-marana* (the sage's demise). This fast unto death must be seen as a course of discipline that is intended to prepare a person for a peaceful and ennobling end, particularly if he is an ascetic. Householders, too, may enter this fast. Once they have renounced all affections, all ill will, all riches, and having confessed their sins before the head of the congregation, they may resort to *sallekhana*.[101] The vow hastens the process of self-realization, but the rigor of this path means that only a few are truly capable of treading it.[102] The texts point out that there are five factors that destroy the efficacy of *sallekhana*—the desire to live longer, the desire to avoid suffering, longing for friends, recollection of past happiness, and the desire for happiness in the next life.[103] When all trace of these factors are gone, salvation appears. It is this end of salvation that distinguishes *sallekhana* from suicide.[104] Suicide is evil. It binds one to the wheel of *samsara,* but *sallekhana* is eternal release.

Conclusion

Jaina ethics comprises right faith, right knowledge, and right conduct. It is manifest as nonpossession, nonabsolutism, and nonviolence. Through faith one discerns the nature of body and soul, and this awareness produces an attitude of detachment and nonpossession. Right knowledge frees one from absolutism and enables one to see things with a liberal and open mind. The discovery of the oneness of all living beings leads to nonviolent conduct. The centrality of *ahimsa* to Jaina ethics makes it truly global. Its practitioners are world citizens. Its message of goodwill is for the whole of humanity:

> May all people thrive in happiness. May the ruler be of religious bent of mind. May there be timely rains. Let all diseases disappear. Let there be no famine, theft or epidemic in this world even for a moment. May this wheel of religion *(dharma-cakra)* move ever and anon, and bring about universal happiness and peace.[105]

Notes

1. S. Radhakrishnan, *Indian Philosophy*, vol. 1 (London: George Allen and Unwin, 1962), 287.

2. J.P. Jain, *Religion and Culture of the Jains* (Delhi: Bhartiya Jnanpith, 1977) 168.

3. Ibid., 10.

4. Ibid., 12

5. Ibid., 13

6. T.K. Tukol, *Compendium of Jainism* (Dharwad: Karnatak University, 1980), 40, 41.

7. H.C. Bharill, *Tirthankara Mahavira and His Sarvodaya Tirtha* (Bombay: Kundkund Tirtha Suraksha Trust, 1981), 69.

8. A.K. Roy, *A History of the Jainas* (Delhi: Geetanjali Publishing House, 1984).

9. H.R. Kapadia, *A History of the Canonical Literature of the Jainas* (Surat: 1941).

10. Jain, J.P., *Religion,* 166.

11. P.S. Jaini, *The Jaina Path of Purification* (Delhi: Motilal Banarsidass, 1979), 90.

12. G.R. Jain, *Cosmology Old and New* (Delhi: Bharatiy Jnanpith, 1975).

13. Muni Devendra, *A Source Book in Jaina Philosophy,* Eng. tr. (Udaipur: Tarak Guru Jain Granthalaya, 1983), 41–45.

14. Ibid., 47.

15. *Tattvaartha-Sutra,* 1.4, Sukhalal Sanghavi, ed., 2d. ed. (Varanasi: Motilal Banarsidass, 1952).

16. D. Bhargava, *Jaina Ethics* (Delhi: Motilal Banarsidass, 1968), 37–38.

17. *Sarvadarsanasamgraha* (Poona: Oriental Institute, 1951), 80.

18. *Uttaradhyananasutra,* chap. 20, Gatha 37, Muni Nathamal, ed., in *Jaina Sutras,* pt. 11, *Sacred Books of the East,* vol. 45, H. Jacobi, trans. (New York: Dover, 1968), 104.

19. H. Glasenapp, *The Doctrine of Karma in Jain Philosophy,* Eng. tr. (Bombay: Jivanlal Pannalal Charity Fund, 1942).

20. *Svetasvataropanisad* (Gorakhapur: Gita Press, 1950), 1.12.

21. Muni Nathamal, *Jaina Darsana: Manana Aur Mimansa* (Churu: Adarsha Sahitya Sangha, 1977), 320.

22. James Hastings, ed., *Encyclopaedia of Religion and Ethics,* vol. 8 (Edinburgh: T.&T. Clark, 1955), 472.

23. Bhargava, *Jaina Ethics,* 63.

24. K.C. Sogani, *Ethical Doctrines in Jainism* (Sholapur: Jain Samskriti Samrakshaka Sangha, 1967), 74.

25. Muni Nathamal, ed., *Desavaikalkasutra* (Ladnun: Jain Vishva Bharti, 1974), chap. 1, Gatha 1, 5.

26. T.G. Kalghatgi, *Jaina View of Life* (Sholapur: Jain Samskriti Samrakshaka Sangha, 1969), 178.

27. Bhargava, *Jaina Ethics,* 25.

28. Kalghatgi, *Jaina View,* 175–176.

29. Bhargava, *Jaina Ethics,* 26.

30. A.N. Upadhye, ed., *Parmatama-Prakasa,* Introduction (Bombay: Rayachandra Jain Sastramala, 1937) 36.

31. A.N. Upadhye, ed., *Kartikeyanapreksa* (Bombay: Rayasandra Jain Shastramata, 1960), Gathas 193–198.

32. Sogani, *Ethical Doctrines,* 170.

33. Sukhalal Sanghavi, ed., *Tattvarthasutra* (Benares: Parshvanath Jain Vidyashram, 1952), ch. 1, vs. 1.

34. S.C. Diwarkar, "Bhagwan Mahavira's Ahimsa and World Peace," in *Bhagwan Mahavira and His Relevance in Modern Times,* N. Bhanawat and P.S. Jain, eds. (Bikaner: Sadhumargi Jain Sangh, 1976), 58.

35. J.P. Jain, *Religion,* 32.

36. *Ratnakarandasravakacara,* sloka 2. (Bombay: Manakchandra Jain Granthmala, 1925).

37. H.S. Bhattacharya, *Jain Moral Doctrine* (Bombay: Jain Sahitya Vikas Mandala, 1976), 83.

38. Kalghatgi, *Jaina View,* 135.

39. Tukol, *Compendium,* 254.

40. S.A. Jain, *The Reality* (Calcutta: Vira Sasan Sangha, 1960), 2, 3.

41. Pholachandra Shastri, ed., *Sarvarthasiddhi* (Varanasi: Bhartiya Jnanpith, 1971), 5.

42. "Nissamkiya nikkhamkiya nibbitigimccha amudaditthiya/Uvaguha-thirikarana vacchalla pabhavana attha"—*Uttaraddhyayanasutta* 28.21.

43. K.K. Handiqui, *Yasastilaka and Indian Culture* (Sholapur: Jivaraja Granthamala, 1968), 248.

44. D.D. Malvania, *Agama Yuga Ka Jaina Darsana* (Agra: Sanmati Jnanpith, 1966), 129.

45. "Tatha pancaviham nanam suyam abhinibohiyam/Ohinanam tu tasyam mananam ca kevalam"—*Uttaradhyayanasutta,* 28.4.

46. Satkari Mookerjee, *The Jaina Philosophy of Non-Absolutism,* 2d ed. (Delhi: Motilal Banarsidass, 1978) and N. Tatia, *Studies in Jaina Philosophy* (Varanasi: Jain Cultural Research Society, 1951).

47. Devendra Muni Shastri, *Jaina Acara-Sidhanta Aur Svarupa* (Udaipur: Tarak Guru Jain Granthalaya, 1982), 293.

48. Bhattacharya, *Jain Moral Doctrine,* 52.

49. J.K. Mukhtar, ed., *Ratnakaranda-Sravakacara* (Delhi: Viraseva Mandira, 1955).

50. Walter Schubring, *The Doctrine of the Jainas* (Delhi: Motilal Banarsidass, 1978), 297.

51. *Ayaro,* Eng. tr., Yuvacarya Mahaprajna, ed. (New Delhi: Today and Tomorrow, 1981), 183.

52. *Sutrakrtangasutra* 1.4.10, also *Sacred Books of the East,* H. Jacobi, ed., vol. 45, 247–248.

53. Muni Hemchandra, ed., *Prasnavyakaranasutra* (Agra: Sanmati Jnanpith, 1973), 2.1.21–22.

54. K.C. Shastri, ed., *Bhagavati-Aradhana* (Sholapur: Jain Sanskriti Samrakshaka Sangha, 1982), Gatha 790.

55. Ajit Prasad, ed., *Purusarthasidhupaya* (Lucknow: Ajitashrama, 1933), vs. 42.

56. H.C. Bharill, *Tirthankara Bhagwan Mahavir* (Songad:Kundkund Trust, 1981), 21.

57. D.S. Kothari, *Some Thoughts on Science and Religion* (Delhi: R.K. Jain Charitable Trust, 1977) 31.

58. P.S. Jain, "Prakrit Katha-Sahitya men Ahimsa ka Drastikoana" in *Amar-Bharti* (Rajgrahi: Virayatana, 1981).

59. Nanalal Acarya, *Samata-Darsana Aur Vyavahara* (Bikaner: Sadhumargi Jain Sangha, 1973).

60. Bhattacharya, *Jain Moral Doctrine*, 53–54.

61. Handiqui, *Yasastilika*, 293

62. V.A. Sammgave, *Jaina Community: A Social Survey*, 2d. ed. (Bombay: Popular Prakashan, 1980), 214, 215.

63. S.B.P. Sinha, "Relevance of Jaina Ethics in the Present Age," in *Mahavira and His Teachings*, A.N. Upadhye, ed. (Bombay: Mahavira Vidyalaya, 1977), 136.

64. T.G. Kalghatgi, ed., *Jainism and Karnatak Culture* (Dharwad: Karnatak University, 1977), 85.

65. J.C. Jain, *Life in Ancient India as Depicted in the Jaina Canons*, 2d ed. (Delhi: Meharchand Laxamandas, 1983).

66. N. Bhanawat, ed., *Bhagwan Mahavira: Adhunika Sandharbha Men* (Bikaner: Sadhumargi Jain Sangha, 1974), 39.

67. Sangave, *Jaina Community*, 384.

68. Thomas A. Mappes and Jane S. Zembaty, *Social Ethics*, (New York: McGraw, 1977).

69. Sangave, *Jaine Community*, chs. 3, 4.

70. Kalghatgi, *Karnatak Culture*, 143–44.

71. Ganesh Lalwani, "Rathanemi" in *Jain Journal*, vol. 15, no. 1 (July 1980), 10–14.

72. Acarya Jinasena, *Adipurana* (Delhi: Bhartiya Jnanpith, 1951), ch. 38, vs. 135.

73. Sangave, *Jaina Community*, 139.

74. "Great Women in Jainism" in *Jain Journal*, vol. 17, no. 2 (October 1982), 67–75.

75. Muni Punyavijaya, ed., *Brahat-Kalpa-Bhasya* (Bhavnagar: Jain Atmanand Sabha, 1938), vol. 4, 43–48.

76. K.C. Jain, *Buddha Aur Jaina Agarnon Men Naree-Jivana* (Varanasi: Parshvanath Jain Vidyashram, 1969), 9.

77. *Adipurana* 16: 98.

78. Muni Nathamal, *Sraman Mahavir,* Eng. trans. (Calcutta: Mitra Parishad, 1980), 150–153.

79. *Suyagado,* second canon, 1.9.27.

80. Jaina Sutras, pt. 11, *Sacred Books of the East,* vol. 45: 140.

81. *Dharma-Pariksa,* 17: 31–33.

82. Sangave, *Jaina Community,* 68.

83. J.P. Jain, *Religion,* 87.

84. There is a Charitable Hospital for Birds in Delhi, run by the Digambra Jain Society since 1935.

85. Sagarmal Jain, *Jaina Bauddha Aur Gita ka Samaja-Darsana* (Jaipur: Prakrit Bharti Sansthan, 1982), 98.

86. Tukol, *Compendium,* 333.

87. S.L. Mamdawat, "Jainism in Economic Perspective," in *Mahavira and His Relevance in Modern Times,* N. Bhanawat and P.S. Jain, eds. (Bikaner: S.J. Sangha, 1976), 172.

88. Ibid.

89. V.P. Kothari, *The Law of Non-Violence and Its Relevance for All Times* (Sholapur: Jain Sanskrit Samrakshakasangha, 1975), 57–58.

90. O.P. Jain, *The Truth* (Indore: Vira Nirvana Granth Prakashan, 1977), 79, 80.

91. P.S. Jain, "Bahubali in Prakrit Literature" in *Gommateshvara Commemoration Volume* (Shravanabelagala: S. D.J. Managing Committee, 1981), 76.

92. S.L. Samgavi, *Pacifism and Jainism* (Varanasi: Jain Cultural Research Society, 1950).

93. Handiqui, *Yasastilikas,* 317.

94. P.S. Jain, "Some Earlier Buddhist and Jaina Legends" presented as a paper at the *First International Conference on Buddhism and National Cultures,* New Delhi, 1984.

95. P.S. Jain, "Jaina Ethics and Human Welfare" presented as a paper at the *God: The Contemporary Discussion* Conference, Puerto Rico, 1984.

96. O.P. Jain, *Truth,* 74.

97. Handiqui, *Yasastilikas,* 262.

98. Robert Lewanski, "The Scientific Basis of Vegetarianism" in *Vegetarian Voice,* vol. 11, no. 2: 5.

99. K.P. Jain, *Ahimsa: Right Solution of World Problems* (Aliganj: World Jain Mission, 1970), 11.

100. T.K. Tukol, *Sallekhana is not Suicide* (Amhedabad: L. D. Institute of Indology, 1976), 11.

101. Handiqui, *Yasastilikas,* 159–60.

102. Kalghatgi, *Karnatak Culture,* 155.

103. Handiqui, *Yasastilakacampu,* 413.

104. Kalghatgi, *Yasastilikas,* 159–60.

105. J.P. Jain, *Religion,* 185, "Prayer of Peace."

Part II
EAST ASIA

4

Confucianism and Contemporary Ethical Issues

CHUNG M. TSE

Introduction

Confucianism has been associated, invariably and rightly, with the name of Confucius (551–479 B.C.), its mentor. But today's Confucianism as it now stands is the result of elaborations, interpretations, speculations and additions by Confucians of later historic periods. From its early form of moral admonitions in the *Analects,* Confucianism has now evolved into a system of thought penetrating the areas of ethics, metaphysics and religion. The term Confucianism should no longer be taken to stand for a particular ethical theory alone; it rather refers to a body of ideas and beliefs about morality, reality, and the Supreme Being. But it is still true that the ethical remains the ultimate concern and foundation of Confucianism.

The ideas and beliefs of present-day Confucianism are found in numerous works authored or compiled by Confucian scholars over a long period of time since Confucius' own day. Along with the work attributed to Confucius, the *Analects,* the most important texts are the *Book of Mencius,* the *Doctrine of the Mean,* and the *Great Learning,* constituting the "Four Books"—the central core of the Confucian literature. Besides these, the ancient classics such as the *Book of Change, (I-Ching)* and the *Book of Odes* have been read "Confucianly" and have been respected as the precursors of Confucianism. Later works by the Neo-Confucians of the Sung (960–1279) and the Ming (1368–1643) give a boost to the original thought, allowing it an extended range of coverage with more sophistication, elaboration, and subtlety. The names of Ch'eng Hao (1032–1095), Chu Hsi (1130–1200), and Wang Yang-ming (1472–1529) are names of prominent Neo-Confucian figures. To the philosophical growth of Confucianism in contemporary times, Professors T'an Chun-I (1909–1978) and Mou Tsung-san, among others, have made significant contributions.

The presentation in this chapter consists of two parts. Part One is developed following this sequence of headings: Basic Moral Concepts, The Metaphysics of Jen, The Concept of the Supreme Being, The Concept of Nature, Summary and Transition to Application. In this part, our treatment of Confucianism is not meant to be historical or comprehensive, but philosophical in intent. The purpose is to lay bare the groundwork of Confucianism by delineating its conceptual threads with regard to such general philosophical topics as the idea of man, the Supreme Being, reality, and physical nature. This calls for a representation and exposition of the basic Confucian concepts and an exhibition of the logic of Confucian thought. In the interests of selectivity, certain things must be omitted. First, since we are not concerned with the history of Confucianism, the chronological development of Confucian ideas and personalities is not part of our organizational focus. Second, as Confucianism, like many other religious and philosophic traditions, is divided on some issues, we can only focus on what appears to be orthodox—the line of thought as fixed by Confucius and Mencius, at one point, and by Lu Hsian-shan and Wang Yan-ming, at another.

Part two attempts to articulate Confucian positions regarding: sexual morality, liberation movements, economic systems, and punishment and justice. The word "attempt" is emphasized because, so far as the author's knowledge is concerned, Confucianism has never dealt with these issues in a philosophical manner; that is to say, by propositions supported by reasons and substantiated by explanations. Moreover, some of the issues, such as sexuality and women's liberation, are quite new to Confucian discourse.

Confucian Metaphysics

Basic Moral Concepts

The concept of jen is basic to Confucianism because it defines or explains nearly all other Confucian concepts, providing unity to the various dimensions of Confucian thought. The concept of jen invariably bears upon the Confucian concepts of man, God, natural and supernatural realities, and morality. It is therefore imperative to begin with an elucidation of the concept of jen as a structural element of the framework of Confucianism.

There have been a number of English translations of the term jen. Some popular ones are: magnanimity, benevolence, perfect virtue (James Legge), moral life, moral character (ku Hung-ming), true manhood, compassion (Lin Yutang), human-heartedness (Derk Bodde), man-to-manness (E. R. Hughes),[1] love, altruism, kindness, and hominity (Boodberg).[2] These renderings, though helpful in identifying some of the meanings of *jen*, are at best partial characterizations of the concept. The concept of *jen* certainly includes the meaning of love, yet it embraces more than that. It is basically an ethical concept, yet it carries rich metaphysical connotations.

In the *Analects* the term *jen* is employed in a number of different ways without providing an explicit definition. Sometimes it is placed in juxtaposition with names of other specific virtues;[3] at other times it suggests a particular conduct;[4] on other occasions it vaguely refers to love, filial piety, or benevolence.[5] Despite this vagueness and ambiguity, several kinds of meanings are distinguishable. First, the term *jen* may refer to a particular virtue of character roughly equivalent to benevolence or love. It is, then, a name of a particular virtue. Second, it stands for a class of virtues, for example, wisdom, courage, confidence, gravity, forgiveness, trustworthiness, earnestness, kindness, etc., and *jen*-virtues. Some of the virtues of the class are more characteristic of and essential to the concept. The virtues of faithfulness, reciprocity *(shu)*, and filial piety, are cases in point. In this capacity, the term *jen* is a generic name. Third, *jen* may also refer to a very special quality in its own right, namely, the quality of moral perfection. By moral perfection is meant, negatively, the quality of having no moral deficiency,[6] and, positively, the ideal state of possessing all possible moral virtues or the state of being absolutely good. The notion of moral perfection defines the ideal of sageness, the highest goal of moral cultivation in Confucianism. In this sense, *jen* is the Confucian ideal.

The three kinds of meaning listed above are clusters of ethical connotations typical of the concept. The roster of meanings, however, could be longer. Often Confucius gave different answers to different students who asked the same question—what *jen* is. *Jen* was variously referred to as: "the subduing of one's selfish ego and restoration of propriety";[7] "[behaving to everyone in such a way that] when you leave home you act as if you were receiving an honorable guest; when you employ people you act as if you were performing a sacrificial ritual; and you do not do to others as you would not wish done to yourself",[8] "[a mannerism] of cautious and thoughtful speech",[9] "[being] sedately grave in private life, and reverently serious in handling affairs, and strictly sincere in dealing with people",[10] and many others. Among the indispensable mani-

festations of *jen* are love and the "Golden Rule"—"Do unto others
as you would wish done to yourself." In general, the concept comprehends nearly all other ethical concepts about human conduct,
moral quality, and character that are deemed desirable in Confucianism. As to the question of where the limits of its range lie and
what the sufficient and necessary conditions of its application are,
there are no obvious and definitive answers. But the concept of *jen*
is invariably associated with the idea of moral goodness and
perfection.

The Metaphysics of Jen

The ethical concept of *jen* covers the arena of individual and social
morality concerning motive, action, character, and feeling. However, the true spirit of Confucianism does not so much consist in
jen being understood in behavioral or dispositional terms, but in
being understood as the ground of morality. For it is in terms of
the metaphysical signification of the concept that the idea of man
(humanity) and the ultimate ground of morality are construed. This
being the case, Confucian ethics is distinguished from ethical nat-
uralism that includes various forms of empiricism, (heteronomous)
authoritarianism, and social conventionalism, and from religious
supernaturalism that posits a distinct deity to account for the origin
of morals requiring faith in that deity, logically and practically, to
precede morality. While it is frequently said that Confucianism is
a type of ethical humanism, the label "humanism" cannot be taken
without qualification. Although Confucianism posits the ground of
morality in humanity itself, it does so in that particular part of
humanity that transcends nature while immanent in it. Confucianism maintains that there is an essential constituent of man, defining
man as man, that transcends the system of natural causality, and has
its own causality, effectually materialized, or to be materialized, in
nature. This statement briefly summarizes the transcendental
humanism of Confucianism.

In the orthodox Confucian tradition, man is thought of as a composite being consisting of two elements in a unique way. In Mencius (371–289 B.C. ?), one of the elements is called the greater *ti*,
the other, the lesser *ti*.[11] By the lesser *ti* Mencius means the physical
body with all its attachments and derivatives. Thus, for example,
the human intellect and all sensuous desires belong to this category.
The concept of physical body is simply a sub-concept of the general
concept of nature *(Ch'i)*, to be explained later. Man has a share in

this natural world and, as such, he is subject to the rule of natural laws. Mencius says, "For the mouth to desire [sweet] tastes, the eye to desire [beautiful] colors, the ear to desire [pleasant] sound, the nose to desire [fragrant] odors, and the four limbs to desire ease and rest—these things are natural."[12] To this extent, man lives in the same kingdom as other animals.

By the greater *ti* Mencius means the moral mind (*hsin, jen*-mind). Mencius' doctrine of mind represents a cornerstone in the development of Confucianism, inaugurating a line of moral philosophical thought uniquely Confucian, culminating with Wang-ming's philosophy of *Liang-Chih* (Good Knowledge). The Confucian concept of mind must be carefully distinguished from other popular concepts. The moral mind posited by Confucianism is not to be understood as a thinking substance *per se,* or a storehouse for sensible ideas, or a bundle of impressions and ideas, or a complex of behavioral dispositions, or a sort of phenomenal consciousness. The Confucian concept of mind is interwoven with metaphysical, ethical, and functional meanings. Mencius thinks that the (moral) mind is given, not biologically or chronologically, but logically and metaphysically, *a priori.* Logically speaking, the mind must be posited before moral precepts and moral conduct are possible. Wangming later makes this thesis clearer and more specific, saying, "Only if there is the mind that sets itself for loving the parents, there is the principle of filial piety; and if there is no such mind, there is no such principle."[13] To say that the mind is metaphysically *prior* is to say that the mind is not to be defined in empirical or naturalistic terms; it is not conceived to be part of, or derived from, nature, although it is supposed to operate through and on nature.

The mind's being consists in its activity (function); it *is* the activity. The mind is defined as nothing but a creatively active faculty for originating moral precepts and principles alone, and commanding and discriminating, accordingly. In order to comprehend such a Confucian concept of mind, the duality of substratum and activity must be eliminated. The mind is the very activity itself, apart from which there is no other entity posited as a substratum.[14] The manifestation of the mind, or, in other words, the effects of this activity itself, occur in the natural world as moral feelings, moral conduct and acts, and moral principles and discriminations. Among the principles that the mind gives rise to are *jen* (in a narrow sense), righteousness, propriety, and wisdom (in an ethical sense), and correspondingly, there are moral feelings of commiseration, of disgrace and disgust, of modesty and yielding, and the sense of right and wrong.[15] These principles and feelings are among the fundamental outcomes of the mind. To illustrate the workings of the mind, Mencius cites an anecdote which has become a classical example:

> When I say that all men have a mind which cannot bear [to see the sufferings of] others . . . if men suddenly see a child about to fall into a well, they will without exception experience a feeling of alarm and distress. [They will feel so], not as a ground on which they may seek the praise of their neighbors and friends, nor from a dislike to the reputation of having been unmoved by such a thing.[16]

The feeling of commiseration in this particular situation appears as a feeling of alarm and distress. In other situations, as with the ruler of a country, the feeling appears as a love for his subjects. The feeling of commiseration is identified with reference to the actual occasions in which it occurs. Similarly, other moral feelings affected by the mind are explained in like manner.

The orthodox "Mencian" school of thought with Wang Yangming and Lu Hsiang-shan as chief proponents, faithfully following Mencius, holds that *jen* is the mind.[17] This identification gives a new twist, reciprocally, to the concept of *jen* and the concept of mind. *Jen* in its ethical sense primarily refers to a group of moral entities, including conduct, principle, character, and quality, but not to a metaphysical entity; it is not a "thing" name, so to speak. The concept of mind, in contrast, refers to an entity—an active moral faculty; it is by analogy a "thing" name. The identification of *jen* and mind results in a compound concept that requires an adequate referent. A reality is the referent, which is an active moral faculty and, at the same time, the most general active moral principle itself. The description, "the active moral reason (or *logos*)," could be helpful to indicate the nature of this reality. In Confucian literature, this reality is generally referred to as the *jen*-mind. Sometimes the term *jen* or the term "mind" alone suffices to carry the messages with the other side of the conjugation understood. The *jen*-mind, then, is a metaphysical reality whose entire essence is the activity of originating moral precepts and principles, and commanding and discriminating accordingly. To use an analogy, the *jen*-mind is like an office of both moral legislation and judiciary that, having its own principle of activity, presents itself as an excelling and commanding entity in relation to the executive.

The Confucian philosophy of *jen*-mind is consummated with Wang Yang-ming's Doctrine of *Liang-Chih* (Good Knowledge), summed up in his renowned "Teaching of Four Lines": the mind in itself is over and above the distinction between good and evil (i.e., the mind is absolutely good), the volition in its exercises may tend to the good or to evil, that which discriminates the good from the evil is the mind of good-knowledge, to have always observed the good and eliminated the evil is called the rectification of the volition in its direction.[18] Note that the volition is a faculty of desire given by nature whereas the mind is a metaphysical being.

The Concept of the Supreme Being

Throughout Confucian literature, the concept of the Supreme Being bears a multitude of names and descriptions. Most frequently seen are Heaven, Tao, God, the Lord, the Heavenly Tao, the Great Tao, the Heavenly Principle, the One, the Ultimate One, the Supreme Vacuity, the Heavenly Mind, the Divine Mind. Some of the names and descriptions are suggestive, some are merely symbolic, while some are misleading. In spite of the diversity, these names and descriptions do help indicate some of the attributes of the Supreme Being as conceived by the Confucians. The term Heaven, for example, is symbolic of what is above, transcending, all-covering, and above all, superhuman. The term mind excludes corporeality and materiality; and the term One may suggest unity, simplicity, originality, or priority. The most widely used term, Tao, may denote a certain way (of doing things), a well-defined process, a normative principle, or a cosmic norm.

The orthodox Confucian notion of Heaven stems from Mencius' saying, "He who cultivates [or extends] his *jen*-mind to the utmost knows his [essential] nature. He who knows his [essential] nature knows Heaven. To attend to one's mind and to nourish one's nature, is the way to serve Heaven."[19] There is a wealth of presuppositions and implications that can be unearthed from this saying of Mencius. For the present purpose it is sufficient to concentrate on one relevant point—a doctrine that has developed from this saying, namely, the doctrine of Man-Heaven Continuum. The doctrine holds that man, as far as his essential reality is concerned, is continuous with Heaven. By continuity is meant that there is no ontological, essential difference between man and Heaven; that man and Heaven, insofar as their essential reality is concerned, are a unity. But, of course, there is some sense in which man and Heaven are distinguishable. The distinction can be drawn in the following ways. Man in his ideal essence is Heaven-*in-concreto;* he is Heaven in individualized form.[20] To say that man is Heaven is not to say that man, as such, is *de facto* Heaven itself, but only that the ideal essence of man is Heaven-*in-concreto*. The doctrine of Man-Heaven Continuum, then, can be expressed as: there resides in man an infinite divinity (Heaven) as his essential reality. Man can be actually and fully identical with Heaven only when he has fully actualized this infinite divinity in him. In the *Doctrine of the Mean* the ideal "Heavenly Man" is admired with the exclamations, "Does he depend on anything else? How earnest and sincere—he is *jen!* How deep and unfathomable—he is abyss! How vast and great— he is Heaven!"[21]

The doctrine of Man-Heaven Continuum is very important for apprehending the Confucian concept of Heaven (God). Now the question as to what the Confucian God is, is explicable with reference to the Confucian view of Man. Confucianism approaches Heaven, the Supreme Being, and man-in-his-essence, reciprocally. The concept of Heaven, by its formal definition, refers to that which is creative, supreme, ultimate, transcendental, universal, and, in short, to a being that is the subject of all infinite attributes. However, the concept is still indeterminate as to its content (object), for these formal predicates of supremacy, ultimacy, universality, etc., are all analytical of the concept of God as the Highest Being. Nothing is said about what God really is. Confucianism takes a humanistic, moral approach to furnish the concept with contents to give a material definition to the concept. Heaven is defined as the *jen*-mind in its infinite self, as man is essentially defined as the *jen*-mind in individuality.[22]

One may recall what Mencius has said: "He who knows his [essential] nature knows Heaven."[23] To know what Heaven is consists in knowing what one's true, essential self is. The knowledge is not gained through philosophical speculation, religious revelation, scriptural doctrine, discursive thinking, or by logical arguments. Rather, knowledge of Heaven comes as a result of diligent cultivation and discipline of the moral self to its fulness. Figuratively speaking, knowledge of Heaven is "lived out," not "thought out," nor "handed down from above." Such cultivation and discipline aim at fully actualizing the *jen*-mind—expanding and extending the activity of the *jen*-mind to its infinite limit where it is unfettered, uninfluenced, unblocked by any alien factors, particularly sensuous desires and selfish calculations. To summarize, Confucian reality is nothing other than the *jen*-mind. Considered in its infinity, it is Heaven; considered in its particularity, it is man's essence.

The Concept of Physical Nature

Nature as a system of physical existents is explained in terms of *Ch'i*. The concept is not altogether transparent and takes on added obscurities when rendered in Western terminology. Attempts have been made to find an equal concept in contemporary vocabulary. It has been variously said, for example, that *Ch'i* is an ether-like substance, or a material substance (matter), or cosmic substance, or material force. What *Ch'i* is exactly may be an interesting topic for philosophical discussion, but the popular opinion tends to define *Ch'i* as cosmic material force.

Despite its obscurity, the concept of *Ch'i* has been utilized to explain the configuration and development of the physical universe. Some Neo-Confucians, such as Chou Tun-i (1017–1073) and Chang Tsai (1021–1077), have constructed, by giving interpretations to the symbolic scheme and text of the *Book of Change*, a neat cosmogony depicting the origin and becoming of the physical universe in terms of *Ch'i*.[24] The cosmogony consists of such key notions as the *Yin* and *Yang* (the two opposing but complementary modes of *Ch'i*) and the Five Elements of Process: metal, wood, water, fire, and earth that are the five basic configurations of *Ch'i*. The cosmogony pictures the universe as an orderly, balanced, and internally harmonious structure, changing and transforming in rhythmic patterns.

Apart from its role in Confucian cosmology, the concept of *Ch'i* bears important implications for Confucian ethical theory and practice. *Ch'i* accounts for the origin of evil, and it is the instrument or vehicle for the actualization of moral existents.

The human body, or in Mencius' word, the lesser *ti*, is conceived of as a special configuration of *Ch'i*—a proposition generally assumed by the Neo-Confucians.[25] *Ch'i*, in the form of the human body, displays many of its dispositions known as man's natural qualities and capacities. Thus, man has emotions, senses, desires, temperament, and instincts as parts of his phenomenal existence. Man in his physical existence—as a configuration of *Ch'i*—is not inherently evil. For *Ch'i* in itself is not an evil being. Evil begins when individuals follow their dispositions of *Ch'i* to the extent that they defy, or become indifferent to, the bounds of morality prescribed by the *jen*-mind. Mencius believes that they are likely to do moral wrongs when they let their lesser *ti* rule over their greater *ti*. For the Neo-Confucians, unchecked selfish desire is the centerpiece of all moral evils.

In contradistinction to the *jen*-mind, *Ch'i* is the category that comprehends all things, occurrences, properties, and events that are not immediately explainable by virtue of the concept of the *jen*-mind in any of its capacities. While the concept of the *jen*-mind accounts for the ground and origin of morality, the concept of *Ch'i* accounts for all those things that are morally indeterminate.

In one of its relations to Heaven (the cosmic *jen*-mind), *Ch'i* serves as a necessary instrument. Heaven is in a constant process of self-actualization. To actualize itself is to materialize itself into concrete particulars that require a principle of individuation. Ch'eng I puts it this way: "The mind is the principle of production. As there is the mind, a *body* must be provided for it so it can produce."[26] The instrumentality of *Ch'i* consists in its being a vehicle with which the cosmic *jen*-mind actualizes itself.

Heaven's self-actualization process translates itself into a process of purposive change and transformation of *Ch'i*. The movement follows a dialectical pattern. Hence, there is the principle of complementary opposites understood from the Confucian perspective.[27] *Ch'i* is thought to differentiate itself into two opposing forces, the *Yin* and the *Yang*, acting, reacting, and interacting on each other. This dynamic opposition is not mutually destructive but complementary as things and events emerge from, and pass into, the process. Ch'eng Hao epitomizes this productive opposition, saying, "Nevertheless, there cannot be anything without the distinction between rising and falling, and between birth and extinction."[28]

The *Yin* and *Yang* are the most general concepts for specific complementary opposites: female and male, winter and summer, night and day, death and life, submission and domination, passivity and activity, receptivity and spontaneity. The principle is employed to explain not only natural things and events but human affairs as well. Hence, there are such opposing but complementary pairs as people and government, worker and employer, wife and husband, the weak and the strong, the emotional and the rational.[29] It is relevant to note that the principle of complementary opposites is supposed to be a normative principle governing human affairs as much as an explanatory principle descriptive of natural process.

Summary of the Confucian Moral Metaphysics and a Transition to its Application

The concept of *jen*-mind is the first principle of orthodox Confucian philosophy. The *jen*-mind is a moral activity-reality, creating, in the manner of self-actualization, existents either immediately good or conducive to goodness. Considered in itself, the *jen*-mind is the Supreme Being—Heaven or God. Considered in its most primary and excellent locus, it is the *jen*-mind in man as the essence of humanity. The *jen*-mind in man acts and affects an outflow of moral feelings, principles, and precepts that result in moral conduct. Among these the feelings of commiseration, of disgrace and disgust, of modesty and yielding, and the sense of right and wrong are most typical and fundamental. Although man has the *jen*-mind as his defining essence, he also has a physical body. The physical body at its best is the vehicle or instrument for the *jen*-mind's activity—self-actualization. The physical body is paradigmatic of (physical) nature.

The Confucian metaphysics of (physical) nature is constructed on the concept of *Ch'i*—a cosmic, material force. The configurations and motions of *Ch'i* constitute the physical, phenomenal universe of which the human body is a part. Man, as far as his physical constitution is concerned, naturally possesses dispositions originated from *Ch'i*. Although such dispositions are not inherently evil, they can become causes of moral evil if they are not properly contained. Excessive selfish desire is the core of all moral impurities, according to Confucian ethics. *Ch'i* is, however, a necessary instrument for the self-actualization of the *jen*-mind, serving as a principle of individuation. The process of the actualization of the *jen*-mind translates itself as incessant transformation of *Ch'i*. The transformation proceeds by way of interaction between opposing forces.

For Confucianism, the ultimate judge of morality is the *jen*-mind ideally unfettered, unbiased, undistorted, and uninfluenced by selfish desires and natural inclinations that are inherent properties of *Ch'i*. As he stands, man is a composite being of the *jen*-mind embodied in a configuration of *Ch'i;* his acts either spring from the *jen*-mind or from dispositions of *Ch'i*. That which is from the *jen*-mind is categorically good, whereas that which is from *Ch'i* is either morally agreeable, indifferent, or objectionable and evil. Hence, the motive of an act carries the most weight when the act is subject to moral judgment; consequences of the act count less towards its morality or immorality. The *jen*-mind responds and reacts to each moral occasion, and it does so in correspondence to the uniqueness of each situation. In Confucianism there are no rigid rules of morality specifying the right and the wrong for all circumstances. Confucian ethics is not teleological or rule-oriented; it is more a theory of act-deontology.

However, there are at least three fundamental and general principles proposed by Confucian ethics. 1) Since man is a *jen*-being in essence, it is therefore his Heavenly vocation and duty fully to actualize the *jen*-mind's activity in his own person and to help do so with other people. More explicitly, it is man's duty to follow the dictates of the *jen*-mind and to help others to do the same, with the final end of realizing a world of Great Harmony—a world where every person is a morally perfect individual. This is Heaven actualized. Moral self-abandonment is a vice, for it is a relinquishment of one's Heavenly duty. 2) If a man is to live up to the name of being human, he must respect his own person and that of others. To be respectful is to be respectful of the essence of humanity. Negatively stated, this means that he is not to act and treat himself and others in a way that erases the essential distinction between man and beast. Knowingly or unknowingly he is not to denigrate the dignity of humanity. 3) The cosmic *jen*-mind is in a constant process of self-actualization, and this results in the coming into being of individuals (i.e., things and persons) underlaid by a moral purpose. Among all the creatures, living human beings are *par excellence* the highest, for it is in a living human being that the *jen*-mind can be truly said to have a locus of actualization. Every individual living person is potentially Heaven-in-particular. Nothing should be done unto a person by oneself or others which might suppress, subvert, or destroy the Heavenly potentiality he has.

The ultimate concern of Confucianism does not lie in the metaphysical as much as in the ethical. Matters of morality—the ground, the ideal, the justification, the principles, the method—are what the philosophy is basically interested in, with the aim to better the world and humanity morally. It does not presume to be able to give final solutions to all ethical problems that emerge out of this ever changing world, but it provides a way of ethical thinking, along with a conceptual framework for the assessment of problems and affairs that call for moral consideration.

Confucian Response to Contemporary Ethical Issues

Morality of Sex

That animate beings, human or nonhuman, have sexual desires, presumably for procreation purposes, and that they are naturally and normally disposed to derive pleasure from engaging in sex, is an indisputable biological and psychological fact. It should be added, that sexual contact is an intimate way of expressing love. Looked upon from these perspectives, sexual activity is quite justifiable and perfectly legitimate. But in the human community, some sorts of sexual behavior call for special considerations that do not apply to the animal kingdom. When activities such as rape, incest, child molestation, extramarital sex, premarital sex, homosexuality, and bestiality occur, then problems of morality arise.

The Confucian position on sexual morality is unambiguously conservative. It views human sexual intercourse as primarily for the purpose of the continuation of the species by means of procreation. Sexual intercourse is the intitial act of procreation and is read as an individualized act of creation of the cosmic *jen*-mind (Heaven), in and through human beings. The whole process, from intercourse to the completion of an individual[30] is regarded as the most basic and highest mode of Heavenly creation. The act of intercourse instantiates many great virtues of the cosmic *jen*-mind and exemplifies the way the cosmic *jen*-mind actualizes itself. In the sex act there is caring, love, intimacy, union, dynamic harmony, exchange of vital energy, give-and-take, joyful consummation, and, above all, creativity. Viewed as such, sexual intercourse is divinely moral, both in itself and in respect to its *telos* (goal).

Although the process of procreation may be said to begin with the act of intercourse, it does not end with it, but ends rather, with the coming into existence of an individual human being. This extended view of the sexual act places solemn responsibilities upon the couple involved. According to Confucianism, Heavenly creation does not essentially consist in the bringing forth of a "thing" or a body," *per se,* but in the bringing forth of individuals (particulars) who are at least potentially Heaven-*in-concreto.* An individual is one who possesses this moral potentiality. Thus, the process of generation that begins with the act of intercourse is followed by conception and all the steps necessary to nurture, care, cultivate, and educate this being, ending finally in the formation of an individual capable of moral undertakings.

The generating process requires a couple to start and bring it to fruition.[31] Hence, sexual activity occupies the highest place in the Confucian scheme of life. Normatively, sexual intercourse must occur for the purpose of procreation and is to be engaged in only by couples of the opposite sex who are permanently bonded, in order to carry through the process of procreation. Simply stated, sexual activity should occur between husband and wife for the purpose of raising a family for which they are willing and able to provide in a manner that meets all needs adequately.

Sexual relationships deviating from this norm are considered in a realm extending anywhere from morally tolerable to downright evil, depending on the nature and degree of the deviation. Incest and bestiality are condemned as evils. The party engaged in incest virtually denies the moral order within the family that Confucianism regards as an extended invidualization of the cosmic *jen*-mind, not to mention the social or genetic consequences of the act. The party engaged in bestiality annihilates the dignity of humanity, completely destroying the distinction between man and beast. This is so because the individual through this act assimilates with an animal and treats it in the same intimate way one would treat a human being.

Both rape and child molestation are morally reprehensible. Rape is sexual contact by force, against another person's will, and is, therefore, both contradictory to the idea of harmonious union, and the source of grave pain to its victim. The latter implies a denial of *jen*-love, i.e., the feeling of commiseration. The attacker not only witnesses the suffering of another, he even derives pleasure from making the person suffer. Child molestation is reprehensible because it is an impediment to the normal process of growth of a child into an individual. It distorts and hinders a particular locus of actualization of the cosmic *jen*-mind.

Consentual homosexuality is morally indefensible, not because the act is antisocial though glossed over as an "alternative life style," but because it countervails the manifest way of Heaven— the way of complementary opposites. It is therefore counterproductive of the Heavenly cause. Homosexual contact by force is blameworthy on two counts, being a combination of rape and homosexuality.

Premarital sex may be morally excusable, provided that the parties engaged in the act do it in good faith, with sincere intention eventually to establish a permanent and normal sexual relationship and to assume all the consequential responsibilities. But there is a kind of premarital sex that is for no other purpose except pleasure. Sexual behavior for the sole sake of pleasure cannot be criticized, for pleasure-seeking is, morally tolerable.[32] But excessive, unrestrained seeking of sexual pleasure, whether premarital or marital, is morally degrading because, in Confucian ethics, it virtually reduces a person to the low position of being an attendant to the lesser *ti*, i.e., sensuous desires. On the whole, premarital sex, though socially questionable, or unbecoming, or even unacceptable in some social settings, is either morally excusable or tolerable, if restrained.

Extramarital sex, in the majority of cases, is morally objectionable for two reasons. First, extramarital sex almost inevitably presupposes or entails other unethical acts, such as deception, cheating, infidelity, unchastity, and, in particular, a conscious disregard for the spouse's right to sexual exclusivity, tacitly implied in a marriage. Second, extramarital sex is mostly for added sexual excitement or pleasure. As far as the motive is concerned, a person who engages in extramarital sex is servile to sensuous desires, and is, therefore, subject to the same criticism as the excessive, unrestrained seeking of sexual pleasure. There is a sense, however, in which extramarital sex may be defended from the above criticisms. Extramarital sex may be negotiated when, for example, the spouse voluntarily waives the right to sexual exclusivity so that extramarital sex need not entail duplicity. It is also permissible when actual circumstances or physical conditions do not allow normal sexual behavior between a husband and wife. In general, there is much rationalism in Confucianism, but not to the extent that there is in Stoicism. Confucianism does allow a *reasonable* outlet for natural desires.

Liberation Movements

In recent times there have been a number of liberation movements for a variety of causes. Among the most popular ones are racial liberation, women's liberation, sexual liberation, ethnic liberation, and proletariat liberation. Each of these movements has its unique motive, features, historical and cultural background, and therefore merit separate discussion. For the present purpose, however, two movements will be discussed from the Confucian perspective, namely, racial and women's liberation.

First, some key concepts must be defined and clarified. A liberation movement is a collective struggle for equal liberty. Equal liberty is defined in terms of equal rights to earthly happiness, or the means thereto.[33] A right is said to be equal when it is, at least in principle, available to all persons who are similar in relevant respects. Oppression is an institution that deprives, in actual practice or theory, certain rights of a designated person or group of persons by organized or legalized mechanisms on consideration of factors connected to that person or group *alone*. Oppression is an extreme form of discrimination. Racism is either the oppression of, or discrimination against, one race by another on consideration of racial difference alone; and sexism (specifically, male chauvinism) is either the oppression of, or discrimination against, the feminine sex by the masculine sex on consideration of sexual difference alone.[34]

That racism is morally wrong can be argued for on the grounds of a number of ethical concepts or principles.[35] For Confucian ethics, racism is morally wrong on account of its *motives*. The motives of racism are many and complex. Racism may arise from a psychology of racial superiority, or an instinctual aversion of unfamiliar creatures and things, or a natural inclination to dominate, or an egoistic self-interest at the expense of others, or, again, a combination of all of the above. These psychological dispositions are indeed natural to human beings *qua* animals. They are morally unacceptable to Confucian ethics insofar as they are unchecked and rise to overpower human morality.[36] But, as such, forms of discrimination can be transformed and gradually reduced as human beings become more and more civilized through rational and moral education.

For Confucian ethics, the most objectionable motive of racism is hatred—a deep-seated hatred of another race as a whole. It is reprehensible because it is a feeling contradictory to the feeling of commiseration (of *jen*-love). In hatred, one is pleased to see and/or to inflict suffering on the object of one's hatred. This mental state is a total denial of the moral feeling of commiseration in which one cannot bear to see the suffering of others. Moreover, racial hatred is contradictory to the Confucian ideal of the universalization of *jen*-love—the gradual extension of *jen*-love, sustained by a moral feeling for the well-being of others. Personal hatred is directed towards particular individuals who are personally relevant, but racial hatred is directed towards a racial group, collectively. Solely in this sense, racial hatred may be considered as a form of "universal hatred," that is, hatred of all without distinction and consideration of individual merits or moral worthiness.

Besides being contradictory to the ideal of universal love, racial hatred commits a moral crime, particularly sensitive to Confucian ethics. According to Confucian ethics, nobody has more worth and deserves more love and respect than those who are virtuous. And in every race there must be some individuals who are exemplary character. Racial hatred imposes upon these otherwise respectable individuals ill treatments that they do not deserve.[37] Furthermore, since the *jen*-mind is presumably universal, every human individual is essentially equal by virtue of the *jen*-mind. Racial difference, among other types, is only a nonessential difference quite irrelevant to the moral worth and definition of an individual. To deprive an individual of certain vital rights for reasons of racial difference implies a depreciation of the respectability and dignity that is warranted by the divinity (the *jen*-mind) inherent in each person. Deprivation also hinders the moral development (actualization of the *jen*-mind) of an individual, for moral development needs material supports.[38]

Although racism is morally wrong, its counteraction, racial liberation, is not necessarily all right. Confucianism does not object to, but neither does it give *carte blanche* to liberation movements. If a liberation movement is motivated by hatred—a reverse hatred—it has no moral superiority over racism except for the fact that the hatred may be only retributive or reactive. Such a movement would be at the opposite end, though within the same category, of hateful racism, and it would be guilty of the same moral crime. Therefore, a liberation movement motivated by racially universal hatred is condemnable.

However, if a racial liberation movement is for the purpose of righting a wrong, the movement will not only be deemed morally justifiable, but morally necessary. Such a movement is one that is not motivated by hateful passions but by a rational idea of humanity. This is the idea of man as a potential locus of actualization of the cosmic *jen*-mind, more—a potential Heaven-*in-concreto*. A racial liberation movement may superficially appear as a struggle for equal accessibility to earthly happiness, but it must be motivated by the moral conception of man and for the good cause of humanity. Only then can it be represented as a moral act to proclaim the equality of humanity. To be sure, no social movement is ever free from passions, nevertheless, it is imperative that the moral conception of man be maintained as its dominant and efficient motive if a racial liberation is to have moral superiority, according to Confucian ethics.

The feminist movement is a struggle for women's equal liberty with men but the movement itself is not unified in its claims. The movement is divided into at least two sides. The liberals (moderates) desire equalities in regard to rights and responsibilities in such matters as social, political, educational, economic, and domestic affairs. Yet they do not deny that there are some roles for which one of the sexes is better fitted, nor do they desire a total overhaul of cultural traditions and institutional establishments. The radicals (extremists) hold some claims that virtually eliminate sex difference in *all* aspects. Liberation for women, it is advocated, requires the total abolition of both artificial and natural differences between women and men. Thus, the traditional institutions of marriage, family, state, and the existing monetary system must eventually be abolished, and the biological differences between the two sexes should be overcome through medical science and technology.[39]

The extreme form of sexism has been called "male chauvinism" by some feminists, and "phallism" by certain writers on the subject.[40] A male chauvinist looks upon women as inferior beings in many ways: defective in morality and intelligence, weak in will power and physical strength, excessive in sentiments and desires. Women are therefore perceived as born to assume roles supportive of the weightier business of men and, as such, can be patronized.[41] Clearly, there is a certain degree of contempt in the chauvinist's attitude toward women.

The Confucian position on this issue is in the mean. It opposes extreme feminism, on the one hand, and sexism, especially male chauvinism, on the other. It believes in what may be called female-male reciprocity. The notion of reciprocity is derived from the principle of complementary opposites. According to the principle, the modalities of *Yin* and *Yang* require each other's contribution because the inherent nature of each makes different contributions. In the Appendix to the *Book of Changes,* is is said, "The way of *ch'ien* [*Yang*] constitutes the male, while the way of *k'un* [*Yin*] constitutes the female. *Ch'ien* initiates the Great Beginning, and *k'un* brings it to consummation."[42] Again, the notion of reciprocity can be explained through the following quotation:

> The system of Change is indeed intermingled with the operation of *ch'ien* and *k'un*. As *ch'ien* and *k'un* take their respective positions the system of Change is established in their midst. If *ch'ien* and *k'un* are

obliterated, there would be no means of seeing the system of Change. If the system of Change cannot be seen, then *ch'ien* and *k'un* would almost cease to operate.[43]

The idea is, simply stated, that the cooperation of two is required if anything is to be accomplished at all.

In Confucianism, the terms male and female do not stand for two categories, or for two grades of biological beings, but represent two kinds of function. They are functional terms more than they are classificatory terms. These two kinds of function presuppose each other, and between them there is no distinction of superiority and inferiority.[44] The *Yin* function has its group of characteristics such as receptivity, emotionality, maternity, inwardness, tenderness, etc., while the *Yang* function has another group of characteristics such as creativity, rationality, paternity, outwardness, sturdiness, etc.

It is now plain that sexism is wrong not because of its stubborn division of sex-roles, but because of its valuational belief and attitude toward the feminine sex. Sexism fails, or refuses, to acknowledge the equality of the functional value of the two sexes. The value is measured not in terms of money or power, but against the existence and well-being of the whole. Without the opposite sex with it complementary function, none of the masculine characteristics mean anything. As is derivable from the principle of complementary opposites and as is observable in common experience, the masculine capability cannot function properly without the sustenance of the feminine. Thus, to be contemptuous of femininity is to fail to see the cosmic way of creation. Ironically, such contempt is equal to the presupposition of masculinity's own existence.

The women's liberation movement is right to the extent that it aims to reclaim the dignity and respect due to them. To that extent the movement represents a moral struggle. The movement is, or ought to be, an effort to demonstrate the proposition that there is no line of command, no distinction of superiority and inferiority, between men *qua* men and women *qua* women. However, if the movement should deny totally the functional differences between men and women, the movement must be judged wrong according to the same principle.

Morality and Economic Systems

One of the most influential confrontations in the contemporary world has been that between Capitalism and Communism. The confrontation, indeed, has many aspects, among which the economic is just one; it also involves a host of other vital issues. The complexity of the confrontation is further compounded by the fact that both Capitalism and Communism are not mere theories for the pleasure of the academicians. They are put into practice, and, more often than not, practices do not square with theories. For the present purpose, the confrontation between Capitalism and Communism is taken as a theoretical controversy in economics.

Karl Marx developed his program of Communism on the basis of his conception of man, his understanding of the agony of workers of his time, and his diagnosis of its cause. Communism was proposed as a therapeutic program. In Marx's opinion, man is part of nature, and nature is primarily a network of material existents. The distinguishing characteristic of man is what Marx calls conscious productive life activity. As a material being, man is determined by material, or materially based, conditions that surround him.[45]

Among all others, the economic condition is the most basic and determinative. The framework of an economic structure lies in its mode of production—a system of interrelationships between and among means of production, ownership, labor, and products. As Marx sees it, the economic reality of his time puts man qua worker (productive being) in adversities: the social institutions and mechanisms of capitalist society effect capitalistic exploitation of the worker; and exploitation chiefly consists of appropriation of surplus value—unpaid labor. The appropriation of unpaid labor alienates man from himself, man from nature, and man from other men.

The causes of alienation are many. In sum, the whole capitalist system is the cause—the system of private property, acquisitiveness, money, capital and land, competition, division of labor, cost and benefit, and so on. In Marx's analysis, the institution of private property is the root cause. Without the institution of private property, the vital capitalistic devices such as ownership, surplus value, acquisition, and profit, would have hardly any practical and motivational meanings. To alleviate the dehumanizing condition, Marx proposes a radical revolution. He envisages a society in which the community as a whole "openly and directly [takes] possession of the productive force. . . ."[46] And this, translated into an action program, means "the *positive* abolition of *private property*, of human self-alienation. . . ."[47]

Capitalism (or better, classical Capitalism) maintains several positions concerning man and economics, summarized as follows:

(1) The doctrine of economic man: Capitalism assumes a Hobbesian concept of man as basically a self-interested ego. It is

accepted as a matter of fact that every individual consults his own interests and is motivated by profit for himself. The economic man is, and should be, free to produce, buy or sell, insofar as his self-seeking activity is within the bounds of common laws.

(2) The doctrine of profit motive: As man is economically recognized as such, the profit motive is thereby accepted as legitimate, not only economically, but socially, morally, and legally. Appropriation and accumulation of wealth by lawful means is regarded as a right. It is also believed that the profit motive is the most effective incentive for people to work and produce.

(3) The doctrine of free economy: Capitalism desires an economic system of free competition, free market, and most of all, a system free from government control. Only with a free economy, it is supposed, can invention, improvement, and progress take place easily. The economy is autonomous, and must be so; economic problems such as those concerning prices, wages, labor disputes, and supply and demand can be solved within the economy itself, for it is self-adjusting.

(4) The doctrine of right to private property: The right to private property is accepted as a basic human right protected by law or constitution. Private property is broadly interpreted to include the means of production and distribution, instruments of exchange, land and real estate, and all material objects deemed relevant to the pursuit of happiness and maintenance of life. In short, Capitalism desires an economic system, along with a supporting political system, in which man as an economic being enjoys the greatest freedom to benefit primarily himself.

The Confucian philosophy of economics is characterized by what may be termed the moral teleology of economics. For Confucianism, the economic prosperity of individuals or the state is desirable, not as an end in itself, but as a contributive factor for moral development. Economic behavior should be directed so as to be able to create an environment in which, positively speaking, material resources are sufficiently available for moral purposes, and, negatively speaking, the maintenance of material life does not constitute a burden on a person. It is conceived that freedom from poverty and the stress of living can facilitate a person's effort to develop his *jen*-nature. The Confucian philosophy of economics can be condensely expressed in this dictum: Be economically free so that one can devote more time and effort to moral undertakings. Specifically, the fundamentals of Confucian economic thought can be summarized in the three following doctrines:

(1) The doctrine of moral primacy. This doctrine assigns a relative position to economic value *vis-à-vis* moral value, giving indisputable priority to righteousness over profit. There are at least two implications. One, the ultimate goal of economic activity does not lie in the sphere of the economy itself but in the sphere of morality. Profit seeking is a means and must be justified in terms of a moral aim. Two, whenever there is conflict between moral and economic values, consideration of morality always precedes and supercedes consideration of economics. In a famous passage, Mencius comments, "If righteousness be put last, and profit be put first, they [i.e., government and common people alike] will not be satisfied without snatching all."[48] For Confucianism, profit seeking can be harmful to individual morality when, if unchecked, it feeds personal greed. It can be harmful to social/national morality when, if unbound, it becomes so pervasive that interpersonal relations are dominated by the consideration of profit (interest). In this latter case, conflicts of interest are always imminent, if not at all times real.[49] Confucianism desires a community with moral relationships, not business relationships, as its basic structure.[50]

(2) The doctrine of private property. This doctrine maintains that, to the morally average person, security of livelihood is contributive to moral development. For only when a morally average person feels secure and worry-free about his means of living can he have a restful mind for moral advancement. Thus, private property not only provides psychological, but tangible security for persons harried by economic woes. Ownership of private property has a positive effect on the prevention of crimes and maintenance of social order.

Mencius well recognizes the truth that lack of property and extreme deprivation are very often principal causes of crime and social turmoil:

> The way according to which the [common] people conduct their lives is this: If they have a secure livelihood, they will have a secure mind. And if they have no secure livelihood, they will not have a secure mind. And if they have no secure mind, there is nothing they will not do in the way of self-abandonment, moral deflection, depravity, and wild license.[51]

Apparently, Mencius seems to have oversimplified the causal relation between economic prosperity (secure livelihood) and moral development. For it is factually true that some people fail to attain a secure mind even when they have a secure livelihood. But the real point of Mencius' saying should be taken in a more general manner, which is that economic prosperity and private property are contributive factors, in one way or another, to matters of morality.[52] Herein consists a moral justification of private property and economic prosperity.

(3) The doctrine of government supervision. The role of the government in business affairs is that of "watchdog," regulator, and guardian against monopoly and exploitation, providing assistance to the trades in times of need, and taxing excessive profits. In such a role, the government is neither a controller nor uninvolved. Confucianism never held the idea of a centralized economy or of a *laissez faire* economic policy. In the famous "Debate on Salt and Iron" *(Yen-t'ieh lun)* is 81 B.C., the Confucian literati made the following argument:

> Never should material profit appear as a motive of government. . . . But now in the provinces the salt, iron, and liquor monopolies, and the system of equitable marketing have been established to compete with the people for profit, dispelling rustic generosity and teaching the people greed.[53]

The debate was on a particular issue, but the general idea behind it was that the government should not gain direct control of business and commerce; that business and commerce should be returned to the hands of the people. Thus, Confucianism favors a relatively free economy.[54] At the same time, the government should see to it that the economy proceeds in a "controlled" manner. For example, "ownership of land should be limited so that those who do not have enough may be relieved and the road to unlimited encroachment blocked."[55] Certain things should not be allowed, for example, outrageous profit, monopoly, exploitation of labor, and concentration of wealth.[56]

To summarize,the Confucian philosophy of economics is neither an openhanded Capitalism nor a totalitarian Communism. It espouses a moral teleology of economics, shares some beliefs with modern Capitalism (private property and free trade), and in some aspects, resonates with modern socialism. How well it works is a question to be answered by facts, not philosophizing.

Punishment and Justice

A recurring topic centering around the concept of justice and its administration is the moral justification of punishment. There are two classical theories of punishment: retributivism and utilitarianism. They agree that punishment of a person for criminal acts is justifiable, yet differ on the grounds for punishment.

Utilitarianism justifies punishment on the grounds of its utility—rehabilitation, deterrence and protection. Some forms of punishment such as imprisonment and hard labor are believed to be able to readjust a criminal to the norms of society. The deterrent effect of punishment consists, it is contended, of deterring offenders from repeating crimes, and deterring common people from doing criminal acts for the first time, or, at least, making a person "think twice" when one is about to commit a crime. Punishment is also said to be able to provide protection for society by isolating and, in some cases, "eliminating" harmful elements from society.

There are some standard criticisms of utilitarian theory from the side of retributivism. It is argued, for example, that utility is one thing and justice is another. Granted that punishing somebody for a criminal act does do good to society, the question still remains whether the act of punishment is itself just. The question arises when, for example, correctness of punishment is brought into consideration. By correctness of punishment is meant that all and only those who have done wrong are punished and that the severity of the punishment is suited to the seriousness of the crime committed. If utilitarian calculation *alone* is followed, then one (or society) can "justifiably" do many things: severely punish a minor offender when such severe punishment appears to produce very desirable effects, nominally punish (or refrain from punishing) a major offender when so doing appears to produce some desirable effects, punish any randomly picked person for no other reason except for demonstrating the punitive power of the society. All these things seem to be justifiable on utilitarian grounds, but they raise questions of justice. Moreover, punishment as deterrence implies the using of a person to achieve a goal (deterrence) to which the very person has no inherent duty.

The retributive theory consists of two basic propositions: that punishment should be inflicted when it is deserved, and that punishment can be inflicted only when, and to the extent that, it is deserved. The first proposition asserts the Right of Retaliation (*jus talionis*);[57] the second calls for Prudence of Retaliation (*lex talionis*).[58] Punishment is justified on the ground of justice, and justice is rendered in terms of dessert. It is assumed that there is a level of justice in human society which requires rebalancing when tipped. The purpose of punishment is therefore to restore the balance when disturbed by offence. The Right of Retaliation is not a right to revenge. Rather, it is a moral necessity to maintain the balance of justice. But punishment, if excessive or deficient, would defeat its very own justification. So, it is imperative that punishment be administered appropriately, without excess or deficiency. Hence, the Prudence of Retaliation.

The Confucian view of punishment is somewhat exceptional. Instead of trying to justify punishment, Confucianism hopes to discard it on moral grounds. When asked about matters of law, Confucius remarked, "In hearing lawsuits, I am no better than other men, but surely the great thing is to bring about that there are no lawsuits."[59] The Confucian ideal is not that punishment be administered justly, but rather that punishment find no place of application in the world. The morally best state of affairs is in getting rid of the need for punishment. The fact that punishment should be imposed on man by man, is itself a moral disgrace to the dignity of humanity.

Confucius voices his objection to the use of punishment, as follows:

> If the people be led by laws, and uniformity sought to be given them by punishments, they will try to avoid the punishments, but have no sense of shame. If they be led by virtue, and uniformity sought to be given them by the rules of propriety, they will have the sense of shame, and moreover, will become good.[60]

The Confucian ideal of human conduct is that people behave following the dictates of the *jen*-mind. Man as a moral being should not be subjected to fear of punishment as a means of behavior control; rather, he should be enlightened and taught to be good autonomously. Confucianism envisions "A World with No Punishment."[61]

This, however, does not imply that Confucianism advocates immediate removal of punishment; there is a pragmatic necessity for the institution of punishment. Mencius notes, "Goodness alone is not capable of governing; laws alone do not enforce themselves."[62] That "goodness alone is not capable of governing" is due to the fact that the actual man is far from being morally perfect and is therefore liable to commit that which ought not to be done. Although the world envisaged by Confucianism is not a morally ideal world, it is, nonetheless, real. Given this, the practical utility of punishment simply cannot be neglected in total favor of the niceties of idealism. In the Commentary of the *Code of T'ang (T'ang-lu shu-i)* the following assertion occurs:

> Virtue and morals are the foundation of government and education, while laws and punishments are the operative agencies of government and education. Both the former and the latter are necessary complements to each other.[63]

Complementary to the moral ideal is the practicality of law and punishment. Confucianism admits of law and punishment on the grounds of pragmatic consideration, not moral consideration.[64]

Finally, it seems appropriate to examine the Confucian position on the much debated issue of capital punishment. Confucianism endorses capital punishment but only with serious reservations. In Confucian ethics, capital punishment is not to be justified by virtue of an argument from deterrence nor on the grounds of retaliatory justice. But there is a sense, perhaps the only sense, in which capital punishment is recommended. Mencius, quoting a passage from the *Book of History,* expresses his opinion as follows:

> "When men kill others, and roll over their bodies to take their property, being reckless and fearless of death, among all the people there are none but detest them":—thus, such characters are to be put to death, without waiting to give them warning.[65]

On another occasion, when asked about King Chou's being executed by King Wen, Mencius responds:

> He who outrages the benevolence [proper to his nature] is called a robber; he who outrages righteousness is called a ruffian. The robber and the ruffian we call a mere fellow. I have heard of the cutting off of the fellow Chow, but I have not heard of the putting of a sovereign to death, [in this case].[66]

On the basis of these two passages, an argument can be constructed representing the Confucian position.

Humanity is essentially defined in terms of the *jen*-mind. A person who has "lost" his *jen*-mind disqualifies himself as a member of the human species and is referred to as a "non-human," or a "beast-equivalent."[67] Being a beast, of course, does not at once imply a justification for the termination of life. But with regard to a person who has "lost" his *jen*-mind through conscious acts that render him dehumanized, Confucianism has little mercy. Such an individual ought to be removed from the human world. The concept of contradiction can be understood in two ways; each, or both together, furnishes sufficient reason for termination of the person's life. By general logic, contradictory terms cannot be in the same place at the same time. It follows that a contradiction of humanity must be disposed of in favor of humanity. (It would be a self-contradiction should we, as humans, dispose ourselves in favor of a contradiction of humanity.) By imperative logic, a contradiction of humanity (defined in Confucian terms), is judged a devilish being;[68] a devilish being is incompatible with the idea or the reality of good (*jen*, Heaven). A devilish being, as an incompatible term of the good, ought to be eliminated.

There remains, of course, a problem as to how to define "a contradiction of humanity" in motivational and behavioral terms. The problem is one of translating the theoretical concept of "contradiction of humanity" into practical terms, giving it an operational definition, following C. S. Peirce. This is a very difficult problem; and it is not inconceivable that a satisfactory solution may not easily come about. But granted that this problem remains unresolved, the argument for capital punishment in principle is not affected in this respect.

Conclusion

As a philosophical system, Confucianism is a type of idealism inasmuch as it posits a mind entity (the *jen*-mind) as the first principle accounting for the ground and end of the universe. Furthermore, it is a moral idealism in that the concept of the *jen*-mind is construed as the concept of a purely moral, creative *logos*. Within its terms, the concepts of man, the Supreme Being, and nature are explained or defined. Viewed from another perspective, Confucianism is also a type of humanism; man in his essential nature is the ultimate reality—Heaven-in-particularity. But the Confucian humanism is distinguished from naturalistic humanism. It is a sort of transcendental humanism in that man in his essence is "over and above" nature.

It follows that Confucianism is anthroposophic, not theosophic, because, given the above propositions, the Confucian way of knowing the Supreme Being and true reality lies exactly in knowing the essential (moral) self. Man's heavenly vocation is to unfold this essential self. The initial way to moral cultivation is introspection. The Confucian ideal for the individual person is sageness and the Confucian ideal for the world is, in Kantian terms, the Kingdom of Ends.

For Confucianism, nature *(Ch'i)* is an instrument for the actualization of the *jen*-mind; it is a principle of individuation (or presentment). It moves forward dialectically—by way of complementary opposites. The Confucian nature is dynamic and teleological. It is a grand process towards a morally ultimate end, and is therefore not a blind mechanism or a Parmenidean being, still less an absurd existence. Evil is not inherent in nature but is derived from dispositions of nature *(Ch'i)*.

Confucian ethics is closer to Kantian ethics than to any other; but, Confucian ethics does not have the type of formalism Kantian ethics has. Confucian morality exalts moral feelings over universal formula. The ultimate ground of morality is posited in the transcendental dimension of man, to wit, the *jen*-mind. Only that which freely springs from the *jen*-mind has true moral merits; hence, Confucian ethics attends more to the motive and spontaneity (autonomousness) of conduct.

Man's natural existence *(Ch'i)*, though instrumental to the actualization of the *jen*-mind, is nevertheless a stubborn object to be transformed morally. Among all the natural dispositions of man, selfish desires are the most pertinacious, constituting a hard core in the way of effluence of the *jen*-mind. Hence the Confucian moral discipline initially and mainly consists of efforts to overcome this selfish ego. Moral discipline is basically a self discipline; helps from external sources are important but not crucial.

Historically, Confucian discourses were mostly devoted to matters of individual morality and seldom to moral issues *per se*. Classical Confucianism has said much about how a person ought to conduct his life, but relatively little about how a given ethical issue should be handled. This is one aspect of classical Confucianism that needs updating. The present writing attempts such a venture, delivering statements representing the Confucian position respectively on four contemporary ethical issues.

On the issue of sexual morality, Confucianism holds it as a basic norm that only that kind of sexual behavior which takes place between a married couple for the purpose of procreation is morally meritorious, and that anything deviating from the norm is anywhere from morally tolerable (or excusable) to evil. On the issue of racial liberation, Confucianism considers racism as morally wrong because racism disregards the essential equality of man in terms of the *jen*-mind, and because it contradicts the ideal of universal love. Racial liberation is right to the extent that it does not commit the same errors attributed to racism. On the issue of women's liberation, Confucianism considers it morally right for women to proclaim equality of women's status, but wrong to deny the distinction between feminine and masculine functions. Confucianism believes that man and woman are axiologically equal, but functionally different. On the issue of economic morality, Confucianism maintains a moral teleology of economics, resisting totalitarian Communism on the one hand, and unrestrained Capitalism on the other. Economic activity must be allowed the greatest freedom but must be guided. On the issue of justice and punishment, Confucianism ideally believes that punishment is morally regrettable and ought to be eventually done away with. But, given the present stage of human moral development, punishment is pragmatically necessary.

Notes

1. These are taken from Y. P. Mei, "The Basis of Social, Ethical, and Spiritual Values in Chinese Philosophy," in *The Chinese Mind,* Charles Moore, ed. (Honolulu: University Press of Hawaii, 1967), 152.

2. Wing-tsit Chan, *Neo-Confucianism, Etc.: Essays* (Hong Kong: Oriental Society, 1969), 1.

3. For example, *jen* is taken as one among the six virtues, i.e., *jen,* knowledge, straightforwardness, boldness, and firmness. See the *Analects,* bk. 17, Yang Ho, chap. 8. Also Legge, James, The Chinese Classics, Taipei Reprint, Wen-hsing Press, 1964, Vol. 1, 322.

4. For example, Confucius says, "He must have *jen,* who can learn extensively with a firm and sincere aim, can earnestly inquire with self-reflection." The *Analects,* bk. 19, Tsze-Chang, chap. 6; see also bk. 13, Tsze-Lu, chap. 19.

5. For example, "Filial piety and fraternal submission—are they not the root of *jen?*" The *Analects,* bk. 1, Hsio R, chap. 1; see also bk. 12, Yen Yuan, chap. 22.

6. Confucius says, "If the will be set on *jen,* there will be no practice of evil." The *Analects,* bk. 4, Le Jen, chap. 4.

7. The *Analects,* bk. 12, Yen Yuan, chap. 1.

8. Ibid., chap. 2.

9. Ibid., chap. 3.

10. Ibid., chap. 19.

11. See *Mencius,* bk. 6, Kaou Tzu, pt. 1, chap. 15. (Legge, vol. II, p. 417–18) The Chinese term *t'i* is rather ambiguous and contextually dependent. In ordinary usage it may mean physical body, or appropriateness-of-speech-and-conduct-in-a-situation, etc.. But in its philosophical, technical usage, it may be used to

refer to some abstract entity, or incorporeal substance, or the very identity of (any) thing or, again, essential reality (existence). The context in which it occurs is important, and oftentimes crucial. Also, precautions must be taken lest one may suppose Mencius and Confucius to maintain a kind of Cartesian-like dualism. In the last analysis, Confucianism has no dualism of substances although it employs some quasi-dualistic language.

12. *Mencius*, bk. 7, Asin Sin, pt. 11, chap. 24, James Legge, tr..

13. Wang Yan-ming, *Ch'uan-hsi Lu* (Record of Instructions) (Taipei: Taiwan Commercial Press; Jen-Jen ed., First printing, 1967; Seventh printing, 1982), chap. 2: 108. This thesis sets Confucian ethics apart from any ethical natural-ism and apart from any heteronomous moral theories.

14. The definition of mind as pure moral activity itself is expounded and articu-lated by Professor Mou Tsung-san in his various works, particularly in his 3 volumes of *Hsin-ti yu Hsing-ti* (The Substances of Mind and of Human Nature).

15. *Mencius*, bk. 6, Kaou Tzu, pt. 1, chap. 6. (Legge, vol. 2, p. 414)

16. Ibid., bk. 11, Kung-Sun Ch'ow, pt. 1, chap. 6. (Legge, vol. 2, p. 414)

17. Mencius says, "*Jen* is man's mind, and righteousness is man's path." *Mencius*, bk. 6, Kaou Tzu, pt. 1, chap. 11. (Legge, vol. 2, p. 414)

18. Controversies over the interpretation of the Four Lines have stretched from Wang's immediate disciples to Confucian scholars of today. An alternative reading of the Four Lines is given by Wing-tsit Chan, as follows: "In the original substance of the mind there is no distinction between good and evil. When the will becomes active, however, such distinction exists. The faculty of innate knowledge is to know good and evil. The investigation of things is to do good and remove evil." See Wing-tsit Chan, *A Source Book in Chinese Philosophy* (Princeton, NJ: Princeton University Press, 1963), 686–687. The interpretation adopted here is based on Mou Tsung-san's elaboration of the Teachings. See Mou, *From Lu Hsiang-shan to Liu Chi-shan* (Taipei: Taiwan Student Book Store, 1979), 233–239. Marked differences between these two interpretations lay in the first and the fourth lines.

19. *Mencius*, bk. 7, Tsin Sin, pt. 1, chap. 1.

20. It can be helpful to use the term *incarnation* to characterize the doctrine. I refrain from using it because the term is heavily loaded with many cultural and religious meanings unfit for Confucianism.

21. The *Doctrine of the Mean*, chap. 32 (Legge, vol. 1, pp. 429–320).

22. Lu Hsaing-shan boldly declares: "The universe is my [*jen*-] mind, and my [*jen*-] mind is the universe." Quoted by Fung Yu-lan, *A History of Chinese Philosophy*, 2d. ed., 2 vols., Derk Bodde, tr. (Princeton, NJ: Princeton Uni-versity Press, 1952), vol. 2: 573. And Wang Yang-ming reiterates the thesis, "The mind of man constitutes Heaven in all its profundity, within which there is nothing not included. Originally there was nothing but this single Heaven, but because of the barriers caused by selfish desire, we lost this orig-inal state of Heaven." *Ch'uan-hsi Lu*, 601–602.

23. See note 19.

24. Chou's *Explanation of the Diagram of the Supreme Ultimate* and Chang's *Cheng-meng (Correcting Youthful Ignorance)* contain such metaphysical discourse.

25. For example, Ch'eng I is reported to have said, "All that has physical form is identical with material force. Only the Way [Tao] is formless." See Chan, *Source Book*, 552.

26. See Chan, Ibid., 569.

27. The idea of complementary opposition that has its early expression in the *Book of Change* is also shared by Taoism, especially the Taoistic religion, and some other "non-Confucian" schools of thought.

28. See Chan, *Source Book*, 534.

29. As a passing remark, Nietzsche's divisions of the Dionysian and Apollonian arts, the slave morality and the master morality, could be regarded as again instances of the Yin and the Yang. Also, the ancient Greek philosophers, particularly Heraclitus, seem to have a similar notion of complementary opposites. Professor Sandra Wawrytko, assuming the polarity of the Yin and the Yang, has ventured to explore the applicability of the Yin principle in many areas including the ethical, the social, the political, and above all, the philosophy of Spinoza. But the Yin-Yang principle she adopts is Taoistic, not Confucian. See Sandra Wawrytko, *The Undercurrent of Feminine Philosophy in Eastern and Western Thought* (Lanham, MD: University Press of America, 1976; 2d. printing 1981), especially chap. 1.

30. To be explained in the next paragraph.

31. Of course, it is not impossible, and indeed it happens often enough, that a child is raised by a single parent. But the process of that child's growing into an individual must be considered deficient as compared to the process of the one who is raised by both parents. For creation is by way of Yin-Yang interaction. A single parent child is lacking one of the influencing forces. The process is deficient, but it does not follow that the product is necessarily deficient.

32. Some other ethical theories would want to make a stronger statement that pleasure is morally good, or even that pleasure is the sole good. But of course, the term pleasure means different things for different ethical positions, and, for this reason, sexual pleasure is not at once good without qualifications on some hedonistic positions like Epicureanism.

33. This concept of liberty is construed on the basis of, though not in exact agreement with, John Rawl's *A Theory of Justice* (Cambridge, MA: Harvard University Press, 1971), 202–204.

34. The term racism, in some contexts, may be used to denote either way of discrimination, i.e., either against or for. The term sexism, when unspecified, refers to discrimination of a sex group by the opposite sex group. To avoid overly extensive discussions, the two terms are specifically defined as above in this essay.

35. For example: the Christian concept of love and brotherhood, the Kantian concept of reversibility, the universalistic principle of utility, the principle of justice (as fairness), and the principle of benevolence.

36. These psychological dispositions all belong to *Ch'i* (the lesser *ti*) and ought to be subdued under the rule of the *jen*-mind (the greater *ti*).

37. The infliction of pain and suffering upon the morally good not only runs
    counter to Confucian principles, but is also contradictory to the Kantian ideal
    of *summum bonum*—the proportionate matching of earthly happiness and
    morality (moral goodness).

38. See Mencius, bk. 3, T'ang Wan Kung, pt. 1, chap. 3 (Legge, vol. 1, p. 239).
    Aristotle makes the same observation when he says, "[Yet] it [i.e., happiness]
    needs the external goods as well; for it is impossible, or not easy, to do noble
    acts without the proper equipment." Aristotle, *Nicomachean Ethics,* in
    Approaches to Ethics, W. T. Jones et al., eds. (New York: McGraw Hill, 3d.
    ed., 1977), chap. 8: 52.

39. Both Margaret Bengsten and Shulamith Firestone are radical feminists who
    hold this view, although they differ in their emphasis. See William T. Black-
    ston, "Freedom and Women," in *Moral Issues,* Jan Narveson, ed. (Toronto:
    Oxford University Press, 1983), 326, 327.

40. See Marilyn Fry, "Male Chauvinism: A Conceptual Analysis." Ibid., 332–44.

41. Many philosophers, including Plato, Aristotle, Hegel, and Schopenhauer,
    have philosophized the "inferiority" of women. We find Aristotle saying:
    "The female is less spirited than the male . . . softer in disposition . . . more
    mischievous, less simple, more impulsive. . . . The fact is, the nature of man
    is the most rounded off and complete, and consequently in man the qualities
    or capacities above referred to are found in their perfection. Hence, woman is
    . . . more jealous, more querulous, more apt to scold and to strike . . . more
    prone to despondency and less hopeful . . . more void of shame or self-respect,
    more false of speech, more deceptive . . . more shrinking, more difficult to
    rouse to action." Aristotle, *History of Animals,* bk. 9, chap. 1: 608b, D'Arcy
    W. Thompson, trans., included in vol. 9 of the *Great Books of the Western
    World,* Robert M. Hutchins, ed. (Chicago: Encyclopedia Britannica, Inc.,
    1971), 133–34. Quoted from Sandra A. Wawrytko, *Undercurrent,* xxi. Again,
    Plato's attitude towards women is expressed through the following statement:
    "We will not then allow our charges, whom we expect to prove good men,
    being men, to play the parts of women and imitate a woman young or old
    wrangling with her husband, defying heaven, loudly boasting, fortunate in
    her own conceit, or involved in misfortune and possessed by grief and lam-
    entation—still less a woman that is sick, in love, or in labor." Plato, *Republic,*
    bk. 3: 395e; in *Plato: The Collected Dialogues,* Edith Hamilton and Huntington
    Cairns, eds. (Princeton, NJ: Princeton University Press; Bollingen Series 71;
    7th printing, 1973), 640.

42. Chung M. Tse, *Book of Changes,* Appendix, pt. 1, chap. 1. (unpublished mss.)

43. Ibid., chap. 12. Translation follows Wing-tsit Chan in his *Source Book,* 267.

44. On this issue, the Confucian position might be labeled "Primitive Sexism" by
    Marilyn Frye. According to Frye, primitive sexists are committed to sexist
    propositions as *a priori* truths, or as ultimate metaphysical principles; and "a
    value-laden male/female dualism is embedded in their conceptual scheme."
    See Frye, "Male Chauvinism," in Narveson, *Moral Issues,* 334. Confucianism
    seems to fit in Frye's description of "Primitive Sexism" with the reservation
    that the qualifier "value-laden" needs to be carefully defined.

45. The notion of material implies an ontology, to wit, dialectical materialism.

But here is no place for detailing this metaphysics as it is not directly related to our interest. It may appear that there is an extension of meaning of the term "material" from "material being" to "material conditions." This extension is justifiable in Marx's logic by saying that material conditions can be ultimately explained in terms of matter, the only substance of the world.

46. Karl Marx, *Socialism: Utopian and Scientific*, E. Aveling, ed., (New York: Scribner's Sons and Co., 1892), 43. Quoted in W. T. Jones, *A History of Western Philosophy: Kant to Wittgenstein and Sartre* (New York: Harcourt, Brace and World; 2d ed., 1969), 182.

47. See Marx, *Private Property and Communism* in Jones, *Approaches to Ethics*, 321. Italics Marx's.

48. *Mencius*, bk. 1. King Hwuy of Leang, pt. 1, chap. 1.

49. Mencius observes, "If Your Majesty says, 'What is to be done to profit my kingdom?' the great officers will say, 'What is to be done to profit our families?' and the inferior officers and the common people will say, 'What is to be done to profit our persons?' Superiors and inferiors will try to snatch this profit the one from the other, and the kingdom will be endangered." Ibid.

50. Compare Marx's vision. Confucianism maintains, in contradistinction to Marxism, that economic, political, and social orders are superstructures built on the basis of moral order.

51. *Mencius*, bk. 3, T'ang Wan Kung, pt. 1, chap. 3. Wing-tsit Chan trans.

52. Ch'ao Ts'o, (178 B.C.?) an eminent statesman of the Han Dynasty, believes the same. He says, "When a man is plagued by hunger and cold he has no regard for modesty or shame." Ch'ao Ts'o, *"Memorial on the Encouragement of Agriculture"* in *Han shu*, 24 A: 9b–13a. Reprinted in *Sources of Chinese Tradition*, W. T. de Bary et al. eds. (New York: Columbia University Press, 1960), 230.

53. "The Debate on Salt and Iron," Ibid., 237. The system of equitable marketing is a system of government marketing. The government controls certain vital resources, and buys and sells certain necessary commodities at prices set by officials.

54. This Confucian economic thought is implicit in the following saying of Mencius: "If, in the market place [of his capital], he levy a ground rent on the shops but do not tax the goods, or enforce the proper regulations without levying a ground rent;—then all the traders of the empire will be pleased, and wish to store their goods in his market place. If, at his frontier passes, there be an inspection of persons, but no taxes charged [on goods or other articles], then all the travellers of the empire will be pleased, and wish to make their tours on his roads. If he require that the husbandmen give their mutual aid [to cultivate the public field], and exact no [other] taxes on them;—then all the husbandmen of the empire will be pleased, and wish to plow in his fields." *Mencius*, bk. 2, Kung-Sun Ch'ow, pt. 1, chap. 5. (Legge, vol. II, p. 218–19).

55. Tsung Chung-shu, "Memorial on Land Reform," reprinted in de Bary, *Chinese Tradition*, 233. Tung (fl. 179–104 B.C.) was a Confucian statesman of the Han Dynasty (205 B.C.–220 A.D.).

56. In *Mencius* there is a story conveying the idea of the need for governmental

restraint on business, as follows: "Of old time, the market dealers exchanged the articles which they had for others which they had not, and simply had certain officers to keep order among them. It happened that there was a mean fellow, who made it a point to look out for a conspicuous mound, and get upon it. Thence he looked right and left, to catch in his net the whole gain of the market. The people all thought his conduct mean, and therefore they proceeded to lay a tax upon his wares." *Mencius*, bk. 2, Kung-Sun Ch'ow, pt. 2, chap. 10. The story could be read as Mencius' expression of disapproval of excessive profit-making and monopoly. Again, Tung Chung-shu passionately charges the economic state of affairs in the Ch'in Dynasty (255–207 B.C.), as follows: "The rich bought up great connecting tracts of ground, and the poor were left without enough land to stick the point of an awl into. In addition the rich had sole control of the resources of rivers and lakes and the riches of hills and forests. Their profligacy overstepped all restrictions and they outdid each other in extravagance. In the cities they commanded as much respect as the rulers, and in the villages their wealth equalled that of the nobles. How could the people escape oppression? . . . Therefore the poor were forced to wear clothing fit only for cattle and horses and eat the food of dogs and swine." Tung, "Memorial of Land Reform," 233.

57. See Immanuel Kant, *The Philosophy of Law*, W. Hastie, trans. (Edinburgh: T. & T. Clarke, 1887), 196. Referred to by John Hospers, *Human Conduct* (New York: Harcourt Brace Jovanovich, Inc.; 2d. ed., 1982), 339. Cf. Kant, *The Metaphysical Principles of Virtue*, James Ellington, trans. (New York: Bobbs-Merrill, The Library of Liberal Arts edition, 1964), 125.

58. See Kant, *The Metaphysical Element of Justice*, John Ladd, trans. (Indianapolis: 1965), 100. Referred to by Robert Gerstein, "Capital Punishment—'Cruel and Unusual'?: A Retributivist Response," in Narveson (New York: Bobbs-Merrill, op. cit.) 136. Cf. Kant, Ibid., 128, 139.

59. The *Analects*, bk. 12, Yen Yuan, chap. 13.

60. Ibid., bk. 2, Wei Chang, chap. 3. James Legge, trans.

61. To borrow the title of a paper by Ariel Yoav, presented at the First World Conference in Chinese Philosophy, August, 1984, Taichung, Taiwan, R.O.C. Professor Yoav sympathetically discussed the Confucian view of punishment, and referred to it as "utopian."

62. Mencius, bk. 4, Le Low, pt. 1, chap. 1.

63. Code of *T'ang With Commentaries and Annotations*, reprinted in Peking, 1890, vol. 2, 14.

64. This distinction between the moral and the pragmatic is attributed to Kant; and the definition of "pragmatic" is also due to him. Kant says, "For those Sanctions are called Pragmatic which . . . do not spring as necessary laws from the Natural Right of States, but from forethought in regard to the general welfare." Immanual Kant, *Groundwork of the Metaphysics of Morals*, H. J. Paton, trans. (New York: Harper and Row, Torchbooks edition, 1964; first published by Hutchinson and Co., Ltd., London, 1948), 84: 417 note; cf. 57: vi.

65. *Mencius*, bk. 5, Wan Chang, pt. 2, chap. 4. James Legge, trans. (Vol. II, 269–70).

66. Ibid., bk. 1, King Hwuy of Leang, pt. 2, chap. 8. James Legge, trans. (Book II, p. 164).

67. See *Mencius,* bk. 2, Kung-Sun Ch'ow, pt. 1, chap. 6; and bk. 4, Le Low, pt. 2, chaps. 19 and 28. (Legge, Vol. II, p. 208–233).

68. A devilish being is a person who intentionally, deliberately acts in opposition to the idea of good. This is based on Kant, *Religion Within the Limits of Reason Alone,* T. H. Greene and H. W. Hudson, trans. (New York: Harper and Row, Torchbooks edition, 1960; first published in 1934 by Open Court), 30. Kant remarks that the designation of devilish being is not applicable to man. He is taken to mean that man is very unlikely to be devilish as such. But one can *hypothesize,* without contradiction, that a man turning devilish is possible. The concept of a devilish animal (man) is not self-contradictory.

Part III
NEAR EAST/WESTERN

5
Jewish Ethics: An Orthodox View
ASA KASHER

General Features of Orthodox Jewish Tradition

Every national identity rests on various traditions and the Jewish identity is no exception. There have always been extensive Jewish traditions of identity, cherished and expressed in numerous ways. These Jewish traditions have absorbed varieties of religious values, attitudes, and practices, and it is with these elements of Jewish life that we concern ourselves in the first part of the present chapter.

However, for our present purpose, not every feature of the religious views or conduct of certain segments of Jews is entitled to be considered "Jewish." We reserve that term for those features of religious life that have proven indispensable to the life of most Jewish religious traditions in some orthodox sense.

Similarly, our discussion of moral and ethical issues (problems, principles, and practices) will be confined to those parts of the Jewish traditions that qualify as essential from an orthodox point of view.

By restricting our survey to the orthodox denomination of Judaism, it is not our intention to depreciate other nonorthodox traditions, denominations, or movements. The Karaites, the Jews of Ethiopia, the Conservative and Reform movements are notable examples of how nonorthodox groups have developed their own religious traditions and approaches to moral and ethical issues. Each of these traditions is, indeed, on a par with the orthodox ones, being richly varied, interesting, and significant in cultural, philosophical, and historical respects. Even so, we discuss religion and its moral and ethical aspects within the sole framework of Jewish orthodoxy, mainly because of its dual role in the history of Jewish religious traditions, both as a full-fledged, viable option within Judaism, and also as an apt starting point for any comparative, historical description and ideological analysis of each alternative Jewish religious tradition. Jewish orthodoxy is a form of life, or rather, a family of forms, comprising various types of practices. These practices are meant to embody the values of the religion. We shall depict the essence of the orthodox Jewish family of practices by describing its form and substance, i.e., by specifying the formal properties of this family and the values it is meant to embody.

Jewish orthodoxy is, first and foremost, normative. By this we mean that any activity within Jewish orthodoxy is characterized by the rules that are followed, rather than with reference to preceding intentions, accompanying volitions, entertained beliefs, or achieved purposes. Rituals are not conspicuous in such a denomination because all of its practices bear the marks of ritual. Thus, rules of such a normative denomination or religion are prescribed in great detail on a par with rules that govern typical rites. Indeed, many of these governing rules are deemed mandatory in the sense that, under appropriate conditions, members ought to follow them.

To a certain extent, this system of mandatory rules is legal. There are several institutional principles for identifying the religious rules. Such principles are involved, for instance, in the establishment and operation of religious codes and courts. They introduce institutional methods for validating the application of general rules to particular cases, under specific circumstances. They regulate the application of sanctions of various kinds to breaches of the religious rules.

Although the practical operation of such complex legal systems often depend on internal expertise, as in cases of litigation and legislation, religious rules within Jewish orthodoxy are, in general, rather public. The rules are meant to be followed not only by the pious or the expert but also by every member of the religion to whom they apply. Clearly, the requirement of publicity, as applied to the religious rules, imposes on them several significant restrictions.

One consequence of the religious rules being public in nature is rather simple: the members of the religious community are capable of understanding the rules to an extent that enables them to follow those rules in practice.

The public nature of the religious rules is also at the base of the religious sense of communal identity. Since the rules are public, there is a common basis for determining mutual expectations, as John Rawls has observed.[1] Every active member of the religion knows what the religious rules demand of the individual and of other persons. A sense of membership in a religious community cannot emerge unless religious rules are mutually expected to be followed up to a sufficient degree.

Some religious systems of public rules are among those rare legal systems that are total in nature. As a matter of principle, the rules of a total system are meant to regulate all aspects of human life, national, as well as other ones. Within a total religion, every instance of human behavior raises the question of what is religiously proper within certain circumstances.

Jewish orthodoxy is total. As such, it is always evolving new religious practices to meet the needs of new situations that keep arising and that require regulation.

The methods used within such a religion for solving new religious problems do not concern us here, but several aspects of the roles played by the solutions that are arrived at need to be stressed.

First, the various processes adopted in the attempt to solve some new religious problem arrive at different ends. In the simplest case, a consensus emerges among members of certain communities as to what practice should be considered the most desirable solution for the given problem. Such general agreement emerged, for instance, when the problem of using electrical appliances during the Sabbath arose. According to the rules generally followed within Jewish orthodoxy, such appliances are not to be manually turned on or off during the Sabbath, under ordinary circumstances.

Where members of the same denomination are widely dispersed, different communities, remote from each other, sometimes reach quite different solutions for the same religious problem. When each of those communities has reached its own internal agreement with respect to the desired solution, having given due consideration to what members of other communities of the same denominations would also consider a religiously proper procedure, a local pluralism might emerge concerning the new religious problem at hand. There develops a variety of practices, each followed by certain communities within the denomination, though not binding upon communities that have chosen to follow other practices with respect to the same religious issue. This, for instance, is the case with definitions of leaven, the use of which is strictly prohibited during the Passover. There are a number of distinct practices, each generally considered binding upon its own followers who belong to certain orthodox communities, but not binding upon the rest of orthodox Jewry.

In certain instances, such local pluralism does not establish itself and what emerges is a cleft within the denomination over a major issue. In this case, a variety of practices are adopted by different communities, and some of these groups refuse to acknowledge the legitimacy of the solutions followed by other communities. Under such conditions, each group within the single denomination claims to be in possession of the only religiously proper solution of the given problem and deems other alleged solutions as innocent mistakes. A conspicuous example of this exclusiveness is the prevailing orthodox view with respect to the religious status of the State of Israel. But in this instance the cleavage is sharp, far-reaching, and, in a sense, even widening.

A schism is an extreme form of such a religious cleft. It obliterates any sense of religious identity between groups holding variant perspectives on some new issue having acute religious significance. For instance, the attitude of some anti-Zionist orthodox groups towards other Jewish groups, including extremely orthodox ones, already bears most features of a schism.

Consensus, pluralism, cleft, and schism are different forms of denominational distributions of religious practices meant to solve some new religious problem confronting diverse members of a total religion. These denominational differences may be wide in Jewish orthodoxy but they all share an important trait of the denomination. When a religious rule has widely established itself as governing religious behavior under some circumstances, it undergoes a radical change. Prior to the rule being accepted as a solution for a given religious problem, it plays the role of a suggested solution under consideration. Alternative suggestions could have been made and other reasons could have been offered for preferring one possible solution over another. However, when a rule becomes widely accepted and followed, it turns into part of the definition of proper religious behavior. It becomes an essential clause of each complete answer to the question as to which rules presently constitute the normative system of the religion. This is part of what is meant when the normative system of Jewish orthodoxy is described as constitutive.

Using the well-known philosophical distinction between regulative and constitutive systems of rules,[2] we can reach an important conclusion with respect to Jewish orthodoxy: since its system of norms is constitutive, it is not globally regulative. The rules of the system do not regulate their followers' behavior the way traffic regulations or health instructions do. The latter are meant to bring about certain results, effectively and efficiently, whereas there is nothing on a par with security or health that can be obtained by following the religious rules. Notice that security and health are definable independently of the systems of rules that are instituted for achieving them. The religious system of rules, in Jewish orthodoxy, should be seen as not serving any independently definable purpose. What, then, is the point of orthodox religious behavior? The answer is: to embody religious values. We will turn to a brief presentation of those values, but first we have to mention two formal aspects of what we have encountered so far.

First, since it is a constitutive system of rules that embodies all the religious values of orthodoxy, those values bear two distinct relations to the normative system. On the one hand, a vivid understanding of those values is operative whenever shape is given to a new mode of behavior precipitated by changes in the external conditions. On the other hand, the only way to master a vivid understanding of the values of orthodoxy is by forming a clear conception as to what values are actually embodied in the orthodox practices at hand. In other words, the rules of the game determine what might count as an embodiment of some value and what could not count as such, from the orthodox point of view. For instance, Jewish orthodoxy has an official manner of expressing its values in the realm of work, namely, through regulations that include those pertaining to the sabbath (and similar regulations). A suggestion to replace this way of expressing those values in the sphere of work by another cluster of practices, which have nothing to do with the seventh day of the week, would be considered as involving a breach of the orthodox normative system, in sharp contradiction with the constitutive nature of the system of rules.

Second, the compound character of the orthodox system of norms being total, value-laden, and constitutive, explains another overt trait of Jewish orthodoxy. The orthodox form of life is, for its participants, a viable routine. In contrast to the dramas by which the Sons of Israel are enthralled in many biblical stories, the orthodox form of life, shaped during later periods and under different conditions, is completely prosaic, but since it is value-laden it is never dull. The seemingly trivial is supposedly treated with as much care as the weighty.

Now, what are the values embodied in the numerous practices of Jewish orthodoxy in which every member considers himself or herself obliged to participate?

A suggestion that might naturally arise is that any attempt to identify the basic values of Jewish orthodoxy, as embodied in its own observed practices, should rest on the observation that many, perhaps almost all of its membership, would describe their religious practices as worship of God. This seems to us a mistaken suggestion, and to understand why it is so is to grasp a major characteristic of Jewish orthodoxy. Strictly speaking, there is no dogmatic theology in Jewish orthodoxy. No theological statement is binding upon the sincere participants of orthodox practice. This fact about Jewish orthodoxy is implicit, but it plays a major role in its life. Most theological claims concerning creation, providence, or the Messianic era, for instance, were explicitly rejected by some eminent members of orthodox Jewry during its long history, though firmly held by others. Only belief in the existence of God has won a seemingly unanimous approval, but actually the unanimity is only apparent. During the history of Jewish orthodoxy, so many diverse and incompatible concepts of God have been upheld by devout practitioners that there is no possibility of identifying a generally acclaimed concept of God nor of identifying a positive consensus that is shared by all those observant of the orthodox rules.

Notice that by denying the existence of a dogmatic theology within Jewish orthodoxy, we do not claim that no theological consideration has ever been instrumental in shaping particular orthodox practices. For instance, *Kabbalah,* the cluster of mystical views created or espoused by orthodox Jews, did exert some influence, even in some daily practices, but none of its elements has gained practical prominence in the sense that all members of Jewish orthodoxy are obliged to affirm its theological conception.

While no particular positive concept of God is fundamental to Jewish orthodoxy, a vivid negative conception of the sphere of the divine is an essential ingredient of it: Nothing "that is in the heavens above or that is on the earth underneath or that is in the waters under the earth"[3] may be worshipped. The command, "you must not make for yourself a carved image or form" of any of those, is just a preventive measure. The main idea is that "you must not bow down to them nor be induced to serve them," that is to say, you must not worship them. The insistent rejection of any form of idol worship is a value shared by all members of Jewish orthodoxy (and, in fact, by the membership of all other Jewish denominations). Many of the religious practices are amenable to interpretation as expressing the basic value of complete rejection of idolatry in particular spheres of life. (The rest of the practices are mostly of a social nature, directly related to the practical establishment of the religious community.)

Clearly, the notion of "idol" is presently used in a very broad sense. One creates an idol and worships it when one considers something in the world as of the utmost importance and manifests this highest regard steadfastly in practice. Any form of religious life which elevates something in the world to a position of ultimacy is thus rejected by Judaism.

In conclusion, we would like to mention two effects that some of the above characteristics of Jewish orthodoxy have had on its historical form.

First, the orthodox tradition is conservative in the strict sense of the term, mainly because of its constitutivity. Developments that take place must not incur the breach of any regulation that is in force. Changes, then, are never abrupt. Novelties are seldom introduced; they must emerge through slow historical accumulation.

Secondly, since Jewish orthodoxy is total in nature and since, for many centuries, the Jews were dispersed all over the world within relatively autonomous communities, there is therefore always a possibility of some practical heterogeneity lurking in the shadows. When a certain practice is presented within Jewish orthodoxy as being religiously enjoined, caution must be used against the possible confusion of the prevalence or hegemony of a practice with its being generally observed within orthodoxy. We should stress the fact that our precaution does not involve any kind of disregard for the obvious, namely, the abundance of practices that are strictly observed by all orthodox communities.

Principles of Decision Making

Our analysis of the general features of orthodox Jewish tradition has pinpointed the two major forces of Jewish orthodoxy, of which at least one can be found at the heart of any orthodox practice. These driving forces are the determination perspicuously to reject all forms of idol worship by adherence to a manifold practice of self-restraint and by devotion to the persistent convictions of the particular community of worshippers, taken to include all or almost all the Jews.

The combination of these powerful religious vectors, so to speak, has resulted in a variety of principles of religious decision making. To the extent that those principles are used for adjudication upon a question that has given rise to a particular conflict, they are moral or ethical in nature. We call a principle "moral" if it pertains only to members of the same religion or denomination, and "ethical" if it applies to all human beings.

Several principles presently deserve special attention, and we take them up in turn.

Two verses in Leviticus were the subject of many discussions in the orthodox traditional literature, "My judicial decisions you should carry out, and my statutes you should keep as to walk in them . . ." And "you must keep my statutes and my judicial decisions, which if a man will do, he must also live by means of them" (18:4–5). The last phrase has attracted most of the attention, "live by means of them." A passage in the Talmud draws the implication, "live by means of them, not die by means of them."[4] The practical significance of this implication is immense. A major consequence, mentioned already in the same Talmudic text, is that the need to save life provides us with a definite reason for overruling Sabbath regulations. Maimonides included in his Code the generalized consequence that the need to save life provides a definite reason for overruling any commandment.[5] An interesting point is mentioned later on in the Code, "When these [breaches of Sabbath regulation, in order to save life] are carried out, they are performed neither by Gentiles nor by children, neither by slaves nor by women . . . but by Jewish leaders and wise men. . . . "[6]

There is an additional context in which the same principle has been used. Another Talmudic tract discusses the case of religious coercion, all too common in Jewish history. The verdict of the sages was clear, "Every religious offense, if a Jew is being told: 'Commit it or else you'll be killed,' he should commit it and not be killed," the standard reasoning hinging on the principle 'live by them, not die by them'."[7] However, the same Talmudic discussion makes three highly important exceptions to that practical principle of compelled commitment of offenses, namely, "idol worshipping, incest, and bloodshed." (Under emergency conditions of a total war waged against the religion, the list of exceptions runs much longer.) The rationale of these standard exceptions is evident: to break the law is to sin, but to worship an idol is to desert the religion. No wonder, then, that the religion prefers any form of resistance to self-destruction. Similarly, shedding the blood of your innocent friend in order to save your own life means, in a sense, the intolerable end of the religious community.

Another biblical verse gave rise to an additional cluster of principles, mostly moral in nature, "You must do what is right and good" (Deut. 6:18). Here is part of what Nahmanides, an eminent Jewish scholar (13th c.), wrote on this verse in his commentary on the Bible:

This is an important issue. Since it is impossible to mention in the Holy Writ all the ways in which a man should conduct himself, with respect to his neighbours and friends, to his dealings, as well as to community or state proprieties, after having mentioned many of them, such as 'you must not go around among your people for the sake of slandering,' 'you must not take vengeance nor have a grudge against the sons of your people,' 'you must not stand up against your fellow's blood,' 'you must not call down evil upon a deaf man,' 'before grey hair you should rise up,' and such like, [the Holy Writ] reiterates, by way of a rule, that he must do what is right and good in every respect, to the extent that he will resort to compromise and supererogation. . . .[8]

Several applications of this principle are discussed in the Talmud.[9] An interesting case is that of Reuben who borrowed money from Simeon and failed to pay his debt on time. A procedure may then be invoked by assessing the value of Reuben's lands and letting Simeon take possession of an appropriate part of those lands. What should happen if after a while Reuben is in a position to pay his debt to Simeon? Solely on the grounds of the principle of doing "right and good," Reuben has a right to reclaim his lands, with no time limitations.

The recommendation and prescription of resort to "compromise and supererogation" are applicable both to personal self-restraint and social cohesiveness. Hence, they enhance the driving forces of the religion, that is to say, the insistent rejection of all forms of idol worship and the persistent maintenance of the particular community of worshippers.

Our final example of a biblical verse to which the orthodox tradition has ascribed various practical principles is from Proverbs, "Its ways are ways of pleasantness and all its roadways are peace" (3:17). The subject of this verse, as determined by one of the preceding verses, is, literally, wisdom; but our verse has been widely interpreted within the tradition as referring to the religion itself. Some of the practical points that were made by alluding to the verse of Proverbs are of an ethical, rather than of a moral, nature in the above-mentioned sense of these terms.

One such principle establishes the wish to avoid creation of hostility as grounds for doing what is otherwise not prescribed by any religious rule. A classical case is that of the famous precept, "Should you see the ass of someone who hates you lying down under its load, then you must refrain from leaving him" (Exod. 23:5). It is not entirely implausible to interpret this precept as applying only to Jews. The related verse in Deuteronomy apparently suggests such an interpretation, "You must not see the *ass of your brother* [emphasis added] or his bull fall down on the road and deliberately withdraw from them" (22:4). However, the Talmudic discussion of the case makes it explicit that this precept applies to Jews and Gentiles alike; the case of the latter ones resting on the principle of avoiding the creation of hostility.[10]

It should perhaps be stressed that this principle is not restricted to cases where feelings of hostility towards Jews in particular are apprehended. The same line of reasoning is invoked also in several types of domestic conflicts, as well as in other cases of social friction. We give the following examples. When a person is completely dependent upon his father for domestic support, it is his filial duty to turn over to his father any find he has made. Otherwise, some undesirable feelings of hostility may arise in his father's heart. An example of a different type involves the Jewish High Priest. The Palestinian Talmud bases the regulation of not anointing two High Priests on the fear of mutual hostility that might lurk in their minds.[11] Mordecai, a thirteenth century Jewish martyr and rabbinical authority, suggested that two wedding ceremonies should not be conducted together, lest one be held in respect more than the other, and this give rise to ill feelings.[12] Mordecai's suggestion has not, however, taken the form of an established orthodox practice. Notice that such careful avoidance of what might precipitate hostility is also conducive to personal self-restraint and to social cohesiveness.

We conclude our brief discussion of the principles of moral or ethical decision making in Jewish orthodoxy by presenting a principle from which a whole cluster of regulations has stemmed. This principle is entitled, "on account of ways of peace," and is applied to a variety of cases, specified in much detail in a series of passages of the *Mishnah,* the canonic collection of Jewish Law, codified c.200 C.E. The cases mentioned in the passages of the *Mishnah,* and also discussed in related Talmudic texts, cover a whole range of practices that, at least in part, address themselves to the matter of the "ways of peace."[13]

First on the list of cases mentioned in the *Mishnah* is that of the ritual of public recital of the Torah (the Pentateuch) in the synagogue. Priests are supposed to be the first to read the appropriate part of the scroll and, *prima facie,* may show respect to other members of the community by waiving, in a certain way, their right to precedence. However, if the priest is not the first to read the scroll, by whom is he to be replaced? This question is bound to arise as part of those all too common problems of honor and priority. Using the "ways of peace" line of reasoning, it was decided the priest must always take his special part in the ritual. For a similar reason, if the members of the community are all priests but one, then the latter member of the community will have the right of precedence over the former ones in the ritual, unless the priests can agree as to who should be given precedence in the ritual proceedings from among their group.

A different type of example, also mentioned in the *Mishnah,* is that of traps and nets. The question might arise as to the ownership of an animal or fish caught in a trap. Again, *prima facie,* whoever has set up the trap must profit from its success; but then, some such devices are not personally identifiable. In such cases, a passerby may, in public, appropriate the trapped prey for himself. Since such practice is bound to cause friction, the "ways of peace" argument is applied and a regulation is established according to which such a removal of animals, poultry, or fish is classified as robbery.

Many regulations that resulted from "ways of peace" considerations pertain to relations with Gentiles. The poor should be supported, the sick visited, the deceased buried and eulogized, and the bereaved consoled, regardless of who they are. In the event these observances were limited to Jews and Gentiles suffering similar vicissitudes are overlooked, the neglect would constitute a clear violation of the "ways of peace."

Our final example is slightly different. Consider the case of a man who found some valuable article in a public place. Who has the right of ownership to it should someone snatch it and take possession? On the grounds of the desirable avoidance of quarrels, a regulation was established that forbids snatching within a certain vicinity of a person. Although the grounds of this regulation are not couched in terms of the "ways of peace," the rationale is identical.

In all of these cases, we encounter ceaseless efforts to shape the religious practices in forms that contribute directly and significantly to orthodox causes. A variety of principles were contrived to minimize both inter- and intra-communal problems. All these principles impose on those who are observant, social restrictions that, by their very nature, deepen their self-restraint. They provide practical expression of commitment to the absolute rejection of all idols, old and new.

Ethical Issues

We turn now to a relatively brief survey of some cognate issues that any value-governed community has had to face in order to provide its members with a general approach and a practical attitude, revealing both its own fundamental views concerning what the case is and ought to be.

In discussing these topics within the framework of Jewish orthodoxy, we should again bear in mind the circumstances of decentralization under which the related tradition developed. As a result of these conditions, differences have emerged between communities distant from each other in terms of space, time, and cultural environment. What follows, then, pertains only to the common core of those orthodox variants.

Sexual Relationships

Notice first that when alleged moral considerations are brought to bear on sexual problems, those considerations are not, in fact, moral or ethical, in our strict sense of these terms. More often than not, such considerations reveal certain value judgments with respect to some sexual behavior, rather than an educated judgment as to what constitutes the best solution to the problem—a solution that should be applied to all members of the community alike (moral judgment), or to all human beings alike (ethical judgment). When an act of voluntary sexual intercourse has no effect upon anybody except the consenting parties, then, strictly speaking, moral or ethical principles are only applicable to the case when some conflict might arise between the parties themselves in respect to their sexual involvement. No third party has an independent moral or ethical standing with respect to that act of sexual intercourse. Therefore, any related value judgment of such a third party carries no moral or ethical significance.

However, since practices and discussions pertaining to sexual relationships abound in the religious tradition of orthodoxy, we outline some major ingredients of the orthodox attitude towards sexual behavior, though most of them are of no moral or ethical significance in the present strict sense.

Since Jewish orthodoxy is total by its very traditional nature, human sexuality is viewed as a natural domain for the expression of basic orthodox values, and thus it should neither be sanctified or banned. The logic of this religious attitude towards sex is essentially parallel to its attitude toward manual labor and food consumption. To quote Maimonides:

> If those of our co-religionists . . . claim they practice self-mortifica-
> tion and abstinence from all pleasures solely to discipline their psy-
> chological powers . . . then they are mistaken, as I shall explain: the
> Torah forbids and ordains what it forbids for no other and ordains
> for no other reason than this: that we should, by habitual practice,
> keep our distance from a given extreme. This is the reason for all the
> dietary prohibitions and for the restrictions on forbidden unions.
> That is the reason for the prohibition of fornication and for the strict
> legal requirements regarding marriage and wedlock. Even this does
> not permit love-making at all times. . . . All this was commanded by
> God solely to keep us well away from the extreme of overindulgence
> and cause us even to depart slightly from the mean in the direction
> of insensibility to pleasure in order that the disposition of temperate-
> ness would be firmly entrenched and ingrained in our souls.[14]

This attitude manifests itself within orthodoxy in many ways. A few examples should suffice.

Celibacy is prohibited. The given facts of life should not be ignored or suppressed, but rather regulated in appropriate value-laden ways. Interestingly enough, the first precept mentioned in the Bible, as early as Genesis, is that of procreation.

Until very recently, baby making involved sexual intercourse. Hence, sexual activity was unavoidable for those who were moved by religious duty to procreate. The recent "test tube baby" reproductive technology that dispenses with copulation does not change the situation from the orthodox view. Although it is too early to expect an official orthodox pronouncement on the use of this new reproductive technique, the opinion has already been voiced by some rabbis that, in the use of the "test tube baby" technique, the observant is not discharging his religous obligation to procreate.[15] There is reason to assume that this view will prevail. Accordingly, in the orthodox view, relations do and will continue to form an essential part of procreative activity.

In addition to procreation, there is the acknowledgment of the role of sexual activity in ordinary human life. The biblical precept that, "if he should take another wife for himself, her sustenance, her clothing and her marriage due are not to be diminished" (Exod.

21:10), was interpreted as early as the second century C.E. as granting a man's wife the right to have sexual relations with her husband, which is tantamount to imposing on the husband a duty to have regular sexual relations with his wife. The appropriate frequency of those required relations was discussed in the *Mishnah* where a determination was made on the basis of the husband's occupation and by other considerations.[16]

On the other hand, legitimate sexual activity is strictly confined to the married couples. Extramarital sex is prohibited, particularly when it is incestuous.

Moreover, sexual activity is prohibited during certain periods, the most usual one being that of the woman's formally-defined menstrual period. That period extends beyond the actual days of menstruation to include "seven clean days," in keeping with the biblical precept that "if she has become clean from her running discharge, she must also count for herself seven days, and afterwards she will be clean" (Lev. 15:28).

Beyond the regulations that prohibit sexual intercourse under certain conditions, religious practices abound that are meant to put a curb on human sexual passions. A whole array of regulations exists, explicitly intended to plant firm checks on the sexual slippery slope. Such a profusion of checks could create the impression that a state of indulgence prevails, but rather it is an admission that sexual drives are powerful and that people are prone to succumb to its forces. This explains the enforcement of regulations that are preventive measures of a somewhat indirect nature, such as the one already mentioned in the *Mishnah* according to which a bachelor should not teach little children who are fetched from school by their mothers.[17]

Liberation Movements

A discussion of liberation movements in the context of a particular religion or denomination should, perhaps, be divided into a discussion of liberation movements within its membership, and a discussion of proper attitudes towards external liberation movements, i.e., ones which are ideologically or politically dominated by forces outside that religion and considered alien to it. In other words, the discussion should, perhaps, have two parts: moral and ethical.

Roughly speaking, there have been no liberation movements within Jewish orthodoxy. In a sense, it would almost be impossible to have an internal, i.e., Jewish orthodox liberation movement because it is essential to such a movement that it carry its unique banner of sweeping reforms. However, within a denomination having a constitutive nature, vast changes cannot be made during one's lifetime. Therefore, even preaching liberation within such a conservative setting would usually not be tolerated.

One apparent exception should be briefly mentioned. The Hassidic movement of the eighteenth century has sometimes been depicted as a social movement of the vein that has more recently been described as a "liberation movement." However, the Hassidic leaders and masses did not carry antinomian banners. They kept observing the orthodox practices and the minor changes they introduced into given religious practices did not involve breaches of religious law. Most of the major ingredients of their new religious style brought forward new emphases rather than novel elements. Interest in mysticism, for example, had been present in Jewish literature many centuries earlier. Indeed, members of the Hassidic movement conferred religious leadership on certain men of charisma, some of whom established Hassidic dynasties. Here the Hassidic movement introduced a new style of religious leadership and a new type of social loyalty and religious community within orthodoxy, but it would be a distortion of historical facts to regard the latter novelties as the culmination of the efforts of a "liberation movement."

There are other reasons why liberation movements in the service of some particular cause could not have been created within Jewish orthodoxy. One example would be that of an anti-racist liberation movement because no internal distinctions by race play a role within orthodoxy. A person of any race may convert to the Jewish religion, and some have done so. The difficulties which the Ethiopian Jews have recently faced in Israel have nothing to do with race.

A completely different example would be that of the Gay movement. Homosexual relations are strictly forbidden within orthodoxy, though the biblical precept with respect to males is more direct and its breach regarded more severely than that pertaining to females. Contrast the male mandate, "And you must not lie down with a male the same as you lie down with a woman. It is a detestable thing" (Lev. 18:22), with the milder ban on lesbianism, "The way the land of Egypt does, in which you dwelt, you must not do" (Ibid. 3).[18] There is no conceivable way a liberation movement within orthodoxy can render such precepts null and void.

The only domain in which some developments may, and have taken place, is that of the social role of women; but the historical processes have taken the form of minute imbibitions, rather than sweeping reforms introduced by a related liberation movement.

Turning to external liberation movements, any analysis of the orthodox attitude would be rather hypothetical since Jewish orthodoxy has not had a real opportunity to establish practices with respect to such external trends. The historical clashes between Hasmonean priests and, later, their theocracy, and the Hellenized Jews, can hardly be depicted as a struggle between a religious establishment and a liberation movement.

In a sense, some modern Jewish movements can be described as liberation movements, but since all of them have been secular in nature, it should come as no surprise that they have experienced the various types of resentment exhibited against them.

Indeed, one may wonder what the orthodox attitude would have been towards certain external liberation movements had there been an orthodox theocracy in power. It is difficult to answer such hypothetical questions because the answer would depend on the nature of the demands made by a liberation movement under consideration, and the context in which they are made. The principles of ethical decision making that were mentioned earlier show very clearly that the orthodox response is bound to be contextual. "Ways of peace," for example, do not offer a single prescription, a practice for all seasons, but rather a very general pattern, adjustable to different situations.

To be sure, some external liberation movements, such as that of the gays, would see orthodoxy ill-affected, but the problem of proper response should still be discussed, even from such an extremely negative point of view.

Economic Order

The orthodox normative system has been required to solve, in religiously proper and practically traceable ways, many problems that have a major economic ingredient but the level on which these problems used to appear was never global. It involved either several individuals or, at most, a community that was not economically self-sustained. Hence, modern history finds orthodox Jews heartily active within capitalistic systems, such as multinational companies and within expressly socialistic frameworks, such as the Israeli Kibbutz movement.

However, major elements for a better economic order can be extracted from the multitude of regulations pertaining to economic relations on lower levels. Those ingredients are of a socialist nature to the extent that socialism, as contrasted with capitalism, is taken to endorse policies of the welfare state. This, of course, is in tune with one of the two basic driving forces of Jewish orthodoxy, namely, the enhancement of social cohesiveness. The other force, self-restraint expressing rejection of all kinds of idol-worship, is manifest as a general attitude towards private property. Neither poverty nor riches have any religiously intrinsic value, and addiction to either is on a par with idolatry. Voluntary poverty verges on exploitation and so does the unrestrained pursuit of wealth. A variety of practices checks both. For example, the obligation to see to it that one's sons master some vocation is intended to cut at one extremity; whereas the whole system of tithes cuts at the opposite end, though it serves other social and ritual purposes as well.

Issues of Violence and Justice

Pacifism, in the utopian sense of valuing universal abolition of war, is not alien to the Jewish orthodox tradition, being expressed in some famous biblical verses, such as Isaiah's prophecy that "in the end days" the nations "will have to beat their swords into plowshares and their spears into pruning shears. Nation will not lift up sword against nation, neither will they learn war any more" (2:2, 4).

However, pacifism in the sense of avoiding use of arms, or of violence in general, here and now, is alien to orthodoxy. Not only is there a definite right of self-defense, which sometimes involves inevitable resort to great force of an appropriate type, but there is also a right to intervene when a person chases another with the intent to kill and when a man pursues a woman with the intent to rape. In both of the above instances, orthodoxy allows for the infliction of death as justification for the defense of life.

On the other hand, the excessive use of power is censured. The biblical precept is that "if a thief should be found in the act of breaking in and he does get struck and dies, there is no bloodguilt for him" (Exod. 22:1–2). The biblical distinction was interpreted as differentiating between a robber who might kill, if resisted, and a robber who would not kill. Whereas in the former case infliction of death upon the armed robber would fall under legitimate self-defense, in the latter case such resort to power would be regarded as murder.

It is interesting to note that a rabbinical authority of the seventeenth century, Simha Luzzatto of Venice, applied a similar line of argument to the biblical specification of the borders of the "promised land": "When the People of Israel entered the land of Israel, their borders were set precisely and they were granted no permission to cross these borders. All other peoples extend their government to whichever place their good luck has carried them and their power has helped them to retain. . . . Only our forefathers remained restrained within their borders, because of the laws of the Torah."[19] Notice that the argument uses the orthodox principle of self-restraint and not some ethical considerations intended to resolve ongoing conflicts with other inhabitants of neighboring territories.

We turn now to a brief discussion of penalites inflicted by physical force. In the orthodox tradition the practice of corporal punishment was not exceptional. As a matter of fact, flogging was the standard sanction applied against whomever violated certain laws. However, the practice of flogging, ensuing from passages of the *Mishnah* and discussions in the Talmud,[20] does not take the harsh form apparently specified by a literal reading of the verse that details "forty strokes" (Deut. 25:3). Instead, it is a mitigated form of a corporal penalty inflicted in a way meant to avoid jeopardizing the life of the offender. For example, the maximum number of strokes permitted is thirty-nine, but that number does not have to be reached in every case of flogging.

It should, perhaps, be stressed that resort to such corporal penalties required a prior due process of religious law, including a very careful examination of the evidence at hand. Moreover, the penalties were applied only in the case where the accused had been previously warned not to commit the crime and had acknowledged in a certain way his having received the warning.

Capital punishment is instituted by the Bible as a penalty to be visited upon felons of certain types. There are four different techniques of execution applied according to the felony of which the accused has been convicted. The details of these techniques, specified in the *Mishnah* and Talmud, may be presently left undiscussed to spare the reader's feelings.[21] What should, however, be mentioned is that the conditions under which capital punishment could be inflicted were severely limited, to the extent that execution was, most probably, a rare event.

One of those conditions·is that a supreme court, called the "Great Sanhedrin," comprising seventy-one members, convened in the

Hewn Stone Hall in the Holy Temple, must be in session. Tradition has it that capital punishment was practically abolished by c. 30 C.E., when the supreme court moved out. Executions were then carried out by Jewish orthodox communities, without the reinstitution of capital punishment, as temporary measures applied to rare cases such as treason.

The theoretical discussion of the death penalty was not ended with the abolition of the practice. It should be mentioned that the *Mishnah,* codified after the abolition of the death penalty, includes the following remarks: "A Sanhedrin which sentences a person to death once every seven years is called damaging. R. Elazar, son of Azariah, says: once every seventy years. R. Tarfon and R. Akiba say: If we had been members of the Sanhedrin, no one would ever have been sentenced to death. Rabban Simeon, son of Gamaliel, says: They, too, increase the number of blood-shedders among the people of Israel."[22] The eminent personalities that have been quoted were active during the first and second centuries C.E., but what they said still sounds intriguing, for more than one reason.

We conclude the present discussion of the orthodox attitudes towards violence by mentioning two cases of attempts to enforce violent acts. The first case is raised by a man who told Rava, a major Talmudic figure of the fourth century C.E., that he had been ordered by the governor of his town to kill a certain person or that he would be killed himself. Rava's response was sharp, "Be killed and do not kill. What reason do you have for regarding your blood redder; perhaps that person's blood is redder?"[23] This religious judgment is very interesting because it involves a conflict between the religiously acknowledged instincts of survival and the constant religious rejection of extreme devotion to anything on earth. Rava's words turned the scales decisively.

A related case is discussed in the *Tosephta,* a contemporaneous supplement to the *Mishnah,* and though some reservations have been voiced with respect to the judgment of the *Tosephta* it seems worthy of mentioning here.[24]

If a group is required to surrender one of its number to be killed and that failure of such compliance would eventuate in the death of the entire group, under those circumstances, all should be prepared to die instead of permitting the sacrifice of one life for the sake of others. Rava's rhetorical question about whose blood is to be regarded as redder is echoed here. However, the *Tosephta* proceeds to raise certain reservations. If the group is required to surrender a certain named individual, it should comply, if threatened with mass death. Assuming that this judgment applies only when effective self-defense has been ruled out for some good practical reasons, one may perhaps interpret it as resulting, not from any utilitarian considerations, but rather from the view that under such circumstances it is the named person's obligation to surrender himself to the enemy, abominable though the latter's demand may be. Of course, the best approach to such tragic circumstances is to do one's best, striving against whatever instigates people to put forward such horrendous demands.

Environmental Ethics

The starting point of any discussion of an orthodox view with respect to environmental issues should be the biblical precept that, "In case you lay siege to a city many days by fighting against it so as to capture it from them, you must not ruin its trees by wielding an axe against them; for you should eat from them, and you must not cut them down . . ." (Deut. 20:19).

The biblical precept was developed into a general obligation to avoid causing destruction, applicable to more situations than trees in the vicinity of a city under siege. The traditional drift is described thus by a thirteenth or fourteenth century author of a famous survey (*Hahinnukh*, The Education) of 613 precepts, as well as their reasons and ramifications, " . . . and whoever destroys anything in a rage was said to be on a par with the idol-worshipper. . . . Everyone must scold one's evil desire and suppress one's passion. . . ."[25] Here, the values of self-restraint and communal cohesiveness go hand in hand.

Bioethical Issues

Before we turn to a brief description of orthodox views with respect to particular problems in this domain, it might be worthwhile to outline the attitude of orthodoxy towards medicine in general.

By now it should be realized that the general attitude of Jewish orthodoxy towards medicine is positive. By using the medical expertise at one's disposal for saving life and securing good health, one obviously renders an essential service to one's community for its existence and well-being.

The theologically-laden religious suggestion to let nature take its course in each and every case, was not accepted by Jewish orthodoxy. The biblical verse that specifies redress for certain torts and mentions compensation with respect to lost time and required healing (Exod. 21:18–19) was used in a Talmudic discussion for granting permission, from a religious point of view, to practice medicine.[26] (Other biblical verses were used by various orthodox authors for the same purpose.) Later on, this permission was extended to form a religious obligation to use medical means when needed. And since medicine is a scientific and technological discipline that cannot be mastered and practiced without appropriate dedication, its study and application were eventually rendered, to a cerain extent, religiously obligatory. It is interesting to note that during the Middle Ages even those traditional figures, such as Solomon ben Adreth of Barcelona, who banned philosophy and natural sciences, excluded medicine from their bans.[27] Indeed, some Jewish orthodox personalities excelled themselves as both religious authorities and medical doctors. The most prominent example is that of Maimonides.

We turn now to particular issues in medical treatment and research.

First, there is the question of the extraordinary prolongation of life by mechanical means. From the orthodox point of view, two distinctions must be made before the question is answered as to whether this should be attempted. To begin with, persons who have shown definite symptoms of imminent death must be distinguished from non-terminal patients. If the life in jeopardy is that of a person in the latter category, certainly attempts should be made to save that life. The more complicated case is that of the dying person. Here a second distinction has to be introduced between those who are in the process of dying and those who have just reached its end, as determined by criteria pertaining to heart failure. In the second case, it is forbidden by orthodox practice to resuscitate life by mechanical means. The first case is not fully settled, but if one follows the most strict measure in practice, the extraordinary prolongation of life under circumstances of dying is considered obligatory.

The question, "How long should life be artificially prolonged?" has been recently answered in orthodox practice to the effect that mechanical means should be turned off periodically to ascertain whether the patient can survive in the absence of mechanical support. If the test is positive, the device should be switched on again, for another trial period.

The second bioethical issue we turn to is euthanasia. A distinction must be clearly made between active and passive euthanasia.

Active euthanasia involves the administration of some means such as drugs to accelerate death. Passive euthanasia is defined as the withholding of certain medical treatment usually intended to prolong the life of an incurably sick person.[28]

Active euthanasia is strictly forbidden by orthodoxy, even when the patient is suffering a great deal of pain or when the patient has requested it while being of a sound mind and with full knowledge of the medical situation.

A possible exception to the ban of active euthanasia is the case of "indirect euthanasia." Here, drugs that are administered in order to relieve a patient from suffering might actually accelerate the patient's death. If the sole intention of the administration of such drugs is to relieve pain, then, it is not forbidden by orthodox practice. A discussion of the relations between this Jewish orthodox consideration and the Catholic argument of "double effect" is intriguing, but beyond the scope of the present survey.

Passive euthanasia is in dispute. The most important sixteenth century rabbinical authority of "Ashkenzai" (mostly European) Jewry, Moses Isserles of Cracow, wrote: "If something causes a delay of demise, it may be removed."[29] The examples he mentions include a noise produced in the vicinity and grains of salt put in the patient's mouth. It is permitted to stop the noise and to remove the grains of salt with the full knowledge that their removal will precipitate the patient's death. Other authors have adopted different positions.

Third, we turn to the bioethical issues of prenatal diagnosis and abortion. Abortion is generally forbidden in Jewish orthodoxy, but there are significant numbers of exceptions. The main feature of many cases in which abortion is allowed within Jewish orthodoxy is when the pregnancy places the mother's life in jeopardy. In such cases, the embryo or the fetus is regarded as being "in chase of" the woman, endangering her life. Since, under such circumstances, the right of intervening may be invoked for saving the life of whomever is chased, abortion is permitted. Abortion during the first forty days of pregnancy is preferable to ones performed later on, *ceteris paribus*. Similarly, abortion during the first three months is preferable to ones performed later, *ceteris paribus*. However, in extreme cases, when the need arises to decide whether to save a woman giving birth or to save the baby being born, there is no doubt that the life of the mother is given priority on the grounds that the baby is not a separate human being. The caution to be used in all these cases is proportional to the stage of pregnancy under consideration. Also, indirect methods of abortion, such as the administration of some appropriate medicament, is to be preferred to direct methods of curettage.

Abortion is also permitted from the orthodox point of view when, not simply the woman's life, but her health is placed in jeopardy. Generally speaking, the anticipation of social and economic hardships is not regarded as a legitimate reason for abortion but it is permissible in the case of certain illicit pregnancies, as when a married woman carries the child of a man other than her husband.

When there is reason to suspect that the baby will be born with severe handicaps and will suffer torments, abortion is permitted during the first three months. Where it is medically demonstrated that the newborn will have the Tay-Sachs disease, abortion has been permitted recently by an orthodox authority, up until the end of the seventh month of pregnancy.[30]

The attitude towards prenatal diagnosis is derived from the attitude toward abortion.

The fourth bioethical issue has to do with human experimentation. From the orthodox point of view, medical experiments that endanger health are prohibited. Scientists and clinicians are forbidden to carry them out and nobody is permitted to serve as their subject.

Other experiments are not forbidden. But though a person should be religiously commended for having volunteered to serve as a subject of medical experimentation, such volunteering is not considered a religious duty by orthodox standards.

Fifth, there is the matter of animal experimentation. The prevailing orthodox attitude towards animals is that no unnecessary cruelty should be inflicted upon them. Certain biblical precepts are interpreted as supporting this attitude. A prominent example is the one that says, "You must not muzzle a bull while it is threshing" (Deut. 25:4). Another biblical passage is popularly quoted says, "In case a bird's nest happens to be before you in the way, in any tree or on the earth, with young ones or eggs, and the mother is sitting upon the young ones or the eggs, you must not take the mother along with the offspring. You should by all means send the mother away, but you may take the offspring for yourself" (Ibid., 22:6–7). This precept shows, actually, that the principle at hand is not one of avoiding cruelty to animals but rather of avoiding unwarranted cruelty to animals. In keeping with this principle, under medically necessary conditions, animal experimentation is approved by orthodoxy.

The sixth bioethical issue deals with genetic interventions. There is good reason to assume that if Jewish orthodoxy is to develop an official view pertaining to various cases of genetic engineering, it will not be sweepingly negative, but neither will it be generally positive.

Crossbreeding, for example, is forbidden by the Bible, "You must not interbreed your domestic animals of two sorts" (Lev. 19:19). It is a safe assumption that other types of hybridization will be viewed similarly. However, though the creation of hybrids is forbidden, the raising of existent ones is not. This leaves a slight opening in the door.

The permissibility for genetic manipulation is much more favorable, albeit under restrictive conditions, when such intervention is justified for urgent medical purposes.

Seventh, in respect to reproductive technologies, there is no single orthodox view that bears upon all modern techniques. Much depends upon the moral implications of each of these techniques. We mention two examples that have attracted the attention of the general public for more than one reason.

Artificial insemination of a women with semen collected from her husband (AIH) is still in dispute but there seems to be a vast majority of orthodox authorities allowing this procedure under certain circumstances. For example, when a marriage is childless for ten years (a period which was determined through the interpretation of certain biblical verses), AIH is deemed permissible. The same holds for a couple concerning whom it is the professional view of experts that AIH is the only way, or the only legitimate way from an orthodox point of view, to circumvent reproduction difficulties.

However, artificial insemination of a woman with semen collected from a donor (AID) is in dispute and does not have the support of major authorities.

There is no clear verdict on *in vitro* fertilization (IVF). The fact of the matter is that there have been only a few orthodox discussions of the issue. The reasons offered by its opponents are that medical personnel are not always reliable with respect to the sources of semen or embryo cultures, or the fact that fertilization does not take place in the uterus. A residual problem in all of this is a deeply entrenched attitude of negativity toward masturbation that the process of fertilization necessitates.

In the event that the IVF and ET (embryo transplant) are successfully carried out and a child is born, from the orthodox perspective problems still abound concerning succession, inheritance, etc. Here, Jewish orthodoxy does not fare any better than any other legal systems that appear puzzled by utterly new types of situations brought about by the combined application of new techniques and surrogacy.

Finally, there is the matter of psychosurgery. Mentally handicapped persons are regarded as sick and their treatment is, accordingly, regulated by principles that apply to the rest of medical practice.

In cases of mentally handicapped persons who are violent, including those who endanger themselves, appropriate measures may be taken. Under certain conditions, brain surgery is permissible for the improvement of health even if the operation involves some risk and might modify the patient's personality to a certain extent. In every case, the best available experts have to be consulted first and permission of the patient's family (who have custodial rights) for authorization of the operation has to be obtained.

It is not difficult to see how many of the regulations and proposals we have surveyed are governed by the basic driving forces of Jewish orthodoxy and thereby reflect all the major traits of this ancient, yet influential, religious tradition.

Notes

1. John Rawls, *A Theory of Justice* (Cambridge: Harvard University Press, 1971), 582.

2. For a presentation and elaboration of the distinction, see John Searle, *Speech Acts* (Cambridge: Harvard University Press, 1969), 33–42, and Naomi Kasher, "Kant and Deontology," *Revue Internationale de Philosophie*, no. 126 (1978), 551–558.

3. For an English translation of the Old Testament, we use the *New World Translation of the Holy Scriptures,* New York, 1961.

4. *Yoma,* 85a–b.

5. Maimonides, *Yad Hahazakah,* hilkoth Shabbath, 2:1.

6. This is the version in Maimonides' Code, *ibid.,* 3. An earlier version appears in the Talmud, *Yoma,* 84b.

7. *Sanhedrin,* 74a.

8. Commentary on Deuteronomy 6:18.

9. *Baba Metzi'a*, 16b.

10. Ibid., 32b.

11. *Yoma*, 1:1.

12. On *Mo'ed Katan*, 1.

13. *Gittin*, v.8.

14. "Shemona Perakin," 4, transl. L.E. Goodman, *Rambam: Readings in the Philosophy of Moses Maimonides* (New York: Viking Press, 1976), 230–231.

15. E.Y. Waldenberg, "Tzitz Eliezer" in *Hilkhoth Ropheim Urephuah*, Avraham Steinberg, ed. (Jerusalem: Mosad Harav Kook, 1978), pt. 4, 3:14.

16. *Kethuboth*, v.6.

17. *Kiddushin*, 4:14.

18. This verse was interpreted as banning lesbianism.

19. Hebrew translation of an Italian "Discourse on the Jews of Venice," (Jerusalem: Mosad Bialik, 1950), 114.

20. *Makkoth*, 22a.

21. *Sanhedrin*, 7:1–4 and 49b, respectively.

22. *Makkoth*, 1:10.

23. *Pesahim*, 25b.

24. *Terumoth*, 7:20.

25. Hahinnukh, 530 (Jerusalem: Mosad Harav Kook, 1977), 647–648.

26. *Baba Kama*, 85a.

27. On the most important ban of this type, see A.S. Halkin, "The Ban on the Study of Philosophy," *P'raqim* (sic)1 (1967–68), 35–55 (in Hebrew).

28. For related philosophical discussions of euthanasia, see Jonathan Glover, *Causing Death and Saving Lives* (New York: Penguin Books, 1977), and James Rachels, *The End of Life*, (Oxford: Oxford University Press, 1986).

29. Glosses to *Yore De'a*, 339:1.

30. Waldenberg, *Hilkoth*, (note 15), xxxiii–xlvi.

6

Blessing and Curse: Toward a Liberal Jewish Ethic

RAMI M. SHAPIRO

Introduction

A certain gentile came before Shammai and said to him, "Convert me on the condition that you teach me the whole Torah while I stand on one foot." Shammai pushed him out with the builder's cubit which was in his hand. When the gentile went before Hillel, he converted him saying, "What is hateful to you, do not do to your neighbor. That is the whole of the Torah, all the rest is commentary; now go and study it."[1]

With this simple statement Hillel reaffirms the heart of Jewish ethical teaching, "You shall love your neighbor as yourself."[2] By reminding us that "the rest is commentary," however, Hillel hints at both the complexity of ethical decision making and the inherent pluralism of Jewish thought. Judaism is not a homogeneous doctrine but a heterogeneous intermingling of sometimes conflicting points of view derived from often highly personal and heavily biased interpretations of sacred text and historical experience in the light of changing secular conditions. Judaism is not static but dynamic, and its dynamism has given birth to many denominations, philosophic trends, and movements, both religious and secular, each with its own flavor and legitimacy.

In this essay we are called upon to present one of these trends, i.e., "liberal" Judaism in modern America. In so doing it is important that we be very clear as to the nature of liberal Judaism as a philosophic idea, for the term "liberal" carries with it several connotations that are not necessarily indigenous to the term Jewish. The very notion of a liberal Judaism, especially in the context of contemporary America, suggests a comingling of cultural influences that fundamentally affects the reading and interpretation of those texts and experiences from which a Jewish ethic is derived. Before delving into liberal Jewish ethics *per se*, then, it is incumbent upon us to probe the word "liberal" and set forth the presuppositions that it brings to Judaism. There are at least four such presuppositions: humanism, rationalism, voluntarism, and egalitarianism.

Humanism

Humanism, simply stated, is the proposition that human life "is too sacred to be treated otherwise than as an end in itself."[3] The implication of being an end unto oneself is, in context, that the human being is radically and irrevocably free. What in liberal Judaism is called *kadosh,* holiness or radical unconditionality, and is said to be the essence of God and the ultimate goal of humankind, is in humanism called freedom, and is held to be the highest goal of human life.

> I have given you, Adam, neither a predetermined place nor a particular aspect nor any special prerogatives in order that you may take and possess these through your own decision and choice. The limitations on the nature of other creatures are contained within my prescribed laws. You shall determine your own nature without constraint from any barrier, by means of the freedom to whose power I have entrusted you. I have placed you at the center of the world so that from that point you might see better what is in the world. I have made you neither heavenly nor earthly, neither mortal nor immortal so that, like a free and sovereign artificer, you might mold and fashion yourself into that form you yourself shall have chosen.[4]

Rationalism

Rationalism implies that life, insofar as it is to meaningfully impact upon humankind, must be open to the reasoning capacity of the human mind, and that whatever truth there may be beyond the reach of human reason is, for all intents and purposes, inherently meaningless.

Human reason is the primary tool of human decision making, and if Life is not open to reasonable investigation then no meaningful decisions can be made. Without informed rational choice and decision making no accountability is possible, and without accountability the entire foundation of ethics crumbles beneath the weight of an overpoweringly irrational universe.

> To be a person means to have a sense of moral responsibility. One needs no special gift or talent to be a person other than that of being aware of oneself as autonomously accountable for one's behavior. Feeling accountable or responsible on the authority of others, under whatever name they exercise that authority, will not do. Being a per-

son implies an intellectual and emotional maturity which is attained only gradually and which has to keep on enlarging its scope. A person is existentially such by virtue of his sense of moral responsibility, and to the extent that he lives up to it.[5]

Voluntarism

Since liberalism is based on an individual's freedom to choose, voluntarism is built into the heart of any liberal ideology. What is, in traditional societies, a given, i.e., that there is a God who has ordained a Life-Way incumbent upon any individual seeking to please that God and gain some reward, is, in modern times, an option chosen or rejected solely on the subjective criteria of the person doing the choosing.

To illustrate our point let us look to the example of Jewish emancipation. In both the ghetto and the eastern European *shtetl,* the notion that one freely chose to be a Jew would be ludicrous. One was chosen by fate to be a Jew, and Jewishness was a matter of destiny, the taken-for-granted aspect of one's identity that was continually reaffirmed and reenforced by both internal pressures and external constraints. One could argue that there was always an escape from Jewishness through conversion to Christianity, but the weight of group values and the continued anti-Semitism of the Gentile community foreclosed this option for all but the most insistent of individuals.

With emancipation, however, all this changed, and Jews began to avail themselves of the options outside the Jewish community. At this point real choice is introduced, and we can begin to speak of Jewishness as voluntary. While the antipathy of Jews toward those who opted to leave the community, and the negative attitudes still extant among Gentiles, checked any mass emigration from Judaism, emancipation went quite far in central and western Europe in the nineteenth century. Twentieth century America, of course, became the arena for full emancipation resulting in an end to any sociologically honest notion of Judaism as destiny and the emergence of the much more fragile idea of Jew by choice. No matter how strong an individual's identification with Judaism may be, given the pluralism of American culture, that identity must be maintained by conscious choice.

Voluntarism is the fact of one's freedom acted out in the sphere of religious loyalties. In the context of liberal religion, voluntarism recognizes no external authority forcing the individual to adhere to doctrines, beliefs, and customs that do not meet one's subjective criteria of reasonableness. Liberal religion, for better or worse, must sell itself to the individual by appealing to reason—even when dealing with the irrational. No matter what the belief or practice, no matter how irrational it may appear to some, it must be perceived by those loyal to it to be completely rational. Even the dictum "It is absurd, therefore I believe" must, in the final and highly subjective analysis of those who uphold it, make sense.

Egalitarianism

Judaism is a civilization far too ancient to be anything but patriarchal, and the inherent biases *vis-à-vis* women, however interpreted, foreclose egalitarianism as an option for normative rabbinic Judaism. Given humanism's respect for individual freedom and autonomy, however, egalitarianism is crucial to our liberal world view and cannot be sacrificed to perpetuate outdated socio-political realities. When we look to make ethical decisions in a liberal Jewish context we do so with an *a priori* conviction that men and women are equal.

Humanism, rationalism, voluntarism, and egalitarianism are the underpinnings of liberalism. What follows, while derived from Jewish tradition, is nonetheless filtered through a secondary yet no less powerful inheritance. Having set forth our biases, let us now set about the task of uncovering the specifically Jewish assumptions about life that shape what will become the principles of ethical decision making in a liberal Jewish context.

Foundation Principles of a Liberal Jewish World View

A liberal Jewish world view (there can be no such thing as *the* liberal Jewish world view) stands upon three things: unity, diversity, and creativity.

Unity

Reality is inherently singular. Things as they are in and of themselves partake of an organic unity, a greater unity which Judaism calls God, where part and whole are seen to be mutually interdependent. Much like an ocean supporting a multitude of waves, unity gives rise to a multitude of forms. And, as with waves upon the ocean, these forms are inherently void of absolute independence. They cannot exist outside the organistic unity of whole and part. This notion of unity is stated directly in Judaism's core liturgical teaching, the *Shema:* "Hear, O'Israel, the Lord our God, the Lord is One."

> The proper intention with which to recite the word 'One' of the Shema is that there exists nothing in the entire world except God, whose 'glory fills all the world.' The main intent is that man make himself into absolute nothing. There shall be nothing of him but his soul, which is 'a part of God above.' Thus there is nothing in the world but God who is One. This is where one's thoughts should be turned while saying 'One'.... [6]

The ideas expressed here by Shneur Zalman, the founder of the HaBaD school of Hasidism, are expanded upon in his commentary of Deuteronomy 4:39, "Know this day and set it upon your heart that the Lord is God in heaven above and on the earth beneath; there is none else."

> Now behold, after these truths, that anyone who carefully considers the matter [will realize] that every created and existing thing should really be considered as nought when compared with the power of the maker and the breath of His mouth in the creature, always giving it being and bringing it forth from nothingness. All these things appear to us to be extant and real only because we cannot conceive or see with the eyes of the flesh the power of God in his creatures or the breath of His mouth in them. But if permission were given the eye to see and conceive, the physical aspect of creatures and their substance would not be seen by us at all. They are completely unreal in the light of the life-flow and spirit within them. Without this spiritual essence they would be as nothing, quite as they were before the six days of creation. And the spirit flowing into them out of the mouth of God alone takes them constantly out of nothingness and non-being, causing existence. Therefore it is said: "There is nothing without Him" (Isa 45:6)-literally. [7]

Diversity

Diversity is Judaism's way of honoring the parts even as it affirms the whole. While it is true that from the vantage point of God the diversity of forms gives way to a greater unity, it is equally true from the human perspective that this greater unity is meaningfully encountered only through the multiplicity of its parts. Judaism values both part and whole, seeing each interlaced with the other. We cannot have meaningful interaction without diversity, but we cannot have morally responsible interaction without a sense of underlying unity.

All moral responsibility involves two referents, a self and an other, and thus accentuates the bipolar character of the human person. On the one hand, it stresses the individuality, the selfhood, the separateness of the human person; and on the other, it negates emphatically any possible encapsulation of such individuality. Instead it emphasizes the role of interaction with other persons as integral to being oneself a person. The role of selfhood is the aspect of personal interdependence.... The proper discharge of moral responsibility consists in arriving at a *modus vivendi* between the self and the not-self ... The function of moral responsibility seems thus to be to have man achieve in his own being an equilibrium between selfhood and otherhood. The actual nature of every single thing, from the electron to the stars in their courses, seems to be its endeavor to persevere in its polarity of individuation and interaction. That is true of the entire universe from the minutest particle to the measureless galaxies.[8]

Creativity

Creativity is the notion that life is not fixed. Novelty, renewal, uncertainty, and change are integral to the scheme of things. As Alfred North Whitehead wrote, "Both God and the world are in the grip of the ultimate physical ground, the creative advance into novelty. Either of them, God and the world, is the instrument of novelty for the other."[9]

The moral implication of the traditional teaching that God created the world is that creativity, or the continuous emergence of aspects of life not prepared for or determined by the past, constitutes the most divine phase of reality. A modern equivalent of the notion of creativity, which tradition regarded as the very essence of Godhood, would be the concept of the latent and potential elements in the universe as making for the increase in the quantity and quality of life. Since a spiritual conception of life is consistent with a world outlook which counts on the realization of much that is still in the womb of possibility, it implies the belief that both man and the universe are ever in a state of being created ...

The belief in God as creator, or its modern equivalent, the conception of the creative urge as the element of Godhood in the world, is needed to fortify the yearning for spiritual self-regeneration ... There can hardly be a more important function for religion than to keep alive this yearning for self-renewal and to press it into the service of human progress. In doing that, religion will combat the recurrent pessimism to which we yield whenever we misjudge the character of evil in the world. It will teach us to live without illusion and without despair about the future, with clear recognition of the reality of evil and creative faith in the possibility of the good.[10]

The implications of creativity for ethics and ethical decision making are far-reaching. If the universe is so constructed as to give rise to novelty, then any fixed notion of right and wrong is, by definition and natural design, ultimately doomed to failure. It is here that fundamental differences between liberal and traditional systems of thought emerge. Traditional Judaism holds that God, creation, and morality are fixed entities, while liberal Judaism sees all three of these open to evolutionary change. This is not to suggest that liberalism rejects the past out of hand:

> Ethical principles require the sanction of history not only to counteract the dogmatism they would otherwise possess, but also to show that they are in line with tendencies inherent in the very nature of man, and in keeping with that character of the world that expresses itself as the power that makes for righteousness;

but that liberalism roots itself firmly in the reality of universal novelty.

> The very notion of finished and rounded-out systems of ethics is wrong. The abstractness and the banality common to ethical systems may be traced to the fact that no two situations are alike, and the only way of knowing right and wrong in each situation is to determine the ethics of it afresh in the light of all the known facts that enter into it. The knowledge of a number of generalizations of past experience cannot make ethics alive and pertinent; a vital ethics must be a process of individual or group reflection and study carried on throughout life.[11]

Having spent some time exploring the general underpinnings of both liberalism and liberal Judaism, we not turn our attention to our presuppositions about humankind.

"What is Man that You are mindful of him?"

When we search for a clear Jewish doctrine of man we are confronted with a wealth of often contradictory material:

"Man has no preeminence above the beast, for all is vanity" (Eccles. 3:20);

"The ideal of man is to be a revelation himself: clearly recognize himself as a manifestation of God" (Baal Shem Tov);

"Behold, even the moon has no brightness, and the stars are not pure in His sight; how much less man, that is a worm, and the son of man, that is a maggot!"(Job 25:5);

"Man, a miniature world, in whom there is the completion of the cosmic order, and its beauty, glory and perfection" (Bahya, *Hobot Ha Levavot,* 1040, 2.4);

"Man, born of woman, is of few days and full of trouble" (Job 14:1);

"Let man ever bear in mind that the Holy One dwells in him" (Eleazar b. Pedat, *Talmud,* Taanit, 11b);

"A man should always carry with him two purses, so that he may reach into the one or the other according to his needs: one purse shall contain the phrase 'I am but dust and ashes,' and another shall contain the phrase 'For my sake was the world created'" (Rabbi Mendal of Kotzk).

The individual is both all and nothing, good and evil, earthly and divine, and it is out of the tension of these polarities that the unique position and possibility of humankind is derived. The quintessential example of this can be found in the Genesis tale of the creation of humanity, "Let us make man in our image, after our likeness. They shall rule the fish of the sea, the birds of the sky, the cattle, the whole earth and all the creeping things that creep on earth. And God created man in His image; in the image of God He created him; male and female He created them" (Gen. 1:26–27). There is much in this short passage that merits detailed commentary, but for our purposes we are interested only in the implications of being created in the image of God.

Rashi, the eleventh century Jewish commentator, explains that God's use of the plural in the sentence "Let us make man" points to God's humility; God consults the angels even though this might lead the reader to erroneously believe that they somehow had a hand in creation. "Scripture thereby informs us that the greater should always consult and receive permission from the lesser" (Rashi on Gen. 1:26). Other commentators note that the word God in Hebrew, *elohim,* is itself plural and therefore the use of the plural in "let us make" is simply a parallel construction. In both cases the attempt is made to explain away any dualism. Yet it is the very dualistic nature of the human being (understood as polarity, i.e., opposites linked in a greater unity) that the author of this passage is trying to teach.

When the writer has God speak in the plural he is not referring to angels, which are nowhere mentioned, but to the rest of creation. "Let us make man in our image" means that man is both Creator and Creation, containing attributes both earthly and divine. Our

physicality ties us forever to creation making the ethical arena a
this-worldly one; our creativity lifts us toward divinity allowing us
to step outside the givens of life and tap the realm of possibility that
we might be agents of novelty and progress in the world. Indeed,
in the Jewish scheme of things, it is the task of humanity to raise
the world with all its creatureliness to the realm of divinity by acting in ways both ethical and just. Paradoxically enough, there are
two sources for this insight in the Bible: God and the Serpent.

The latter tells us through Eve that it is the destiny of humanity
"to be as Gods, knowing good and evil" (Gen. 3:5); the former
supports the claim ("You are gods and all of you sons of the most
high" (Ps. 82:6), and in fact carries it one step further when he says,
"Say unto all the congregation of the people of Israel, You shall be
holy; for I the Lord your God am holy" (Lev. 19:1–2). But just
what does it mean to be holy?

Kadosh, the Hebrew word for holy, suggests a fundamental "otherness." In most cases it refers to that quality of being that separates
God and humankind, yet in Leviticus it is holiness and the human
attainment of holiness that links God and humanity in a greater
unity. According to Martin Buber, *Kadosh* refers to the state of
unconditionality and freedom that is God's nature and humanity's
goal. Being created in the image of God means having implanted
within us the seeds of holiness. Becoming like God in holiness
means bringing those seeds to fruition through deeds based on ethical decisions in this world. In other words, the goal of life is to
become God, "and there is no other way to this goal but the way
of decision and unconditionality. . . ."[12]

> The more man realizes God in the world, the greater His reality.
> This seemingly paradoxical formulation . . . is instantly grasped
> when the words "'You are My witnesses' says the Lord" (Isa. 43:10)
> are complemented by the interpretation given them by Rabbi Simeon
> bar Yohai: "If you are my witnesses, I am the Lord, and if you are
> not my witnesses, I am not the Lord." God is man's goal; therefore
> the force of all human decision flows into the sea of divine power.
> In the same spirit, the words of the psalm, "Ascribe you strength
> unto God" (Ps. 68:34), are explained by the statement that the righ-
> teous increase the power of the upper dominion.[13]

We are dealing here with *imitatio Dei,* the imitation of God, or
better the realization of humanity's innate divinity, as the key to
Jewish ethical action, liberal, traditional, or otherwise. The prophet
Joel tells us, "And it shall come to pass that whosoever shall himself

call by the name of the Lord shall be delivered" (3:5). While written in a manner that makes the plain meaning a matter of interpretation, the rabbinic commentators moved beyond the simple implication of calling out to God for salvation and chose instead to understand the prophet as saying that whosoever calls himself Lord shall be delivered.

> But how is it possible for man to call himself Lord? Just as God is called merciful and gracious, be yourselves merciful and gracious, and give gifts to anybody without expecting a return; as God is called righteous . . . be yourselves righteous; as God is called loving, be yourselves loving.[14]

The authors of Deuteronomy enjoin us to walk in the ways of the Lord (11:22), and the authors of Exodus assist us by elaborating on His ways, "The Lord, the Lord, God merciful and gracious, long suffering and abundant in goodness and truth; keeping mercy until the thousandth generation, forgiving iniquity and transgression and sin and He clears away sin . . . " (*Exod.* 34:6). The radical humanism of the rabbis is nowhere more evident than in this notion of divine likeness and *imitatio Dei,* for, as Hermann Cohen has noted, the qualities of God are here transformed into norms for human behavior!

We are, each one of us, a blend of the conditioned and the unconditioned, the earthly and the divine. We are, each one of us, evolving from conditionality toward unconditionality and holiness. And those actions that effect the transformation of conditionality into unconditionality, those decisions for holiness that present themselves to us daily, are the fundamental challenges of a religious life conceived as *imitatio Dei.*

> The act that Judaism has always considered the essence and foundation of all religiosity is the act of decision as realization of divine freedom and unconditionality on earth. The late-Jewish saying, "The world was created for the sake of the choice of him who chooses," is only the mature formulation of an idea that, though still unformulated, already existed and was basic in biblical times. Just as the sequence of Sinaitic laws opens with the call to an exclusive and unconditional decision for the One, so do Moses' great words serve to support the same demand: "You shall be whole-hearted with the Lord your God" (Deut. 18:13) and "You shall serve the Lord your God with all your heart and with all your soul" (Deut. 11:13) . . . The Mishna interprets [this] to mean: with both your inclinations, the "good" as well as the "evil"; that is with and by your decision,

so that the ardor of passion is converted and enters into the unified deed with all its strength. For no inclination is evil in itself; it is made evil by man when he surrenders to it instead of controlling it.[15]

Here we have the ideas of unity and diversity played out in the creative decision-making power of the human individual. Our perceived nature is dualistic, containing inclinations for "good" and "evil," yet this perceived dualism is in fact a unity of polarities that, when taken together, give rise to a greater harmony: the divine holiness of God. "Only when you are undivided," say the rabbis, "will you have a share in the Lord your God" (*Sifre* on Deut. 33:5). Only when you unite the polarities of your earthly nature with the divine power of decision making will you enter into that state of holiness that we are called to achieve.

Inertia and indecisiveness are called the root of all evil . . . The man who has fallen prey to it but later, by a wrenching decision, extricates himself from it; who has sunk into the abyss of duality but later hews his way out of it to unity; and who, taking himself into his own hands, like an inert earthen clod, kneads that self into a human being—that man above all is dearest to God. Or, in the words of the Talmud: "Even the perfectly righteous may not stand in the place where those who have returned [from duality to unity, from indecisiveness to decision making] are standing." The great decision is the supreme moment in the life of man, indeed, in the life of the entire world. "One hour of return in this world," it is stated it the Sayings of the Fathers, "is better than the entire life in the world to come." For the latter is merely being, whereas the former is the great becoming. Sin means to live not in freedom, that is decision making, but in bondage, that is, being acted upon, conditioned. The man who "returns" rises to freedom; he rises from conditionality into unconditionality; he is, as the Zohar calls it, "alive all around, at one with the tree of life."[16]

Being "alive all around" is the goal; deciding for holiness is the means to reach that goal. The power to decide, to unify seeming opposites into polarities of a great unity, to imitate God, these are absolute and fundamental to a liberal Jewish ethos. Where traditional religion may see obedience to the word of God as espoused by his ordained spokespeople to be the highest state of ethical attainment, liberal Judaism sees God as the Unconditioned and obedience to God as the ongoing struggle to liberate ourselves from the conditioned responses often demanded by those spokespeople. But unconditionality and freedom of decision does not mean, and should not be mistaken for, simple rebellion against norms and

precedents. Disobedience takes God's *word* as its starting point
and then rebels against it. Unconditionality takes God's *world* as its
starting point and embraces it.

The freedom to choose is real only in this world of choices. We
may well choose the path of precedent, but not because it is precedent. Our choices, whether imitative or innovative, are based on
our existential situation in the world as we perceive it. We and we
alone are the arbiters of our fate, and even God as authority must
give way before us if true holiness is to be attained.

> On that day Rabbi Eliezer brought forward all of the arguments
> in the world [in favor of his position on a certain matter of ritual
> cleanliness], but they [his colleagues] did not accept them from him.
>
> He said to them: "If the law agrees with me, let this carob-tree
> prove it." The carob-tree leaped a hundred cubits from its place in
> the garden. The sages replied: "No proof can be brought from a
> carob-tree."
>
> He said to them: "If the law agrees with me, let this stream of
> water prove it." The stream of water began to flow backwards. The
> sages replied: "No proof can be brought from a stream of water."
>
> Again he said to them: "If the law agrees with me, let the walls of
> this schoolhouse prove it." The walls began to shake and incline to
> fall. Rabbi Joshua leaped up and rebuked the walls saying: "When
> disciples of sages engage in legal dispute what is your relevance?" In
> honor of Rabbi Joshua the walls did not tumble. In honor of Rabbi
> Eliezer they did not right themselves, and are still inclined even to
> this day.
>
> Again Rabbi Eliezer said to the sages: "If the law agrees with me,
> let it be proved from Heaven." A divine voice came forth and said:
> "Why do you dispute with Rabbi Eliezer, for in all matters the law
> agrees with him!"
>
> But Rabbi Joshua rose to his feet again and exclaimed: "It is not
> in heaven" [Deut. 30:12; implying that the divine law is now in
> human hands and open to human interpretation regardless of God's
> position].
>
> Some time later, Rabbi Nathan met the prophet Elijah and asked
> him: "What did the Holy One, blessed be He, do when rebuked by
> Rabbi Joshua?"
>
> Elijah replied: "He laughed with joy saying 'My children have
> defeated me, my children have defeated me.'" [17]

Here we have a far more radical situation than simple rebellion
against authority; here we have the defeat of God. And his defeat
is pleasing to him! The very nature of Creation and the creative
process as enacted by God in Genesis demands that we become as

God and take up the awesome responsibility that unconditionality and decision making demand of us.

> In the unconditionality of his deed man experiences his communion with God. God is the unknown Being beyond this world only for the indolent, the decisionless, the lethargic, the man enmeshed in his own designs; for the one who chooses, who decides, who is aflame with his goal, who is unconditioned, God is the closest, the most familiar Being, whom man, through his own action, realizes ever anew, experiencing thereby the mystery of mysteries. Whether God is "transcendent" or "immanent" does not depend upon Him; it depends upon man . . . "The Lord is close to all that call upon Him, to all that call upon Him in truth" (Psalm 145:18). That means, in the truth they *do*.
> In the truth they do. This truth is not a What but a How. Not the matter of a deed determines its truth but the manner in which it is carried out: in human conditionality, or in divine unconditionality. . . . Every deed, even one numbered among the most profane, is holy when it is performed in holiness, in unconditionality.[18]

Unconditionality is the "specific religious content of Judaism,"[19] but it is often lost beneath the weight of tradition that comes to replace lived experience and freedom of choice with conditioned responses and formulaic beliefs. Liberal Judaism seeks to return to the unconditional and to rekindle the urge to unite with it. Liberal Judaism, while respecting the past, seeks to free itself from the past that Judaism might regain the power of decision making that is our divine right. Traditional Judaism seeks a return to religion, to tradition; liberal Judaism seeks to return to religiosity, i.e. the ardent desire for unconditionality lived out in the everyday decisions and struggles of ordinary human beings.

> Religiosity is . . . man's urge to establish a living communion with the unconditioned; it is man's will to realize the unconditioned through his deed, and to establish it in his world . . . Genuine religiosity is doing. It wants to sculpt the unconditioned out of the matter of this world. The countenance of the God reposes, invisible, in an earthen block; it must be wrought, carved, out of it. To engage in this work means to be religious—nothing else.[20]

To engage in this work, in the work of carving out and revealing the countenance of divine unconditionality inherent in life and the choices life presents to us; in the work of bringing God into the world by deciding for holiness, is to engage in the work of ethical decision making. And it is to this work that we now turn.

Liberal Jewish Approaches to Ethical Issues

As we set about articulating possible liberal responses to concrete ethical concerns, it is well to keep in mind the three central principles of a liberal Jewish ethic. The first principle is that human life is an end in and of itself, "One who saves a life saves an entire world, one who takes a life destroys an entire world" (*Talmud*, Sanhedrin). The second principle is that all things are interdependent, part of each other and of a greater whole, "If I am I simply because I am I, and you are you simply because you are you, then I am I and you are you. But, if I am I because you are you, and you are you because I am I, then I am not simply I and you are not simply you" (Reb Mendel of Kotsk). The third principle is holiness and *imitatio Dei*, making the attributes of God into norms for human behavior, "If you sanctify yourself it is as if you sanctify Me" (*Sifre*, Kedoshim 1, 86b). These three principles together will inform our approach to each of the six ethical issues we have been asked to address.

Sex: A Matter of Covenants

In a world where the roles of woman/wife/mother/lover and man/husband/father/lover are open to both anxious questioning and dramatic experimentation; in a world where marriage is no longer the sole arena for sexual intimacy or child rearing; in a world where marriage is no longer the necessary outcome of a long-term relationship but is simply one alternative among others for the achieving of human intimacy; in such a world we must find a higher moral standard with which to challenge people's sexual ethics toward holiness than the now sociologically "deviant" two-parent family. This standard must broaden the limits of acceptable unions and at the same time hold out the promise of holiness as shared intimacy between self and other. Such a standard is suggested by the Jewish idea of sexual union as *yadah*: "knowing" self and other in the deepest and most intimate sense.

> When are people called whole? When they are male and female together. Hence, they should have a single inclination at the hour of their union. There should be joy and play in their joining, for so joined they become one body, one soul, one mind. From this we know that a person who is not convenanted is not whole. But when male and female are joined, God abides upon their oneness and endows it with a holy spirit.[21]

At the moment of sexual union, at the moment when the divine manifests itself in the merger of male and female both as external sexual beings and internal psychological states (i.e. masculine and feminine), at that moment *yadah* is realized. *Yadah* is the knowing of another as oneself, and of oneself as part of the other and the All. The nurturing of such knowledge, the arrival at a single inclination shared fully and simultaneously by two people, cannot happen without much preparation. *Yadah* requires lovers to be of one mind as well as of one body, and such intimacy is not easily achieved. It takes much time and effort outside the confines of an explicitly sexual union.

One cannot, therefore, expect *yadah* to occur outside a covenantal relationship, for it is only a relationship based on covenant (Hebrew: *brit*) that demands the time and encourages the risks that are necessary for *yadah*. Casual sex is by definition sex without *brit*, without commitment. Casual sex by its very nature is a relationship without the intention or possibility of attaining *yadah*. While this places casual sex in an ethically grey area (is the casual sex partner a means or an end?), it opens the door to ethically sound and spiritually sensitive relationships that for one reason or another do not find their consummation in traditional marriage.

In other words, to take but one category of ethical concern, living together outside the bonds of matrimony need not preclude the establishment of *brit*, the attainment of *yadah*, or the possibility of holiness. And, if *brit*, *yadah*, and holiness are the intended goals of the relationship, then the relationship may have as much of a claim to ethical legitimacy as one that is legally sanctioned.

Yacov Emden (1697–1776), a noted rabbi, mystic, and social critic, in commenting on Deuteronomy 23:18, "There shall not be a harlot among the daughters of Israel," stated that there may be conditions under which it is permissible to have sexual relations outside of matrimony. Rabbi Emden sets forth four criteria for such a relationship:

1. the woman must follow the laws pertaining to menstruation;
2. the relationship must be monogamous for as long as it exists;
3. the relationship must be public and involve cohabitation; and
4. a rabbi must be consulted in each case.

Rabbi Emden even goes so far as to say that the teaching of nonmarital cohabitation is a *mitzvah*, a divine commandment, since it offers a way of sanctifying relationships that will occur in any case. This inclusivity is a hallmark of a liberal Jewish ethic: accepting the social facts of life and seeking to challenge them to higher levels of holiness and responsibility.

Rabbi Emden's requirements offer us a guideline for a liberal sexual ethic for couples choosing to live together outside of wedlock. The first requirement, taking for granted an acceptance of Jewish ritual purity on the part of the woman, implies that we are dealing with responsible human beings: the keeping of the laws of purity was, in Rabbi Emden's time, a sign of conscious devotion to the ideal of holiness.

The second requirement, monogamy, takes us deeper into the relationship's potential for *yadah*. The psychological and spiritual intimacy demanded by *yadah* strongly suggests that lovers restrict their sexual activity to themselves alone. While not condemning out of hand non-monogamous unions, a liberal Jewish sexual ethic would question the ability of such relationships to achieve *yadah*, the highest level of human encounter. Monogamy, however, must be understood in a deeper sense than simple physical constancy. To achieve *yadah* one's heart and soul must be turned toward one's lover; this union of self and other on the psycho-spiritual level is the true essence of monogamy as the singular commitment of lovers to the quest for knowing.

Public cohabitation, Rabbi Emden's third requirement, is directly related to the idea of *brit*. The fact that one chooses to live with another human being is itself covenantal. Doing so openly suggests a communal sanction (*de facto* if not *de jure*) that furthers the *brit* between the lovers and between them and their community. A liberal Jewish sex ethic would urge the couple to enter into a written, albeit extralegal, covenant (a *ketuba*) that commits one to the other and sets forth the ground rules for their life together.

The very public nature of this union leads to the involvement of a rabbi. Ideally, the liberal rabbi would be able to help the couple explore the implications of living together and help them establish a *brit* that would bind them body and soul in the quest for human intimacy and *yadah*.

Who would seek out such a covenant? Elderly singles who cannot afford the financial loss a change in marital status would bring *vis-à-vis* their Social Security, to name one; homosexuals legally blocked from matrimony, to name another. A liberal Jewish ethic committed to holiness and human intimacy can have tremendous relevance to people in search of true union, helping the legally disenfranchised gain the moral courage and confidence to pursue their commitment to each other and to *yadah*.

Liberation Movements

As with the other ethical concerns addressed in this essay, liberation movements present us with a large and unwieldly field of reference. The mere proclaiming of one's group as a liberation movement does not guarantee one moral legitimacy. Still, given the three principles of a liberal Jewish ethic we can devise a guideline for judging such movements.

The goal of any liberation movement is autonomy and self-determination for those it seeks to liberate. Whether we are talking about Palestinians, Gays, Women, Blacks, Zionists, or White Supremacists we are talking about people seeking some sense of autonomy. The question a liberal Jew must ask is: How is the liberation being undertaken and to what ends will autonomy be used?

From the liberal Jewish perspective a liberation movement must promote, in word and deed, the following three objectives: universal human dignity, universal human autonomy, and universal human community. In other words, the consequences of freeing the constituency of any given liberation movement must enhance the greater freedom and self-determination of humankind. To the extent that it does so a liberation movement can be considered ethical.

Economic Order

In dealing with questions of economic order we must deal with both the abstract principles and the concrete facts of historical experience. The former suggests that there is a criterion for judging the ethical claims of various economic systems, the latter shows just how those systems operate when it comes to furthering human dignity, freedom, and holiness.

We begin with the notion of the "work ethic." From earliest times Jews have valued labor as essential to human dignity since it is through labor that one attains self-sufficiency and autonomy. Even study, the highest of Jewish occupations, must be coupled with more mundane labors, if it is to bear fruit.

> Splendid is the study of Torah when combined with some worldly occupation, for toil in them both puts sin out of mind. But study of Torah that is not combined with work falls into neglect in the end, and becomes the cause of sin (Pirke Avot, 2:2).

Given this positive attitude towards work, it is not surprising to find Judaism addressing the obligations of both workers and employers for the upholding of the dignity of both self and other.

You shall not abuse a needy and destitute laborer, whether a fellow
countryman or a non-citizen in your community. You must pay him
his wages on the same day, before the sun sets, for he is needy and
urgently depends on it; else he will cry to the Lord against you and
you will incur guilt (Deut. 24:14–15).

Whoever withholds an employee's wages, it is as though he has
taken the person's life from him (Talmud, Bava Metzia, 112a).

If a person hires workmen and asks them to work in the early morning or late eveining, at a place where it is not the local custom to
work early or late at night, he cannot force them to do so. Where it
is the custom to provide food for workmen, he must do so. If it is
customary to give them dessert, he must do so—it all depends on
local custom (Mishnah, Bava Metzia, 7:1).

Just as the employer is enjoined not to deprive the poor worker of
his wages or withhold it from him when it is due, so is the worker
enjoined not to deprive the employer of the benefit of his work by
idling away his time, a little here and a little there, thus wasting the
whole day deceitfully . . . Indeed, the worker must be very punctual
in the matter of time (Maimonides, *Code*, Laws Concerning Hiring,
13:7).

If a laborer began to work and then changed his mind, he may stop
work [this was understood to mean quit or strike]—even if it is in
the middle of the day, for it is said: "For it is to Me that the Israelites
are servants; they are My servants" (Lev. 25:5). They are God's servants and not servants unto servants [i.e. they do not belong to their
employer] . . . but this is applicable only when no irreparable loss is
incurred. In a situation where irreparable loss may be incurred, the
worker is not permitted to change his mind. [This ruling is used to
support the right to strike among most workers, while forbidding
strikes among those such as police officers, fire fighters, etc., who
provide essential services.] (Maimonides, *Code*, 9:4).

To round out this brief survey of ethical attitudes toward work
and dignity in the marketplace we must deal with the issue of honesty. The Torah is very clear on this matter:

You shall not have in your pouch alternative weights, larger and
smaller. You shall not have in your house alternative weights, larger
and smaller. You must have completely honest weights and completely honest measures if you are to endure long on the soil that the
Lord your God is giving you. For everyone who does those things,
everyone who deals dishonestly, is abhorrent to the Lord your God
(Deut. 25:13–16).

The Jewish concern with honesty in business is summed up neatly in the following quotation:

It is evidently proper for a man to praise his wares or, by reason of persuasion, to earn for his labor as much as he can. We say of such a man that he is ambitious and will succeed . . . But unless he is very careful to weigh his actions, the outcome is bound to be evil instead of good . . . But, you will say, how in the course of bargaining can we avoid trying to convince our neighbor that the article we want to sell is worth the price we are asking? There is an unmistakable distinction between fraudulent and honest persuasion. It is perfectly proper to point out to the buyer any good quality which the thing for sale really possesses. Fraud consists of hiding the defects in one's wares. . . . (Moses Hayyim Luzato, *The Path of the Upright*)

From these few citations it should be clear that Judaism is intimately concerned with the well-being of workers and employers, sellers and consumers. The economic justice demanded by Jewish law and tradition encompasses all brands of Judaism and one would be hard pressed to find a specifically liberal Jewish ethic at odds with the themes expressed in the traditional material. Of greater interest now, however, is the question: "Which economic system is most compatible with this ethic?"

In answering this question from the Jewish perspective one need only look to Jewish history. Taking the Jew as our test case for measuring an economic system's commitment to human freedom and dignity, we need ask: Under which economic systems did the Jews achieve emancipation? Only capitalism emancipated the Jews.

Although the ideas of individual freedom and equality spread as ideas throughout Europe from the very moment they were born in the great capitalist revolutions of the seventeenth and eighteenth centuries, they had concrete liberating effects only after the penetration of capitalism. . . . Where capitalism triumphed, Jews received emancipation with little or no prodding from themselves; but where capitalism made little headway, no amount of appeal to the ideal realm yielded results.[22]

While presenting itself as an economic system, capitalism carries with it a set of ideas that go far beyond the sphere of economics. Capitalism, (and here we are dealing exclusively with developmental capitalism) tends to favor individual autonomy and dignity, the free exercise of reason and intellectual curiosity, the adaptation of scientific knowledge to the practical world via technological innovation, freedom from and freedom of religion, and human creativ-

ity. Capitalism embodies the very values that make up the principles of a liberal Jewish ethic. But capitalism does not operate in a
vacuum, and the reality of racism or anti-Semitism can often bring
about a weakening of developmental capitalism's liberating potential. Nevertheless, this does not negate the fact that to the extent
that developmental capitalism (capitalism based on the inalienable
rights of individuals to freedom and dignity) becomes the dominant
economic system of the land, to that extent people enjoy liberation
and individual autonomy.

Developmental capitalism, driven as it is by the entrepreneurial
spirit and the need to make profits, creates a state of permanent revolution, a state in which all givens are open to challenge in order
to produce the "better mousetrap." Entrepreneurial capitalism is
rooted in the inalienable right of the individual to pursue, as John
Locke put it, life, liberty, and property.

> To develop the capitalist spirit of enterprise, a climate of total indi-
> vidual freedom must be created, even for those who do not choose
> to be entrepreneurs. Since entrepreneurial talent is not necessarily
> inherited, the ideal capitalist society must foster fresh entrepreneurial
> talent. To allow freedom to some and not to others threatens to
> choke off the very breath of capitalism, entrepreneurship.[23]

Given all the vagaries of history and the political climates within
which capitalism is forced to work, it can still be demonstrated that
only in countries where capitalism and capitalist ideals of freedom
and individual autonomy took hold did Jews begin to receive some
measure of emancipation; and the extent of that emancipation is
directly tied to the degree to which the ideals of capitalism were
allowed to flourish. There is not one instance of Jewish liberation
in any precapitalist environment.

This is not to say, however, that Jews embraced capitalism themselves. Indeed, the capitalist spirit of individual autonomy and freedom is not compatible with the closed nature of traditional Judaism. While home to a variety of theological formulations,
premodern Judaism was a severely bounded world view not open
to the radical humanism and voluntarism that capitalism demands.
The Jew's embrace of developmental capitalism was most often at
the expense of traditionalism, thus giving birth to liberal Judaisms
more at home with the capitalist ideals of individual freedom and
autonomy.

Like traditional Judaism, and unlike capitalism, Marxism is a
closed system of belief based on the exegesis of the written word

rather than an open system of intellectual entrepreneurship. For this reason, Marxism cannot meet the demands of liberalism.

Marxism grew out of the crash of the capitalist ideal on the rocks of nation-state imperialism. To achieve the entrepreneurial ideal capitalism must restructure societies for freedom. Old ruling classes must be challenged, traditional hierarchies must be dismantled, impediments to individual growth and autonomy must be removed. Unfortunately, nation-state capitalism opted for another route and set about exploiting colonial peoples. This left the Communists with the cry for revolution and human dignity. Suddenly they and not the capitalists were the champions of freedom.

In practice, however, the freedom promised by Marxist ideals is a hollow one. Marxism is not rooted in the inalienable rights of individuals, but rather in the inalienable rights of class. It is class and not the individual that provides the primary category for Marxist values and analysis. No status is assigned to an individual outside class needs and concerns. There is no *a priori* commitment to intellectual freedom: reality is found in the works of Marx and Engels, and any challenge to those works is by definition irrational. Communism is, like traditional Judaism, a closed system of belief. What is possible is what is already known. Novelty, change, and creativity are severely limited since reality is the function of exegesis and not open-ended entrepreneurial investigation.

Marxism, while taking over the cry for liberation, is internally incapable of fostering liberation. Capitalism, with all its compromise and abuses, is still the only system internally geared to the perpetual revolution of the human spirit.

Since it is the revolution of the spirit and the dignity of the individual that lie at the heart of any liberal Jewish ethic, it is only common sense to believe that of all known economic systems, capitalism, not nation-state exploitative capitalism, but global, developmental capitalism, holds out the promise of an ethically just world.

Violence and War: In Search of the Fourth Side

Forced by limits of space and practicality to seek the heart of the matter, we shall confine our consideration to the moral status of global nuclear conflict. Since the fundamental principle upon which our ethics is based is the sacredness of individual human life, it will be that principle that shall guide our discussion.

When you take the field against your enemies . . . then the officers shall address the troops as follows: "Is there anyone who has built a new house but has not dedicated it? Let him go back to his home, lest he die in battle and another dedicate it. Is there anyone who has planted a vineyard but has never harvested it? Let him go back to his home, lest he die in battle and another harvest it. Is there anyone who has paid the bride-price for a wife [i.e. become engaged] but who has not yet married her? Let him go back to his home, lest he die in battle and another marry her." The officers shall continue to address the troops saying: "Is there anyone who is afraid and disheartened? Let him go back to his home, lest the courage of his comrades flag like his." When the officers have finished addressing the troops, then army commanders shall assume command of the troops (Deut. 20:1–9).

The humanity of this doctrine of war is startling. Can we imagine a modern day commander addressing his troops in such a manner? Can we imagine a draft law as liberal as that suggested in Deuteronomy ever passing Congress and being signed into law? And yet, while recognizing conditions of national emergency that might force all people to take part in battle regardless of these exemptions, the sages of the Talmud actually expanded the Bible's list of exemptions and excused those listed above from working even in noncombatant positions.[24]

Here is a humanism of unprecedented clarity. Given the nature of nuclear conflict, however, we can no longer make the neat distinctions between soldier and civilian. While not all people are combatants in a nuclear exchange, all people are potential targets. Is it possible to follow the ethical mandate of Judaism in this situation?

A similiar question is raised when we take up the ethics of laying seige.

When siege is laid to a city for the purpose of capture, it may not be surrounded on all four sides but only on three in order to give an opportunity for escape to those who would flee to save their lives. . . .[25]

Given the nature of global nuclear war where is the fourth side?

It is forbidden to cut down fruit-bearing trees outside a (besieged) city, nor may a water channel be deflected from them so that they wither.[26]

Not only one who cuts down fruit trees, but also one who smashes household goods, tears clothes, demolishes a building, stops up a spring, or destroys articles of food with destructive intent, transgresses the command "Thou shalt not destroy."[27]

Certainly the destructive intent of nuclear war put it in the category of transgressing the law against wanton destruction. And yet the rabbis go even farther, looking beyond the intent to which a weapon is employed to the very nature of weapons themselves.

> It is forbidden to sell to idolators any weapons of war. Neither may one sharpen their weapons nor make available to them knives, chains, barbed chains, bears, lions, or anything that might cause widespread injury. One may sell them shields or shutters which are purely defensive.[28]

> That which is forbidden for sale to idolators is also prohibited for sale to Jews who are suspected of then selling such materials to idolators. Likewise, it is forbidden to sell such weapons to Jewish brigands.[29]

It is important to realize at the outset that the prohibition against selling weapons or other means of destruction to non-Jews and Jewish brigands presupposes the actual socio-political status of the Jewish people of the time. Jews were politically disenfranchised and militarily impotent. The only Jews Maimonides could imagine who would have any use for weapons would be Jewish outlaws. Thus the ban on weapons sales to Gentiles and outlaws was a practical ban on their sale altogether. In addition, we should note that the items banned are not simply weapons, but other items which have the potential to cause widespread destruction even if they are not actually purchased with that intent in mind. If such a ban is valid for lions and bears, how much the more so for plutonium and nuclear hardware?

Following up on the notion of injury to the many, we discover in rabbinical literature a tremendous concern for the rights of both combatants and noncombatants. In commenting on the biblical tale of Jacob and Esau the rabbis paid special attention to Jacob's consternation at the possibility of having to kill his brother: "Then Jacob was greatly afraid and distressed" (Gen. 32:8).

> Yet one might argue that Jacob surely should have no qualms about killing Esau, for it states explicitly, "If one comes to slay you, forestall it by slaying him" (*Talmud,* Sanhedrin 72a). Nonetheless, Jacob did indeed have qualms, fearing that in the fray he might kill some of Esau's men, who were not intent on killing Jacob but merely fighting against Jacob's men. And even though Esau's men were pur-

suing Jacob's men, and every person has the right to save the life of
the pursued at the cost of the life of the pursuer, nonetheless there is
the law that states "if the pursued could have been saved by maiming
a limb of the pursuer, but instead the rescuer killed the pursuer the
rescuer is liable to capital punishment on that account."

Hence Jacob feared lest he might instead have restrained them by
merely inflicting injury upon their limbs.[30]

The rabbis are concerned here with the use of appropriate force
even in the heat of battle! The rabbis also read their concern for
human life into the story of Abram's participation in the War of
the Kings (Gen. 14). God calls out to Abram saying "Fear not,
Abram ... " (Gen. 15:1). Why was Abram afraid? "Abram was
filled with misgiving, thinking to himself, Maybe there was a righteous or God-fearing man among those troops which I slew. . . . "[31]

From these passages one cannot help but note the overriding concern of Jewish ethics for individual human life. This concern is carried even further in the notion of submitting oneself to defeat at
the hands of an enemy if the alternative to such defeat is one's own
death.

A major source in the Torah for the law of self-defense is the provision exonerating from guilt a potential victim of robbery with possible violence if in self-defense he struck down and, if necessary, even
killed the attacker before he committed any crime (Exod. 22:1).
Hence, in the words of the rabbis, "if a man comes to slay you, forestall it by slaying him" (Talmud, Sanhedrin 72a). Now this law confers the right of self-defense only if the victim will thereby forestall
the anticipated attack and save his own life at the expense of the
aggressor's. But the defender would certainly not be entitled to frus-
trate the attack if this could be done only at the cost of both lives;
for instance, by blowing up the house in which he and the robber
encounter each other. Presumably the victim would then have to
submit to the robbery and even to death by violence at the hands of
the attacker rather than take preventive action which would cause
two deaths. In view of this vital limitation of the law of self-defense,
it would appear that a defensive war likely to endanger the survival
of the attacking and the defending nations alike, if not indeed the
entire human race, can never be justified. On the assumption, then,
that the choice posed by a threatened nuclear attack would be either
complete mutual destruction or surrender, only the second alternative may be morally vindicated.[32]

While liberal Jews may argue conscientiously about the moral
status of nuclear weapons as deterrents to war, they will most likely

agree that the actual use of such weapons which will, at best, result in the wanton destruction prohibited by Torah and Talmud and, at worst, escalate into mass suicide for the entire human race, is an action totally at odds with Jewish ethical behavior.

But what about this notion of surrender? Can it be, to put it in the vernacular, that a liberal Jewish ethic would be the moral equivalent of "Better Red than Dead"? Two events in the history of the Jewish people illustrate the implications of Rabbi Jacobvits' above stated position. The first is Masada, the second is Yavneh.

Located on the summit of an isolated rock on the edge of the Dead Sea Valley and the Judean Desert, Masada was King Herod's royal citadel and the last stronghold of the Jewish Zealots in their war against Rome (66-70). After a long siege, a breach was finally made in the fortress' wall and the Roman legions prepared for a final assault. Rather than be killed or taken into slavery, the Jews of Masada chose suicide over surrender. Nine hundred and sixty men, women, and children sacrificed themselves the night before the Roman attack.

During the same war Jerusalem was besieged by Vespasian, the soon-to-be-emperor of Rome. Vespasian tried to reason with the inhabitants of the city, asking for only a single bow and arrow to be delivered to him as a sign of tribute and surrender to the rule of Rome. The city's leaders refused, but a minority, led by Rabbi Yohanan ben Zakkai, believed that the Jews could not win militarily and should seek a different kind of victory.

After failing to convince Jerusalem's rulers to give in to Vespasian's request, Yohanan ben Zakkai sought to escape the city. Since it is forbidden to keep a corpse in the holy city over night, Yohanan pretended to be dead, and had his disciples smuggle him out of Jerusalem in a coffin. Having heard from his spies that Yohanan was opposed to the war with Rome, Vespasian welcomed him and offered him a boon. Yohanan asked that he and his disciples be allowed to establish a school in Yavneh and there perpetuate the teachings of Judaism.[33] Not long after, the city of Jerusalem was sacked and burned, her Temple razed and her people slaughtered or taken into captivity.

What was the victory Yohanan ben Zakkai won through surrender which the Zealots lost through dying? The future. Masada is gone. Vespasian is gone. The Roman Empire has fallen. But the houses of study, the wisdom and teachings of Torah, the prayers and values of the Jewish people that Yohanan ben Zakkai established at Yavneh, and that his disciples and their disciples carried throughout the world, live on. While on the smaller scale of individual integrity we may argue for the need to die for some causes, on the global scale of total nuclear annihilation we would opt for the wisdom of Yohanan ben Zakkai and live that we might work for the redemption of the future.

Environmental Issues

In dealing with the ethical dimension of environmental issues it is important to highlight three areas of concern. The first is ownership, the second is humility, and the third is harmony.

Judaism is quite clear as to who owns creation. "The earth is the Lord's and the fullness thereof" (Ps. 24:1). And yet it is equally clear as to whose job it is to till and tend this creation: "And the Lord God took man and placed him in the Garden of Eden to till it and to guard it" (Gen. 1:10). Humankind is God's partner in creation, a position that a second psalm makes plain: "The heavens are the heavens of the Lord but the earth He has given to the children of man" (Ps. 115:16).

The rabbis, however, were not unaware of potential conflicts over "ownership," seeing the natural tendency of people to forget the greater unity that they share with creation and begin to act as lords themselves, exploiting the earth for short-term gain while sacrificing life in the process.

Thus it was that the sages required that a blessing be said before using any of the fruits of creation.

Man is forbidden to enjoy anything without pronouncing a benediction, and whoever enjoys anything in this world without a benediction commits a trespass against sacred things [and] . . . is as guilty as if he would have derived enjoyment from the things dedicated to Heaven, for it is written, "The earth is the Lord's and the fullness thereof." Rabbi Levi raised the question: In one place it is written, "The earth is the Lord's and the fullness thereof," and in another place it is written: "The heavens are the heavens of the Lord but the earth He has given to the children of man." The answer is that the former verse applies to the status prior to man's pronouncing a blessing; the latter verse applies after one pronounces the blessing.[34]

The purpose of blessing an object before using it is twofold. First, it heightens the individual's awareness of the sacredness of creation, and second, it unites the user with the object used in a greater holiness. When pronouncing a blessing one is in effect saying: "I am not the creator of Life yet I can be creative with it; I am not the owner of Life yet I can participate fully in it." And, once the category of holiness has been brought into consciousness in such a way as to unite the person doing the blessing with the object over which the blessing is said, then "the earth is given to the children of Man," i.e., then the creation is open to the input of humankind as creative agents for now their actions will be infused with a sense of holiness.

This awareness of the sacred quality of all being leads to a sense of humility on the part of humankind. Recognizing that life is too grand to be "owned" by us, we begin to sense the awesome grace by which we exist on this planet. We may lay claim to the earth, settling her with farms and cities; we may buy and sell property as if we were its masters; but in the end, if we are to live in harmony with creation, we must recognize that living "as if" does not alter the truth of our situation. Thus the Torah prohibits the selling of land in perpetuity, since such an act implies final ownership, "And the land is not to be sold in perpetuity, for all land is Mine, because you are strangers and sojourners before Me" (Lev. 25:23).

Note that the text does not say "you are strangers and sojourners on the land"; our sojourner status comes only in relation to God, the whole of which we are a part. We are not strangers on earth, we are not alien to nature—we are nature achieving self-consciousness. But self-consciousness should not blind us to the bigger picture. By requiring blessings the sages are opening us to the awareness of our place in the scheme of things, humbling us by our responsibilities toward creation and our smallness before God. "Beloved is man for he was created in the image of God. But it was by a special love that it was made known to him that he was created in the image of God."[35]

Bioethical Issues

Bioethical issues follow directly from our discussion of environmental concerns, for serious consideration of them demands a recognition of our humility. Whether we are seeking the prolongation of life or its early termination, the preservation of an older life form or the generation of a totally new one, we are tampering with the givens of nature. How do we know if our actions are for the good? The fact is we cannot know, thus we must take great care and proceed with true caution, honoring our ignorance even as we increase our knowledge.

But we must be very careful here. Rhetoric should never be mistaken for knowledge, nor ideological purity for wisdom. What is it we truly know about life that allows us to take it or create it? Being created in the image of God means we have the power to play God. Knowing that we are in the image of God overwhelmingly reminds us that this is no game. God is our goal, *imitatio Dei* is our plan, but how, in fact, do we proceed?

Suicide, abortion, and euthanasia, whether passive or active, is the acceptance of an early termination of life. Are we putting an end to suffering? Or are we murdering hope? Does a person have the right to avoid intolerable suffering and a prolonged dying? And who is to decide when suffering is intolerable? If the individual is to decide, when must a decision be made? If a third party is to decide, how are we to know whether they act out of compassion or their own sense of frustration? If we allow abortion for reasons of quality of life, who is to define quality? The mother? The state? Who shall be the fetus' advocate and how shall they not do an injustice to the mother?

When we genetically alter a fetus for whatever reason, we are assuming an ideal human being and judging the viability of another's existence against that ideal. Who will set that ideal? What are the long term consequences of eradicating disease by genetic engineering? Once we begin to fix human beings in the womb, where will we draw the line on what is in need of fixing? Will skin color ever become a liability open to genetic makeover? Or sex? Is it too wild to imagine, given the history of female infanticide, that certain societies will take advantage of genetic engineering to assure the birth of males and the continued subjugation of females?

Admittedly these are farfetched questions. But when dealing with technologies with the potential to alter the evolutionary process we cannot fail to be farfetched. So what do we do?

First we admit our ignorance. It is one thing to be able to state unequivocally that polluting the environment is ethically untenable. It is quite another to state just as unequivocally that abortion is wrong. Or that abortion is right. There is a time for ethical equivocation. And this is it.

Our radical humanism demands that we allow individuals the freedom and autonomy to make these horribly painful decisions for themselves. Or, if they cannot do so, to choose a third party to act on their behalf through, for example, a Living Will. But this does not solve our ethical dilemma; it simply shifts the responsibility.

The fact is there cannot be a liberal solution to these kinds of bioethical problems. Admitting this is the second thing we must do.

And what is the third? The third is to allow the individual the full force of her agony in having to make a decision that for thousands of years we were lucky enough to leave in the "hands of God." We allow her the dignity of her struggle, offering neither ethical niceties nor moral judgments, but rather honest compassion and support. We respect her as a maker of decisions and help her weigh the alternatives and deal with their consequences. Whether we are talking about abortion or any other bioethical decision falling upon the shoulders of an individual, the life of one who is forced to decide takes precedence over our opinions and our pronouncements, and we must show that person the dignity and compassion that is her due as a person struggling toward holiness.

Assuredly this is not a solution to bioethical conundrums, nor is it meant to be. On the contrary, a liberal ethic must admit its own limitations, and in the areas of bioethical issues these limitations become most apparent. It is easy, for example, to declare abortion to be immoral. It is just as easy to declare it moral. But neither declaration really aids the woman struggling to make a decision that she can live with in her heart of hearts. If liberal Jewish ethics is to be true to its radical humanism, it must admit to ambiguity when such an admission is warranted, and then turn its attention to the person forced to decide and help her to know her heart that she might act in accordance with it.

The situation is slightly different when we come to the area of genetic engineering and recombinant DNA. Here we are dealing not so much with individual ethical choices as we are with societal policies that may well affect the future evolution of the race. The liberal is committed to creativity and novelty as fundamental principles of life. We cannot foreclose life options, even ones that we ourselves create. Homo sapiens may well be the vanguard of the evolutionary process, called upon to do consciously what nature has hitherto done "unconsciously," i.e. seek out the grand mutation that will become the next stage of evolutionary development. But whether or not one sees humanity as the avant-garde of evolutionary creativity, one must in all honesty admit that the implications of our actions are unknown.

We are, or should be, humbled both by our intelligence and by our ignorance. And we must honor both. It is foolish and counterproductive to think that we can turn off the human drive to know.

We cannot place areas of knowledge off limits without thereby betraying the soul of humankind. But let us not imagine that the pursuit of knowledge is the same as the pursuit of the good. Knowledge brings with it the potential to act on what is known, and in that capacity there is the possibility of danger. But note we are talking about possibilities not inevitabilities. The human person is a maker of decisions. To know does not mean we have to act on what is known. We can learn and then choose to refrain from acting on what is learned. Indeed, what is learned may motivate us to refrain from certain actions once we are aware of the possible consequences of those actions. So a liberal Jewish ethic must uphold our right to inquire while forever calling us to the task of making informed and rational decisions.

"Behold I place before you this day blessing and curse, life and death; therefore choose life." In this statement the Torah sets forth our predicament. We have before us knowledge, both good and evil, knowledge that can lead to blessing or curse, life or death. It is up to us to make the choice. We had not choice in learning, this is our nature. But how we use what we have learned is up to us. The crucial issue is how do we, with the rush of knowledge clamoring for our constant attention, carve out the time and space to begin to make the choice for life?

Let me suggest a model for doing just this. The model is the Jewish notion of the Sabbatical Year:

> Six years you sow your field, and six years shall you prune your vineyard, and gather in the produce thereof. But on the seventh year shall be Sabbath of solemn rest, a Sabbath unto the Lord, you shall neither sow your field, nor prune your vineyard.[36]

The impact of the Sabbatical Year in the context of choosing life is twofold. First, it reminds us that we are not the owners of life but its recipients. Second, it allows us time to reflect, to breathe, to consider our situation thus far that our future actions will be informed by reason and not habit, and will, as best we can surmise, lead us toward life.

It is the nature of the human being to inquire, to experiment, to explore. Our curiosity and inquisitiveness are essential to our meaningful survival as a species. The liberal need not, indeed cannot, put limits on curiosity, but we can punctuate it with reflective pauses.

The concept of the Sabbatical Year applied to genetic engineering and other bioethical issues would be as follows: For six years we shall carry out our research and struggle with the ethical immediacies of having to make often terrifying choices and awesome decisions, but on the seventh year we shall impose a moratorium, a Sabbath unto the Lord, a time for considering the holiness of creation and our place in it. Our Sabbatical year shall be set aside for serious wrestling with the moral complexities of our research and the decisions for action that we are called upon to make.

The institution of Sabbatical Year would be applicable to areas outside the biomedical sphere as well (weapons, weapons testing, to name but two). Our goal will be to see if, in our rush to do what we have given so much of our time and energy and money to doing, we are enhancing life and human dignity, or if we are simply doing because we can do and have so done in the past.

A Sabbatical Year would give us a chance to do what human beings are uniquely qualified to do: reflect, consider, reason, and renew. It might, in the long run, be the respite we need to help fashion the world we so ardently desire.

Conclusion

The principles of a liberal Jewish ethic rest on three pillars: the dignity and freedom of the human person and the humility of humankind.

The first demands of us an ethic that is radically humanistic, concerned with people as ends not means. The second envisions religion and tradition as catalysts to innovation and entrepreneurial creativity. The last calls for a new kind of religiosity, one rooted not in the word but in the deed, not in the revelation from God but in the revelation of God.

Together they require of us a love of self that extends to a love of other, and then a wisdom that sees both as part of a greater whole.

Together they evoke a sense of perspective and a heathy respect for our ignorance. We cannot know whether we pursue the holy or its shadow. We cannot know whether the good we imagine is in fact the good we need. We operate *as if* we knew and are continually brought up short by the Is of reality. Together they urge us to patience; we must be willing to wait and see that we might honestly judge the fruits of our actions. Together they prevent us from playing God even as they challenge us to be God. Together they provide us with the courage and vision to choose wisely—to choose life.

Notes

1. *Babylonian Talmud*, Shabbat, 31a. (All Talmudic references are from the *Hebrew-English Edition of the Babylonian Talmud*, New York: Traditional Press, 1982.)

2. Lev. 18:19, (Translations from the Hebrew Scriptures are taken from *Tanakh, A New Translation of the Holy Scriptures*, New York: Jewish Publication Society, 1985.)

3. Mordecai Kaplan, *Judaism as a Civilization*, Philadelphia: Jewish Publication Society, 1981, 463.

4. Pico della Mirandola, *Oration on the Dignity of Man*, translated by Elizabeth L. Forbes in Ernst Cassirer, Paul Oskar Kristeller, and John H. Randall, Jr., eds., *The Renaissance Philosophy of Man*, Chicago: Univ. of Chicago, 1948, 169ff.

5. Mordecai Kaplan, *The Greater Judaism in the Making*, New York: Reconstructionist Press, 1960, 492.

6. *Liqqutim Yeqarim*, Jerusalem edition, Brooklyn N.Y.: Kehot Publication Society, 1974, 161.

7. Shneur Zalman, *Tanya*, Section 2, chapter 3, Brooklyn, N.Y.: Kehot Publication Society, 1984, 283.

8. Mordecai M. Kaplan, *The Greater Judaism in the Making*, New York: The Reconstructionist Press, 1960, 499–500.

9. Alfred North Whitehead, *Process and Reality*, New York: Macmillan, 1929, 519.

10. Mordecai M. Kaplan, *The Meaning of God in Modern Jewish Religion*, New York: Reconstructionist Press, 1936, 62–63.

11. Mordecai M. Kaplan, *Judaism as a Civilization*, 464.

12. See Martin Buber, *On Judaism*, New York: Schocken Books, 1972, 85.

13. Buber, *Ibid.*, 85–86.

14. *Sifre* on Deuteronomy 5:33, see Martin Buber, *On Judaism*, 85–86.

15. Buber, *On Judaism*, 81–82.

16. *Ibid.*, 82.

17. *Babylonian Talmud*, tractate *Bava Metzia* 59a-b.

18. Buber, *On Judaism*, 86–87.

19. *Ibid.*, 87.

20. *Ibid.*, 93.

21. *Zohar* on Genesis 5:1–2, Volume I, 37b, New York: Soncino Edition, 1970.

22. Ellis Rivkin, *The Shaping of Jewish History*, New York: Scribners, 1971, 159–160.

23. *Ibid.*, 167–168.

24. *Mishnah*, tractate *Sotah* 8:4, New York: Judaica Press edition, 1964.

25. Maimonides, *Code*, Laws of Kings and Wars, Ch. 6, Law 7.

26. *Ibid.*, Ch. 6 Law 8.

27. *Ibid.,* Ch. 6 Law 10.

28. *Ibid.,* Laws of Murder and Defense, Ch. 12 Law 12.

29. *Ibid.,* Laws of Idolatry, Ch. 9 Law 8.

30. *Sifte Hahamim,* Genesis 32:8, Jerusalem: Mesora edition, 1968.

31. *Genesis Rabbah,* 44:4.

32. Immanuel Jacobvits, in *Tradition,* Vol. 4, No. 2, Spring, 1962, p. 202.

33. See *Avot de Rabbi Nathan,* Ch. 4, for details of this story.

34. *Babylonian Talmud,* tractate, *Berakhot* 35 a/b.

35. *Mishnah,* tractate *Pirke Avot* 3:18, New York: Judaica Press edition, 1964.

36. *Lev.* 25:3–4.

7

Ethical Consequences of the Christian Way

GEDDES MacGREGOR

Foundations of Christian Ethics

The foundations of morality within the Christian tradition are exceedingly complex. Christianity, no less than Hinduism, is the name given to a vast clearinghouse of religious ideas. Therefore, when we seek to unearth the foundations of Christian ethics we may be sure that we are not to expect underpinnings such as the stone or brick substructure of an ancient building, all clearly definable and analyzable as in an archaeologists's report, but, rather, an old tree whose enormous roots have gathered sustenance from a bewildering variety of sources far distant from the living tree.

Of course all forms of Christianity, from Eastern Orthodoxy to American Methodism, from medieval Latin Catholicism in France to twentieth century Anglicanism in Australia, purport to have as their focus the Person and Work of Jesus Christ and, in one way or another, claim to look to the Bible as their supreme documentary standard of authority, their "rule of faith." The Bible however (like every other written document, and to a greater extent than many) demands interpretation, the principles of which inevitably change through the centuries with increasing knowledge of the circumstances out of which that large body of literature called the Bible was developed. True, the Christian Way was from the first rooted in its Hebrew heritage, but that heritage itself was complex and had become very much more so in the centuries immediately preceding the birth of Jesus. For although the Hebrew people were strongly inclined to resist foreign imports, influences from abroad affected Jewish thought and practice in many ways, not only among Jews of the Diaspora, scattered as they were over much of the known world, but (thanks to armies of occupation in Palestine) even in the Jewish homeland.

We cannot intelligently speak of Stoic or Hellenistic ideas added to a basically Hebrew outlook, as one might talk of adding pepper or salt to a bowl of soup. So ancient and complex are the roots of the Christian heritage that no scholarly student of Christianity would ever feel entirely confident in attempting to identify all the ingredients in the ideological mix. How did Christianity acquire, for example, the severely ascetic aspect that is expressed in the Catholic monastic ideal with its vows of poverty, chastity, and obedience? That seems, superficially at any rate, closer to certain forms of Buddhism than to the classical Hebrew outlook in patriarchal times. Whom are we to praise or blame for it?

In the popular mind, Paul seems, perhaps, a convenient whipping boy, but of course Paul was thoroughly Jewish. Then was it, as people formerly were disposed to image, something that came into Christianity from the pagan world? Yes, some influences from the great Mediterranean world, a religious melting pot at the time Jesus and his disciples lived, certainly had their effect on Christian attitudes and beliefs. But then Christianity has also been accounted by some as too lax, too ready for ethical compromise. Some, like Nietzsche, have found it too feminine, and it is not difficult to argue such a case. But then it has often been charged with being too masculine, too ready to engage in holy wars, indeed the source of much of the violence in history. That, too, can be argued. One can easily show that it has been too ritualistic, too preoccupied with liturgical pomp and the trappings of architectural splendor; yet no less justly can one portray it as too puritanical, too beautiless, too drab, "grown gray with" the breath of the "pale Galilean," as Swinburne depicts. If it can be and has been all these things, and much more, can it have any identifiable meaning?

Christians who, in the fashionable idiom of today, are accounted "liberal" do have a tendency to call "Christian" any action of which they approve, and to call "unchristian" whatever seems to them morally objectionable, somewhat in the way in which, according to Voltaire's satire, a "bad thinker" is "one who doesn't think the way you do." Yet it can also be argued that although humility, for example, is a virtue that all religions, at least in theory, admire and would seek to foster, Christian humility is not necessarily the same as, say, Zoroastrian or Jain humility. Why not? Because the quality of a particular form of any moral virtue is deeply colored by, not to say derived from, the philosophical and theological beliefs that lay behind the concept of virtue. In short, does not ethical behavior, whatever it is, acquire its deepest meaning and value from the metaphysical background or belief system from which it springs? It certainly seems to be much easier to argue in favor of suicide or abortion-on-demand, for instance, if one happens to believe that one's body is one's own sole property, than it is if one holds that our life is not our own to do with as we will, but belongs to God the Creator, being given to us in trust through his gracious bounty.

That ideas about morality, be they dubbed Christian or otherwise, depend upon such underpinnings is at least a notion that warrants investigation. People argue endlessly about ethical questions without ever being able to reach any kind of agreement except within very restricted boundaries. We can all agree to live by a certain form of the Highway Code, driving on the left in England and on the right in France, as we learn to accept the rules of golf or tennis, which are of course all mere conventions. When we talk, however, of a certain course of conduct as morally right or wrong, we do not mean that it happens to conflict with or conform to the rules of a game. Religious people, including Christians, are saying something more than and different from that. Christians, despite the enormous differences in their interpretation of Christian belief and practice, do not condemn matricide and incest as merely graver forms of the kind of misconduct that we call traffic violations. No, they condemn such acts as sinful or evil not because they violate a conventional code but because they contravene in some way what is taken to be the will of God or, as the followers of some other religions would more characteristically express it, the karmic law. Any community can choose to change its traffic laws at any time it pleases or finds expedient; for instance, not many years ago most states disallowed a right turn on the red, which is now much more commonly allowed. No one but a religious fanatic, not to say maniac, would ever claim that permitting or forbidding a right turn on the red accorded better or worse with the will of God. Few people if any, other than those unduly affected by certain academic ethical theories, would really put murder and rape in the same category as traffic violations. They are not merely graver; they are of a different *order*. Even drunk driving, despite its often terrible consequences, is not of the same order as murder or mayhem or child abuse, although it may deserve no less punishment.

Christian View of God

So let us look at the Christian view of God. Plainly it has deep, central roots in the biblical tradition. The early Hebrews were too preoccupied with the business of sheer survival to have much time for philosophical reflection about the nature of Yahweh, their God. Yet, for one reason or another, their idea of God developed along certain specific lines. They had no word for "nature" so that what we would call natural phenomena were attributed directly to the activity of Yahweh, who sent plagues and earthquakes as he causes the sun to shine on the just and on the unjust. Yahweh could be seen to move in mysterious ways, planting his footsteps in the sea and riding upon the storm. All this may seem very primitivistic, yet towards Yahweh was gradually developed, under the influence of prophets and other religious seers, an attitude to God that is notably different from that of the vast majority of Israel's neighbors. God is seen to be nothing if not wholly other than man. He is also seen to be not a collection of powers and influences, but One.

By contrast, the gods of polytheistic societies were invested by their devotees with highly specialized and limited qualities. Their state is indeed portrayed as very superior to that of mortals; they live at ease and do everything more easily than we do even at our best. Nevertheless, they are grandees who are specialists only within their own domain. Mars is the undisputed god of war, Venus of love. They are foci of special kinds of power. They quarrel with one another in their striving for a higher place in the Olympian hierarchy, where Zeus reigns as a sort of first among equals, yet by no means with absolute security as such.

Yahweh, however, as he comes to be depicted under the influence of the prophets, is both unchallengeable and universal in his dominion. The metaphors used to state all this have a tendency on the whole to be authoritarian. There is a certain aloofness about a judge and even a father, at least an oriental father in the ancient world. As shepherd, Yahweh may seem to have assumed a gentler and more loving mien, and so of course he has; yet he looks so from a human standpoint only. Presumably, to a sheep he looks no less authoritarian than would a sultan to his subjects. We can hardly feel comfortable today with the notion that we are mere sheep in the house of the Lord, no matter how benign are the qualities poetically attributed to the shepherd.

The central philosophic difficulty that arose in polytheistic models of power was that it was very difficult to make the idea of godly power cohere with the idea of godly impassibility, that is, the idea that a god or goddess must move with such consummate swiftness and ease that he or she ought not really to have to move at all. For even the least effort is some effort. Even the swiftest and most thunderbolt-like action is some action. When Zeus nods, all Olympus trembles; but while that may seem at first to exalt Zeus, it also limits him, for if he were really godlike, ought not he to attain his purpose without even a nod, indeed without even a thought, but merely by an unuttered *fiat*? Even the Greek poets saw something was wrong and the philosophers taught people to smile at the gods although not necessarily at what lay behind the poetry of the pantheon.

Among the Greek thinkers to whom we look as the cradle of Western thought, not even Plato provided a thoroughly satisfactory solution to the philosophical puzzle tht the Greek pantheon had presented. Aristotle, his pupil, did so by an extraordinary stroke of genius. To the question, "How can that which is impassible and immutable ever pour forth or send forth anything or set anything in motion?" Aristotle gave his celebrated answer: *kinei hos eromenon*, it moves by being loved. In this ingenious phrase Aristotle expressed his "magnet" theory of the nature of God. All that exists strives, through the cosmic force of *eros*, to follow the divine Being that attracts it, pulling it like a magnet to itself. Deity need not move and does not; it draws everything to itself in one way or another through the longing that everything has for God. As a beautiful woman has no need to chase after or seek out admirers, since they all desire her by the *eros* in them that seeks her out, so God draws everything to himself so surely that all things are held together by him without his exerting himself at all.

This impressive model eventually had an enormous influence on the Christian concept of God, and so inevitably affected the development of Christian concepts of the moral life. When, in the thirteenth century, Thomas Aquinas sought to reconcile the religious tradition of his day with its scientific though as represented by the then recently rediscovered Aristotle, he found in this, as in so many of Aristotle's modes of thought, a model that was not only consistent with biblical thought and Christian tradition, but in some ways a peculiarly felicitous expression of that thought and that tradition. For it provided a means of expressing the notion of love *(agape)* that is so central to biblical and of course more particularly, New Testament teaching.

We cannot doubt that Dante, a century later, had this model in mind when he concluded the *Paradiso* of his *Commedia* with the sublime reference to God as *l'amor che muove il sole e l'altre stelle:* the love that moves the sun and all the stars. That love "moves" them (that is, sustains them in being) not as a boy drives his top by feverishly whipping it, but causes them to whirl around it as bees are drawn to honey. God, therefore, remains self-sufficient, yet the author and creator of all else. From Homer to Plato, the Greeks had sought this answer to which Aristotle gave metaphysical expression: God, as the universal magnet, is the "first" and "final" cause of all existence.

From the earliest days of the missionary expansion of the Christian faith, the notion that God's power is the power of an infinite and all-encompassing love, not a physical or chemical or political power, had dominated the Christian mind. It was prominent in the teaching of Paul as it had been central to Jesus's own understanding of the nature of him whom he called "Father." What Jesus taught about moral behavior in, for example, the so-called "Sermon on the Mount," which is a collection of his typical sayings, did not radically depart from teaching that was either explicit or implicit in the Torah and the subordinate literatures that go to make up what we now call the Bible. However, early in the history of the development of Christian thought about God, philosophical questions were posed about the consequences of belief that love constitutes the "heart" of God, so that anything that might be properly attributed to him, such as creativity or power or strength or intelligence, must be a special, unique *kind* of creativity and power and strength and intelligence, made unique by the uniqueness of the self-giving love that governs all things from the deep core of divinity itself.

In the first few centuries of the development of Christian thought about God, the intellectual fashions of the Greek world prevailed. Hebrew modes of thought were alien to the Gentile world. They were little understood even among the best scholars. Although Jerome, who translated the Bible into Latin about the year 400, learned Hebrew, even he could have had little real understanding of the Hebrew heritage. The average person had virtually none at all, so that in the Gentile world the Old Testament remained for long virtually a closed book, except for picturesque stories such as that of Jonah, and deep outpourings of the human heart, such as the Psalms. The Greek Fathers of the Church used the learning of their day to try to express the nature of God as they found it in the Bible and their attempts reflect the philosophical subtlety of the Greek mind and the adaptability of the Greek language to the expression of that subtlety. When theological ideas were transmitted to the West in Latin the situation was very different indeed, for Latin was not at all so ductile a means of expression, being suited, rather, to historical narrative and law. Glaring examples are: the rendering of the New Testament *charisma* as *gratia* (from which we get "grace"), which means literally "thanks" rather than anything charismatic, and the translation of the Greek *mysterion* as *sacramentum* (from which we get "sacrament") that was in fact a soldier's loyalty oath rather than anything in the least like what could ever have been understood by the mysteries of Baptism and the Holy Eucharist.

Augustine (354-430), Father of the West and revered as such both by the Latin Church and by the Reformation Fathers, did not know Greek, but he had been deeply influenced before his conversion by Neoplatonism, as the school of the third-century Plotinus came to be called. Neoplatonism was in fact a serious rival to Christianity and, but for the fact that it was too intellectual to have wide popular appeal, might even have had in the long run a more numerous following. Plotinus had taught that the aim of religion is to enable the soul, which here on earth is a pilgrim far from its true home, to go on to be with its kin in a realm in which it can more fully participate in the life of the eternal and immutable reality, that is, God. Of course there are hints of such a notion here and there in the Bible, yet nothing quite so emphatic or specific. Here, then, is an idea that was to influence Christian thought and Christian hope immensely. Stoic ideals and attitudes, which also had affected Augustine, played a considerable part in the development of attitudes toward God in his relation to humanity and the universe. The vision of God comes to be seen as the climax to an intellectual process: the ladder from the lower to the higher, the probe from the outer to the inner. Both Plato and Plotinus affected both Jewish and Christian thought; but through Augustine all interpretation of the Bible came in a Plotinian mold.

The Trinity

The most notable development in Christian thought as the Church tried to express biblical traditions in terms of the intellectual modes of the day was toward the doctrine of the Trinity that, by the fifth century, had received its full formulation. The doctrine of the Trinity, which was to become so specifically and peculiarly Christian, is never expressly stated in the Bible except in a solitary passage (1 John 5:7-8) known to be a very late interpolation into the New Testament text. Modern translations generally omit it. It is certainly not to be found in Paul who uses phrases such as "in Christ"

and "in the Spirit" indifferently. The identification of the pre-exis-
tent Christ with the Spirit of God is characteristic, indeed, of much
early Christian literature. The evolution of the Doctrine of the
Trinity is a lengthy process in early Christian thought and occurred
amid much acrimony. Yet, despite its philosophical limitations and
the controversial bitterness attending its development, the doctrine
can be seen as a brilliant attempt to provide a way out of the intellectual puzzles created by affirming that God, who is the source of
all created things, is also essentially love. The labyrinthine history
of the evolution of this much misunderstood doctrine is beyond the
scope of this essay.

Triadic notions in connection with deity are, we all know, prominent in the thought of other religions. For instance, the Gnostic
Trinity, which includes *Sophia* or Wisdom (sometimes identified in
Christian lore with Mary), along with God and Christ, is well
known to scholars. To what extent, if any, such notions affected,
by devious paths, the development of Christian thought on the eve
of Europe's entry into the Middle Ages, is no doubt highly debat-
able, but in any case the *functioning* of the doctrine of the Trinity in
Christian theology is unique. Complex as were the circumstances
leading to its development, it would not have been developed at all
but for the need to express in intellectual terms the affirmation that
God is both the eternal ground of all being and the love that governs and cares for all things. It says in effect that despite the cruelties
and injustices that confront us wherever we go, and notwithstanding the pain and suffering that are inseparable from the human condition and permeate all life, all is in the hands of One who is neither
a mere creative principle nor a mere "pure will," but a heart of love
that so cares for his universe that not even a little sparrow can fall
to the ground without his concern. What the doctrine is designed
to express above all else is what a much later Catholic piety was to
express in a more romantic and popular way in the devotional
imagery of the Sacred Heart. Nothing could be more alien to the
doctrine of the Trinity as classically expounded than any tritheistic
interpretation. What Augustine and other Fathers of the Christian
Church emphasize in the Trinity is that it is a Unity: the trinitarian
aspect is an intellectual way of describing the nature of the Unit
that is God.

So Christianity, whatever form it takes, is essentially in the
monotheistic tradition. Jesus, its central focus, habitually spoke in
terms of that tradition. If there is anything distinctive at all in

Christian ethics, it must be distinctive within that monotheistic framework. To what extent and in what ways, if any, it is distinctive, is what we have still to explore.

How Should a Christian Make an Ethical Decision?

If modern biblical studies have taught us anything at all, it is that we have far less exact information about the life and words of Jesus than our forefathers supposed. That conclusion is as clear to those scholars who intelligently revere and may even acclaim as unique the Person and Work of Jesus Christ as to those who, in the tradition of Herman Samuel Reimarus (1694–1768), have sought to denigrate and discredit the traditional Christian claims. In the words of R. H. Lightfoot, when we read the Gospels we touch only the hem of the garment.

Moreover, every age has seen Jesus through its own spectacles, not least our own twentieth century, in which he has often been transformed in popular imagination into a social reformer or a quixotic visionary, even into the founder of modern democracy. Further, biblical scholarship has also shown us that whether we read the Bible with skepticism or loving devotion or both or neither, we must recognize that the form in which it has reached us today is the product of a complex evolutionary process over the course of a thousand years or more, and of repeated editing and literary reconstruction during that time. This does not make it any less worthy of reverence, nor any more worthy of it, but the veneration we give it must be of a different, not to say of a better, kind. For if we are to venerate it at all and to recognize it as in some way containing the revelation of God to man, we must see the revelatory process as much more complex than a dictation of God to a series of inspired scribes, as has been the way it has often been seen in popular imagery.

This reference to evolutionary process directs us to another consideration to which we must briefly attend before going to the core of the subject of this section. We are today separated from *all* the thought of our forefathers by the great nineteenth century discovery of the evolutionary nature of all things. The work of Darwin, extremely important though it was, was only a part of a more general discovery. Not only is life governed by an underlying evolutionary process, so also is the entire universe. Evolution is a key principle to an understanding of physics, no less than to that of biology. Not least is it a fundamental principle in the development of man who turns out to be not so much a species, as our forefathers thought even up to a century or so ago, but part of a process. This kind of awareness of the evolutionary nature of the environment outside us, as well as of the spiritual reality within us, inevitably changes our outlook and our understanding *at all points*. Even what we have more recently learned of the vastness of outer space and of the mysteries of the submicroscopic dimension of life do not so radically alter our outlook as much as the discovery of the evolutionary nature of all things altered it to those in the vanguard of though more than a hundred years ago. This, as we shall see later, most profoundly affects our approach to any ethical system that has Jesus as its principle focus.

First, however, we must look at what may be called the traditional principles by which Christian moralists have sought to derive a Christian morality from the Bible in general and in particular from the life and teachings of Jesus. The derivation is more from the life than from the teachings, for the latter have for long been seen to be consonant with and expressive of the most enlightened and spiritually vigorous aspects of Judaism in Jesus' own day. One of the sayings attributed to him that is likely to express a central point in his thinking is that he came not to destroy the law (the Torah) but to complete it. More of the specifically ethical teaching of Jesus could have been given by many rabbis of his day. What is much more distinctively Christian is what is attributed to him by the evangelists and apostles of the Christian Way who, in the New Testament and other early Christian literature, attest their belief that in one way or another he is ontologically unique.

Uniqueness of Jesus

Of course all human beings are God's children and all unique in their way; every one of us has a distinctive fingerprint and vocal timbre, even (if he or she be a writer or artist) a distinctive style, so that in reading a work one can say, "that could not possibly be Tennyson" or, "that's pure Emerson," or the like. What is attributed to Jesus, however, is a special relationship to God. Again, of course we all may be said to have a special relationship to God as his children, for all relationships are special and the relationship of John to his mother is never identical with the relation of his brother Peter to their mother. The relationship of Jesus to God has been generally held by Christians, however, to be of a fundamentally different kind from even that of the greatest of the many prophets and teachers in the history of humankind.

The mode in which the New Testament itself expresses this uniqueness varies. Not always is it expressed with such dramatic power and poetic beauty as in the Prologue to the Gospel according to John. Nevertheless, we do find a general concurrence in the view attributed by John (John 7:46) to the officers sent by the chief priests to apprehend Jesus, "Never man spake like this man." Any attempt at constructing any system of Christian ethics must surely therefore take into account that it must be rooted not so much in a system of teaching that can be extracted from the New Testament reports, as in the life of Jesus insofar as it can be ascertained from a study of these sources. Moreover, since all early Christian proclamation is centered upon the affirmation that Jesus Christ is risen and lives in the Christian community, Christian ethics must also be centered in the life of the Church itself. After all, the Church, in one form or another, was already well established in various centers throughout the Mediterranean world by the time (about A.D. 50) that the earliest of the New Testament documents was written. Whatever else may be said about the principles to which we must look in trying to construct a Christian ethic, we must recognize that it certainly cannot be extracted from a written document. At best the documents can provide only pointers.

To Jesus is attributed by Matthew (Matt. 7:16–20) the saying that "by their fruits ye shall know them"; that is, when you see thorns and thistles you know they cannot have come from the roots of a healthy fruit tree. This was no doubt an effective answer to those who charged him with healing people by the power of some evil agency. But then are we always capable of recognizing good fruit on sight or even on taste? We can become so accustomed to a poor diet that only with some education can we come to accept a more nutritious one. Not every Eskimo would take at once to even the best of Polynesian food, nor do all Americans ever acquire a taste for French cuisine. The notion that we have any better powers of discrimination in the spiritual realm must depend on some presupposition such as that there is a "natural" law written into the heart of every human being enabling it to discern good conduct from bad instinctively.

Such a notion, which has roots in Stoic doctrine and was made familiar in the West through the writings of Cicero and others, has played a considerable part in the teachings of the Roman Catholic

Church, which inherited from Stoic and other sources the concept of *ius naturale,* "a natural" law implanted in every human being independently of any moral education. The case for such a law is no doubt arguable, yet what may be even a more telling consideration that has found expression by the Fall is that such moral discrimination is either partly or wholly destroyed. So then if, as the ancient collect says, "we have no power of ourselves to help ourselves," how are we to know how to behave? The traditional answer was along such lines as, "Check your moral instincts against what is commended in Holy Writ," or, even more simplistically, "What would Jesus have done?" As we have seen, however, such injunctions are not so easily fulfilled as our forefathers tended to suppose. In a relatively homogeneous society such as England or France, people gradually acquire certain fixed ways of looking at things and determining what is desirable or undesirable conduct. When to this is added a general adherence of any such society or nation to the Christian faith in any of its forms, what is Christian conduct tends to seem comparatively easy to determine. In the more heterogeneous circumstances in which we find ourselves today, and with the perspectives to which modern biblical scholarship has led us, it is by no means to be so easily ascertained. It was not entirely easy even in seventeenth century France and Spain when special schools of moral theology such as "probabilism" and "probabiliorism" provided rival interpretations of the rules for making moral decisions. In a society such as our present global one, into the melting pot of which have come a bewildering variety of presuppositions and (among Christians) interpretations of the nature of the Person and Work of Christ, even the most temperamentally decisive Christian is often in grave doubt, as we shall see in the next section of this chapter.

Principles of Moral Conduct

True, when all is said, nothing could be more obvious than that Christianity shares with other religions certain general working principles about moral conduct. In public international relations one sees, alas, very little morality of any kind. In private and personal relations, however, a Christian can often find that a Muslim or Buddhist would seem to agree with him on most ethical questions. Murder and adultery are very generally disapproved in all religious traditions. Lying and cheating of every kind are in principle as much deplored in Hinduism as in Judaism, in Christianity as in Islam. Even the subtler forms of moral virtue tend to be commonly applauded: if I come across to a Muslim or Buddhist as a gentle and humble person, he is more likely to see me as a brother than if I appear arrogant and bellicose. Externally, my habits and manners are likely to seem outlandish and strange to a Chinese unaccustomed to my Western ways, but we can very quickly learn to accept each other's ways as one accepts different fashions in dress, so long as they can be seen as expressions of an interior attitude that accords with what both of us see as right.

We must ask, however, how much this tells us. Let us look at sexuality for an analogy that may help. Men and women may be described, from one standpoint, as functioning in identical ways. A woman chews and digests her food in the same way as does a man. Her liver, heart, and kidneys function in no notable respect differently from the way in which these organs function in her brother. Her nervous system is organized on the same lines as a man's. Except of course in the reproductive system men and women can be described in almost identical terms. Yet because of the male hormones and the reproductive role of the male, the whole male body is permeated by its maleness and because of the female hormones and the reproductive role of the female the whole female body is permeated by its femaleness. It is as if a man were steeped in a blue dye and a woman in a pink one. So even when a woman frowns or smiles, her frown betrays her femininity as a man's his masculinity, although both physiologically and psychologically it would be difficult to state the difference in scientific terms. Men and women are both capable of passionate love and to say "he loves her" seems the same as to say "she loves him." Grammatically the predicate is identical. The subjects, as we have seen, can be called the same except in one respect; yet so vital is that respect that, as everyone knows, a woman's love and a man's love are by no means the same, so that "she loved him" is indeed very different from "he loved her."

So despite the common ground of morality that we can find among the religions of the world, it is difficult to say (even where the adherents of one religion clearly concur with those of another on ethical questions "on paper"), that they are saying the same thing when they concur. It is one thing to condemn adultery because it is destructive of the marriage relationship and a violation of the vows relating thereto and that it entails cheating and lying, such as everyone deplores; it is another thing to condemn it for these same reasons, but *also* because, as Paul puts it to the Corinthians, our bodies are the temple of God and of his Holy Spirit (1 Cor. 3:16; 6:19). To refrain from sexual misconduct because I believe it to be socially destructive is commendable, but it is quite different from refraining from it because I believe my body to be the temple of God and therefore not my own to use as I think fit. Likewise, to refrain from murder and other violent acts against fellow human beings because I believe them to be members of the same species to which I belong and to which, therefore, I have special moral duty is also commendable, but it is not the same at all as refraining from so treating my fellowman because he and I have been created spiritual brothers through the Fatherhood of God. The theological presuppositions of any form of Christianity do radically affect the motivation behind any virtuous or vicious act that I may do.

So when a Christian's humility is engendered by his or her awareness of the awesome love of God expressed in the self-giving of Christ and indeed by his or her gratitude for the gift of life itself, the virtue we call "humility" has a radically different and, to a Christian, superior character. This does not mean that humility not so motivated is bad. On the contrary, humility is to be praised and ought to be envied by many a Christian who sorely lacks it, yet its profound goodness does not make it Christian humility.

The deplorable and often outrageous turpitude of Christians, not least in the hierarchy of the Church (the ignorance, arrogance, and hypocrisy of many bishops, for instance), far from diminishing whatever truth there be in what has just been said, brings it into even bolder relief. So Kierkegaard's celebrated *Attack Upon Christendom* (in which, shortly before his death in 1855, he pilloried the Church with uniquely savage bitterness) is one of the most deeply Christian writings in all Christian literature, from Paul's letters down to writers of the present day. If Christian virtue has a unique quality in it, no less surely has churchly vice.

Augustine claimed that virtue gives perfection to the soul, that the soul obtains virtue by following God, and that following God constitutes the happy life. Happiness is seen to be the unquestioned goal of humanity. Thomas Aquinas, following Augustine in this as in much else, argues that man's ultimate happiness consists in the contemplation of God as the source of all good. Calvin, who was really no more predestinarian in his theology than was Thomas but only has seemed so because his predestinarianism was more prominently displayed in his writings and so came to be more preached about, taught above all else that man's duty, though it includes of course relations with his fellowman, is even more fundamentally towards God. His chief end, as the old Scottish catechism has it, is "to glorify God and to enjoy him for ever." One glorifies God by doing his will and his will is to be discovered by prayerful reading of Holy Scripture under the guidance of the Holy Spirit.

In all such central Christian teaching on ethical questions we can see clearly that our duty to our fellow man ensues from our duty to God. "Love God and do what thou wilt," is too easy a formulation of it. The question is: How does one know precisely what is the will of the God one seeks to please? That was in many ways easier for our forefathers to decide than it can be for us if we have taken on the responsibility that ensues from a study of the Bible and of the variegated pattern of Christian tradition, although even to them it was never by any means as easy as it might at times have sounded. Yet a Christian can never settle any ethical decision without reference to the focus of his faith, which is Jesus Christ, about whom most Christians are, and seem content to remain, even more ignorant than we need be.

Contemporary Issues

Classical Christian principles of morality, as we have seen them in the foregoing sections, do not change with the passage of centuries, but their application certainly does with the enormous expansion of human knowledge and the circumstances of modern life. One or two examples will exhibit the kind of changes we must expect in the application of Christian ethical principles to life today. Then we can consider some of the perplexing questions that arise in our time and whose scope is likely to be greatly enlarged in the near future, not least in the field of their application to medical situations.

Crime and Punishment

Traditionally, crimes against a human being, from murder to merely minor assault, have been very sharply distinguished, both by moralists and jurists, from comparable offenses against horses, dogs, and other animals. Punishment for first-degree murder has been either death or a long prison sentence, and even a minor assault can be taken very seriously by the courts. The same offenses against a horse or a dog would be treated as they always have been, quite differently. Unless they involved great cruelty, they would not be crimes at all, and they would be civil torts only to the extent that someone's property rights in the animals were affected. Christians have generally been indifferent, when not positively cruel, to nonhuman animals, and our laws reflect an attitude that imposes a duty on human beings to respect the rights of other human beings to be protected from violence, while recognizing no such rights for what was traditionally called "the lower creation." Indeed, any duty to be kind to "our four-footed friends" was really seen as a duty to ourselves, a duty to avoid injury to our own sensibilities as civilized human beings, not a duty arising out of any rights that the animals themselves might have.

All this was understandable when man could be viewed as a separate species, the ultimate creation of God, having no direct connection with an evolutionary stream preceding man. Scientifically, we cannot make that kind of distinction today. We can make a good case for the view that, since life is one, dogs and cats participate in it as do we and that if our laws are to protect the sanctity of human life, they must protect in some way also the sanctity of all life. Is the life of a faithful dog or a fine horse less sacred than that of a vicious rapist and murderer? Christian moralists ought to address themselves to such questions long before legislators may be expected to do so.

Let us look at one more such example before we consider more pressing issues. Christians have recognized from early times (although practice has lagged behind moral theory) that since human beings are the special handiwork of God, every Christian must treat all human beings as brothers, irrespective of the color of their skin or the cut of their jowl. It is not a question of slavery that arises here, for slaves might well belong to the same race as their masters, so that slavery is a different question. What is at issue here is, rather, that Christian moral theory has always excluded the notion that there can ever be a hierarchy of castes based upon race or any other anthropological distinction. The reason is simple. All human beings are brothers and sisters with God as their common Father because spiritually he has fathered them. Even if some are less advanced than others at a particular time, they are all entitled to God's love, therefore they are entitled to and ought to receive ours, such as it is. What sort of family would give less love to a baby than to a child of twelve? Of course Christianity is not alone in all this. Buddhism teaches something similar, and Islam so highly regards man that, according to the Qur'an, he is higher than even the angels.

With our adventures into outer space, however, and the likelihood that there is intelligent life on other planets in other galaxies if not in other solar systems, we must ask what would happen to our traditional view of man and our duty to the human race as such if we did discover extraterrestrial intelligent life? Would not our traditional view seem intolerably parochial, like the view of an island tribe that accounted itself the supreme handiwork of God? If we encountered in outer space intelligent beings far below or far above us in mental and moral development, should we hail them too as our brothers in Christ under the common Fatherhood of God? Has Christ gone to them to save them as he has saved us and, if not, should not we send Christian missionaries to enlighten them? Christ is "True God and True Man"; but for them he would presumably have to be "True God and True Martian" or whatever. Once again, the traditional view of humanity is in more than one way parochial.

Euthanasia

These reflections may help to prepare us for a consideration of more immediate ethical concerns. Take first of all a typical contemporary ethical puzzle: the morality of euthanasia and anti-dysthanasia, that is, the passive role of merely permitting death to occur. We are not the first generation to face such puzzles, but in the past they were less complex. Traditionally, Roman Catholic moral theology is uncompromisingly opposed to euthanasia as viciously immoral, being accounted contrary to the natural law *(ius naturale)* as well as to Scripture. (If life is held to begin at conception, abortion falls under the same condemnation.) Nevertheless, anti-dysthanasis has been by no means so strongly opposed in Catholic tradition. Many moralists have insisted that the mere prolongation of life is useless and that "extraordinary" means of preserving it are not obligatory.

Protestant opinion, although it may seem more divided, is classically much the same, being grounded, as in Catholic opinion, on Scripture. Official pronouncements by the American Council of Christian Churches, by the Lutheran Church (Missouri Synod), and by the General Convention of the Episcopal Church in the US, could be cited in firm opposition to euthanasia. Many distinguished leaders within the Reformation heritage, however, have urged reformative legislation. As long ago as the thirties, W. R. Inge, the celebrated Dean of St. Paul's Cathedral, London, did so and, among American churchmen, Harry Emerson Fosdick, David Roberts, Ralph W. Sockman, and Henry Pitney Van Dusen all sought to pioneer reformative legislation. These were, nevertheless, exceptional voices, although they have elicited much sympathy from lay people in "liberal" circles. Official Christianity within the Reformation heritage, notoriously divided though it is on so much, has been virtually unanimous in a fundamental opposition to euthanasia and abortion. Dietrich Bonhoeffer and Emil Brunner opposed euthanasia: the latter implicitly, in denouncing suicide, and the former explicitly. No doubt, both were affected by an acute awareness of Nazi crimes committed under a cloak of euthanasia. Anti-dysthanasia, however, is widely supported even by the most conservative of Protestant churchmen as by religious leaders of other groups.

The traditional distinction between "ordinary" and "extraordinary" means in the prolongation of life becomes artificial when one perceives that what were "extraordinary" measures in prolonging life fifty years ago are often now accounted "ordinary" ones. Almost any form of intensive care would have been accounted "extraordinary," while today many forms of it would be routine. A hundred years ago, leeches were still quite widely used in the alleviation of a variety of disorders, while what were then accounted avant-garde, highly experimental, and therefore "extraordinary" measures, would be in many cases today taken for granted as what any competent physician would feel bound to prescribe as a matter of course. How can one say that a poultice is an "ordinary" measure but penicillin an "extraordinary" one, except in reference not only to the date, but to the place and circumstance? What might be an "ordinary" measure in a New York hospital might still be a very "extraordinary" one indeed in a missionary outpost in an undeveloped country of today.

Other circumstances demand consideration no less than does advancement in medical knowledge and practice. Suppose that I am the only son of a very rich father and am well aware of the terms of his will to bequeath his entire estate to me. A loving son, I have in fact no avaricious designs on his estate. I perceive, however, that he is dying, in acute agony, and unable to declare his wishes. My natural instinct as a humane person with filial devotion would be to expedite my father's death and so avoid his further suffering. In the eyes of society, however, and certainly of a court, if my case came to trial, my action would be likely to be highly suspect. The same action on the part of a son who had nothing at all to gain from his father's death would be likely to be received with much more general approval or, at least, sympathy on the part of the average person.

Such reflections lead to the recognition, by no means novel in the history of Christian ethical thought, that moral precepts can never be more than guidelines. This recognition is at the heart of the teaching of Jesus as reported in the Gospels. The whole Torah, with the Ten Commandments and the hundreds of rituals and other injunctions and prohibitions developed out of it, can be summed up in the Deuteronomic precept: love God with all my being and my neighbor as myself. This precept lies behind all Christian attempts to deal with ethical conundrums, whether these attempts take the form of the seventeenth century Roman Catholic ones (probabilism, probabiliorism, equiprobabilism, tutorism) or twentieth century Protestant ones, such as Joseph Fletcher's "situationalism" and Paul Lehman's "contextualism." No age, no society has ever been able to escape moral problems that arise from the codification of moral injunctions and prohibitions. What is peculiar to our contemporary scene is only tht such rapid advances in science and technology have demanded a rethinking of the traditional guidelines themselves, a new orientation, a new understanding of many of the basic working models of morality that have been long taken for granted. To the libertine all this may seem to warrant making the contemporary outlook less restrictive than in the past, but to the Christian it must be seen to make the old puzzles more poignant than ever, turning us more and more to the underpinnings of all Christian ethics. No Christian in any age can dispense with moral guidelines, but every Christian in every age needs constantly to be reminded of that to which the guidelines have always been intended to guide him, which is God as seen in the Person and Work of Jesus Christ. That, we have already seen, is less easy than it sounds to untrained ears.

Abortion

The conventional arguments for and against euthanasia reflect much the same presuppositions as those used for and against abortion. In the past, abortion was often attended by disastrous consequences that none could deny, so that even from the most "secular" standpoint, it could be plausibly denounced. Today the "right-to-life" stand requires the enunciation of the traditional principle that all human life is sacred (difficulties about which we have noted) and the affirmation (for which there is much medical testimony) that life must be regarded as beginning at conception. In the case of abortion, however, a special consideration emerges: no one can predict the quality of the future offspring. The seemingly most favorable circumstances may result in a physically deformed, or mentally deficient child, while the most unfavorable ones may issue in a genius. Illegitimate children are very likely candidates for abortion and a remarkable number of the greatest figures in human history have been so classified. One risks, therefore, destroying a future Leonardo. Jesus indeed would have seemed to many a prime candidate. Champions of a "right-to-life" stance often noted that their opponents are generally vigorously opposed to capital punishment of proven criminals of the lowest and most incorrigible type yet seem eager to facilitate the destruction of a helpless fetus embarking on human life.

Yet even if one takes the "right-to-life" principle as seriously as do so many Christians, on the ground that human life is the precious gift of a gracious God, so that there is no essential difference between on the one hand, abortion and, on the other, infanticide or other categories of murder, there do seem to be special cases. For example, is the innocent victim of a brutal rape by a syphilitic maniac required by any Christian principle to carry the offspring of that crime to full term? Moreover, one may well ask why, if abortion be so contrary to the will of God and the sanctity of human life, contraceptive devices are not, after all, in the same category, since they impede the creation of life. That, of course, is the sort of consideration that enters into traditional Roman Catholic objection to mechanical and chemical methods of birth control.

Advanced medical technologies, as we all know, have made possible a variety of formerly unthinkable procedures such as *in vitro* fertilization and surrogate motherhood. Predictably, such procedures induce vehement protests by horrified Christian traditionalists. Yet might not one argue that they are but extensions of the aids that have been used for centuries with the approval of Christians, who have never discountenanced the various forms of midwifery, primitive or advanced, that have been used in assisting the creative purposes of God. There may be indeed moral objections to them on Christian grounds, but if so, more than the fact that they look artificial may be needed to show that they are inadmissible. Intravenous feeding is a highly artificial method of providing the human body with nutrients. Vaccination is a highly artificial method of inoculating the human body against smallpox, and even that was opposed on conscientious grounds by some Christian traditionalists when it was first made mandatory, although it is very generally accepted today.

Sexual Relationships

Sexual relationships and their consequences are, however, in a very special case, for whatever we are to say of the Christian ethic on sex we must recognize that not without reason have Christians always accounted it a particularly sacrosanct area of human life. In the ancient world and in the Middle Ages it was so, not for any romantic reason (the kind of romantic love celebrated in poetry and fiction and song is a comparatively modern notion), but because men and women instinctively connected it with divine creativity and understood it in such terms. In many ways they were wiser than they knew and certainly a great deal wiser than those who today would treat it casually. Christians from the first lived in societies in which they were surrounded by sexual profligacy of every kind. They perceived that chastity is more than sexual deprivation or repression and they saw no less that undisciplined submission to our sexual impulses can injure not only the framework of society but our own souls, by diminishing spiritual sensitivity and capacity for growth. Chastity was seen as ministering to the self-denial that is the basis of all Christian living.

Nevertheless, sexual morals were modified according to the conditions of the age. In patriarchal times, in the Hebrew heritage in which Christianity was cradled, polygamy had been not only permissible but encouraged. By the time of Christ, the virtues of the monogamous household had come to be praised as they are in the later Old Testament literature. So we read (1 Tim. 3:2) that a Christian bishop is to be "the husband of one wife." Concubinage, widespread in the pagan world, was contrary to this ideal. With the example of Jesus, Paul, and others, the ideal of celibacy, abhorrent in classical Hebrew society, was admired.

Yet concubinage, prostitution, and other deviations from the ideal were tolerated as concessions to human frailty despite disapproval of them in principle. (In Judaism, polygamy was not officially forbidden till the tenth century of the Christian era, although by then it had been for long in desuetude.) Moreover, in terms of the societal structures of the ancient world, women were (from our modern perspective) more respected and liberated in Hebrew society than among neighboring peoples. Christianity inherited and, through devotion to Mary, fostered respect for femininity according to the social and political circumstances of the day. In the ancient and medieval world, while Christian moralists applauded and revered the ideal of perpetual chastity for those men and women who had a vocation to strive for this ideal, they were by no means blind to the practicalities of life. They saw the sexual urge as natural, as divinely implanted in men and women, and the act of coitus as sanctifiable in marriage. Some, as we have just seen, even tolerated, however reluctantly, certain forms of extramarital copulation as a necessary social evil. Homosexuality, however, was condemned as unnatural, belonging only to a corrupt and decadent pagan society and having no place in the Christian Way.

In developing a Christian sexual ethic for our contemporary circumstances, therefore, we need not be bound by a strict, legalistic adherence to everything that we may find enjoined or forbidden in the documents of the Christian Way, for (as we have seen) Christians have throughout adapted in various ways to the circumstances of the age. Nevertheless, when all that is said, we must recognize that, in Christianity, there is an underlying attitude toward sex that goes far deeper than any mere ministration to the well-being of this or that social structure in which Christians happen to find themselves. Christian marriage is an expression of the basic reverence for the role of sex in human life The family is a means for personal spiritual growth as well as for the economic welfare of a society. Yet, above all, chastity, both within and outside marriage, is at the heart of Christian morality. Far from being a mere neurotic notion (although, like everything else, it may be developed along neurotic lines), it is the indispensable condition of that spiritual love that all Christian moral action must have as its spring.

Freedom and War

Politically, the free world is ideologically very much separated from that in which Christianity was cradled. When students today first encounter Plato's ideal Republic, what strikes them at once is its totalitarian character; the state always comes before the individual. Inevitably so, the kind of political freedom we enjoy today in the West was unknown to the ancients. It was developed in the West

in the later Middle Ages through the felicitous circumstances that
Church and State came to be sharply distinguished as rival powers,
so that the individual could learn to see himself as a citizen of both
and, to some extent, play the one off against the other . (By contrast, in the Byzantine East the situation was quite different, so that
early medieval conditions prevailed in Russia, for example, right up
to the Bolshevik Revolution in 1917, making the change from a
Tzarist totalitarian empire to a Leninist totalitarian empire a comparatively easy transition.) The Christian political outlook on society was from the first very different from what it would be today
in the United States, for example, and the saying attributed to Jesus,
"Render to Caesar the things that are Caesar's and to God the
things that are God's" (Mark 12:17), must have seemed very
straightforward, not to say obvious, to many Christians in the political situation in which they found themselves. Not much could be
expected of the state by way of moral integrity or spiritual discern-
ment. The most that could be said was said by Augustine in his *De
Civitate Dei:* it is better than anarchy, since it affords a certain degree
of protection from marauding murderers and brigands, domestic
and foreign. So slavery, for example, was accepted by Christians
from New Testament times as part of the social scenery: what dif-
ferentiated Christian conduct was how a master treated his slaves
and how they treated their master. War, too, was an unavoidable
evil inherent in the human condition. The individual had almost
no political freedom at all. Only in a society with the kind of freedom to which we are not accustomed in the free world do questions
about the Christian attitude to war and poverty, for example, arise
as they do in typical contemporary discussions. Our expectations
are quite different from those of Christians in the New Testament
times.

Moreover, there is nothing specifically Christian, for instance,
about objections to nuclear war. Indeed, some of the strongest
opposition to the development of nuclear power has come from
"secularist" sources. A nuclear holocaust is feared by every intelligent human being who understands at all what it would entail for
humanity. Nor of course was pacifism, even before the nuclear age,
limited to Christians. War of any kind is abominated by all
thoughtful people and was hideous enough even when waged with
bow and arrow. Poverty, famine, disease, and war plagued past societies of every kind, whether dubbed Christian or Islamic or otherwise, as they plague our societies today, whether we label these cap-

italist or socialist. The only societal circumstance that can help a Christian show to the world the spiritual advantage and efficacy of the Christian Way is the degree and quality of the freedom of the individual within society.

For the Christian Way is, in the last resort, an individual choice based upon an individual response to the eternal One believed to be revealed in the Person and Work of Christ. All Christian moral decisions must be made in terms of that individual responsibility and capacity for spiritual growth. It is a way into the interior dimension of our being. True, it has in time certain external consequences and some of these may be more quickly attained than others, but no formula for the release of humankind from its various predicaments, no nostrum for the world's ills, can be Christian that begins from any other starting point. Where Christians recognize and act upon this insight, they deviate least from the best in the teachings of other religions, and from the best in Christian teaching.

8

Islamic Ethics

ISMA'IL R. AL FARUQI

Foundations of Morality

Essence of Religious Experience

In Islām, ethics is inseparable from religion and is built entirely upon it. The Islāmic mind knows no pair of contraries such as "religious-secular," "sacred-profane," "church-state"; and Arabic, the religious language of Islām, has no words for them in its vocabulary. The first principle of Islāmic knowledge is therefore the unity of truth, just as the first principle of human life is the unity of the person, and the first principle of reality is the unity of God. All three unities are aspects of and inseparable from one another. Such unity is the ultimate principle. The existence of God was not a question for Islām. It had correctly assumed that man was indeed a *homo religiosus,* a being whose consciousness has always worked around a pivotal presence of the Godhead. But its call for the unity of God was fresh as most men repeatedly mixed up the Godhead with other beings, powers, or human wishes, thus spoiling its unity. However, anxious to save mankind and the whole of human history from any assumed loss before its advent, it affirmed this divine unity to have been known to Adam, the first human, and his descendants, and called its absence, wherever divine unity was not in evidence, a human aberration.

The presence of this unity in the mind is what Islām calls religious experience, *īmān,* or certain conviction. It is not an "act of faith," a "decision" that man makes when the evidence is not conclusive. Nor is it dependent as it were on him and his assessment of a case from which apodeictic certainty is ruled out—not a wager *à la* Pascal! It is so crushingly compelling by its own evidence and reality that man must acquiesce to it as to the conclusion of a geometrical theorem. Perception of the divine unity, Islām holds, happens to a man just as the presence of a "hard datum" enters consciousness. Its "truth" is as rational, as critical, and as inevitable. The meaning of divine unity is that God alone is God; that nothing, absolutely nothing in creation, is like unto Him in any respect whatever, and hence absolutely nothing is associable with Him. He is Creator of all that is, Lord and Master, Sustainer and Provider, Judge and Executor. His will is the law in nature, and the norm in human conduct. It is the *summum bonum,* the sublime.

Such awareness on the part of man is at once enchanting to him and the world around him. It is possessive, its object being both *tremendum* and *fascinosum.* To be seized by it is to live one's whole life, not excluding the most personal secret moments of it, under the all-seeing eye of God, under the all-relevant norms of His divine will, under the shadow of impending judgment according to a scale of absolute justice. There can be no more perfect self-discipline, no more effective self-motivation. In the perspective of this awareness of divine unity, everything in the universe is created for a purpose and sustained at every moment of space-time by the Author of that purpose. No law of nature operates mechanically, for its necessity derives not from blind fate or clockwork cosmos, but from the benevolent God Whose will is to provide man with theater and materials wherein his action is ontologically efficacious. Hence, the doors of natural and humane science and technology are wide open to the most thoroughgoing empiricism possible without the least alienation or separation from the realm of moral and esthetic value. Fact and value are here synthesized as one datum proceeding from God and fulfilling His will. The world is, under this view, animated; every atom of it moves by the divine agency, in a divine dependence, for a value that is divine desire.

This, in brief, is the essence of Islām, the unchangeable core of the religion and ethic, of the *sharīʿah* or law, of the culture and civilization. The Muslims have called it *tawḥīd* or unization, meaning the three unities of God, truth, and life. It is at the base of their representation of reality, of their collective mind, action, and hope. The question, what ought man to do? is answerable only in its light.

Purpose of Man's Creation

Islāmic ethics therefore begins with the identification of the divine purpose in man. What is his *raison d'etre?* the purpose of his creation, of his continued sustenance in life and history?

Using the religious as well as the ancient Semitic terminology, Islām holds that man was created to serve God. God said in the Qur'ān, the scripture of Islām, "I have not created men and *jinn* except to serve Me."[1] In philosophical terms, this is tantamount to saying that the purpose of man's existence is the realization of the *summum bonum,* or the plenum of values. Obviously, what is being asserted here is the purposefulness of human life. Its denial is the cynical assertion of meaninglessness. It is another matter whether the meaning of human life is heroism, saintliness, or covering the world with yellow paint. Indeed, this question itself cannot be raised without assuming a positive answer to the first, namely, that there is meaning or good in human life. Such meaning or good, which is the purpose of all creation, is according to Islām, fulfillment of divine will. Whereas this fulfillment takes place involuntarily with the regularity of natural law in the nonhuman realm, it takes place in man both involuntarily as in the physiological and psychic functions, and freely, as in the ethical. The ethical functions realize the moral values and these are the higher occupants of that realm, the higher imperatives of divine will. The divine will includes imperatives of a lesser order such as food, growth, shelter, comfort, sex, etc., for everything in creation partakes of the divine purposiveness, and in fulfilling them, in the hierarchical order proper to them, man realizes the divine will. But his vocation lies in the moral realm where fulfillment of the divine will can take place only in freedom, that is, under the real possibility of man's capacity to do otherwise than he ought. It is in this sense that he is God's *khalīfah,* or vicegerent, on earth; for only he can realize the ethical—and hence higher—values, and only he can have as an objective the realization of the whole realm in its totality. Hence, he is a sort of cosmic bridge through which the divine will, in its totality and especially the higher ethical part of it, can enter space-time and become actual.

In a dramatically eloquent passage of the Qur'ān, God tells us that He offered His trust to heaven and earth, but these shied away from it; man alone accepted it.[2] The Qur'ān also tells us in another passage that the angels objected to God's plan for creating man, knowing that man was equally capable of evil, which they are not. God, however, rejected their claim and assigned to man a higher destiny.[3] In cosmic economy, man's capacity for evil is indeed a risk. But this risk is incomparable with the great promise that he may fulfill if endowed with freedom. What the Qur'ān meant to say is that only man may realize ethical value because only he has the freedom necessary therefore; only he may pursue the totality of values because only he has the mind and vision requisite for such pursuit. Upon his creation, God gave him of His wisdom, proved him superior to the angels, and ordered the latter to prostrate themselves in honor of him.[4] No wonder then that in Islām man is regarded as the crown of creation, higher than the angels precisely on account of his unique ethical vocation and destiny.

Man's Innocence

Islām holds that man is created innocent and lays out the drama, as it were, after his birth, not before. No matter who his parents were, who his uncles and ancestors, his brothers and sisters, his neighbors or his society, man is born innocent. It repudiates every notion of original sin, of hereditary guilt, of vicarious responsibility, of tribal, national, or international involvement of the person in past events before his birth. Every man is born with a clean slate, it asserts, basing its stand on the absolute autonomy and individuality of the human person. No soul, the Qur'ān declares, will bear any but its own burden.[5] To it belongs all that it has itself personally earned, whether merit or demerit. None will receive judgment for the deeds of another, and none may intercede on behalf of another. Islām defines man's responsibility exclusively in terms of his own deeds and defines a deed as the act in which man, the sane, adult person, enters into bodily, consciously, and voluntarily, and in which he produces some disturbance of the flow of space-time. That guilt and responsibility are ethical categories and are incurred only where a free and conscious deed is committed is a "hard datum" of ethical consciousness.

A number of modern Christian thinkers sought to reestablish the old doctrine of original sin by giving it a new, descriptive base. Such base, they claimed, was furnished by the discoveries of biologists and psychologists and their analyses of human nature. The will to live, to survive, to satisfy the instincts, the desire for pleasure and comfort, man's will to power, his egotism, and even the undeniable fact of his imperfection and otherness than God—all these have been claimed to constitute in their opinion so many loci of original sin, which they then define as the self-centered direction of all these natural or psychic inclinations.

Surely, man is made of all that the biochemist, physiologist, pathologist, psychologist, and all the sciences study in him, and the object of their studies is certainly a "given," another "hard datum," predetermined before birth. But all this, whether physical or psychic, is natural and necessary. Man does not have it by choice.

The baby and the adult are determined by their bodily frames, the one not to climb a mountain and the other not to carry an elephant. But it would be repugnant to reason to call either of them "guilty" of their failures to climb the mountain or carry the elephant. The Qur'ān has declared that no man may be responsible for any more than he can bear.[6] Determination by nature is consonant with innocence and constitutes no valid ground for incrimination. For, ethical responsibility is commensurate with capacity for the controlled use of one's natural equipment with a view to produce the objective contemplated by consciousness. Where there is no capacity, there can be no freedom and hence neither responsibility nor guilt. Modern advocates of original sin have often fallen back upon the endowment of nature for justification of their theory. Their most common plea is: Consider the self-centeredness of the newborn infant, not to speak of the adult person. Topping all modern Christian apologetics in bombast is the grandiose claim of Paul Tillich who defined original sin as the personal guilt incurred by passage from essence to existence of the idea of man within the mind of God.[7] The sweeping assertion of some Indian thinkers, not forgetting Gautama, the Buddha, that man—indeed the whole realm of nature—is both evil and unreal, is of the same kind.[8]

Imago Dei

The Qur'ān claims, in agreement with the Jewish and Christian views, that man is created in God's image.[9] Like Judaism, and unlike Christianity, however, it regards this image as innate in all men and permanent, that is to say, being part of nature, it cannot be lost. Islām does not follow Christianity in distinguishing between a natural imago dei (as actus) and an ethical one (as reatus). Neither does it allow either or both of them any ontological status, as the theological term inquinamentum indicates. The Christian distinction is needed to make the fall something ontological, something true of all human beings, and this would constitute the necessary predicament from which no man can save himself by his own effort—which is the assumption of the Incarnation.[10] Islām did not share these assumptions and could hence regard every man at all times as embodying the divine image.

Islāmic thought built upon this notion of God's image in man its philosophic anthropology. The Qur'ān asserted that man was endowed with a soul, and defined the latter as "of the breath of God."[11] Man's soul was then analyzed into an animal component that gave man his sentience and desires, and a rational component that gave him his mind. The Qur'ān told of man's endowment with the senses, with a capacity for knowledge of nature, of God and of His will, strong enough to be trustworthy—indeed to substitute for revelation or to be its equal.[12] Muslim philosophers have universally equated the two. Reason was the part of man which made him Godlike; being the breath of God, reason is man's most Godlike organ and hence the faculty by which like can know like, by which man can know God.

This divine image is ubiquitous in all men. It cannot ever be destroyed or lost and it constitutes man's essential humanity. It is his noblest and most precious possession. It is divine. Where it is missing, there is no human being; where it is deficient, the condition of the patient is called insanity. Here Islāmic humanism is one with the philosophic humanism of the Greeks (Socrates, Plato, and Aristotle), with the difference that, whereas for the Greeks the highest object of rationality was *Paideia* or culture, for the Muslims, it is *taqwā* or piety. On second look, however, Islāmic piety turns out to include Greek *Paideia,* for in Islām, the recognition of God as God, i.e., as Creator, Lord, and Judge, is the highest rationality ever.

Islām is radically different from Greek humanism where the latter recognized the free citizens and assigned the slaves to another inferior category. It is equally different from Jewish humanism that while asserting the *imago dei* to be present in all men by nature, differentiates between men on the level of birth and nature by assigning an elect status to its own adherents. It is different from Christian humanism where the latter distinguishes between *imago dei* as a natural *zelem,* possessed by all men and an acquired *demuth* that only its adherents possess as a result of their faith and baptism. Finally, it is different from secular European humanism that defines itself in terms of European culture exclusively, and this relegates the Asians, Africans, and other non-Europeans to a bushman level. Even the great Kant, the noblest prince of the Enlightenment, the advocate of the categorical imperative, was unable to push his own rationalism to its logical conclusion and assigned inferior status to the Asians and Africans. Islām regards all men alike, and God never tires of reminding man in the Qur'ān, "We have created you all from one pair—all from dust—Higher among you is he who is higher in righteousness . . . and knowledge."[13] "Those who know and those who don't, are they equals?" Qur'ān asks rhetorically.[14]

On the day of his Farewell pilgrimage, the Prophet received a revelation signalling the completion of the revelation and of Islām. On
that solemn occasion he found fit to remind the Muslims who were
all Arab in race but a handful, all Arab in language and culture
without exception, "No difference whatever between an Arab and
a nonArab, a black man and a white man, can exist except in
righteousness."[15]

The second faculty constitutive of the soul as mind or reason, is
man's capacity for responsibility. The Muslim philosophers insisted
on defining this capacity as *qadar* or capacity for action, and the
theologians, as *kasb* or capacity for acquisition of the consequences
of action, action being exclusively a divine prerogative. The difference between *qadar* and *kasb* is a theological nicety. On the ethical
level they are equal for both have the same effect of attributing
responsibility to man for his deeds.

Man's capacity to know the good or the will of God, his capacity
to fulfill or not to fulfill the imperative, and his responsibility for
his deeds constitute his humanistic "equipment." All men are
endowed with this equipment without exception.

Islām has no soteriology. "Salvation," in its purview, is an
improper religious concept devoid of equivalent term in the Islamic
vocabulary. It is a fabricated hope in a state of impotence and
despair. Islām therefore rejects the view that man stands in any
predicament from which he cannot ever extricate himself, and from
which he stands to be "saved." Adam, the first man, committed a
misdeed (eating from the prohibited tree), but he repented and was
forgiven.[16] His misdeed was an ordinary human mistake; it was the
first error in ethical judgment, the first misconduct, the first crime.
But, for all its firstness, it was the deed of one man, and hence his
own, personal responsibility. It had no effect on anyone else besides
him. Not only was it devoid of cosmic effect, but even of any effect
upon his own children. It constituted no "fall," neither for Adam
himself, nor for anyone else. It did send Adam from Paradise to
earth but it changed nothing in his nature, his capacities, his promise, his vocation, or his destiny. Man is not "fallen" and hence there
is no need to "save" or ransom him. Rather, man stands under an
imperative, an ought-to-do, and his worth is a function of his fulfillment or otherwise of the imperative. Rather than "fall," Islām
asserts innocence, rather than "salvation," felicity. Being an exact
function of his own deeds, man's felicity or infelicity is totally his
own work. Such felicity does not depend upon anyone's blessing or

agency; it is not the effect of a sacrament, or of an ontic participation in a mystical body such as the Church. Islām is free of both.

The moral imperative to which man is subject neither looks towards, nor refers to, any past event whether a "fall" or a "ransom" effected by someone else. It does not arise out of such past events but is totally constituted by something present or future. Hence, Islām knows no "justification by faith," no history of salvation, or *Heilsgeschichte.* The only relevant past it recognizes is the revelation of divine commandments and past men's felicity or infelicity as obedience or violation of these commandments.

Instead of flowing from faith in a salvific drama that happened in the past, man's morality comes from the Muslim's faith that God is. In his perspective, the existence of God is the existence of truth and value, both of which lay claim to his loyalty and energy. Such claim consists in the positive disturbance of space-time to the end of actualizing therein the divine pattern. Faith and all the attendant faculties by which values and their relations are cognized and their materials are selected and assigned are only preparations for concretization. Spirituality itself, the whole realm of it, Islām asserts, is nothing unless it is concretized, actualized in real men and women. Assuming that at birth man stands on the threshold of ethicality, at the zero point of the ethical dimension, Islām conceives of his duty as positive deeds, as the doing of something new, not as the undoing of something past. Its ethic is wholly forward-looking, even when it is arch-conservative and stagnant. It is this ethical affirmativeness which gave the Muslim his *élan.* Not weighed down by shackles from the past, he became an exemplar of worldliness and activism, an inveterate enemy of world-denial and history-deprecation.

Actionalism

Carrying the internalizing ethical insights of Jeremiah and later Semitic men of religion to their logical conclusion, Jesus (upon whom be peace!) was sent as prophet to the Jews in order to promote the personalist ethic of intention against the growing externalism and literalism of the Pharisees and Sadducees. It was natural that such extremism was contrasted with an opposite extremism in order to expose the aberrating exaggeration. Jesus taught the principle that the moral character of an act is a function, not of its effects or consequences, which are measured by the values of utility, but of its accompanying and motivating intent, exclusively. In numerous parables, he illustrated beautifully the point that what seems to be evil in its effect is really not so because of its motivation; where the intent is pure, where the heart is determined by the noble purpose of love of God and obedience to Him, the act is wholesome and the person saved. It was thus that Augustine could say, "Love God and do what you will" and Immanuel Kant, "The only intrinsically good thing is a good will." Jesus' sublime effort was therefore oriented toward the internal, radical self-transformation of the person. It was not part of that ethic to deprecate the effects of moral action and hence of the world, of space-time, and history. Its strength lies in its singleminded determination to cleanse and purify the spring of all action—the will. If it defined the moral good as a state of the will when it is determined by the love of God, it did rightly. For the slightest violation of this principle is *ipso facto* vitiation of any deed whatever. This was Jesus' divine answer to rampant externalism, to a law-enthusiasm that had lost the spirit of the law.[17]

Islām acknowledged the revelation of Jesus, and confirmed its ethical insights with enthusiasm. Indeed, in the interest of furthering that insight, it ordered its adherents to pronounce verbally, before entering into every morally or religiously significant deed, the formula, "I intend the projected act for the sake of God." Whether a ritual of worship, or removal of a nuisance from the public road, Islām declared no act ethically meritorious unless it was so prefaced, so dedicated to "the Face of Allah." Islām has thus institutionalized the good intention, and almost externalized it in the process—a practice adopted thereafter by Judaism in the Middle Ages under Islāmic influence—in order to guarantee its presence in the moral agent.

This notwithstanding, Islām went beyond intentionalism to an ethic of action. Having assured the good intention as a *conditio sine qua non* of morality, it prescribed passage from the will to action, from the realm of personal consciousness of space-time, to the rough and tumble of the market place, the murky business of history-in-the-making. Values, or the divine will, must not only be the object of human intention. It must become actual, and man is the creature meant to actualize it in freedom and for the sake of God. He must therefore disturb the ontological poise of creation. He must re-knead and cut nature so as to actualize therein the moral dimension of the divine pattern revealed to him. He must bring the world's latent tendencies to full fruition or self-realization. The extent to which he is successful in achieving this is the criterion of his *falāḥ,* or ethical felicity. While the good will is an entrance ticket to the arena of ethical striving and endeavor, actionalism or the efficacious actualization of the absolute in history is the entrance ticket to Paradise bearing the closeness to God of one's residence therein. This is not a return to the utilitarian or casuistic ethics of consequences. For the good intention is presupposed. It is a "plus" that Islām is seeking, not a substitute, nor a "minus." The ethic of Jesus correctly saw that personal conscience is the ultimate judge of one's moral status on earth. For only conscience knows the determinants of the will and its judgment is alone capable of setting the will right. Action, on the other hand, is by nature public, altruistic, and goes beyond the self. It is visible to the world and measurable by external means, whether its object is self, other selves, or nature. Hence, it is necessary that it be regulated by public law—the *sharī'ah;* administered by a public office or state—the caliphate; its disputes adjudicated by a public judiciary—*qaḍā'.* With this in mind, Islām declared action the necessary concomitant of faith.[18] God's commandments to act are innumerable in the Qur'ān, and leave no room for doubt. God's condemnation of *qu'ūd* (rest, inaction) is no less emphatic.[19] Even where solitude, self-isolation, or inaction is sought for cultivation of the personalist virtues of the inner self, as in the case of Christian monasticism, Islām condemned it blatantly. "Monkery," the Qur'ān said, "is the invention of priests, not a divine prescription ... [Moreover] they [the Christians] have abused it."[20]

Ummatism

Actionalism, we have seen, demands man's transcendence of himself to what is other than himself. When this other-than-self is nature, Islāmic actionalism means to transform the world into Paradise. Everything that natural science and technology prescribe for such transformation becomes a religious duty incumbent upon every Muslim. When the other-than-self is another human being or beings, Islāmic actionalism means to transform humankind into heroes, saints, and geniuses, in whose life and activity the divine will is fulfilled. This involvement with other humans is not what is meant by ummatism. Moral altruism, or such involvement with the welfare of others, can well be, and is in many cases, the concern of non-ummatists, indeed of monastics. The Christian need for

Near East/Western

such altruism was the chief concern of Pachomius, over the personalist isolationism of Antonius, in early Christian Egypt.[21]

It is in what concerns the doer or agent as subject of action that Islām brought the new notion of ummatism, requiring that the doer involve others in the action as co-doers or co-operators. Its purpose was to make actionalism collective, to bring the other self or selves into sharing the action as subjects, and hence incurring its moral merit or demerit. If an altruism seeking to improve or perfect man as object will not do, a regimented society whose members act together as subjects out of habit or custom, or from fear of a political tyrant, will not do either. Since the desired end is moral, its achievement must be the work of the subject in a condition of moral freedom. It should be willed, and so for the sake of God, if it is to be moral at all. The achievement of the automation of duty is morally worthless, and so is that of a collective of subjects acting out of any kind of external coercion. Only the action that can be other than it is, depending on the unencumbered vision and will of the subject, has moral worth.

Islām therefore prescribes that the other selves be invited, educated, warned, and adequately moved to join in every deed, willing the objective in question. While coercing them might well realize the utilitarian values in nature, and regimenting them might well realize the moral altruistic objectives in men, the realization itself would never be moral. And yet, that is precisely what Islām requires. It can be achieved if and only if the other selves are approached with a view to convincing them of the desirability of the action; and once convinced, they would engage in it and bring about the real-existents or matériaux of values voluntarily and consciously. Since realization of the divine will is infinite, relevant to all activities, to all persons, at all times and places, it follows that the society Islām projects is one perpetually stirring to convince and be convinced, to pursue and actualize value in freedom. Such society is society properly speaking in the Gesellschaft sense of the term, not the Gemeinschaft sense. Such society is the ummah Islām seeks.[22] Its members constitute a threefold consensus: in the mind or vision, in the intention or will, and in the realization or action. It is the brotherhood of the believers under the sharīʿah, or law of God, set into perpetual motion. It is a school, grosser stils, where the business of "convincing" the mind is eternal; a gymnasium of the heart where the will is eternally subject to disciplining and cultivating, and an arena where destiny is seized by the horns and history is made. Unlike the political theories of liberalism, the ummatist theory is one where government governs most not least, and where sovereignty belongs to God and His law, not to the arbitrary will of majority or minority, and where the ultimate good is the divine pattern, not the *eudaemonia* of the members. Into membership of the *ummah* the individual Muslim is not a conscript, but a volunteer for life, perpetually mobilized to bring about actualization of the absolute on earth.[23] The *ummah* is a society where actionalism is totalist, not totalitarian, authoritative but not authoritarian.

All this flows from the fact, proclaimed in the Qur'ān, that human life is not a sport, that existence is not a game, but a deadly serious matter.[24] The *engagé* Muslim is a serious being who lives for a cause. God said in His Book, "We have not created you, mankind, except that you may prove yourselves the worthier in the deed."[25] Hence, the Muslim's career is replete with danger. But his precarious existence is his pride, and his vision of the divine will, his nourishment. His constant awareness of God is not a hollow obsession. Under it, he sees himself as the cosmic median between God and creation. Because of it, he is the vortex of cosmic history.

Principles of Ethical Decision Making

Universalism

The totalism of the divine will leaves no human being outside of its relevance, just as it leaves no point outside of space-time. The whole world is object, and the whole of humankind is object and subject of moral striving. The earth is therefore object of the Muslim's endeavor, and all humankind is to be involved in its and their own transformation. The universalism of Islām is absolute and without exception just as God is Lord and Master of all without exception. The world can hence be either within or without the world order of Islām. That is why classical Islāmic theory regarded the world as divided between a Dār al Islām (The House of Islām) and Dar al Ḥarb (House of War). For there is no third alternative between the order of ethical freedom, responsibility, and peace, and that where these are denied, no middle ground between lawfulness and lawlessness. Just as the individual stands under the obligation of transcending himself to the others, so does society. Isolationism is moral lethargy and uncharity for both individuals as well as societies. When it is practiced in face of injustice, aggression, crime, hunger, ignorance, and non-actualization of values, it is downright criminal, a thumbing of one's nose at God or defiance. Cynicism is diametrical contradiction of God's affirmation of His purposiveness, of the meaningfulness of all that is. However, the real opposite of universalism is particularism, which has taken the form of henotheism and tribalism in the past, and of racism and nationalism in our day. The Hebrew-Jewish tradition has occasionally been accused of a strand of particularism because its people have regarded themselves as the elect of God. And their modern descendants have upheld the biological definition of Jew in face of their claim to an equal status that they had hitherto been denied by the nations.[26] The Christians of history have on the whole heeded the advice of St. Paul, "In Christ there is neither Jew nor Greek."[27] It must be admitted though that from Augustine to the Crusades, Luther, Calvin, and American Puritanism, the doctrine of pre-destination has served as cover for crass racism against other Christians and non-Christians. The Christians' conduct toward one another throughout their history, and toward the Africans, Asians, and Amerindians during the last centuries, has brought dishonor to Paul as well as to Jesus who answered, when he was requested to give special attention to his kin because they were sons of Abraham, "God is able of these stones to raise up children unto Abraham"[28]

Islām has always been universalist, and the Muslims have as far as this problem is concerned, the cleanest record in history. The religion, as represented by its supreme authority, the divine word or the Qur'ān, speaks with utmost emphasis and clarity. "O mankind, We have created you of one pair, male and female, and constituted you in tribes and peoples that you may complement one another. Nobler among you is only the more righteous."[29] "O men, Fear your Lord Who created you all from one and the same soul."[30] The qualities and equipment constitutive of humanness are recognized by Islām to be possessed by all mankind by nature. It does not discriminate against anybody on the grounds that the said qualities or equipment were never present, or were once present but subsequently lost because of a guilt incurred by the individual or by his ancestors or fellows. Nor does it bind this egalitarianism to a specific culture or civilization. The ethical principles constitutive of Islāmic humanism are not denied of any human being even though he may belong to another faith; to another culture, civilization, or age; or if, by some accident of his people's involvement in history, he was or still is, a slave.[31] The universalism of Islām transcends all human distinctions. It reaches to the *fitrah,* or the state of nature in which every man is born. There, it recognizes what nature has given, or what by virtue of being born, the man is entitled to.[32]

Certainly Islām assigns privileges to knowledge and wisdom, to piety, virtue, righteousness, good works, and self-exertion for God's sake. "Unequal are those who have spent their wealth and exposed their lives in the cause of Allah, and those who remained behind. . . . "[33] And it states unequivocally that such differentiation remains true only as long and in so far as the adherent is wiser, more pious, more righteous, and self-exerting. "If they turn away from this cause, then God will bring forth another people [to take their place] who will not be like them."[34] All Semitic religions have represented the God-man relationship in terms of a covenant wherein man is to serve God and God is to bless man with crops, children, well being, and happiness, and all of them were keenly aware of the opposite, namely, that where man does not serve God, he would be invested with suffering and punishment. Only Judaism and Christianity have altered the "Covenant," a concept which implies the two directional activities of God and man into the "Promise." For Judaism, this is the one-directional commitment on the part of God to favor the Jews regardless of their piety or righteousness—nay, even in their a-whoring after other gods, to use the image of Hosea. And for the Christians, this is the unilateral commitment of God to love and ransom His "partner," namely man, even though he sins—nay, *because* he sins— against God. Islām has maintained the Mesopotamian "Covenant" that gives rise to obligation on both parties, the one to serve and the other to reward, and to privileges to both parties, the one to defy and not-serve, and the other to punish.[35]

Comprehensiveness

The will of the Creator is relevant to everything in creation, for it constitutes its *raison d'etre*. And since nothing stands outside of creation, it follows that all beings and all events ought to fulfill one part or another of the divine will. In this sense, nature is ever-obedient to God by necessity and human life ought to be so in freedom. Whether on the personal or social level, at home, in the city, or in the world at large, every human activity ought to fulfill that element of the divine will assigned for it. Man's pursuit of material value, of intellectual, spiritual, and esthetic value, ought to be determined by the divine. No activity may escape this determination. The divine will, the realm of values, lays claim to everything in

space-time seeking to subject it to its determination; i.e., to assume
the form or pattern God wishes for it. Of course the degree or
intensity of determination differs. Besides the main division of
necessity and freedom, determination differs within the latter. The
ought-ness that belongs to the recognition of God and His unity,
or to the preservation of human life, is of a different degree from
that which belongs to knocking at the door and seeking permission
before entry or to speaking always with a soft voice. But an ought-
to-be pattern for both does exist and is an integral portion of the
divine will. Cynicism, libertinage, and egotism, for example, mis-
takenly deny the comprehensiveness of the realms of value when
their objection really concerns the order of rank of the value in
question. It is both natural and commonplace to let anyone eat what
he likes, to dress and sleep as he likes, but not to injure or dispossess
as he likes. This is not due to the relevance of value to the one and
irrelevance to the other. Value, or the divine will, is relevant to
both; the intensity or degree of the relevance, the order of rank
belonging to them, is different.

Equally, this is the common mistake of differentiating between
law and ethics. The claim that law, unlike ethics, carries sanctions
against its violators, omits the fact that ethics does no less. The
sanctions of the latter are applied by God whether in this world or
in the next. To the believer, both are equally real, and indeed,
God's sanctions are the more dreadful. The ought-ness of the legal
prescription and that of the ethical is one, though their differing
order of rank may make observance more urgent and violation
more condemnable. The same equivalence applies to offenses
against conscience (e.g., jealousy, resentment, etc.) as those against
the law. Both are violations of an ought-to-be that is part of the
divine will, though the one concerns intention, the other action.

The sharī'ah, or law of Islām, is a complete system of desiderata,
principles, rules, and laws regarding human activity. Its coverage is
more comprehensive than any other law, for it includes ritual,
criminal, political, economic, social, physical, as well as personal
behavior. Naturally, it prescribes sanctions according to the order
of rank of the value concerned but it leaves hardly anything to fall
outside its purview. For some violations, it prescribes specific punishments, for others, it leaves the punishments to the discretion of
the judge. It classifies human deeds into obligatory (wājib) and recommended (mandūb), prohibited (harām) and recommended
against (makrūh), prescribing sanctions for neglect of the former

and commitment of the latter. The left out area—namely, the permissible *(mubāḥ)*— is thus reduced to the barest minimum, but never escaping the relevance of the *sharīʿah*. This comprehensiveness of the *sharīʿah*, or the totalist determination of space-time by the divine will, sanctifies human life by adding to it a dimension of the eternal. The Muslim does not therefore regard himself as existing and acting, as it were, by his own right. Pure eudaemonism is for him a ridiculous ideal, hedonism is downright despicable, and the division of human activity into secular and religious is a rebellion against God. The life that is worthy of man is one totally dedicated to the pursuit of the divine will in all its detail. Observance of the laws of traffic is as religious as that of the laws affecting property, life, worship, or war and peace. The sanctity of life is inseparable from its unity, and its unity, inseparable from the will of the Creator of all life.

Life- and World-Affirmation

It follows from the essence of religious experience in Islām that God has placed man in a world that is to be the theater for his service to Him. If God is not to be a malevolent trickster, man's service must be possible. This possibility requires that the world be malleable, capable of receiving man's action, transformable into the pattern which God has revealed. A complete ontological fitness of man and world to each other is a necessary consequence of the divine arrangement.

Unlike speculative Hindu thought and unlike Buddhism and Jainism, Islām does not regard the world as alien to righteousness or religious felicity. In itself, the world is not to be denied and combated. On the contrary, it is innocent and good, created precisely to the end of being used and enjoyed by man. The evil is not in it, but in its abuse by man. That is the villain that deserves to be denied and combated; the immoral use of the world. That is why the ethic of Islām is not that of asceticism. The Prophet has directed his followers against overextended rituals of worship, against celibacy, against exaggerated fasting, against pessimism, and the morose mood. He ordered them to break the fast before performing the sunset prayer, to keep their bodies clean and their teeth brushed, to groom and perfume themselves and wear their best clothes when they congregate for prayer, to marry, to take their time to rest and to sleep and recreate themselves with sports and the arts. Naturally, Islām ordered its adherent to cultivate his faculties; to understand

himself, nature, and the world in which he lives; to satisfy his
innate craving for food, shelter, comfort, sex, and reproduction; to
realize balance and harmony in his relations with men and nature;
to transform the earth into a producing orchard, a fertile farm and
a beautiful garden; to express his understanding, his craving, his
doing, and realizing in works of aesthetic beauty. All this is history
as well as culture. To make history and create culture and to do so
well is the content of the divine will. It is righteousness. Indeed,
Islām regarded every act capable of adding, however little, to the
total value of the cosmos, as an act of worship, of service to God,
provided of course it is entered into for His sake. Hence the Muslim
has no inhibitions about his body, or the satisfaction of his instincts.
As conscious believer, such satisfaction is for him a "taste" of the
joys of Paradise to come if he continues to fulfill his duty to God.
"Who dared prohibit the niceties of this world and the delicacies
of His providing?" the Qur'ān asks rhetorically, and answers
emphatically, "They are indeed rightful for the enjoyment of the
faithful in this world, and will all be purely theirs on the Day of
Judgment.³⁶ Repeatedly, the Qur'ān commands, "Eat, drink and
enjoy yourselves, but do not abuse."³⁷

This clearly presupposes honoring work, success, and achievement in the transformation of nature. If the world is to yield its
fruits, it must be cultivated. Thus the ancient Mesopotamian principle of agricultural service to God is recrystallized as the general
transformation of the earth into the orchard wherein man is to find
his nourishment and pleasure. The Qur'ān affirms that God has created the world for man, hence, everything in creation is for man to
use and to enjoy. The oceans, the rivers and mountains, indeed the
skies and stars, sun and moon—all have been created for man's usufruct and esthetic (zīnah) pleasure.³⁸

The ummatism of Islām blesses man's will to power. "He who
has not participated in at least one bay'ah (election of a caliph) dies
a non-Muslim," a famous tradition of the Prophet says. It is God
Who instituted the state, political order, and participation in the
political process as a religious duty. The ruler is to execute the law
of God; the ruled is to obey the law and advise the ruler and help
him in upholding the law. Both are to mobilize their efforts perpetually to extend this application depthwise in fulfillment of the
requirement of totalism, and breadthwise in fulfillment of those of
universalism. This is the ultimate realization of the absolute Islām
seeks and declares possible in this world and in time. It has no use

for a "kingdom of God" conceived as an alternative to this kingdom, as a messianic age where what is denied here will be realized, an "outer world" in which the *summum bonum* is realizable at the cost of "this world." Such otherworldly categories Islām has rejected altogether. With this rejection went equally all mortification of the flesh, world-denial, monasticism, and asceticism. So strong was this rejection by Islām and so strong was its world-affirmation that it was too often accused of "pure worldliness." The truth is that Islāmic worldliness is not "pure," but tempered; and that is precisely the role played by the consciousness of God and spirituality in Islāmic life. Pursuit of the world, Islām commands, must be carried out as fulfillment of God's commandment to pursue the world and hence, in obedience to the ethical limits set by God's other commandments. This is really what Islāmic spirituality means: not a disembodied life of constant prayer and meditation, of self- and world-denial, and of pining after a kingdom hopelessly unrealizable in space-time, but a full and innocent enjoyment of this world, combined with persistent activism for its betterment, and regulated by ethical precepts opposed to exaggeration, injury, injustice, hatred, and discrimination.

Justice

The three great Semitic faiths are eschatological. Judaism looks forward to a "Messianic Age" where the Jews will be restituted and vindicated since their formative age was one of defeat and persecution. Christians look forward to a second advent of Christ incepting the "Kingdom of God" where the absolute will be realized since it cannot ever be realized in history. In both cases, the Judgment will take place, but in both cases it is only a preparation for the *eschaton,* the age when everything will be as it should have, but has never been. Unlike its predecessors, Islām looks forward to the Judgment, but it does not do so as to another "Kingdom," but merely as judgment coming at the termination of history. What happens after the Judgment, *viz.,* eternal bliss in Paradise or eternal suffering in Hell, is only a consequence of judgment. It does not conceive of the "Other World," whether Paradise or Hell, as an alternative to this world, for this world is not an evil that should not have been but one that should have been as it was and is. The "Other World" or "Life Eternal" or Paradise-and-Hell is only the consummation of the verdict of judgment, the latter remaining purely and simply what it is, namely judgment. The Prophet

Muḥammad and his companions lived their lives under the awesome shadow of the Judgment. God as Lord of the Judgment determined their consciousness in a preeminent way. "God as the Judge" continues to dominate the consciousness of all Muslims.

This tremendous role that the Judgment occupies in Islāmic consciousness is based on Justice, on an absolute scale that knows no favoritism, no intercession, no partisanship, no weakness, and no inclination in the Judge or in His process of meting out judgment.[39] Because it is judgment of all men and all history, any exception to the law of justice would cause the collapse of the whole system. Even if it is divine, a mercy or love which transcends justice makes of man a divine puppet. Islām does not deny God's mercy, but it regards it as an arbitrary measure belonging to an almighty transcendent being. Justice-transcending mercy contradicts the notion of seeking one's salvation "in fear and trembling."

On the other hand, Islām regards justice as the norm and pattern of God's judgment. No man, Islām asserts, may live his life assuming that divine mercy will eventually come to the rescue. It constantly reminds the Muslim that blest or unblest, every man will receive on the Final Day exactly what he himself had earned.[40]

Man and God are not competitors with each other, as in the Promethean view. Nor is man, even if he is a Muslim, the favorite of God who remains His favorite regardless of morality and despite his "hardness and stiffneckedness" as Deuteronomy claimed on behalf of the Jew. Nor is man the object of a divine love that sacrifices a divine being as an oblation for him as in the Christian view. Though not Prometheanly arrogant, man is not helpless. He can "save" himself by his own effort, that is, he can realize the divine pattern in himself, in the world, and in history. On this real possibility a different dignity is based. Rather than the Christian, "I am the being whom God had ransomed with His own Son," the Muslim asserts, "I am the being whose fate has been put entirely in his own hands." When the former asserts with Luther that "God's righteousness is His mercy," the latter rejoins, "God's mercy is His righteousness." Divine Justice is the guarantor of the Muslim's dignity and self-esteem and is the lock on the door barring human complacency in matters moral.

This, in brief, is the groundwork of the ethics of Islām. The principles on which we have touched in the foregoing analysis constitute the prolegomena, the metaphysic. As values, these principles are the word of God, His will and hence divine, eternal and immutable. As embodiment of them, the *sharī'ah,* or law of Islām, is divine. But it must be borne in mind that the claim for divine status of the *sharī'ah* concerns that of which it is the embodiment, the figurization, the prescriptivization. As figurized, i.e., as translated into concrete directives for application to daily life and affairs, it is human, except in those relatively few cases where the Qur'ān and/ or the Prophet has furnished the figurization as well as the principle contained in the figurization. In the realm of translating the divine imperatives into rules applicable in concrete situations, man is to use his God-given faculties of rational, intuitive, and empirical insight. He may always fall into error. But that is his God-granted prerogative. And he may hit the truth and do right. As the Prophet had said, "Whoever exercises his mind [in understanding and interpreting the law of God] and errs, has earned one unit of merit. Whoever does so and falls on the truth has earned double." In all cases, Allah certainly knows best!

Ethical Response to Some Contemporary Issues

On the Political Front

It follows from Islām's religious experience that all humans are equally the creatures of God placed in the world (His manor) in order to serve Him, by fulfilling the patterns of His will as revealed or established through reason. All humans are equal in that race for value. Thus Islām countenances no ethnocentrism, no nationalism, no isolationism, no protectionism, and no cultural relativism. It tolerates any diversity of political structures but it judges them all on the basis of the *sharī'ah:* How far they contribute to the preservation of peace? to the usufruct of nature and enjoyment of God's bounty? to the ethical felicity of the citizens? How much do they enable or at least require the people to give of their material, intellectual, and spiritual wealth to the rest of humankind? How open are they to envelop humanity as their citizens? Islām's political ideal is the world-state where man is free to move and dwell wherever he pleases without exit, entry, or customs permit; where the order is peace and competition is in righteousness. From its purview, the present division of the globe into parties competing for world dominion at the risk of world-destruction, for nationalistic (egotistic) monopoly on God's bounty, is not only crazy. It is Satanic.

On the Economic Front

It follows from Islām's world-affirmative stance, that God's bounty
in creation is to be had and enjoyed, partly as reward for one's work
and obedience to God, and partly as the theater in which the modalities of obtaining and consuming God's bounty realize or violate
ethical value. Human instincts and needs are there to be satisfied.
Humans are free to choose their occupations, as well as to acquire
wealth in any amount their talents and efforts make possible. Poverty is the Promise of Satan, and, according to the Qur'ān,[41] chas-
tises those who are poor because of laziness and lack of daring.[42] As
to those who are poor by necessity, God has assigned to them a
"right" in the wealth of the affluent."[43] The limitations upon
enjoyment of God's bounty are not material but ethical. Cheating,
robbing, and beguiling in production or distribution are crimes and
so are monopoly, profiteering, cornering the market, and marking
profit without assumption of risk (interest-levying). Ethical limitations are also imposed by Islām on consumption. All acquired and
held wealth is subject to zakāt, a purifying tax of 2½% per year to
be spent on the needy and welfare of the public. Beyond this tax,
charity is most commendable, the principle being that man ought
not to keep of his appropriated wealth any more than he needs to
satisfy his current needs and those of his dependents.[44] Indeed, the
more he legitimately earns, the more he legitimately consumes and
lets others consume with him, the greater is his merit with God.
Islām therefore approves of an interest-free capitalism[45] in which
production and consumption are maximized, the benefits of which
are distributed to the widest possible range of humans, and where
the opportunities for employment are equally available to all
humanity. Since the world is God's manor, and humans are His
servants and stewards, it is their right to usufruct nature and benefit
from it, not to rape, pollute, or spoil it. Islām demands of its adherents that they leave the world better than when they received it.
The realization of the absolute being both desirable and possible in
this world, it is imperative that the cumulative effect of man's usufruct of nature not bring about depletion of its resources.

On the Social Front

Islām regards human instincts as innocent and their satisfaction as
legitimate. As mentioned earlier, celibacy is prohibited and the
ascetic ideal discouraged. Marriage is a divine pattern,[46] ordained to
make human life continuous through generation and providing an

infinite realm of relations in which ethical values may be realized. Sexual pleasure is therefore a good, a gift from God.[47] Its obtention outside of marriage, however, turns it into an evil, for marriage is a solemn contracting of responsibility from which adultery is an escape.[48] Women are full, legal persons, entitled to act as such in all circumstances and to preserve their separate identities on an equal par with men. Their marriage does not affect their legal status at all. Moreover all women, whatever their age or wealth, do not have to earn their livelihood. They stand forever exempt, for they are entitled to their livelihood from their male relatives, on an equal level. If, in addition, Islāmic law has allocated to them an inheritance half the size of their brothers, it is indeed as a further, even extraordinary, guarantee of their autonomy and independence.

Likewise, Islāmic law regards everyone as supporter or dependent of another to the full extent of demonstrated kinship and need. That is why the Islāmic family is an extended one covering numerous members and several generations, thus making socialization and acculturation easier. Equally, the extended family makes work outside the home for any member (male or female) possible without disruption of family life and child care, and prevents solitude and the feeling of being unloved from playing havoc with psychic health. To consolidate these gains further, Islāmic law prescribed the rights of the neighbor to be visited when sick, to be assisted when in need, to be protected (person and property) when in danger, and to be given a proper funeral and burial in death.

On the Juridical Front

Islām gave the minority the name of dhimmī (covenanter for peace and security under the guarantee—dhimmah—of God and His Prophet). It recognized the dhimmī's right to dissent, to have his own religion, culture, ummah (ordered community), and institutions. The sharī'ah not only recognizes the law of non-Muslims as legitimate, but enforces them wherever there are dhimmīs. It was the first to teach a pluralism of laws, not merely a pluralism of ethnic restaurants and costumes. And it still is unique among the legal systems of the world in its tolerance and legitimization of other laws than those of its own system.

True, the sharī'ah is harsh on crime. But punishment is a necessary evil. Its enforcement brings the further benefit of prevention and pedagogy by example. It is a deterioration of justice when it takes capital (fees, etc.) to obtain it, or when it takes months and years to reach it. Islāmic justice, *per contra,* is both swift and free. Since Islāmic law is the law of God, derived rationally from the texts of the Holy Qur'ān and Sunnah of the Prophet, any one may question the constitutionality of any provision of it, whether Muslim or non-Muslim, citizen or noncitizen. The same reasoning enables every human being on earth to enter into contract with the Islāmic state to realize any legitimate common advantage, as well as to sue in any Islāmic court that Islāmic state which fails to uphold the full provisions of the *sharī'ah* in any of its departments.

On the Bioethical Front

Every human being is entitled to marry and to raise a family. This means, among other things, the right to be the means for the creation of new life, a right that is inseparable from numerous responsibilities. Impregnation, therefore, must imply that one has assumed the duties of caring for the mother and child, and for the upbringing, acculturation, and socialization of the offspring. It may not take place outside of marriage, but in it, i.e., under a contract proclaiming and specifying the responsibilities of the parents toward each other, their progeny, their next of kin, their community, and society.

Since God is the cause of life, and life is a gift that He grants to whomsoever He please, the *sharī'ah* regards it as a universal and inviolable right that the person has from the moment of conception. Abortion is not permissible except in two cases: where pregnancy endangers the mother's life, and where it is the result of a rape that does not result in marriage. Every person born is entitled to carry the father's name, and to receive sustenance, care, education, and protection from parents and family. Legal personality is the corollary of life (the gift of God), and may not be violated or changed. Hence, Islām sees no need for adoption, for the law holds the relatives responsible in all cases. It encourages hosting, giving to, and caring for children, but prohibits tampering with their legal personalities.

Islām is confident that there is no disease but God has provided a cure for it—except old age and death. Muslim physicians have reinforced the Hippocratic oath and used its expanded form to save life. Saving and enhancing life is in fact a personal duty for everyone. Curing the sick and relieving the sufferers of their ailments is a task incumbent upon all humans without distinction. Transplants from the dead to the living are permissible insofar as life is sustained and promoted through them. However, physical life may not be extended limitlessly in the absence of "brain" life or sentience. Any situation should be avoided which seems to be a human defiance of God's verdict of death. To respect that verdict whenever it comes and thus to die in dignity in one's own home and in the presence of kin, is both a right and an obligation. *Per contra,* Islām has no countenance for euthanasia. Life is the gift of God which only He can take away.

God is not only the Creator of life. He is equally the Organizer of its patterns. It is His decree that life be reproduced to embody configurations of genes according to His order. It is admissible to argue that the manipulation of genes in plants and animals may lead to a greater yield, or to the betterment of stock, both serving the interest of humanity. It is not admissible to hold the same regarding manipulation of human genes, since man does not belong to himself as animals and plants were ordained to serve and "belong" to him. The human race belongs to God alone Who created them to be as they are and to serve Him within the capacities He implanted in them at birth.

Notes

1. Qur'ān, 51:56; "God commanded that He alone be served" 17:23, 12:40; "Serve God! For it is He Who created you" 2:21, 23:32; "There is no other God than Me! Me, therefore, do you serve" 20:14, 21:25, 92, 29:56.

2. "We offered Our trust to the heavens, to earth and mountains; but they refused to carry it and were frightened by it. Man did indeed come forth to carry it" (33:72).

3. "When God said to the angels, 'I plan to place on earth a vicegerent,' they retorted: 'Would you place on earth a being who does evil and who sheds blood while we give praise to You and hallow Your name?' God answered, 'I know much of which you have no knowledge'" (2:30).

4. "God taught Adam all the names, presented reality to the angels and asked them to name its constituents and thus show their knowledge of the truth. The angels said: Praise to You, O God, we have no knowledge other than that which You have granted to us. You are the Knower, the Wise. God then called on Adam to tell the names. When he did, God said to the angels: Have I not told you thus before? I have knowledge of all heaven and earth, knowledge of all truth. . . . And when We ordered the angels to prostrate themselves in honor of Adam, they did . . . "(2:31–34).

5. Qur'ān, 2:48, 123, 281; 6:164.

6. Qur'ān, 2:286; 6:152.

7. For a thorough discussion of original sin, of the role it played in determining

(as Peccatism) the ethics of Christianity, see I.R. al Faruqi, *Christian Ethics: A Historical and Systematic Analysis of its Dominant Ideas* (Montreal: McGill University Press, 1967), Pt. 2, chap. 6: 193–247. Concerning Paul Tillich's and other contemporary views, 166.

8. I.R. al Faruqi, Wing-tsit Chan, Joseph Kitagawa, P.T. Raju, *The Great Asian Religions* New York: The Macmillan Co., 1969), chap. 6: Buddhism, 70.

9. Qur'ān, 32:9.

10. For a discussion of the "lost-found" image of God in man in Christian thought, see Faruqi *Christian Ethics,* 157–192.

11. Qur'ān, 32:9.

12. "It is God indeed Who gave you birth from the wombs of your mothers, Who gave you hearing, sights [internal and external] and hearts [perception of all values] that you may render [i.e., acknowledge His endowment with] praise and gratitude" (Qur'ān, 16:78). See also Qur'ān, 3:190; 29:19–20.

13. Qur'ān, 49:13, 6:50; 35:19.

14. Qur'ān, 39:9.

15. Muḥammad H. Haykal, *The Life of Muhammad,* trans. I.R. al Fārūqī, (Indianapolis: American Trust Publications, 1977, 487.

16. Qur'ān, 2:35039. It may be noted here that Islām does not identify the prohibited tree as the tree of knowledge. Knowledge and wisdom in Islām are supreme values; and their acquisition is virtue. Adam's fault was one of disobedience only.

17. The moral breakthrough of Jesus, and Paul's *apolytrosis* from the law, common themes of Christian ethics, are discussed in Isma'il R. al Faruqi, *Christian Ethics: A Historical and Systematic Analysis of its Dominant Ideas* (Montreal: McGill Univ. Press, 1967).

18. " . . . Whoever believes in God and *does* the good will have his desert with God. Such persons have no cause to fear; neither will they grieve" (Qur'ān, 2:63). Similar statements stressing *actionalism* are found in the Qur'ān, 5:72, 18:89, 19:60; 20:82, 28:67, 80; 34:37; 25:71, 41:32, 16:111; 39:70. The direct command *i'mal* or *i'malū* (literally, Act! addressed in the singular or plural) occurs in Qur'ān, 34:11, 41:5; 6:135; 11:93; 121; 39:29; 9:106; 23:52.

19. "Not equal are those believers who do not *act*—except the invalid—and those who *act* for the sake of God, sacrificing their wealth and their selves. God loves the actors and prefers them [to the non-actors]"(4:94). Other condemnations of inaction are to be found in 10:12; 9:84; 5:27; 9:47, 87.

20. Qur'ān, 57:27.

21. Details of their controversy may read in Aziz S. Atiya, *History of Eastern Christianity* (Notre Dame, Ind.: University of Notre Dame Press, 1968) 158; F.J. Foakes Jackson, *The History of the Christian Church from the Earliest Times to A.D. 461* (London: George Allen and Unwin, Ltd., 1957), 585–588.

22. "Let there be of you an *ummah* calling mankind to the good, enjoining the good deed and prohibiting the evil deed. For such are truly felicitous" (Qur'ān, 3:104). "We have thus made you [O Believers] a median *ummah* that you may witness unto the others and that the Prophet [Muḥammad] be witness over you in your witnessing" (Qur'ān, 2:143).

23. "Say," God commanded the Prophet Muḥammad, "My worship, my adoration, my life itself and my death, all belong to God, Lord of the universe, and are dedicated to Him" (Qur'ān, 6:162).

24. "We have not created heaven and earth and all that stands between them in sport. Had We sought to make jest, We would have done so alone. Rather, We did so that the untrue may be confounded by the true, the evil by the good" (Qur'ān, 21:16–17, 44:38). "Or, did you think We have created you in vain" (Qur'ān, 23:116).

25. Qur'ān, 18:7; 11:7; 67:2.

26. For a detailed analysis of Jewish tribalism, see I.R. al Faruqi *On Arabism: 'Urū-bah and Religion* (Amsterdam: Djambatan 1967), 16, and *Christian Ethics* 50.

27. Gal. 3:28

28. Matt. 3:9.

29. Qur'ān, 49:13.

30. Qur'ān, 4:1; 6:98; 7:188; 39:6.

31. Qur'ān, 31:28.

32. Qur'ān, 30:30.

33. Qur'ān, 4:94; 57:10.

34. Qur'ān, 9:40; 47:38.

35. Qur'ān, 78:18–40; 82:13–19; 84:6–15; 84:10–12; 88:1.

36. Qur'ān, 7:32.

37. Qur'ān, 7:18, 31; 2:57, 60, 168, 172; 7:159; 20:81; 6:142; 16:114; 5:91; 23:52; 34:15; 52:19; 69:24; 77:43; 4:3.

38. Qur'ān, 37:6; 16:8; 18:7; 16:14; 35:12.

39. Qur'ān, 2:286; 4:111; 6:160; 35:18; 82: 19.

40. Qur'ān, 2:233; 82:19; 6:164.

41. Legitimization of wealth and consumption may be read in Qur'ān, 5:5–6; 7:31; 8:26; 16:72; 40:64; condemnation of poverty in 2:268.

42. Qur'ān, 4:96.

43. Qur'ān, 51:19; 70:25.

44. Limitations upon acquisition of wealth may be read in Qur'ān, 6:152; 7:84; 11:84; 15:19; 55:7–9; 104:1–4. Passages dealing with limitation upon consumption of wealth are more frequent than may be surveyed. The command to spend of one's wealth for the sake of God (*zakāt, infāq* and their derivatives) occurs more than two hundred times. The command to spend all but the necessary occurs in Qur'ān, 2:219.

45. Qur'ān, 2:279.

46. Commendation of marriage is ubiquitous; e.g., Qur'ān, 16:72; 30:21; 78:8. Condemnation of celibacy occurs in 57:27.

47. Qur'ān, 7:188; 30:21.

48. Condemnation of adultery occurs in the Qur'ān, (as *zinā, fāḥishah* and their derivatives) over fifty times; e.g. Qur'ān, 4:14; 7:32; 16:90.

Part IV
AFRICA

9

The Ethics of African Religious Tradition

JOHN K. ANSAH

Introduction

The title of this essay might suggest that the subject discussed here covers the whole of traditional Africa. Some writers on African traditions speak of African Traditional Religion in the singular; others prefer to speak of African Traditional Religions in the plural. The latter form better reflects the heterogeneous population of Africa. The fact is that if African peoples were counted by tribes, one would find that, "there are about one thousand of African peoples (tribes)."[1] In terms of religion, it means the same number of religious affiliations because "each people has its own religious system with a set of beliefs and practices."[2] One might also discover that these traditional religions are peculiar to the peoples from whom they originated and, therefore, are tribal or national, not universal.[3] Such a complex situation renders a claim to write about the religious traditions of all of Africa a trifle bold without a matching knowledge of these diverse peoples. I make no pretensions of such wisdom.

My purpose is to approach the subject paradigmatically. I will present the religious traditions of two ethnic peoples of Black Africa as examples of African traditional religious thought on ethical issues. The specific ethnic groups to be considered are the Akan and the Ewe of West Africa.[4]

At the same time, some of the things that are notable about these two tribes may be applied to many other African peoples. For, no matter how many African ethnic groups there are and how different they may be from one another, certain religious and ethical ideas, beliefs, attitudes, and practices know no boundaries, be they ethnic or national.

History attests to the fact that man, whether of early or advanced culture, has always had a religion and an ethical code. In Africa, these are preserved in customs, regulations, taboos, proverbs, myths, art, signs, and symbols originating with the peoples. We

241

shall therefore turn to these sources for our understanding of the
religious and ethical conceptions that are to be discussed.

Foundations of Morality

The Doctrine of God

Religion is a potent factor in the African tradition, exerting, perhaps, the greatest impact on the thinking and life of the Ewe and
Akan peoples, as indeed on all Ghanaians. In the traditional life of
these African peoples, there are no agnostics. The Akan notion that
a child simply grows up to know God is captured in their proverb,
"no one shows God to a child" *(Obi nkyere abofra Nyame)*. Everybody knows that God exists, including children. This knowledge is
believed to be innate in man.

God is basically conceived by the Akan and Ewe as the Supreme
Being. They say, "he is first among all beings," "he alone the Great
God," and he is far greater than other beings and all other gods. He
is omnipotent, omniscient, and omnipresent. The Akan depict these
attributes of God in the names they give him: "the Gigantic God,"
"the Immovable Rock," "One who sees or knows what is in front
and back of him," "One who is now and from ancient times," "the
One you go away from and return to meet." God's attributes are
also depicted in proverbs, "if you want to tell God something, tell
it to the wind," "if you run away from God, you are still under
him."

God is worshipped as a fully ethical being. In praise-names and
proverbs, the Akan and Ewe show that they believe that God dis-
likes evil; that he loves but can be angry; that he punishes but for-
gives; that he takes care of human beings, providing for them, and
so is loving.[5]

God is thought of as possessing two paradoxically complimentary
attributes. He is transcendent and immanent, remote and near. This
concept is expressed in a myth presenting God as living in the sky
above the level of human beings, but, nevertheless, being involved
in the affairs of his people. God's paradox means to these peoples
that he is so "far away" (transcendent) that he cannot reach them,
yet, he is so "near" (immanent) that he lives with them.

God is also the Creator. Two Akan praise-names of God, *Borebore*
and *Oboadee,* describe him specifically as Excavator, Hewer, Carver,
Originator, Inventor, and Architect. Hence, God is called "owner
of heaven and earth."[6] All things and every human being come

from his creative hand and exist because he keeps them in being. Even death comes from him, though not directly, but through agents whom he permits to cause death.[7] Thus the Akan say in a proverb, "unless God permits that you die, they who try to kill you do so in vain."

As Creator, God is the giver of life. The Akan and, particularly, the Ewe give sufficient evidence of this belief. They take many indigenous personal names that affirm God as the source and owner of life. For example, *Mawuena* (Ewe) and *Nyamekye* (Akan) meaning "it is God *(Mawu, Nyame)* who gives" or "God has given"; *Mawuto* (Ewe) "God's own," "that which comes from God"; *Sesime* (Ewe), "God *(Se)* controls man's life and destiny"; *Sefiamo* (Ewe), "God shows the way of life"; *Segbedzi* (Ewe), "man's life is as God wills or orders it."[8]

Because human life and destiny are seen to be in the hands of God, he is considered the final helper in the time of adversity. He is responsible for events and phenomena whose consequences affect groups and individuals. Sunshine, rain, and good harvest are all considered the handiwork of God. But calamities, disease, drought, and famine are also feared as his visitations. This is why, when the skies rumble, the people say, "God thunders," and when it drizzles, "It is God who is spitting."

Traditional Akan and Ewe theology have complex views of the Godhead. For the Ewe, God has a dual nature: female *(mawu)* and male *(lisa)*. *Mawu* (female) is the principle of life; *Lisa* (male) is the principle of power. Thus, God is given a dual name *Mawu-Lisa,* expressive of his two-in-one nature.[9] The two natures are considered complementary and gender-balancing. Together they form one substantial unity of being.

Likewise, the Akan hold to the dual nature of God, exemplified in the name, *Nyame Obatan pa. Nyame* refers to the male component, and the phrase, *obatan pa,* refers to the female, signifying "a kind (good) nurturing mother."[10]

Trinitarian motifs are also present in the theology of these people. For the Ewe, God is three: *Mawu Dzifovito, Mawu Sogbla* and *Mawu Sodza.* The first name represents the Supreme Being, and the latter, the male and female respectively. Corresponding to the Trinity are three skies or heavens, the Supreme Being residing in the highest heaven. God *Sogbla,* the male, is viewed as the dispenser of punishments, therefore, he is feared and seldom invoked. By contrast, God *Sodza,* the female, is sought through many prayers, for she is kind, blesses people, and protects them and their farms.

The triune God is acknowledged in words, actions, and taboos. There are the sacred words such as, "where there are three, there is life." There are symbolic actions, such as the sprinkling of water on anything three times; and the threefold spitting of the medicine man on his medicaments, to bless them, along with the saying, "three is life." And then there are the taboos that are identical in all three cases, which clearly establish the unity of the three beings. However, though the three divine beings are one, they are perceived differently. Whereas the Supreme God is thought of as beyond all forms and images, and therefore not capable of being worshipped as a visible reality within the walls of some temple built for him, it is thought possible to represent the male and female beings through particular images and to erect temples for their worship.[11]

Though the Supreme God is conceived as self-caused and self-existent, he is celebrated as having a birthday. Birthday names are a feature of Ghanaian traditional society, and God is thought of as being born on Saturday. As such, he is known as *Kwame*—the name for boys born on Saturday. The full name of the Supreme God is *Kwame Nyame,* among the Akan and *Kwame Mawu,* among the Ewe. Yet, this folksy theology should not suggest that the people look upon God as having a cause. Such a view would go counter to the basic belief that God is the Creator of everything. The fact is that the Akan and Ewe find no incompatibility in holding that God was born on a certain day, and at the same time believing that he gave birth to himself.

The idea of God in African traditional religions is bound up with the concept of minor deities. It is common knowledge that the existence of these lesser gods is recognized by every tribal religion in Africa. They are generally believed to be created by God. The Akan call them *abosom,* and the Ewe term is *trowo.* To these African tribes, God as the High (Supreme) God, the Big God, acts through envoys in the same way as a traditional ruler acts through the medium of a spokesman, or as an elder in the chief's palace. Thus, the minor deities perform the roles of intermediaries between God and human beings. Their duty is to protect human beings as well as to bring afflictions upon them. It is common for individuals to solicit their favorite god for protection against such misfortunes as sickness, infertility, and poverty.[12] Through these intermediaries, the people feel God's presence.

The Doctrine of Man

The theology of the Akan and Ewe is reflected in their anthropology. Man is believed to have preexisted. Before he was born into this world, he existed in a prior one called *Bome, Bofe, Dzofe, Sefe,* and *Amedzofe,* by the Ewe, and *Asamando,* by the Akan. Man lived in this first world in childlike innocence and is destined to return to his original home after his stay in the present world. Thus, man is the denizen of two homes. According to the Ewe, a woman called Bomeno, meaning "the mother of Bome," has dominion over man's original home. It is she who moulds all children and sends them into the world.[13]

Man is believed to be immortal because, in addition to the material elements, he is also composed of spiritual elements. This belief is embedded in the myth describing human creation. In the Ewe account, God formed man out of clay (*ame*-molded object). In the molded clay, he put life *(agbe),* and the object of this creation became a living being. So, man is called *amegbeto (ame+agbe+to).* He is living molded clay. Further, since Se or Mawu-Lisa, as the Ewe call the Supreme God, is the principle of life, man is endowed with a part of Se. He thus participates in the life of God. This element of God in man is embodied in his soul which the Ewe call *Se* or *dzogbese,* and the Akan call *okra.*[14] The *Se* or *dzogbese* (soul) is indestructible. After death, the individual returns to *Bome,* its original home.

Other elements add to the constitution of the human being, aside from clay and soul. According to the Akan, a person derives an element each from mother and father and two from God. The mother provides *mogya* (blood), the father *sunsum* (spirit), and God provides the *okra* (soul) and *honhom* (the breath of life). Together, these elements constitute the individuating marks of a child, particularizing it into a unique entity. If one element were misssing, the child could become something other than a human being. The soul is considered a particle of God, the principle of animation that makes a being a human being. The breath of life is the principle of life. It accompanies the soul and is the force that makes a human being a living human being. It also sets the process of disintegration in motion; when it exits, breathing stops, the person dies, and the remaining elements disintegrate. The soul then returns to God, its creator. The spirit *(sunsum)* becomes a ghost or an ancestor, and heads for the home of ancestors. The body is buried in the ground,[15] and, in the vivid speech of the Ewe, it now becomes the property of the termites.

This concept of the person has certain implications for the ethical life of the Akan. Because the blood is believed to be derived from the mother and the spirit from the father, brothers and sisters are viewed as having identical blood and spirit. The upshot of this consanguineous relationship is that marriage between close relatives is forbidden, and beating parents is taboo. Perpetrators of these acts must acknowledge their faults and appease the angered gods and spirit of the parent, or else evil consequences must follow.

Destiny also plays a part in the life of a person. The individual does not enter the world with a clean slate; he carries a blueprint, a ready-made plan of action. The traditional Ewe belief, which is substantially the same for the Akan, is that before a person leaves *Bome* for this world, he determines the kind of life he will lead in his new world. So he comes into the world with plans that are well laid out for himself. The self-chosen pattern for existence is called *dzogbese* in Ewe, and *hyebre* in Akan. Some people are said to opt for being good, loving, kind, hardworking; others, for becoming rich, happy, having long lives, and successful marriages; but some choose to be lazy, dishonest, disrespectful, and wicked. The Akan hold that an individual can also have his life patterned by God. They call this God-given destiny *nkrabea*.

It is significant that the Ewe call man "molded clay with *life* in it" *(ame-gbe-to)*. As the indigenous Akan and Ewe conceive it, man possesses infinite value and worth. Human life exceeds all other values. The Ewe make known the high value they place on life by giving names that exemplify this significance.

In view of the dignity of the person, there are acts which should not be committed against any individual. A husband, for example, should not strike his wife with with his sandal or kick her with his foot, and neither should the wife do the same. Infractions of this law incur the defilement of the dignity and worth of the person. In the case of a male, there is the additional possibility of his becoming impotent, a chilling thought because sexual potency is believed to be the source of parental immortality.

The Doctrine of the World

The world view held by the Akan and Ewe is not monistic. It may be described as pluralistic or as being inclined toward a pluralism that claims that the world is composed of a multiplicity of things, and ultimately of specifically different elements. That this view is prevalent, at least among the Ewe, is corroborated by other studies of the Ewe.[16] According to these people, the world comprises both visible and imperceptible entities, and though the latter are experienced as ghosts, gods, spirits, and the living-dead, they are, nevertheless, real. Yet, the world is ultimately constituted of two opposing elements, forces, or qualities that unite to complete each other. From their union emerges an individual, substantial being. Accordingly, the Ewe see the world to be fundamentally dualistic. It is a world formed on the note of unity in diversity, and is reducible to unity in duality. This view of the world has its source in the concept of God as a dual being, but One who is unified.

It is believed that such a world is not the product of chance but is a creation of God. The world appears to cause harm by sometimes bringing catastrophes and untold sufferings on man. However, on the whole, the world is good to man for God has created a benevolent order to meet all human needs.

Much more has been left unsaid about the thoughts of these African peoples on the subjects of God, man, and the world, due to the limitations of space. What has been said and what has not been said lay together at the foundation of the peoples' religions and form the background for their ethical thought.

Principles of Ethical Decision Making

People must necessarily make decisions in order to act. If these actions are to be meaningful, they must be rationally ordered. This requires guidelines that are provided by ethical principles. Whether these principles are taken as fundamental truths, laws, doctrines, or assumptions, they are possessed of an organizing and guiding force. Principles direct activity toward a chosen end. Their function is to provide a map for the path of ethical pursuit. The Akan and Ewe people, as with all the other people of Africa, follow traditional principles on the basis of which they arrive at ethical decisions.

In traditional Akan and Ewe societies, religious beliefs provide the reflective background against which they determine their ethics. This is a corporate effort in which a number of persons participate, usually from the ranks of members known as elders (*nananom* in Akan; *ametsitsiwo* in Ewe). These individuals are principally councilors at the chief's court. The practice of group reflection on ethical matters in traditional societies derives from two principles stated in proverbial language. They are, "One head does not take counsel," and "Knowledge is like a baobab tree; one person cannot embrace it." The latter maxim, common among the Ewe, is that just as the trunk of a full-grown baobab tree cannot be encircled by one's arms, a single person cannot claim to know everything about good and bad, right and wrong. The equivalent of this principle in Akan is that "one person does not possess all the wisdom" *(nyansa nni baako tiri mu)*. Thus, both societies have a healthy respect for the finite character of human knowledge, and hence the need for ethical collaboration.

The policy of joint deliberation is well illustrated in the procedures at the chief's court, colorfully described as "going to consult *aberewa,"* meaning, going to seek advice from the old lady who, in Ghanaian mythology, is regarded as full of wisdom because of the wealth of experience she has accrued through her long life. The fact is, in Ghanaian culture, old age is synonymous with wisdom. The court procedure requires that before the traditional jury, made up of the chief and his elders, gives a decision in a case it must withdraw to the jury chamber in order to deliberate jointly. Therefore, the verdict the jury finally returns is one that has been reached through corporate reflection. Such decisions are considered much fairer than those that have been arrived at individually.

Notwithstanding their emphasis on collective counsel, the Akan, the Ewe, and some other African societies make room for situations that need immediate attention. It is recognized that sometimes a matter does not allow consultation because it is so urgent that it demands a decision here and now. In such cases, these African peoples rely on the guidance of God's wisdom in dispensing single-handed decisions. At such times they will say, "God knows" *(Nyame na onim,* Akan).

Just as moral and judicial decisions are arrived at by a process of joint thinking, so moral values are formed by reflecting on human experience, especially the past. Here, too, elders in the society are deemed best qualified for the task. They reflect on events of life and extract the moral teachings they convey. Often the teachings are couched in proverbial sayings. Experiences in life are believed to be pregnant with moral lessons. The Ewe personal name, Agbefianu, says precisely that. It means, "life (experience) teaches a lesson."[17] A person is expected to learn a lesson from his mistake, otherwise he lacks wisdom. In the Ewe proverb, "only the fool falls down on the same mound twice."[18]

Because these indigenous ethical methods and principles appear to proceed largely from common sense and plain reason, the question is raised as to their religious status. The answer, as already made, is that religion is among the most influential factors in traditional African life and thought. African peoples do not divorce aspects of their life from their religion. Although certain ethical values, norms, and principles may not originate from a divine being, it is believed that they do receive the sanction of the Supreme God, of other deities, and of ancestors. In this way all public wisdom is connected with religious sources.

Response to Contemporary Ethical Issues

Sexual Ethics

In traditional African societies, human sexuality is looked upon as sacred. This religious sanctification shapes the thinking of the people in respect to all aspects of sex. Akan and Ewe societies are quite typical in this regard. By examining their taboos, we can construct a fairly clear picture of their attitudes toward sex, their morality of sexual relationships, and their meaning of marriage and family.

In general, taboos are found in every African society, a phenomenon that anthropologists tell us is global in its proportions. In the indigenous societies of the Akan and Ewe, taboos form an extremely important part of their ethical code and are practical and effective ways of dealing with ethical matters. As prohibitions, laying down what must not be done in society, taboos cover almost every aspect of life. They are charged with a high degree of religious fervor, being associated with divine power. Their infractions are considered offenses against the deities, the ancestors, or the Supreme God who, in turn punish the whole society with epidemics, drought, famine, and excessive rainfall.

Sex taboos form a code of sexual conduct that is so highly respected that any deviation from it is deeply detested. The code stipulates the time and manner for having sex and also the persons with whom one may or may not enter into sexual relationships.

The sacredness with which sex is held is so fundamental an idea that it is a necessary condition for understanding the high premium the people place on sex, and all of the regulations and customs they have concerning it and marriage. For instance, initiation ceremonies serve the dual purpose of informing the youth and his society that he has crossed the boundary from adolescence to adulthood, and they also serve the important purpose of introducing young people to the facts of sex, marriage, and of the family. Such ceremonies are eminently educative. Through the impartation of appropriate knowledge and meaningful experiences, the youth are equipped with ethical weapons (critical judgments) to do battle against the challenges of sex life.

Prior to the performance of the initiation ceremonies known as puberty rites, a young person, particularly a girl, is not expected to indulge in sexual relationships. A girl who has sexual experience before the initiation is liable to punishment. The same applies to a girl who becomes pregnant prior to puberty rites.[19] In such cases, in addition to being penalized, the erring maiden must be ritually purified. All of this elevates the importance of virginity that a young woman must prove in the act of consummating her marriage in order to win respect.

Even after being publicly declared an adult through participation in puberty rites, the young person is not licensed to indulge in sex. He and all other persons are expected to practice continence.

The sacred character of sex makes it an exclusive prerogative of married persons. An unmarried individual who becomes sexually active is considered as going beyond his bounds into a territory that only married adults may enter. He is considered as usurping a right. Premarital sex is forbidden by traditional Akan and Ewe societies.

How and where sex is performed are also matters of concern to some African peoples. Because sex is sacred, the Akan and Ewe believe that sex must be performed well. It is therefore a taboo to have sexual relations in the bush, on the farm, or on the bare floor. Sexual acts done in any of these places are treated as abominable offenses that will call down the vengeance of the gods (earth is the goddess *Asase Yaa*). It is possible that the gods can cause the land to become infertile, and this is followed by famine.

Again, because sex is sacred, there is a taboo against its performance in the open, even with one's own wife. Sexual acts are to be done in private—in a room and on a bed. Generally, traditional Africans do not display affection toward the opposite sex in public. Love play is reserved for the privacy of the bedroom. It follows that demonstrations of feelings through kissing and petting in public are viewed as indecent by many traditional Africans.

A sex act is proper when it is engaged in by two consenting parties. A man should never force himself on a woman who rejects his advances. This may explain why rape is not widespread in Akan and Ewe societies. When this occurs, the guilty person is fined heavily.

There are also prohibitions in respect to menstruating women. It is a taboo to have sexual relations with a woman during her period because she is then considered unclean. The man who breaks the taboo defiles his own sanctity. Among some tribes, such as the Akan of Ashanti, the menstruating wife must not cook for her husband. She is also expected to stay away from the house if it enshrines a god or a sacred stool, symbol of ancestors, otherwise she will defile the gods or the spirits of the ancestors.

Among the most appalling sex offenses in traditional Akan and Ewe societies is incest. The concept of incest is variously perceived among the indigenous peoples. The Ashanti of Akan-speaking people extend the notion to the whole lineage. The Akan and Ewe societies publicly scorn sex between a man and his mother, his daughter, or his sister, even between an uncle and his niece. The forbidden relationship is also extended to a man having sex with a woman and her daughter or with two sisters, a father and his son with one woman, and two brothers with the same woman. The taboo is more serious when one has prior knowledge of the other's relationship.

The term for incest among the Akan is "mixing blood" (mogya fra). It is a crime and a sin that attracts a heavy fine in addition to having to fulfill the ritual obligation of appeasing the gods and ancestors by offering a sheep for sacrifice. It is believed that the consequence of mixing blood through sexual relations will incur a severe accident or illness leading to death. Those who commit the offense are not to see each other when one is sick. If they do, it is predicted that the sickness will worsen and the ill person will eventually die unless the crime is confessed and purificatory rites are performed. Incest prohibitions are extended to include all persons who might be regarded close relatives.

From these illustrations it should be clear that the function of taboos among the Akan and Ewe is to protect and strengthen the sacredness of sex and also to nurture due respect for it.

By the same token, marriage is an exceedingly important institution in Africa. This becomes apparent in the celebration of marriage as an affair of the entire town or village. A fundamental notion among traditional Africans about marriage is that "everybody must get married and bear children."[20] Emphasis should not be placed so much on marriage as upon procreation within marriage. A married person must at some time transform his or her conjugal life into parental life. Marriage and procreation in traditional Africa are deemed inseparable. It is this idea behind African marriage that gives meaning to many others ideas, practices, and customs, such as polygamy, marrying a widowed sister-in-law, and bridewealth.

The Akan and Ewe peoples provide good examples for these. A marriage must produce children. An unproductive union is a matter of grave concern. Children are prized, not only because father and mother pass on the torch of life through them, but because it is in the children that the Akan and Ewe couple see themselves immortalized—something particularly important for the male. Since marriage must be fruitful, care is taken during the engagement period to remove any problems that might impede marital productivity. Family feuding might pose such a problem, so any contending parties are reconciled during this period.[21]

If there are indications that a couple will remain childless, help may be sought from the gods. The wife then goes to the gods and implores them for a child. Offspring as a result of petition and divine intervention are usually given special names by the Ewe, such as Klu, Soklu, and Kpetsu, for boys, and Klufe, Kosi, and Dasi, for girls.

Marriage is carefully regulated so as to avoid the offense of incest. In the Akan society that adopts the matrilineal system, marriage is forbidden between members of the same matrilineage. In the patrilineal Ewe society, marriage is forbidden between members of the same patrilineage.[22] The reason for these restrictions is that persons of the same lineage are considered family members since they have a common ancestor.

As a rule, marriages among the Akan and Ewe of Ghana are outside one's own group (exogamous). This provides a way of creating wider group affiliations. The only near relatives sometimes permitted to marry are cross-cousins. It is permissible for a man to marry his mother's brother's daughter or his father's sister's daughter. The reason for this exception to the prohibition against intragroup or close-kin marriages appears to be the usefulness of cross-cousin marriages as a way of responding to some common, but significant, marriage problems. Quarrels are reduced and conflicts are more easily dealt with since the mother's brother is also father to the woman, and father-in-law and uncle to the man, and he is therefore in a position to exert necessary influence on the marriage. Further, the spouses are quite familiar with each other's character and family background, having known each other from childhood. This tends to make for marital stability. It also means that property is kept within the family, thus solving the problem of inheritance that is particularly vexing within matrilineal societies in which property does not go to the children of the man but to his nephews and nieces.

An important marriage practice is the giving of a marriage gift or bridewealth to the bride's parents or relatives. This custom is found everywhere in Africa.[23] The kind of gift presented and the function it plays may vary from society to society, but the custom is widespread. Among the Akan and Ewe, this social convention solves a number of problems. It is the traditional seal to the marriage contract, legalizing the union. Consequently, it earns for the husband exclusive rights over his wife. After the gift has been presented, the husband has the right to claim adultery fees from the accomplice of an adulterous wife. Bridewealth also confers legitimacy on children. The husband becomes the legitimate father of all the children born of the marriage, including the offspring of an adulterous relationship engaged in by the wife. In patrilineal Ewe society, children belong to the man. Even in matrilineal Akan society, children bear the man's name.

If bridewealth legalizes marriage, it also serves to ratify divorce. In general, bridewealth is refundable. Where it is customary to give it back upon divorce, its return formalizes and legalizes divorce.

In the patrilineal and exogamous society of the Ewe, the wife becomes part of the family of her husband. The bridewealth fills the vacuum created in her father's home by her departure. The gift is supposed to take her place to some degree. Among the patrilineal peoples, the gift can be exceedingly large. The Nuer of Sudan, for instance, are reputed to give forty cows as bridewealth. Such expensive gifts serve to buttress the matrimonial bond. They stabilize the marriage by causing the husband and wife to behave well. The husband is fully aware of the fact that should he be the cause of divorce, he loses both his wife and the bridewealth. The wife is similarly cognizant that if she is to be blamed for the divorce, she might not be in a position to reimburse the gift.[24] Thus the practice of giving costly gifts among the Akan, and to a lesser degree among the Ewe, is a custom that answers some real needs in their marriage institutions.

The existence of polygamy[25] in Africa is no secret to anyone who knows something about the continent, nor is the practice a square peg in a round hole. Mbiti explains, "the custom fits well into the social structure of traditional life and into the thinking of the people, serving many useful purposes."[26] The custom finds a suitable place in the lives and thoughts of African peoples by playing a useful role in their societies. This makes it another of traditional Africa's mechanisms for handling its questions of sex and marriage. In the thinking and life of the Akan and Ewe, polygamy helps to prevent or, at least, to reduce unfaithfulness. For one thing, it is considered an abominable thing to have sexual relations with a menstruating woman, and, consequently, with a menstruating wife. For another, sexual relation is prohibited during the time of nursing a baby, which may last months and perhaps years. Marrying two or more wives ensures the normal enjoyment of married life. Moreover, the social structure of these African peoples is such that an unmarried woman has no respectable standing. The title "Mrs" elevates a woman to social heights. Polygamy takes care that as many women as possible are married and thereby achieve status in the eyes of the people. Polygamy also has something to do with economic life. Many wives mean many children, and many children mean many hands to run the family business, and so make the family richer. Whatever else, polygamy is an economic asset.

This is by no means an attempt to justify the practice of polygamy or to present it as better than monogamy. What has been said here is simply an exposition of the meaning this practice has for these African peoples, and what it could mean for other Africans in their attempts to tackle the many problems connected with marriage. Today, young people tend to view this ancient institution differently. It has lost some of its traditional appeal for young men. They are finding it difficult to cope with the practice in the context of modern living.

As in the case of sex, numerous marriage taboos exist to reinforce the dignity and sacredness of marriage. The Ewe have prohibitions that make for intimate bedroom relationships in order to enrich the ties between husband and wife. For instance, among the bedroom taboos is the sanction against a husband having sexual relation with another woman on the same bed that he shares with his wife. The same applies to the wife. The reasoning behind this sanction is that such an act downgrades the offended spouse in the eyes of the illicit lover. There is also a whole class of taboos to safeguard against acts done in anger by the husband or wife. For example, if, in anger, a husband refuses to eat the food his wife has cooked but later changes his mind and partakes of it, he commits an act of defilement against the woman and the relationship between them. If a distraught wife throws her husband's food away but later cooks some more of the same, she is also guilty of the offense.

The Family

The family emerges from the marriage concept as a natural product of the union entered into by a man and a woman as husband and wife. As stated above, marriage must lead to children, according to the Akan and the Ewe. When this happens, the family emerges, consisting of parents and offspring. However, the African concept of family is much wider than that of the immediate family. It embraces grandparents, nephews, nieces, uncles, aunts, and other distant relatives. The African family is therefore an extended family. In traditional Africa, the nuclear family is the foundation for the extended family. In the case where a man is a polygamist, he may have many small families and therefore more than one extended family. What Westerners designate as the "family tree" is just the family in the extended African sense of that term.

The Akan and Ewe believe strongly in the unity and solidarity of the family.[27] There is the recognition that a person's taproot is the family and that personal identity develops within its fold. Hence, in Ewe traditional society there is a strong sense of family values such as cohesion, cooperation, and helpfulness that are indoctrinated in the growing child.

The extended family structure responds to the social and moral problems of solitude and destitution. Nobody, old or young, really feels unwanted, uncared for, or completely destitute. The child is born into the wider family and the whole family is responsible for him. This is why children may be sent to live with another member of the extended family—an aunt, uncle, grandparent, brother, or sister. Old people's homes are unknown in traditional Akan and Ewe societies. The greatest disservice an adult child can do to the parents is to neglect them in their old age. It is a conduct that invariably incurs the displeasure and disparagement of the community. In some cases, parents are taken in their old age into the homes of their children, or a grandchild is sent to live with them and serve them. The extended family system thus ensures seniors against the anxieties of want and old age and, to that extent, serves as a "life insurance policy" within Akan and Ewe societies.

All of the concerns we have just looked at pertaining to sex, marriage, and the family, are seen to be religious in essence or are regarded as religious duties and responsibilities. Therefore religious attitudes are adopted towards them. Taboos associated with them serve a single purpose: to safeguard their sacred character. Any violation of these regulations is viewed as an offense against the gods and ancestors (the living-dead) who are considered part of the soci-

ety. The offense is deemed a destabilization of the smooth relationships that should exist between the divinities and human beings.
Reconciliation of offenders to these spirit-beings and to the community, and consequently, restoration of the broken relationship, is
achieved through rites of purification.

Liberation Movements

Women We now turn to the position of women in traditional
Akan and Ewe societies. The status of these women must not be
confused with that of their educated sisters. For the most part, these
women are semi-illiterate. They form the bulk of the rural folk
among whom are devotees of traditional religions. The traditional
socio-political society in which they live is male dominated. These
women have been left untouched by women's movements that
have uplifted the social, political, and economic status of literate
African women and their counterparts elsewhere. The popular slo-
gans of women's liberation movements, such as, "what men can do,
women can also do," are not heard among these women who do
not really question the roles that tradition ascribes to them, and
therefore they hardly attempt to change their male-controlled societies. Even so, along with the inequality that is found in many areas
of traditionally socio-political life, some equality does exist between
the sexes. For instance, women can choose their husbands as men
choose their wives, and the same applies to divorce. Should a husband wish to take a second wife, he must first obtain the consent of
his wife. But in the case of adultery, the wife's offense is taken more
seriously.

In traditional religious life, women have even less from which to
be emancipated. Traditional religions treat women much more
equitably. Although discriminatory elements are not wholly ruled
out, women are accorded much of the same dignity that is given to
men. As has been seen, women are represented in the gender of
God. God is conceived of as both male and female. He is attired in
masculine and female clothing. He is father and mother. Thus
women are given a prominent place in the imagery of the Highest
Being. Likewise, femininity is given expression in the hierarchy of
divine beings. For example, Earth is conceived of as a female deity
(Asase Yaa), and, as the spouse of God, she holds a rank second only
to that of the Supreme Being. The priesthood, too, is not an exclusively male domain. Women can be ordained and perform priestly
duties of the same order as their male counterparts such as divina-

tion, healing, and officiating at sacrifices. Where some sacerdotal functions are performed only by priests or by priestesses, it is simply a matter of convenience or division of labor, rather than one of gender preference.

Notwithstanding the glorification of womanhood in theory and practice in the indigenous life of these African peoples, there are traces of meanness, signifying inequality of the sexes. For instance, the widowhood rite of the Akan and Ewe and that of many other Ghanaian tribes, prescribes a period of ceremonial mourning for the deceased spouse. Among the Southern Ewe, the Buem, Atwode, Krachis, and Nchumuru, a man is required to observe a seven-day to twenty-four day ritual, whereas a woman must observe the ritual for a period ranging from twelve to eighteen months. She must abstain from sexual relations throughout that period. Again, a striking display of discrimination between the sexes pertains to that aspect of life peculiar to womanhood, namely, menstruation. Tradition has said that a woman in her menstrual period is unclean. This places certain restrictions upon her, such as the prohibition against being in the proximity of sacred places and objects. For this reason a menstruating priestess cannot perform her sacred functions. Hence, notwithstanding the fact that women are not barred from the priesthood, only those who have reached their menopause and have thereby become "men," are eligible for the highest sacerdotal office in the religious tradition of people such as the Southern Ewe. On the contrary, any priest, regardless of age, can be elevated to the office of the high priest.[28] Certainly there is room here for some traditional African women's movement to challenge these customs which denigrate women on the grounds of their biology.

Homosexuality "Gay life" hides in the shadows of traditional Africa. It is seldom visible, but this should not suggest that it does not exist. It is believed that witches of the same sex do mate. The observation of Barrington Kaye that homosexuality is known to exist among some children in their early adolescent years in Ghana, may also be said of adults without fear of falsity.[29] All the same, it is unintelligible to the indigenous Akan and Ewe peoples that a person can have sexual desire toward another person of his own sex. Even animals, they contend, distinguish between male and female in their sex life.[30] Since "African peoples are very sensitive to any departure from the accepted norm concerning all aspects of sex,"[31] homosexual relations constitute a sexual abberation that horrifies and evokes contempt, but not hostility. Viewed in this light, homosexuals in these societies conceal their sexual orientation or identity. It will thus be unimaginable to these African societies to anticipate the day a "Gay Rights" movement may develop.

Issues of Violence and Justice

Pacifism The Akan and Ewe traditional view of Reality is that nature is made up to two opposing elements that unite harmoniously for the good of nature. Thus, although nature is fundamentally dualistic, within it is harmony and unity. Struggle and tension are real possibilities, but ultimately this resolves itself into harmonious relationships. This mode of thinking supplies the foundation for the Akan and Ewe theory of pacifism. It can be said that the indigenous life of these people is founded on peace. They attach great importance to peace, ranking it among their highest values.

Akan and Ewe societies genuinely embody their pacifist values. The Ewe have a ritual herb called *ma* that is believed to possess the quality of coolness, that is to say, it has a good taste without any harmful effects. God's "cool" nature is likened to it. God is said to be even "cooler" than it—more peaceful. A person of calm and gentle disposition is spoken of in terms of *ma*. When a child is obedient, he is said to be as cool as the herb; this is true also in the case of a successful marriage. Since *ma* is the symbol of coolness and peaceful existence, it is used in rites of reconciliation. In traditional religious ceremonies, the herb is kept in the water with which the participants are sprinkled with the blessing of peace.

Ewe commitment to peace is further demonstrated in their designation of two days of their four-day week as "cool days." On these days, called *Domesigbe* and *Asiamigbe*, "cool" activities are performed, such as weddings, engagements, the laying of foundation stones for buildings, and the naming of newly-born babies. The values that this custom posits are peace and blessing. In Akan society, which observes a seven-day week calendar, two days are set apart as days of peace, Monday *(Dwoda)* and Saturday *(Memreda)*. Saturday is particularly a day of peace because it is also the day of the Supreme God *Kwame* (Saturday-born) *Nyame*. Furthermore, pacifism among the traditional Akan and Ewe is evidenced in the personal names they give, especially to females who are "the symbols of harmony and peace," such as: *Fafa* ("coolness"), *Fafali* ("there is coolness"), *Dzifa* ("the heart is cool"), *Akofa* ("the chest is cool"), *Afeafa* ("the house is cool").[32]

Other examples reinforce the predominance ascribed to "coolness" among the Ewe as the regulating value for all levels of social intercourse. They look upon the well-being of the individual and that of the society as mutually dependent. Therefore they consider all acts that foster social harmony, unity, and peace as of utmost value.[33] In the event that disputes and disagreements arise between individuals, family members, and in society, efforts are made to solve the conflicts quickly by the head of the family or clan by summoning the disputing parties and some kinsfolk for arbitration. Occasionally, the restoration of harmony is celebrated with communal drinking of local wine or whisky. By contrast, recourse to force or violence as a means of achieving justice is strongly disapproved because such a method is contrary to the spirit of forgiveness and brotherhood which is an important value in traditional religion. The Akan and Ewe societies are religiously persuaded that nonviolent methods are preferable for the achievement of peace and justice. Of these means, the people further prefer the way of sitting the parties down to talk around the table. This facilitates mutual understanding. Their philosophy teaches that force leads to counterforce. In the end the cost may be too high for everybody.

Crime and Punishment

African peoples share the belief that there is good and evil in the world, but some, such as the Akan and Ewe, focus on the latter. The explanation seems to be that evil acts are seen as bringing destruction to the individual and to society. This notion is expressed by words that are often used by the Ewe for evil—*gble* (destroy) and *gbeble* (destruction). "A bad thing" is *nu gbeble,* and "a morally bad person" is *ame gbeble.*[34]

Crime waves, well-known in the West, are slowly breaking into the modernized towns of Africa. They are yet unknown in the traditional societies of the Akan and Ewe, but taboo-crimes do exist and are taken very seriously, their gravity varying according to the degree the crime does or does not involve the deities, the ancestors, or the Supreme God. Abuse of a chief, murder, suicide, incest, and intercourse with a girl under the age of puberty belong to this class of crimes.

Punishment of crimes is qualified by the consideration of whether the crime infuriates some divine reality. Here, a distinctively indigenous characteristic manifests itself. Traditionally, the Akan and Ewe make the distinction between voluntary and involuntary acts. They are aware that some acts are done knowingly with the consent of the agent and that some are done unknowingly and unwillingly. However, in the ethics of these African tribes, the factor of knowledge and will (consent) plays a less vital role in determining responsibility and punishment for some acts. It is essential to underscore "some acts," because it is not seldom that the jury of a traditional court acquits a person of a crime on the ground that he did not do the act deliberately *(wanhye da, ommoa pa)*. Yet, in regard to these crimes (taboo/non-taboo) that are believed to anger the gods, or ancestors, or the High God and to bring evil consequences from them, the distinction between known and willed acts evaporates. By the mere fact that a person commits a crime, regardless of whether it is voluntary or involuntary, the offender is held responsible and punished. To illustrate: it is a taboo to fish in some lakes and rivers on certain days of the week. If this taboo is broken by someone who is completely unaware of the offense he is committing, he is culpable none the less and is punished. The logic at work is that the gods or ancestors have been offended, although unknowingly, and must be appeased in order to ward off their vengeance on the perpetrator or on the whole village or town.

The same reasoning applies to punishment for committing taboo offenses by a lunatic or child under the age of reason. What is regarded as important is the anger that has been incurred of the deities, the ancestors, or of the Supreme God, and the evil outcome of this in the form of epidemics, drought, famine, and other calamities. Punishment for an act done by a person with defective knowledge of the deed and lack of consent to it is a religious obligation that must be fulfilled. When a person infringes a taboo, he has done something that is gravely contrary to the accepted norms of behavior. He has broken a rule or gone against a belief of his society. He has harmed the relationship between him and society, and between him and the divine beings. When this criminal conduct is known, the traditional Akan and Ewe punish; but they also have a process of reconciling the wrongdoer with society and the divinities, and of restoring the social and religious order that has been disturbed. The process is the rite of purification. The offender, alone, or the entire society, can undergo the rite. If it is performed to purify the offender and so avert the anger of the gods, it is known in Akan as *mmusuo yi,* and in Ewe as *nugboedodo.* If the whole village or town undergoes the rite, it is known as *dubabla* in Ewe ("tying a village or town").

Environmental Ethics

Land, Forest, Food, Water Human beings do not just happen to live in the world. Their existence is made possible through their environment. They drink its water, eat its food, breathe its air, and subsist on a variety of its products. It means, then, that nobody can ignore the environment in which he lives, or can live completely cut off from it and still enjoy a well-adjusted life. Such a person is sure to perish in the end. Indigenous African peoples recognize this fact of life. Their whole meaning of existence is tied up with their environment.

The societies of the Akan and Ewe are not affected by the problem of air and water pollution that plague industrialized and technologically developed nations. On the other hand, these African societies have a concern, evidently religious, for land, forest, food, and water. The concern arises from the importance of these things to them. They prize them and count all that contributes to their attainment and enjoyment as high values. The great esteem they have for these essentials of life explains why they revere, and sometimes worship, land, forest, sea, rivers, and lakes, for these resources of nature help in the realization and satisfaction of the basic biological needs of life.

Land and forest are given reverence and worship as the donors of various foodstuffs and, above all, as the abode of the gods. Sacrifices are occasionally offered to them. The fishermen of Keta, in Southern Eweland, and of Cape Coast, in Southern Akanland, are known to make offerings to the sea in order to have good harvests during the fishing season. The sacredness, reverence, and worship associated with forest, land, rivers, and lakes, protect them from destruction and misuse. This function of religion could therefore be called an Environmental Protection Agency.

Bioethical Issues

Euthanasia and Abortion To African peoples, no other human value surpasses the value of human life. It has been said of them that "there was always the awareness that human life was the greatest value."[35] Evidence in confirmation of what human life is to the indigenous Africans is given by the traditional Akan and Ewe. They have numerous indigenous personal names and forms of greetings that contain the word life. A few examples of such names are:

- Agbexoasi (agbe = life; xo = takes; asi = price): Life has value; life is precious.

- Agbenyega (agbe = life; nye = is; ga = great): Life is the greatest thing.
- Agbenyefia (agbe = life; nye = is; fia = king): Life is king.
- Agbewu (agbe = life; wu = surpasses): Life surpasses everything.
- Agbeko (agbe = life; ko = the only thing): Life is the only thing.
- Agbeyewoanu (agbe = life; ye = is that which; woa = does; nu = thing): Life does everything, i.e., with life men can do things.
- Agbesinyale (agbe = life; si = with; nya = word; le = is): Life has the word, i.e., everything depends on life.
- Sunkwa (su = cry, weep; nkwa = life): Cry for life, i.e., look for life alone in the world.

In greeting and bidding good night, the Ewe show their awareness that human life is the most important value. They say *ele agbea?* (ele = are you; agbea = alive): "How do you do"; *do agbe* (do = sleep; agbe = life): "Good night". For all this, the best evidence so far of the significance of human life is that the indigenous Akan and Ewe regard any quality of life as valuable. The Ewe proverb, "the person with a miserable life is never tired of it," is a succinct summation of this value.[36]

The traditional Akan and Ewe attitude towards euthanasia and abortion is conditioned by these tribes' understanding of human life. The high regard these ethnic peoples have for human life means to them, on the one hand, that they value whatever nurtures human life and, on the other, do not value anything that destroys it. To them, euthanasia and abortion have only one end, namely, the destruction of life. They are, in Ewe terms, *nu gbegblewo* (bad acts) or *nuvowo* (acts to be feared).

The absolute prohibition of euthanasia is summed up in the teaching of the proverb that no form of life should be considered unworthy of living.

The issue of abortion is weighted with even more concern than euthanasia for these Africans because of its more frequent recurrence. From the moment a pregnancy is known, there is no doubt in the minds of these people that new life is in existence. Thereafter, the pregnant woman is treated with singular care and is given all the special attention she needs. Taboos and regulations surround her, such as abstinence from certain foods and the avoidance of encounter with ugly persons, for it is believed that the baby will then be ugly, too. All of these measures are for the protection of the unborn life. In the context of such thinking, abortion cannot be anything other than a heinous act. Of course, the complexity of the problems surrounding abortion do not arise for these people. They tolerate spontaneous abortion or miscarriage because it is nobody's fault, nonetheless, they consider it a regretful loss of life. But direct abortion carries the taboo of murder because it involves the deliberate destruction of human life.

There is another reason why abortion does not find favor among the traditional Akan and Ewe societies. As has been observed, the purpose of marriage is for the begetting of children. New life is the glory of marriage because through offspring, parents, particularly the father, become immortalized. The man's name is never lost, for children bear it even in matrilineal systems, and thus perpetuate his line of life. Hence, the more children one has, the greater the glory, and the more immortalized are the parents. For this reason, abortion is tantamount to suicide. It is seen as self-extinction, the erasing of one's own name from the registry of life. In the eyes of the Akan and Ewe, abortionists and pro-abortionists are therefore enemies to themselves and to the whole human race.

In the light of the above, it is not uncommon to find among these traditional African tribes unmarried women who are pregnant or with children. Parents may wax indignant over the incident that has brought their family into disrepute, but the woman with child never becomes an outcast. Society accepts her and this support imparts to the expectant mother the courage to keep her baby. Communal acceptance of unwed mothers thus minimizes the need to resort to abortion and, to that extent, serves as a sort of anti-abortion pill.

Conclusion

There are no unethical people. There are no persons whose lives are void of ethical qualities with no reference to morals. Unless the society is anarchic, a people must live and act according to certain ethical norms and principles expressed in definite codes of conduct.

The traditional lives of the Black African peoples discussed in this chapter are regulated by customs, forms of behavior, rules, observances, taboos, and values. These constitute the moral codes of the peoples and are held as sacred because they are believed either to be handed down or to be sanctioned by the Supreme God, by the lesser divine beings, or by the ancestors.

The world today is experiencing an unprecedented revolution. Changes are taking place in almost every area of life. This has given rise to myriads of new problems and has given a new face to old ones, including ethical problems. Africa is part of this world, and Akanland and Eweland are part of the African world. Like people all over the world, traditional Africans respond to the ethical problems with which they are confronted. In doing so, the Akan and Ewe seek the guidance of a dominant force in their life—religion.

Certain ethical issues loom uppermost for the Akan and Ewe. Among these are matters of sex, marriage, and the family. The sacredness ascribed to them explains the sensitivity with which they are approached. The area of bioethics, particularly the questions of abortion and euthanasia, attract considerable attention. For, like witchcraft, sorcery, and bad magic, euthanasia and abortion are seen as intrinsically destructive of human life. In Akan and Ewe traditional thought, human life is "the pearl of great price" that must be preserved at all cost.

Notes

1. John S. Mbiti, *African Religions and Philosophy* (New York: Doubleday & Company, 1970), 1.

2. Ibid.

3. Ibid., 5.

4. The Ewe people as a tribe are found in the West African countries of Ghana, Togo, and Benin (formerly Dohomey).

5. See J.B. Danquah, *The Akan Doctrine of God: A Fragment of Gold Coast Ethics and Religion,* 2d ed. with a new Introduction by Kwesi A. Dickson (London: Frank Cass & Co. Ltd., 1968), 40–41, 45, 48–56.

6. Ibid., 28, 30.

7. Peter Sarpong, *Ghana in Retrospect: Some Aspects of Ghanaian Culture* (Tema: Ghana Publishing Corporation, 1974), 11.

8. The most common names for God among the Ewe are *Mawu* and *Se;* and among the Akan, *Nyame* or *Onyame.*

9. N.K. Dzobo, *Black Civilization as Cultural Product of Conceptual Creativity,* unpublished paper (Cape Coast, 1977), 9–10.

10. Ibid., 11.

11. See S. A. Motte, *Mia Denyigba* (Accra: Bureau of Ghana Languages, 1968), 91–95.

12. Mbiti, *African Religions,* 98. See Sarpong, *Ghana,* 14–17.

13. It is pointed out that *Bomeno* is in reality the same as the High God who, besides the name Mawu-Lisa, is also called Dada Segbo, which means "the Great Mother God." See Dzobo, *Black Civilization,* 41. The male-female nature of God is here again expressed. Dada (Mother) added to Segbo indicates the femininity of God.

14. Ibid., 41–42.

15. Sarpong, *Ghana*, 37.

16. See Dzobo, *Black Civilization*, 7–9, 12.

17. N.K. Dzobo, "Introduction to the Indigenous Ethics of the Ewe of West Africa," in *The Oguaa Educator: A Journal for the Promotion of Educational Thinking in Africa*, vol. 6, no. 1 (October, 1975) 84, col. 2.

18. Ibid.

19. Among the Buem, a tribe in Ghana, a pregnancy preceding puberty rites is termed "street pregnancy" *(ogbami kafo)* and the child born of such pregnancy is called "a child of the street" *(ogbami kafo ubi)*.

20. Mbiti, *African Religions*, 176.

21. Dzobo, "Introduction," 91, cols. 1 and 2.

22. Meyer Fortes, "Kinship and Marriage among the Ashanti" in *African Systems of Kinship and Marriage*, A.R. Radcliffe-Brown and Daryll Fortes, eds. (London: Oxford University Press, 1950), 278–279.

23. Mbiti, *African Religions*, 183.

24. Ibid., 183–184; Sarpong, *Ghana*, 83–84.

25. The term is used here in the same sense of polygyny, that is, one man having two or more wives. This is the popular sense in which it is used in Africa, for polyandry (one woman with two or more husbands) is non-existent among Black Africans.

26. Mbiti, *African Religions*, 186.

27. Dzobo, "Introduction", 87, col. 2; 88, col. 1.

28. A woman in her menopause being seen as a man is not particular to the Ewe. Some other African peoples, for example, the Zulus of South Africa and the Annang of Nigeria, regard women who have ceased menstruating as men, most likely because women of that age have "lost" their distinctive trade-mark and in this regard are not different from men.

29. Barrington Kaye, *Bringing up Children in Ghana* (London: George Allen and Unwin Ltd., 1962), 208.

30. It is hard to understand the logic of admitting homosexual relations for witches and not for persons since witches are human beings turned spirit-being of some sort.

31. Mbiti, *African Religions*, 193.

32. Dzobo, "Introduction," 93, cols. 1, 2.

33. Ibid., 86, col. 2; 87, col. 2.

34. Ibid., 95, col. 1.

35. K.A. Busia, *Purposeful Education in Africa* (London: Mouton and Co., 1964), 17.

36. Dzobo, "Introduction," 85, col. 1, 2; 83, col. 1.

10

Ethics in Yoruba Religious Tradition

SAMUEL O. ABOGUNRIN

The Yoruba people constitute the largest single ethnic group in West Africa. The principle that regulates the lives of these more than thirty million persons is religion. "As far as they are concerned, the full responsibility of all affairs of life belongs to the Deity; their own part in the matter is to do as they are ordered . . . the interpreters of the will of the Deity."[1] Religion is both dominant and pervasive. "It forms the themes of songs, makes topics for minstrelsy, finds vehicles in myths, folktales, proverbs and sayings, and is the basis of philosophy."[2]

The Yoruba are proud and conscious of their historic past, their noble ancestry, and their rich traditions. Emmanuel Bolaji Idowu correctly remarks, "They have been enjoying for centuries a well organized pattern of society, a pattern which persists basically in spite of all the changes consequent upon modern contacts with the Western world."[3] However, it will be untrue to claim that the Yoruba people have remained uninfluenced by Westernism, Christianity, and Islam. Nevertheless, the effects of these external influences on the Yoruba culture and religious beliefs and traditions are still minimal. In actual fact, it is the Yoruba culture that significantly sets the pattern for the forms of Christianity and Islam in Yoruba land. Our task, therefore, is not just a discussion of the mythological, glorified past of the Yoruba race or an attempt to rediscover the past, but an examination of things that still persist in the society. Our discussion of the subject will cover the following areas: Foundations of Yoruba Ethics, The Principles of Ethical Decision Making, Basic Moral Values, and Modern Trends.

Foundations of Yoruba Morality

Our major source of information about Yoruba moral values comes from the Ifa literary corpus.[4] According to Yoruba mythology, the person who introduced the Ifa divination system into the world was

Orunmila, one of the sixteen divinities who first inhabited the earth.[5] Orunmila was the only divinity present when God created the universe. It was in his presence that God decreed what each creature's mission would be on earth. This is why he is called *Eleri Ipin* ("The witness of the nature of being," or "One who knows the essence of being of every creature"). Orunmila is therefore the repository of all myths and moral tenets including the moral and physical laws governing the universe. He is the aged historian, counselor, and custodian of all divine wisdom as contained in the Ifa literary corpus. Hence, Orunmila is referred to as:

The Counselor, who teaches like his relation.
The Wisdom of the Earth.
The Aged Historian of Ife land.

The recital of each verse or subchapter form is followed by stories and sayings elaborating the meaning and purpose of that section. The Ifa system represents the different stages in the historical and spiritual developments of the Yoruba nation and what some have described as God's body of revelation to the Yoruba. We shall therefore refer to Orunmila from time to time.

In the religion of the Yoruba, Olodumare is Ultimate Reality. He is the Creator, Controller of the universe, the Preserver of man's life, and the Determiner of human destiny. The Yoruba have various myths about the origin of the universe and the beginning of all things, but every myth points to the fact that Olodumare is the Source-Being who gave being and existence to all else. According to Orunmila, this earth was the seventh and last planet created by God. He created Esu (Satan)[6] from the beginning and gave him the opportunity to live in the first six planets, but each time Esu was evicted for his mischievous deeds. When God created the seventh planet (earth), which was first peopled by sixteen human beings created by God,[7] Ela, the only begotten Son of God,[8] pleaded with Olodumare to give Esu the final opportunity for repentance by allowing him to dwell on earth. It was Ela who taught the aboriginal sixteen men and women that they needed good character, patience, endurance, humility, and love to be able to dwell peaceably on earth. But Esu misled and deceived them.

For the Yoruba, religion does not exist in the intellect alone but includes man's awareness of his own moral responsibilities. The Yoruba civilization is dominated throughout by religion. Their conception of the universe governs every aspect of national and civic life and every aspect of social intercourse. For the Yoruba, the matter of the connection between religion and morality is a redundancy, for morality is considered intrinsic to religion. The ethicoreligious conception of the universe prevails in Yoruba traditional society. The general assumption is that morality rests upon the commandment of the Deity. The Yoruba have no opposing schools of ethical thought, nevertheless, the Yoruba have taken a keen interest in the moral aspect of the world. Our forbears might not have indulged in ethical speculations but that did not diminish their strong ethical consciousness. The Yoruba make no distinction between religious, civil, and moral laws. Morality is not just the fruit, but the root of religion. Whatever religion sanctions, society sanctions; and whatever religion forbids, society forbids.

According to the Yoruba tradition, Olodumare, who made man, gave him the qualities inherent in him. One of these qualities is the sense of moral values, known as *ifa-aiya* (the oracle of the heart) or *eri-okan* (the testimony of the heart). This is similar to what St. Paul calls conscience or the law of God written on the heart (Rom. 2:15). The Yoruba realize that social relations are God's concern and are defined by moral obligations. This provides the source for Yoruba taboos. Most Yoruba religious taboos have moral implications. Every moment, man stands face to face with the question, "What ought I to do?"; and each time the question comes, one is bound to answer.

The word that better explains the Yoruba conception of ethics is *iwa*, meaning "character," "nature," "being," or "the beginning of being." *Iwa* refers to man's essential nature, his psychic self, and the origin and totality of what a person is as an individual. The Yoruba speak of *iwa rere* "good character," "good natured;" *iwa pele* or "humble character," "well behaved;" and *iwa buruka* "bad character," "ill-natured."[9] When the Yoruba say that someone lacks character, it means that such a man lacks morals and all the good qualities required of a normal person. A man endowed with good character is *omoluabi,* which might be a shortened form of *omo-olu-iwa-bi* ("the begotten of the source of good character, or the begotten of the Source-Being"). According to T. A. Awoniyi, "To be an *omoluabi* is to be of good character in all its ramifications. Good character in the Yoruba sense includes respect for old age, loyalty to one's parents and local traditions, honesty in public and private dealings, devotion to duty, readiness to assist the needy, and sympathy."[10]

The personification of things and abstract ideas is a common feature among the Yoruba. It is purposely done to concretize abstract ideas for the ordinary mind to understand. Two distinct but related myths in the Ifa literary corpus personify *iwa* (character) as the wife of Orunmila in *Ogbe Alara*.[11] According to the two myths, Iwa (character) was a daughter of Suru (patience) who himself is the son of Olodumare. Thus, Iwa (character) is seen as a grandchild of God. This means that God is the embodiment and source of good character, and this automatically links religion with ethics.

According to the first myth, Iwa was exceedingly beautiful, patient, and kind. Iwa agreed to marry Orunmila on the condition that he would not ill-treat her, would take good care of her, and would not throw her out of his house. Orunmila promised to be a loyal, loving husband. But soon after Iwa arrived at Orunmila's house, he started to ill-treat Iwa. When Iwa could no longer endure the sufferings, she fled into heaven, her home. Orunmila then went round the whole earth and finally to heaven, searching for Iwa, and singing:

It does not matter how difficult the task may be;
O Iwa! Iwa is the greatest thing we seek for, Iwa.
The search may be terribly dangerous;
O Iwa! Iwa, you are the only one we seek for, Iwa.
Alara, please tell me if you have seen Iwa?
Alara said he had not seen Iwa;
Orangun, King of Illa, did you see Iwa, tell me.
Orangun said that he did not see Iwa;
Iwa! Iwa you are the only one we seek for, Iwa.
Orunmila visited Alara, the King of Ara;
He went to Ogbere the King of Owu;
The journey took him to Oseminigbokun the king of Igbomina;
The search took him to Atakumosa, King of Ijesa;
He came to Osepurutu, the King of Remo;
Lastly, he came to Aseegba, King of Egba;
Asking, whether any of them had seen Iwa for him.
He was told at last that Iwa had gone to her home in Heaven.
O Iwa! Iwa you are the only one we seek for, Iwa.

When Orunmila eventually found his wife in heaven, he pleaded for forgiveness and asked Iwa to return with him to the earth, but she refused. She urged Orunmila to return to the earth and henceforth to be of good character, to take care of his future wives and children. Iwa told Orunmila that she would no longer dwell on earth, physically, but in spirit. Men's attitude to her (*Iwa* = good character) would determine the fate of the earth.

In the second myth, however, despite her beauty, Iwa lacked good character. She had divorced many divinities before marrying

Orunmila. She had a sharp tongue, was intolerant, very lazy, and rough. When Orunmila could no longer tolerate her, he drove her away. Consequently, however, Orunmila lost his friends and respect in society. He became poor and wretched. Orunmila therefore went out in search of Iwa, singing:

> Psychic Wisdom, the priest of Alara's household,
> Consulted the Oracle for Alara.
> Counsellor, the priest of Ajero,
> Consulted the Oracle for Ajero.
> Where did you see Iwa, Tell me.
> O Iwa! Iwa, you are the only one we seek for, Iwa.
> He therefore concludes that: If you have wealth but lack good
>   character,
> The wealth is not yours but others;
> O Iwa! Iwa, you are the only one we seek for, Iwa.
> If you have children but lack good character,
> The children are not yours, but others;
> O Iwa! Iwa, you are the only one we seek for, Iwa.
> If we build mansions, but lack good character,
> The mansions are not ours, but others;
> O Iwa! Iwa, you are the only one we seek for, Iwa.
> If we have clothings, but lack good character,
> The clothings are not ours, but others;
> O Iwa! Iwa, you are the only one we seek for, Iwa.
> We may have all the good things of life, but lack good character,
> All the good things are not ours, but others.
> O Iwa! Iwa, you are the only one we seek for, Iwa.

After a long search, Orunmila found Iwa and brought her into his house; he regained his wealth, respect, and friends.

In the two myths, the symbol of good and bad character is a woman. In Yoruba folklore, women are symbols of beauty, love, tenderness, care, and devotion; at the same time, they are symbols of death, wickedness, jealousy, deceit, and disloyalty. In the two myths, Iwa represents these opposite poles of emotional involvement. In the first myth, she is a paragon of patience and good character. In the second myth, though beautiful, she is an embodiment of evil character and unfaithfulness. Although the myths look contradictory, they are true to life. The Yoruba realize that good moral character is connected with the psychic side of man and is something that flows out of the spirit. Hence, the Yoruba speaks of a good, kind man as Oninurere (the man with a good bowel) and the wicked person as Oninububuru (the man with an evil bowel). The bowel or stomach, as well as the heart, for the Yoruba, are seats of thoughts, emotions, wisdom. It is, therefore, significant that in the first myth, Iwa (character) says that she would no longer dwell with man physically, but spiritually, and that the fate of man's society would depend on the attitude of man to good moral character. In the second myth, it was the lack of good moral character that rendered Iwa useless. Orunmila was forced to look for the evil woman in spite of her bad character. Evil is real in the world, but the problem is not solved by isolating evil men as Orunmila did with Iwa, but to seek to reform them. Orunmila rated good moral character above all earthly possessions because a man who possesses them, but lacks *iwa,* will lose them all to the winds. In the two myths, the most precious thing to seek after is *iwa* because, without it, life is meaningless. Man should seek it regardless of the cost. The first hymn represents Orunmila's repentance and longing after good character. The second is an appeal by Orunmila to his wife to repent and to change for the better.

Principles of Ethical Decision Making

Yoruba ethical principles are regulated by a system of taboos and a strong sense of community. The word *eewo* (taboo; that which must not be done) explains the principles of ethical decision making among the Yoruba. The simple exclamation, *eewo!* means, "It is taboo;" "It is forbidden;" "Hold it;" "It must not be done." It is also called *owun* (that which brings condemnation when the taboo is broken). These two words cover anything that can be considered as sin or sinful. Sin, to the Yoruba, is not an abstract concept. It is connected with man's acts to his fellow man, and to other creatures that are also of concern to the Supreme Deity and to the divinities. An act of inhumanity is therefore also an offense against the divinities and the Deity.

On the question of moral values, the divinities come first. The Yoruba believe in one Supreme Deity but they also believe in the existence of divinities. The Yoruba speak of 200 divinities, 401 divinities, 460 divinities, and 1440 divinities. It is not clear whether these numbers refer to different opinions on the number, or to the four major divisions among the divinities.[12] The divinities, like biblical angels, assist Olodumare in the theocratic government of the earth. Each of the divinities has its special role to play in the governance and control of the universe. Many of the divinities are guardians of morality. For example, Sango or Jakuta, the thunder

divinity among the Yoruba and related groups, represents the wrath
of Olodumare on thieves, liars, traitors, evil doers, etc. Sango visits
God's wrath on such people to punish them for their evil deeds by
striking them with lightening. Another divinity is Obaluaiye (King
of the earth) or Olode (the Lord of the Open). The main scourges
of this divinity are smallpox and chicken pox. The dreadful diseases
are seen as the most objective symptoms of the wrath of the divinity
upon the victim or the community. He visits God's wrath on such
evils as witchcraft, sorcery, the keeping of poisonous medicines at
home, and other such wicked acts.[13] There is also Ogun (the Metal
divinity) who visits divine wrath on people for false swearing, oath
breaking, and adultery. Such offenders always pass away through
accidental death incurred by gunshots, motor accidents, and other
fatal accidents. Belief in the reality and presence of these divinities
as agents of God in executing his judgment upon offenders, helps
individuals refrain from evil acts. Moreover, there are taboos
imposed on the worshipper. For example, the devotees of Orisanla
(the arch-divinity) must not drink palm wine or other strong
drinks, and men must be monogamists.[14] There are also many food
laws that devotees are expected to observe. Part of the initiation
into the cult of any divinity is called *gbigba eewo* (receiving the
taboo), which actually refers to the receiving of the terms of the
covenant from the divinity concerned. During the initiation ceremony the taboos are related to the new entrants. The covenant
between the devotees and the divinity is sealed by eating and drinking in communion with the divinity concerned. Once the covenant
is sealed, it becomes binding.

Yoruba ethics is also a community ethics. Individualism is not
encouraged since an evil deed by an individual can heap disaster
upon the whole community. The breaking of a taboo may not only
bring judgment on the sinner but upon his immediate community,
and even upon his future generations. Hence, harsh punishments
are often meted to evil doers as part of the remedy for removing
divine wrath. In addition, the Yoruba believe in divine retribution,
and that an evil doer cannot escape the punishment of the All-
Knowing Olodumare, either in this life or in the life to come. The
Yoruba believe in leaving a good name behind as the children's
greatest inheritance.

All of the above form the major principles of ethical decision
making among the Yoruba.

Basic Moral Values

Respect for Elders and Authority

This is one of the most important aspects of Yoruba ethics. The Yoruba child grows up in a community where he respects all elderly men and women as fathers and mothers. The term "parents" in a Yoruba community does not refer to the biological parents alone. Respect and care for parents and the elders are regarded as sacred duties. Those who neglect these parental duties will lose not only the respect of their immediate society, but must bring curses upon themselves. That is why Orunmila says in *Odu Irete Eguntan:*[15]

> Render due honour to your mother and father,
> So that your days may be long on earth.
> Ifa says: "Offer sacrifice to your mother and father,
> The sacrifices of true care and humility;
> Because this will be to you a spiritual re-birth."
> Ifa says: "Offer sacrifice to your mother and father,
> The sacrifice of concern and obedience;
> So that you may not bring their curses upon yourself.
> The curses of your mother and father are the curses of the Almighty."
> Ifa says: "Offer sacrifice to your mother and father,
> The sacrifice of true love; so that you may have perfect peace,
> And in order that you may have the richest blessing."[16]

In this verse taken from one of the 256 chapters of the Ifa literary collection, it is clear that the most acceptable sacrifice to God is care for parents, for the poor, and for aged relatives. It is significant that throughout the verse the mother is mentioned before the father who is the head of the home. In Yoruba values, the mother comes first in respect to parental importance, attachment, and care for the aged. A Yoruba adage says, *Orisa bi iya kosi* ("There is no goddess like the mother"). Likewise, a popular Yoruba school children's song singles out the mother for praise:

> The mother is my comforter who took care of me while I was a baby.
> She carried me on her back. Mother, thanks for the job well done.
> I will show my mother my deep appreciation by bowing down in
>   humility.
> I will never again disobey my mother.
> Never! Never! Never!

But, as stated earlier, Yoruba ethics also teaches respect for elders, regardless of blood relationships. Elders are valued as indispensable

because they are always the source of wisdom, strength, and guidance. The following verses capture the traditional sentiment:

Give respect to the elders because of grey hair.
Give respect to the elders; they are fathers.
Give respect to the elders; the elders are saviours.
In the days of plenty, the elders give support.
In the days of scarcity, the elders give support.[17]

In Yoruba traditions and customs, respect for the elders rates
high. The Yoruba hold the elders in the highest esteem, almost to
the point of adoration. Beginning from childhood, a Yoruba man
is steadily schooled to give the elders his due regard. He must not
talk to them sternly, must not be rude to them, and must not stare
them in the face. Respect is a sacred duty that every young person
owes the elders. To live long on earth and to have success, respect
for the elders is a necessary condition. This is made clear in the
following passage from *Odu-Ika-Idi*—a chapter of the Ifa literary
corpus.

A vain youth is fond of roguery.
He could, if so desires, slap the face of an aged priest who he meets
    walking on the road.
Moreover, if by chance, he meets a veteran physician on the way,
Let the rogue give the physician a thorough beating.
If, during an aimless wandering, he sees an elder *alufa*[18] bending down
    to pray,
He could push him down, if he so desires.
But the oracle has this message for the rogue.
Who says that he is above the law?
"Know ye not, that there is no long life
For a youth who beats an aged priest;
There is no old age for the youth
Who beats a veteran physician.
The child who beats an elderly priest is courting an instant death;
An instant death, the way a worm dies instantly!"[19]

Outside what we know from the Ifa literary corpus, the Yoruba
language is very rich in proverbs and parables, most of which are
meant for moral education. The Yoruba believe that is is only
respect for the authority of the elders, customs, and traditions that
can create peace and harmony in the world. Hence the saying,
Aifagba fenikan niko je ki aiye ogun (Refusal to accept the authority
of the elders is the major cause of chaos in the world). There is also
the saying, *Agba ko si ilu baje, bale ile ku ile di ahoro, Imado ibase bi*

elede a ba ilu je: eru ibajoba, eniyan iba ku okan (There are no elders, hence the city is in ruin; the head of the family is dead and the house becomes desolate. Were the hippopotamus the pig, the city would have been ravaged; were a slave to be crowned king, no man would have survived). The elders are symbols of cohesion and harmony in Yoruba communities. Whenever young, inexperienced people try to play the role of the elders, chaos is bound to occur. Moreover, whenever fools and those who are not committed to the good of the community control the destiny of a people, this must lead to calamity. But young people who accept and respect the authority of the elders will drink from their fountain of wisdom. *Aimo owo we, lai ba agba jeun; eni ba mo owo we a si ma ba agba jeun* (He who does not know how to wash his hands, cannot eat with the elders; but he who knows how to wash his hands will eat with the elders).

However, respect for the elders is not a one-sided affair. The elders must conduct themselves well and act as examples to the community in words and in deeds. They can not attempt to dominate the community, but must respect its wishes and traditions. The elders know that the young people are indispensable, and hence the saying, *Owo omode ko to pepe; ti agbalagba ko wo akeregba* (The hand of a child cannot reach the ceiling, and likewise the hand of the elder cannot enter into a gourd). In other words, there are things that the young people can do that the elders are unable to perform. Thus, neither the elders, nor the youths, are self-sufficient.

As for the civil authority, the Yoruba regard their *Oba* (Kings) as possessing divine authority. They are addressed as *Alase, ekeji orisa* (The Power-wielder, the vice-regent of the Deity). The ruler of Ile-Ife, "the ancestral home of mankind," which first appeared out of water, is, in Yoruba tradition, called Olofin-aiye (the Supreme Pontiff of the earth), representing the Olofin-orun (the Supreme Pontiff of heaven) on earth. The Alafin of Oyo, the one-time rulers of the two-century old Yoruba empire that extended up to present Ghana, are known as *Iku baba yeye* (Death, the father of goddesses).[20] Yoruba traditional religion enjoins respect, obedience, and loyalty to rulers who represent the authority of the divinities and the ancestors. However, the Yoruba have no place for tyrannical rulers. Hence the Yoruba have a system for removing rulers who become despots.[21] With regard to the authority of kings, Orunmila says:

The sword sucks the blood of those who despise the king.
To the king belongs the sword, to the king's authority.

Therefore, tread softly; I say tread softly,
Lest your own self-conceited wisdom pushes you against the king's
   sword.

Orunmila says further:

The crown is the judge of the monarch;
The throat of the sage may lead the sage into trouble;
It is only Mr Know-all that refuses to respect the king.
He was urged to offer sacrifice,
In order that the king's sword might not suck his blood.

Orunmila says that the earthly king is the messenger of the heavenly King.

Orunmila says: "As for me,"
I say, as for me too;
I have obeyed the king's command;
I will certainly find favour with the king."[22]

Disrespect for the rulers and elders is therefore regarded as one of the most heinous crimes. Some Yoruba myths even associate the origin of sin with disobedience to or disrespect for the elders. A youth who does not honor the elders, as has been shown above, can never attain old age. He will suffer several calamities, including sudden death.

Sex and Marriage

Marriage is ordained by God for the procreation of children and for mutual help. Marriage is obligatory. Every man and woman is expected to marry. Even deformity or being handicapped must not prevent marriage. It is a curse for any man or woman not to marry. Marriages are even arranged for eunuchs. But such cases of impotency are usually part of the family secrets. These marriages are consummated by the man's brothers or closest kinsmen. The offspring are considered the legitimate children of the impotent husband, not those of the actual fathers. Polygamy is allowed as long as a man does not marry more than the number of wives he can comfortably maintain.[23] Levirate marriage is also part of the Yoruba marriage custom. Polyandry is totally forbidden. Among the Yoruba, betrothal precedes marriage. This may even be from the period of the pregnancy or birth of the girl.[24] The duration of the courtship is usually not less than four years. Beginning with the time of the betrothal, the girl is regarded as the legitimate wife of the man.

A wife is expected to be humble and submissive to her husband. She is to respect the elderly men and women, as well as the senior wives in the extended family. All the children born into the husband's extended family before the day of her wedding, whether male or female, are regarded as her seniors and she is not expected to call them by their personal names. She must resort to such nomenclature as "my husband," to the use of common nicknames, or invent names of her own.[25] She is to be honored and to be shown kindness by her husband and other members of the extended family. She is a member of the large family and not a slave.

It is said that the most important thing a woman takes to her husband's house is *iwa* (good character). According to one saying, "Character is a goddess and she rewards each one according to his/her character" *(Orisa ni iwa bi ati hu si ni ise gbe ni)*. Another phrase says, "Good character is the beauty of a woman; a beautiful woman without character is worthless" *(Iwa l'e wa omo eniyan, b'obinrin dara bi o ni iwa asan lo je)*.

The Yoruba have many myths of childless, deified women. Such women, though barren or childless, were known to love and care for the children of others. One such childless woman who has been deified is Olomoyeye (Mother of countless children). Throughout her life, this woman made beancakes every morning and distributed them in charity to hosts of children. This is why, though childless, this lady was nicknamed Olomoyeye. Hence, in *Ogbe Egunda,* Orunmila declares:

Behold the children of Iwa are countless!
Behold the children of Iwa are countless!
Iwa is carrying many on her back; Iwa is carrying many in her hands;
Behold the children of Iwa are countless![26]

The building of the home and the care of the children are regarded as the joint responsibility of the husband and wife or wives. They are assisted by members of the extended family. A Yoruba adage says, "It takes wisdom to set up a home; it takes understanding to make it a real home" *(Ogben ni a fi nko ile, oye ni a si fi ngbe inu re)*. While the Yoruba love children, they believe that quality is very important, and so the saying:

"I have twenty children"; but they may not be worth more than grass.
"I have thirty children"; but they may not be worth more than giant-grass.
Instead of being a parent of 2,000 worthless children, I prefer to have just one who ranks above the best of children.

A similar adage says, "A thousand giant-grasses can never make a big forest tree; one good child is far better than a thousand vain children" (Okan soso araba ki i se egbe egberun osunsun; omo kansoso ti o yanju o san ju egberun omolasan lo).

Good home training for children is the sacred duty of parents and elders. It is their responsibility to train those who will succeed them after their death. Hence the saying, "When the fire-brand dies, it is covered by ashes; when a banana tree dies, it is survived by its little ones" (Bi ina ba ku a fi eru b'oju, bi ogede ba ku a fi omo re ro po). The wish to be survived by good children is a prayer that can be heard from all of the Yoruba people.

With regard to sex in terms of Yoruba values, virginity is the glory of a young woman. The maiden who loses it prior to marriage loses her pride and glory and is a shame to her family.[27] A husband who finds his wife chaste at marriage will go to the bride's family early on the morning following the consummation of the marriage, with a white cloth stained with "virginity blood" as proof that their daughter has retained her "glory" until the marriage bed. The husband and his friends will thank the family for giving their daughter good moral education. The wife also receives special gifts from her husband for remaining chaste. But if she is found to have lost her "glory," the husband will not pay the parents the "thanksgiving visit." Instead, he will send her parents half a piece of yam cut in two or a half-full keg of palm wine or water to show that their daughter was not found "full" at marriage. In some places the erring woman must perform certain rituals in order to appease the divinities and thus remove the curse. The man responsible, if known, is also punished in accordance with the custom of that community.

Sexual purity within marriage is mandatory. Since Yoruba custom sanctions polygamy, sex by a man with several women who are his legitimate wives is considered normal. But since the society rejects polyandry, extramarital sex by any woman is abnormal and, if detected, may be severely punished. Membership in various religious cults nurtures this sort of sexual morality. Apart from the fact that one must not do evil to a fellow cult member nor betray him, extramarital sex with the wife of a cult member is a taboo. Traditionally, a man must not sit on a chair that the wife of a fellow cult member or friend has just vacated. To do so is tantamount to committing rape or adultery with the woman in question. For example, Orunmila declares in Ogbe Atewa:

After initiation into the cult of Ifa, the initiate must not seduce the
wife of a fellow cult man.
He cannot snatch the wife of a herbalist.
He cannot go in stealthily to seduce the wife of a fellow priest.
It is a taboo to plan wickedness with the wife of a fellow covenanter.
Whenever you are summoned by the cult leader, you must tell the
truth and nothing but the truth.[28]

Harlotry is strictly forbidden by tradition and was, until recently,
quite unknown in Yoruba land. Harlots are referred to as, "Death!
that cuts a man's throat without a knife" *(Iku! apaniyan lalaisobe)*.
An adulterous woman is regarded as a murderess. Orunmila
declares in *Ogbe Oyeku Palaba:*

A destroyer of the husband's house, a destroyer of the husband's
house,
A destroyer of the concubine's house, a destroyer of the concubine's
house,
She kills the husband; she kills the concubine.
Afterwards, she kills and buries herself in a bottomless grave.
Thus declared the Oracle to the female harlot, the messenger of
death.[29]

It is also a taboo to seduce the betrothed wife of another man.
After the betrothal, a woman, though not yet married, is the legal
wife of a man. A myth of how Orunmila seduced the betrothed
daughter of Eledidi-Agbo is told in *Odu Idingbo*.[30] Orunmila was
cautioned not to woo the betrothed wife of another man, but he
refused. After marrying Princess Ese, Orunmila was forever barred
from entering the city of Edidi-Agbo. Orunmila recounts his
experience:

Gentle wind drive me on, drive me on nonstop;
Strong wind drive me on, drive me on nonstop.
Thus declared the Oracle to Orunmila,
When he was going to marry Ese[31] the daughter of Eledidi-Agbo.[32]
After Orunmila had married Ese, he was permanently barred from
Edidi-Agbo.

All forms of abnormal sex are forbidden. Incest is abominable,
and therefore it is strictly a taboo. Sex or marriage with any relation
is not allowed. One of the duties of the two families involved in
the negotiation of a marriage is to find out whether or not there is
any blood relation between the two families before a marriage pact
is sealed. Even sex and marriage with descendants of slaves or immi-

grants who have become part of the extended family is regarded as incest.

Homosexuality, lesbianism, and having sex with animals are not only taboos, but are regarded as mental illnesses that require as much treatment as given to those who eat sand or potsherd.

In the past divorce was very rare among the Yoruba. Marriage is considered a pact between two families. Neither the man nor the woman can make an independent decision to divorce. The few divorces in the past were due mainly to barrenness or to cases where, after the death of the husband, there were no brothers or close blood relations to take over the young wives or to play the role of husbands. Other reasons for divorce might be connected with the danger of contracting diseases such as leprosy, or the committing of shameful acts. Today the situation has changed considerably.

The debate about the equality of the sexes is still limited to a very few westernized elites who often exhibit complete ignorance of the various African societies they try to describe. Among the Yoruba, the husband is both the head of the home and the breadwinner for the family. The women are not just housekeepers. Those in villages tend their own farms or engage in other moneymaking ventures. The grandmothers are at hand to help care for the children. Those in cities also have their trades or business enterprises. It is believed that each woman, like a man, must have a vocation.

Among many religious cults, men worship under the priesthood of women. However there are also many religious cults from which women are barred. In most cases, these are cults dealing with ancestral worship.

It is generally believed that women are emotional and cannot keep secrets. Women are also regarded as unclean during menstruation, but men are also expected to abstain from sex for a certain number of days prior to officiating in some religious worship. The Yoruba believe in an orderly society with everybody performing his or her role for the growth and development of the society. Cruelty to women is not allowed. There are mechanisms at the extended family level to iron out differences between husbands and wives. Nevertheless, it will be untrue to claim that women have attained equality with men in every sphere of life. The Yoruba society is guilty of the notion that women are a weaker sex needing both care, love, and concern, as well as the domination of men.

Truthfulness

Truthfulness is another important moral value around which all other moral principles revolve. To the Yoruba, truthfulness means dedication, devotion, loyalty, honesty, and faithfulness. It is the most important moral principle guiding religious worship, practice, covenant-making, friendship, business, service, family relations, and love affairs. Truthfulness is the measuring rod for determining whether an action is good or bad. Yoruba religious tradition stresses the importance of speaking the truth at all times and the dangerous consequences of lying. According to Orunmila, no religious duty is as important as telling the truth and engaging in honest business. Anyone who expects God's blessings must be truthful. Orunmila therefore enjoins man thus:

> Be truthful and honest.
> Ifa says: "Be truthful, be honest."
> Only the truthful ones are blessed by divinities.[33]

Individuals are expected to be transparently honest in matters relating to friends, members of the same family, fellow cult members, and all men in general. Through several myths, Orunmila declares that it never pays to be dishonest. God is all-knowing and watches over the conduct of humans. Because Olodumare knows all things, he will certainly bring to judgment every evil deed. Orunmila say in *Ogbe Ogundabede:*

> Lying slays the liar, betrayal slays the betrayer.
> The eyes of Olodumare sees what is buried under the earth.
> Thus declared the Oracle to the man who steals under the cover of
>   darkness.
> And thinks that no earthly king sees him.
> Though the earthly king sees you not,
> Know you not that the Heavenly King sees you?
> Orunmila says further:
> Tale bearing—they slay the slave.
> Curses—they slay the thief.
> Covenant breaking—they slay the friend.
> The tutelary divinity kills one who harms his relation.[34]

In all business transactions, man must be truthful and honest. Dishonesty always leads to sorrow and tragedy, while truthfulness leads to abundant blessings. This can be illustrated by the following myths. The first one tells about three men: Eke (Liar), Odale (Covenant-breaker), and Oninure (Kind-hearted). All three decided to go to the town called Otito (Truth) to do business. They consulted Orunmila who assured them that they would be loved and respected by the citizens of Otito and that they would return prosperous if they remained truthful in all their dealings in Otito. Only Oninure (Kind-hearted) heeded Orunmila's warning and returned from Otito, prosperous, but Eke (Liar) and Odale (Betrayer) perished in Otito (Truth) city. Therefore, Orunmila says:

> The Liar died; he was buried in hot ashes.
> The Covenant-breaker died; he was buried in a pot of burning sun.
> The Kind-hearted died; he was buried with a coffin of brass,
> With his back leaning on a pot of jewels.
> Thus the Oracle declared to Orunmila
> When he was going on business to the city of Truth.
> His diviners told him not to embark on the journey,
> Because all those who went to the city of Truth never returned;
> Those who went to the city of Truth always perished there.
> But Orunmila replied that he would go to the city of Truth.
> He went. He was truthful in all his dealings and he became
>   prosperous.
> Orunmila returned safe and sound.[35]

The second myth in *Eji-Ogbe* tells of three men who decided to go to another country to do business.[36] They were Eke (Liar), Odale (Covenant-breaker), and Otito-inu (Truth). They consulted the Oracle and Orunmila told them that all would return prosperous, provided each of them was truthful in his business dealings. When they reached that country, each of them behaved according to his natural character. Mr. Liar told lies. Mr. Covenant-breaker never kept his promises. Both of them languished in misery and eventually died in poverty and penury in the foreign land. But Mr. Truth was honest in all his business transactions. He returned to his country a rich man because he took the advice of Orunmila. Therefore Orunmila says:

> The Liar went to a foreign country but never returned.
> The Covenant-breaker went to a foreign land but perished there.
> Thus declared the Oracle to Truth
> Who said: rectitude is more profitable than lying.

Riches and Poverty

The Yoruba believe in the dignity of labor, in being industrious, and working hard to earn one's living. This is made clear in the following sayings, "Weeping will not save anyone from penury," "the indolent deserve hunger," "the pretended illness of the indolent is incurable," "labor is the cure of poverty," "one who puts his hope on inheritance will die in penury" *(Ise o gb'ekun; ebi jare ole; ojojo ole o san boro; ise logun ise; agboju le ogun f'ara re fun osi ta).*

Young people are especially urged to understand the value of labor. Several sayings encourage them to become self-sufficient:

Do not while away the time of your youth.
It is through hard work that one becomes a respectable person.
Your mother may be wealthy;
Your father may have a stable of horses;
If you rest your hope on inheritance, you are daydreaming.

Yoruba ethics enjoins honesty in moneymaking ventures. It is possible to have all earthly riches and lose the respect of the community. An adage says, "There is difference between money and high respect; there is difference between wealth and honor" *(Oto l'owo, oto niyi, oto l'ola, oto l'o la).* The source of wealth and what one does with it is what determine the people's attitude to a wealthy man. Another adage says, "Never strive to become rich in haste; never rush to become a wealthy man overnight" *(Ka ma fi ikanju l'owo; ka ma fi waduwadu loro).*

Money is an earthly thing that will pass away, therefore it is possible for a rich man to become poor again. That is why it is important for a wealthy person to give liberally out of his wealth to the poor. Hence the following proverbs, "Money comes and goes like showers of rain," "times and seasons do not remain unchanged," "earthly things do not remain fixed like a straight rod" *(Ojo lowo; igba ki ito lo bi orere; aiye ki ito lo bi).* Since nobody knows what tomorrow will be like, it is important to do good today. "It is because tomorrow will never be like today, that is why the priest consults the Oracle every five days" *(Bi oni tiri, ola ki ire be, oun ni babalawo fi ndifa ororun).*[37] The greatest inheritance a rich man can leave behind is a good name because "the good man never dies, the good man lives on forever." Many Yoruba myths speak of the calamitous ends of misers to show that a miserly life does not pay in the end. A proverb says, "If you have given me, it is by your giving and my giving that the world lives on" *(Bi o ni o bun mi, bun mi n bun o lo l'aiye).* A wretched afterlife awaits anyone who lives miserly on earth with no concern for the poor. It is believed that whatever you give to help the poor on earth is stored up in heaven for you. The story of the rich man and Lazarus (Luke 16:19–31) gives the true picture of the Yoruba conception of the afterlife.

Destruction of Life

To the Yoruba, life is sacred and it is divine in origin. God is not only known as the Creator but as the Source Being. The name Orisa or Orise (Deity) literally means, Source Being. The name Oluwa, commonly rendered "Lord" or "Master," can also mean the Source Being (Olu-iwa). God is known as Eleda or Aseda (the Creator). He is called Elemi (the owner of life). God gives life to every living thing, nothing exists without him. He controls and orders people's lives from the beginning to the end. He gives life and takes it back. The promise about what one hopes to do in the future often begins with, "If the Owner of Life does not take it" *(Bi Elemi ko ba gba emi)*. What the person concerned is saying is, "I shall do such and such a thing, if God spares my life."

With regard to the creation of man Olodumare gave Obatala the task of molding man's physical body with clay, cold water and snail water, while he reserves to himself the prerogative of giving man life and his essence of being. Obatala was given the sole right of making human figures perfect or defective and to give their various colors. Hence, the Yoruba sing in praise of Obatala:

He who makes the eye, makes the nose;
It is Orisa I will serve.
He who creates as he chooses;
It is Orisa I will serve.[38]

A story is told of how Obatala decided to spy on Olodumare in order to know the secret of how Olodumare gives man life and his essence of being. One day, after molding the physical bodies, Obatala refused to vacate the chamber where the lifeless bodies were, as he was supposed to do before the arrival of Olodumare. Instead, he hid himself in a dark corner of the room. But before Olodumare arrived, Obalata had fallen into a deep sleep and did not wake up until Olodumare had given existence to the lifeless bodies and had left the chamber. Since then, Obalata contented himself with making physical forms alone.[39]

The Yoruba believe that no living being should be destroyed without a just cause. Children are not only taught to be kind to fellow human beings but also to animals and other living things. One of the Yoruba poems that I learned in school as a young child nearly forty years ago, says:

Turn, turn your foot aside,
Do not step on the insect.

That insect for which you have no regard;
It is only God who can create it.
The same God who gives you your life,
Also bestows his great love upon that insect.
He created the sun and the moon for all his creatures,
And made the land to grow vegetable for the sake of man and insects.
Therefore spare them and allow them to enjoy all their blessings.
Oh! never wantonly take a life which you cannot create.[40]

Human life is sacred for the Yoruba because man is regarded as Heaven's masterpiece. The Yoruba never think of themselves as belonging to the animal kingdom, but rather see themselves as those occupying the unique position of leadership over all other living things. It is a great insult to refer to a human being as an animal. In *Ogbe Oyekulogbo,* Orunmila says:

The benefactor says, "Thank you, thou true son of man."
It is only the seed of man that is not only the hearer
But the doer of what he is told.
We persistently reprove the seed of the animal; he rejects correction.
He is constantly beaten, but he will not listen.
Repeatedly we warn the seed of a graven image; he refuses to yield.[41]

The above verses are explained by a myth that states that, at the time when people were still few on the earth, they felt that the method of populating the world through childbearing was too slow. Therefore, they appealed to Olodumare to change the method or to send more persons rapidly to populate the earth. Olodumare asked them to bring two hundred animals and two hundred graven images. Olodumare turned them into human beings and sent them down to earth. When these four hundred individuals reached the earth, they behaved like animals and dumb idiots. The lesson people learned by this experience was that humans are God's special creation, and they became contented with God's ordained method for populating the earth. This is in keeping with the Yoruba myth of creation, that man is the only creature with the spark of God within him.

While animals can be killed for food, the killing of human beings is strictly forbidden among the Yoruba. He who sheds blood must pay with the shedding of his own blood. Sometimes blood and life are used interchangeably. For instance, the phrase, he took his life *(o gba emi re)* or he took his blood *(ogbe eje re)* means that the person committed murder. A murderer is said to have blood hanging on his neck *(o l'eje l'orun),* which means the murderer is guilty of blood. The Yoruba believe that it is impossible to escape divine punishment for shedding blood and the consequences for the murderer may even extend to generations yet unborn. Murder is considered to be the most heinous crime. Those wielding the powers of life and death are expected to exercise such powers with caution because of the possibility of an evil repercussion, not only on them and their descendants, but on the entire community.

The following are capital offenses. Anybody who wilfully kills another human being must also lose his life. Thieves are often exiled for life from their towns and villages or sold into slavery. But notorious armed robbers are often condemned to death or permanently maimed. Other offenses requiring capital punishment are witchcraft or sorcery. Self-confessed witches or sorcerers are often beheaded, stoned to death, or poisoned. The most common method of execution for capital offenses is beheading.

The breaking of certain taboos might also demand capital punishment, and this varies from community to community. Taboo-breaking is thought to bring a curse on the whole community, unless it is atoned for—in order to remove the curse and avert the wrath of God. As a parallel, the Old Testament tells of Achan who brought a curse upon Israel when he broke faith with Yahweh. In order to remove the curse, Achan and his family were stoned to death. The ancient Israelites thought that that was the only way to appease Yahweh. This story somewhat explains the attitude of the Yoruba toward the breaking of taboos. Even so, capital punishment for taboo-breaking is quite rare among the Yoruba. Rather, the prevailing belief is that every individual will reap what he sows. This attitude has served to mitigate all punishments meted out to offenders.

In spite of the high regard the Yoruba have had for human life, human sacrifice has been practiced traditionally in several communities. It must be mentioned here, however, that human sacrifice was not, at any time, universal among the Yoruba. The significance of human sacrifice for the Yoruba can be summarized in the words of Caiphas to the Jews about Jesus, "You know nothing at all; you do not understand that it is expedient for you that one man should die for the people, and that the whole nation should not perish."[42] The reasoning is that human sacrifice is the supreme sacrifice—the best that man can offer Deity as a last resort.

The victims of human sacrifice were believed to be different from animals. Since the Yoruba believe in life after death, such victims were, in effect, sent to plead their cause before the Deity. In some cases, victims of human sacrifice were deified after their death. On occasions, during the founding of new towns or markets, human beings were used as "foundation sacrifices." Such victims were regarded as protectors of such towns and markets, and they, in turn received sacrifices, though not necessarily human sacrifices. There were few occasions when individuals volunteered to be offered as sacrifice on behalf of the community. It was regarded as a privilege to die for the community and thus become their representative before the Deity or divinity. However, more often than not, it was the Ifa Oracle that did the selection. For example, the person selected for the foundation sacrifice at the inauguration of Ibadan, the largest black city in Africa, was said to be the diviner himself who had been consulted to know the type of sacrifice needed. He willingly surrendered himself, and today is still worshipped in Ibadan.

From the moment the priests took custody of the victims of human sacrifice, the victims were treated as sacred. Before a victim was sacrificed on behalf of the community, the priest would lay hands on him, confessing guilt, and messages would be sent through the victim to the Deity. In the case of the foundation sacrifice, the victim was either sacrificed or buried alive at the gate of the center of the city, and he thus became the protector of the community. So, too, the biblical story tells us that when Jephta offered his only daughter to Yahweh, he sincerely believed that he was giving his best to Yahweh.[43] Only later, with the expansion of people's mental, moral, and spiritual horizons, did they realize that human sacrifice or any other form of blood sacrifice was unnecessary, and that it is the offering of one's life that the Deity demands.[44]

On the question of abortion, which is gradually becoming a social problem, particularly among young, unmarried girls, there is no specific answer from Orunmila and other oral traditions. This is because, until recently, abortion was foreign to Yoruba society. Even in cases where married women had miscarriages, these were attributed to witches or sorcerers. Girls were expected to remain virgin until the time of marriage. Abortion to the Yoruba is as grievous as murder. It is a recent practice, now covered by the criminal law of Nigeria.

Euthanasia, a related matter, is not common among the Yoruba. Yoruba ethics classifies euthanasia as an act of murder. It is considered the duty of relatives and of all those in charge of health care delivery to nurse a sick person until life is naturally terminated by death. For herbalists, euthanasia is contrary to their professional ethics. However, it is believed that some individuals possess mysterious powers that make them refuse to die even after their bodies have started to decay and they have lapsed into prolonged periods of unconsciousness. In such cases, family members investigate what needs to be done to help the stricken individual die. This might take the form of removing certain rings from his finger, removing charms from his house, or resorting to such measures as the ingestion of fresh eggs, snail water. It is admittedly difficult to ascertain how the above cases can be treated as subjects of euthanasia. What is much clearer is that the forms in which euthanasia is currently practiced would be deemed murder because they involve the act of taking life, which is only the prerogative of man's Maker.

Similarly, in regard to suicide, the Yoruba believe that no person has the right to terminate his own life for any reason. The individual who commits suicide is looked upon as an accursed person who dies an accursed death. The curse is conveyed to the whole family and to the entire community, and therefore all persons collectively related to the person who has done this deed must engage in the removal of the curse through the performance of prescribed rituals. Further, persons who die by hanging, those who cut their throats, shoot themselves, or take poisons are not permitted burial at home or in the town, but only in groves by the Ifa priests. All belongings of the deceased are also accursed and are removed from the home. By tradition, the Yoruba bury their dead in houses, except for children. To do otherwise would be keeping the departed under the rain and sun in the world of the dead. Only individuals who are counted accursed are buried in the bush. These include persons who have died of smallpox, those killed by lightening, those killed by fallen trees, victims of fire disasters, pregnant women, and someone who collapses and dies in the market on a market day.

The above instances show that killing in all its forms is strictly forbidden among the Yoruba except for the purpose of sacrifice. No one has the right to terminate another person's life, not even his own, for all life is sacred. It is impossible for a man to shed blood and escape divine wrath.

Justice, Reward, and Punishment

In common with other people, the Yoruba have occasional misgivings about doing good. Here we are concerned with the problem

of why the righteous suffer and the wicked prosper in a world that
is ruled and controlled by the just God, Olodumare. This problem
is expressed and explained in many legends and sayings, such as,
"When the wicked prospers on earth and the good does not prosper, one feels that it does not pay to do good" *(Bi ile ba ngbe osika
ti ko gbe oloto, ore a ma su ni ise)*. The Yoruba believe that one may
even suffer death in the course of doing good, "Before the Mother-
Earth slays the wicked, the good man might have been ruined completely" *(Ki ile to pa osika, eni rere ti baje)*. Although the Yoruba
emphasize truthfulness, it is simultaneously recognized that man,
by nature, prefers falsehood to truth. Hence, the saying, "Truth is
displayed unsold in the market, but falsehood sells like hot cakes"
(Otito d'oja okuta, owo lowo l'a nra eke). Yet, it is enjoined that man
must, under all circumstances, do what is right, "It is better to tell
the truth and die, because it pays to tell truth; it never pays to tell
lies *(Ka s'otito k'a ku, o san, nitori otito ni gbeni, iro ki gbe ni)*. Again,
"A lie may have run the race of falsehood for twenty years; it will
take the truth only one day to catch up with it" *(Bi iro ba sare l'ogun
odun, ojo kan soso ni otito yio le e ba)*.

It is possible for one to serve his fellow men with sacrificial devotion, though this may not be appreciated. According to a myth, the
vulture was originally a domestic bird. At one time, there was a
terrible famine because there was no rain. Man was asked to offer
sacrifice to Olodumare. When every bird refused to carry the sacrifice to Olodumare, it was only the vulture that volunteered. It
carried the sacrifice to heaven. Olodumare accepted the sacrifice,
and by the time the vulture returned to earth, it had started to rain.
The vulture went round knocking on every door, but nobody
allowed it in. Instead, people started to hit its head with sticks. That
was how its head became bald and it became a brush bird. That is
why Orunmila says:

> It was in consequence of kindness that the vulture became bald;
> Because it did not exercise caution.
> It was in consequence of kindness that the hornbill developed goitre;
> Because it did not exercise caution.[45]

A Yoruba proverb says, "Good trees never live long in the forest"
(Igi rere ki i pe n'igbo). This is always true with regard to human life.
It is clear from the above that the Yoruba recognize the fact that
the righteous may suffer adversities and even violent death in consequence of their good deeds. It is realized that the wicked may
prosper in this world in spite of their wickedness. But the mere

recognition of this fact of life does not answer some of the questions that always agitate man's mind as to why the righteous suffer while the wicked prosper in the world. This, therefore, leads us to the matter of reward and punishment in Yoruba tradition.

Olodumare is not just the Creator of the ends of the world, but is the judge of all men. He is the only righteous judge whom no man can escape. It is said of him, "The Lord is a silent Judge; the Judge of the ends of the world, the Judge of the earth, is never a wicked King" (Adake dajo l'Oluwa, Adajo aiye, Adajo ile ki i se Oba ika). Olodumare is known as "God the rewarder " (Olorun e san). He is called, "The King whose blessings know no discrimination on earth; but the King who blesses only the selected few in the after-life" (Oba ajoke aiye, Oba asake orun). Olodumare is all-knowing. He is "The One who knows man in and out; the One who knows the heart" (Arinurode, Olumo-okan). According to Ogbe-Iro-sun wase, "No one knows the heart of man, except the Source-Being, except Olodumare" (Ohun ti mbe ni inu akole e rii, a fi Orisa, afi Olodumare). For the Yoruba, the day of reckoning with God is certain.

The Yoruba believe that death does not write "finis" to man's life. If one escapes judgment in this world, he cannot escape reckoning with God after death. It is said, "Whatsoever we do on earth, we shall recount, kneeling before Olodumare.[46] Again, "Do not feed on centipedes, do not feed on earth-worms; it all depends on one's character in this world," meaning, it is useless wishing the dead eternal bliss since their deeds on earth will determine that. To the Yoruba, death means the separation of the body and the personality-soul. The body will decay and return to the earth from where Obatala took it, but the essential person will return to Olodumare, its Creator. The abode of the dead, of God, and of the divinities is known as "heaven" (orun), the after-life (ehin-iwa), or heavenly home (ile-orun). But there exists two separate heavens for the dead. The righteous go to good heaven, white heaven, the heaven of the ancestors. Each dead person must first report at the gate of heaven, and if the gateman finds him worthy, he will open the gate for him to enter into eternal bliss; but if he is found unworthy, the gateman will refuse him entry and will ask him to take a narrow road that leads to the heaven of hot ashes or the heaven of potsherds or bad heaven. It is believed that at the death of a wicked person, all those whom he had wronged on earth will be waiting for him at the gate of heaven to testify against him. The personality-soul

(ori) of those still living and who are wronged by the wicked will
also be there to testify against him. Heaven or the afterlife is very
important to the Yoruba, "The world is a market, but heaven is the
home." Man is constantly reminded to remember the afterlife in all
his doings. This is exemplified in the following saying:

> Covenant-breaking may not prevent one from living long,
> But the dreadful thing is the day of "sleep" (death.)
> Also, in *Ogbe-Oyeku-Meji,* Orunmila affirms:
> Do not lie against a person in his absence;
> Do not deal deceitfully with someone with whom you are in a
>   covenant relation;
> Do not betray a friend;
> Because of the day that one is to "sleep" (death).[47]

Concerning witches and murderers, Orunmila says in *Odu-
Ejiogbe:*

> Even if the witches die peaceful deaths on earth,
> Their afterlife is sorrowful in heaven.
> Thus declared the Oracle to Ejiogbe[48] and Obatala
> Who distribute the gift of children.
> Be well-informed that the human flesh you have eaten
> Will become real persons to bear witness against you;
> Real persons they will become.

In Yoruba theology, the dead receive their judgments, rewards,
and final destiny immediately after death and do not have to await
the resurrection day.

But the above does not mean that all judgments for wicked deeds
are postponed until after death. The Yoruba religious ethics are also
community ethics. As it happened in the story of Achan (Josh. 6:7),
the Yoruba believe that the breaking of a taboo can bring calamity
not only on the sinner but on the entire community. The outbreaks
of epidemics are often attributed to such things. This is why the
oracle is consulted every five days in order to know what sacrifice
to offer so as to avert the wrath of the divinities, should some
unknown people have committed sins or broken taboos.[49] The
Yoruba also believe that rewards and punishments may be extended
to generations yet unborn. It is believed that suffering, poverty, barrenness, violent deaths, etc., may be the result of the evil deeds of
the parents or grandparents. It is said, "For the sake of Tomorrow,
one must be kind Today." A popular song among the adherents of
Yoruba Indigenous Religion says:

Refrain from wickedness in this life because of tomorrow;
We will certainly render account at the gate (of heaven).
Ma sika laye o, nitori ola;
Bi a de bode a o rojo.

Modern Trends

The average Yoruba man today is, to some extent, a deculturalized person, living in a no-man's-land. The present Yoruba society is becoming increasingly materialistic, and traditional moral values are losing their fundamental meanings. A major cause for this degeneration is the impact of Westernism upon Yoruba society through the introduction of Christianity and colonialism.

Before the advent of Christianity in 1842,[50] there were a few thousand Muslims scattered over the Yoruba land. Islam had thus far made very little impact on the Yoruba society. But the introduction of Christianity and Westernism brought about radical changes in their religious perception, moral values, education, industrialization, and economic developments. By an accident of history, Christianity was introduced into Yoruba land at a time when Christianity and Western culture were seen as a matter of "cause and effect," as "root and branch." Therefore, the Christianization of Africa was deemed tantamount to its westernization. Christianity first found ready recruits in the liberated slaves who later formed the largest number of early Christian missionaries in West Africa. These simple folks were not in a position to distinguish between what was essential Christianity and its Western trappings. Therefore they unwittingly aped the white man in all things and could not escape thinking that the more Western they became, the more Christian they were. This fateful equation prompted the following observation by Orisatuke Fadumo at the "Conference on Africa" at Common Theological College, Atlanta, 1875.

> That which distinguishes a Heathen from a Christian is not moral character and allegiance to Christ, but an outward dress; the stove-pipe hat, the feathered bonnet, the high-heeled shoes, the gloved hands, and all these, under the burning tropical sun, make a man a Christian gentleman.[51]

Today many people are questioning whether society any longer takes seriously the values such as honesty, dedication, devotion, loyalty, and chastity that have characterized Yoruba society in the past. It is pointed out that the status of ethics was far healthier prior to the advent of Christianity and Westernism. At the same time, it is recognized that morality has not broken down completely, especially in the rural areas where traditional ethics still influence the daily life of the people.

In 1943, Chief Fagbenro Beyioku, the *Araba Ifa* of Lagos, stated in his work, *Orunmila, the Basis of Jesuism,* that Christianity was based on an Ifa Oracle. He claimed that the Bible is essentially an Ifa book on the grounds that the Gospels have parallels in the Ifa Oracle. Since Orunmilaism is older than Jesuism, it is argued that Orunmila is the Savior of Africa. He, therefore, urged Africans to purify themselves from multifarious imported religions. There can be no political freedom without spiritual freedom. He, therefore, urged people to believe in Orunmila and be saved.[52] But such a narrow view does not take into account all the factors that have led to the present moral crisis and the change of values in the society.

In spite of the deculturalization of the Yoruba man and the fact that the majority of them today are either Christians or Muslims, the common Yoruba man has not lost his soul. The traditional beliefs still wield much influence upon him. A High Court Judge (ret.), Justice Olu Ayoola, during the 1980 Annual University of Ibadan Religious Studies Conference, stated that during his years on the bench he had observed that, whereas most Christians and Muslims who swore on the Bible or the *Quran* generally told lies, those who swore by cutlass or iron, told the truth.

Even so, the Yoruba society of today is morally much weaker than in earlier years. The value systems of the land have broken down. The churches and mosques appear helpless. Christianity and Islam have done little to check the sartorial extravagance of the affluent minority in a society where the majority still live in poverty. Recently, in Ibadan, a woman was found in a well. Nobody could explain how she got there. After she was rescued, she claimed to have received a message from Yemoja, the Yoruba river goddess, to the effect that Yemoja was against extravagant dressing by women. Yemoja forbade the use of expensive attire and jewelry. The message came with the warning that Yemoja would carry away women who disobeyed. Surprisingly, most Christians and Muslims complied religiously for a few weeks. If, in the short run, the message of the Ibadan woman was to prick the conscience of the rich, it achieved its purpose. The incident dramatizes the urgent need to take into account the principles of ethics that have been enunciated in the Yoruba religious traditions if an ethical reorientation of Yoruba society is to be achieved.

Notes

1. They are found mainly in Nigeria and the Benin Republic (formerly Dahomey), but their cultural influence extends beyond their borders.

2. Emmanuel Bolaji Idowu, *Olodumare: God in Yoruba Belief* (London: Longmans, 1962), 5.

3. Ibid.

4. Ifa refers to the divination instruments and belief system that Orunmila, the Oracular divinity, introduced into the world. The name is sometimes used for Divinity Himself or His paraphernalia. The Ifa literary corpus contains what may be described as the unwritten sacred scriptures of the Yoruba. It contains sixteen major divisions and two hundred and fifty-six chapters. Each of the major divisions has at least 1,680 sayings attached to it. (Cf. Wande Abimbola, *Sixteen Creed Poems of Ifa* (UNESCO, 1975), 2; Patriarch D. Olarinwa Epega, *The Basis of Yoruba Religion* (Nigeria:Ijamido Printers, Abeokuta, 1971), 4. The book is a revision of the 1932 edition of D. Onadele Epega, *The Mystery of the Yoruba Gods* (Hope Rising Press).

5. Some traditions put the number at 256.

6. E.B. Idowu has claimed that Esu is quite different from the Devil of the New Testament and that a closer analogy is with Satan of the book of Job in the Old Testament. But we know much more about Esu in Yoruba mythology than we do about Satan in the Bible. In Yoruba mythology, Esu is a complex figure having both the characteristics of the Satan of the Book of Job and the Devil of the New Testament. The thesis of Idowu cannot stand in the light of the totality of the Yoruba myths. (Cf. Idousu, *Olodumare*, 80–85; *Meditation on Job* (Ibadan: Daystar Press, 1966).

7. Some traditions put the number at 256. Cf. D.O. Epega, *Basis*, 11.

8. *Ela* literally means a Savior, or that which saves. It also refers to an entity that can break itself into several units and still remain a whole unit. Again, it refers to something or someone who resolves knotty problems. The word also has the sense of *Logos* as employed by St. John. Some Yoruba Christian theologians have advocated the rendering of *Logos* in John 1:1–18, and the identification of Ela with Jesus.

9. Cf. C.L. Laoye, *Eda Omo Odua* (Ibadan: Onileowo Publishing House, 1967), 2.

10. T.A. Awoniyi, "The Fundamental Basis of Yoruba Traditional Education" in *Yoruba Oral Tradition: Poetry in Music, Dance and Drama*, Wande Abimbola, ed. (Ife Languages and Literature Series No. 1, 1975), 364, 365.

11. *Ogbe Alara* is the title of one of the 256 chapters of the Ifa literary corpus.

12. The three numbers most probably refer to the major divisions among the divinities because the Yoruba speak of the 400 divinities on the right hand, the 200 divinities on the left, of the 460 divinities to whom homage is due, and of the 1,440 divinities for whom metal rods are sounded and for whom horns are beaten. Cf. E.B. Idowu, *Oludumare*, 67.

13. J. Herkovits, *Dahomey*, vol. 11 (New York: J.J. Augustine, 1938), 136; G.

Parrinder, *West African Religion* (London: Epworth Press, 1969), 26; E.B. Idowu, *Oludumare*, 85.

14. E.B. Idowu, *Oludumare*, 71.

15. *Odu-Irete Eguntan* is one of the 256 chapters of the Ifa literary corpus.

16. Samuel A. Adewale, "Ethics in Ifa," in *Religion and Ethics in Nigeria*. Samuel O. Abogunrin, ed. (Ibadan: Daystar Press, 1986), 60, 61.

17. Samuel O. Abogunrin, "Man in Yoruba Thought," Original Essay (Department of Religious Studies, University of Ibadan, 1972), 55.

18. Alufa = a priest, most often referring to a Muslim or Christian priest.

19. Samuel O. Abogunrin, "Man in Yoruba Thought," 55.

20. The reference to the Alafan Oyo as Death means that he has the power of life and death. However, the Yoruba kings rule in-council and are not dictators. Their pronouncements are expected to reflect the decision of the king-in-council.

21. In the past, tyrannical kings were either exiled or requested to commit suicide. If he was to commit suicide, a covered empty calabash would be sent to him in order to demosntrate that the whole community—ancestors and divinities—have rejected him. He should, therefore, take the honorable course by dying quietly or being beheaded. Cases of this type are rare. Such an action would only take place in the case of the most heinous ruler.

22. Samuel A. Adewale, "Ethics," 67.

23. But there are exceptions. As pointed out earlier, priests and devotees of Orisanla or Obatala must be monogamists. According to Obatala, Olodumare's vice-regent, the reason for chaos in the world is polygamy. If every man, therefore, can be a monogamist, there will be peace on earth.

24. Occasionally, the mother or father of a young boy of between the ages of one and six could tell a pregnant mother or her husband that if the expected child were a girl, she or he is proposing marriage to the unborn child on behalf of the young body. Or, the marriage proposal could be anytime from the day the girl was born. However, when such girls grew up, they were allowed to make their own decisions, but they rarely went against the earlier decisions made by their parents.

25. The day of a woman's wedding is treated as the day when she is received into her husband's family as a member. Hence, all those born before the hour of her stepping into her husband's family are regarded as her fathers, mothers, senior sisters, senior brothers, and senior wives as senior colleagues. She is expected to respect them thus.

26. *Ogbe-Egunda* is one of the 256 chapters of Ifa literary corpus. Cf. E. Bolaji Idowu, *Olodumare*, 155.

27. Ibid., 71.

28. The language and style of the poem is different from those of the Ifa literary corpus. It is probably a composition of one of the early Yoruba educators or a translation of a foreign poem.

29. *Oyekulogbe* is one of the 256 chapters of the Ifa literary corpus.

30. *Odu Ipingbe* is one of the 256 chapters of the Ifa literary corpus.

31. *Ese* refers to something or to somebody that leads another person into trouble or calamity.

32. *Eledidi-Agbo* is the king of a group of four small towns known as Edidi-Agbo in Kwara State in Nigeria.

33. E.B. Idowu, *Olodumare*, 161.

34. *Ogbe-Ogundabede* is one of the 256 chapters of the Ifa literary corpus. Cf. E. B. Idowu, *Olodumare*, 161.

35. Cf. Samuel A. Adewale, "Ethics," 65.

36. *Eji-ogbe* is one of the sixteen major chapters of the Ifa literary corpus.

37. The Yoruba five days is the Western four days. This is because the Yoruba count the days from the beginning. Hence there are eight days in a week instead of the Western seven days.

38. Obatala, otherwise known as Orisa-nla is God's agent in creation, especially the earth and its inhabitants. He is God's vice-regent on earth. He molds man out of clay and shapes him according to his good pleasure. But it is the sole responsibility of the Deity to give breath to lifeless bodies formed by Obatala. Cf. E. B. Idowu, *Olodumare*, 71–75.

39. E.B. Idowu, *Olodumare*, 71.

40. The language and style of the poem are different from those of the Ifa literary corpus. It is probably a composition of one of the early Yoruba educators or a translation of a foreign poem.

41. *Oyekulogbe* is one of the 256 chapters of the Ifa literary corpus.

42. John 11:50.

43. Judg. 11:29–40.

44. Human sacrifice is now virtually a thing of the past in Yoruba land.

45. Samuel O. Abogunrin, "Man in Yoruba Thought," 75, 76.

46. Edumare is another form of the name Olodumare, the Supreme Deity.

47. *Ogbe Oyeku Meji* is one of the sixteen major divisions of the Ifa literary corpus.

48. *Eji-Ogbe*, one of the sixteen major divisions of the Ifa literary corpus.

49. The Yoruba five days stand for the Western four days. See note 37.

50. There had been Spanish missionary activities in Nigeria as early as the 15th century, but Christianity was successfully planted in Nigeria with the missionary efforts that began in 1842.

51. *African and American Negro*, J.E. Bowen, ed., n.p. 126–127.

52. E.G. Parrinder, *Religion in an African City* (Oxford: Oxford University Press, 1955), 128–135.

Contributors

SAMUEL O. ABOGUNRIN, Ph.D., Senior Lecturer, Department of Religious Studies, University of Ibadan, Ibadan, Nigeria.

JOHN K. ANSAH, Ph.D., Lecturer, Department of Religious Studies, University of Cape Coast, Cape Coast, Ghana.

S. CROMWELL CRAWFORD, Th.D., Chairman, Department of Religion, University of Hawaii, Honolulu, Hawaii.

ISMA'IL R. AL FARUQI, Ph.D. (deceased), Professor, Department of Religious Studies, Temple University, Philadelphia, Pennsylvania.

PREM SUMAN JAIN, Ph.D., Associate Professor and Head, Department of Jainology and Prakrit, Sukhadia University, Udaipur, India.

ASA KASHER, Ph.D., Professor, Department of Philosophy, Tel Aviv University, Tel Aviv, Israel.

GEDDES MACGREGOR, D.Phil., Emeritus Distinguished Professor of Philosophy, University of Southern California, Los Angeles, California.

P. D. PREMASIRI, Ph.D., Associate Professor, Department of Philosophy, University of Peradeniya, Peradeniya, Sri Lanka.

RAMI M. SHAPIRO, Ph.D. Rabbi, Temple Beth Or, Florida.

CHUNG M. TSE, Ph.D., Professor, Department of Philosophy, Tunghai University, Taichung, Taiwan, Republic of China.

Index

Abortion: African religions tradition on, 261, 262–263; Buddhist view of, 57–58; Christian view on, 206–208; Hindu ethical principles and, 23–27; Islamic view on, 234; Jewish orthodoxy on, 150–151; justifiable, 26–27; liberal Jewish view on, 182–183; Roman Catholics on, 204; Yoruba view on, 287
Acarya Amatigati, 78
Acarya Samantabhadra, 72
Acarya Somadeva, 81–82
Acaryas, Jain, 68; on social issues, 77–79
Actionalism, Islamic, 219–221
Adhikara, doctrine of, 9
Adoption, Islamic view on, 234
Adreth, Solomon ben, 149
Adultery: Buddhist view on, 60; Islamic view of, 233. *See also* Extramarital relations
Adultery fees, 253
Affection, displays of, 250
African religious tradition, ethics of, 241–265
Agape, notion of, 192
Ahimsa: concept of, 14–16; dominance of, 6; Jain idea of, 80–84; primacy of, 74–75
AIDS epidemic, interdependence and, *xiii*
Akan tribe, 241–264
Ambalatthikarahulovadasurra, 49–50
Analects (Confucius), 91
Ananda, 8
Anekantavada (theory of nonabsolutism), 73, 80
Anguttaranikaya: on care of parents, 59; on ideal marital relationship, 60
Animal experimentation, 151–152
Animal rescue, 82

Animal sacrifice, 81–82
Animals: Yoruba on sex with, 280; Yoruba view on, 284–285
Anti-dysthanasia, 204, 205
Antonius, 222
Aparigraha (nonattachment), 80
Arahanta, 40
Aristotle, 192–193
Artificial insemination, 152
"Ashkenzai" Jewry, 150
Ashramadharma, 10
Attack Upon Christendom (Kierkegaard), 201
Augustine: on good intentions, 220; neoplatonism of, 194; on the state, 210; on virtue, 201
Authority: civil as divine, 275; Yoruba sense of, 273–276
Awoniyi, T. A., 268

Bahitikasutta, 49
Barbour, Ian, 32
Bestiality, 104
Betrothal, 276, 279
Beyioku, Chief Fagbenro, 293
Bhagavid Gita. *See* Gita
Bhargava, D. N., 71
Bhattacharya, H. S., 72
Bhavanas (virtues), 76
Bhikku (monk), 46–47. *See also* Monk, Buddhist
Bible, 188, 193, 194, 197
Bioethical issues: in African religions tradition, 261–263; Islamic view on, 234–235; Jewish orthodoxy on, 148–153; liberal Jewish view on, 181–185. *See also* Euthanasia; Genetic engineering; *In vitro* fertilization; Surrogate motherhood
Birth control, 57
Bodde, Derk, 93
Bonhoeffer, Dietrich, 205